Passport To Pittsburgh

The New Airport

The International City

Featuring the Photography of Roy Engelbrecht

The New Airport
Passport To Pittsburgh
By Beth Marcello ▪ Corporate Profiles by Earl Bohn
The International City

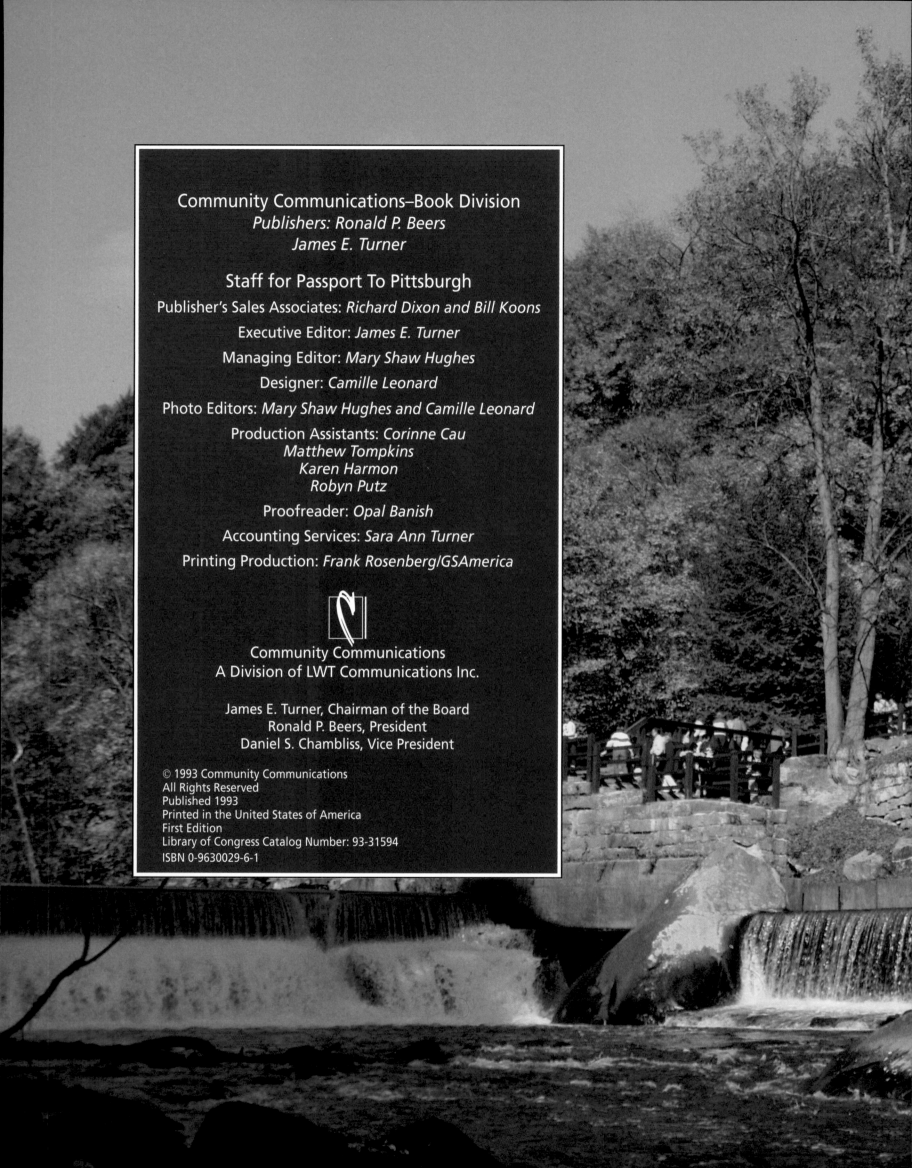

Community Communications–Book Division
Publishers: Ronald P. Beers
James E. Turner

Staff for Passport To Pittsburgh

Publisher's Sales Associates: *Richard Dixon and Bill Koons*

Executive Editor: *James E. Turner*

Managing Editor: *Mary Shaw Hughes*

Designer: *Camille Leonard*

Photo Editors: *Mary Shaw Hughes and Camille Leonard*

Production Assistants: *Corinne Cau*
Matthew Tompkins
Karen Harmon
Robyn Putz

Proofreader: *Opal Banish*

Accounting Services: *Sara Ann Turner*

Printing Production: *Frank Rosenberg/GSAmerica*

Community Communications
A Division of LWT Communications Inc.

James E. Turner, Chairman of the Board
Ronald P. Beers, President
Daniel S. Chambliss, Vice President

Contents
The New Airport
The International City

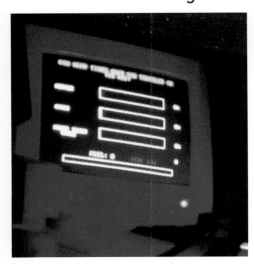

■ *Preface Page Photos By:*
Roy Engelbrecht: 2-3, 10-11, 12-13, 14-15, 16-17
Herb Ferguson: 4-5, 160-161

Contents

Pittsburgh's Enterprises

Ⅳ

Pittsburgh's Enterprises is an advertorial section and is not a complete listing of Pittsburgh firms.

Foreword

Accomplishment and pride. Pittsburgh at its finest. We present *Passport to Pittsburgh: The New Airport and The International City*, a publication to demonstrate the area's astounding accomplishments en route to its destiny in the global frontier.

Written to commemorate the opening of the new Pittsburgh International Airport, *Passport to Pittsburgh: The New Airport and The International City* is a contemporary work capturing where Pittsburgh is today and where it is going in the next century.

Paging through the book, readers will find a profile of the city, the airport, and major businesses throughout the area.

Highlights as diverse as Pittsburgh's historic legacy, competitive advantage, high technology, international connection, state of the art health care, sophisticated educational system and quality of life are incorporated into this publication to give the reader a broad overview of the strength, diversity and opportunity offered by the Greater Pittsburgh area.

Readers will also be introduced to the companies, the entrepreneurs, the products and the people who have helped Pittsburgh become a leader in business...both nationally and internationally.

This extraordinary publication featuring the best of what Pittsburgh has to offer to the local and international scene promises to be the definitive book on the area for years to come. A powerful, image-building tool for the region, *Passport to Pittsburgh* documents the essence of a city that has responded successfully to both structural and economic change.

We would like to thank the authors of *Passport to Pittsburgh: The New Airport and The International City*, the Greater Pittsburgh Chamber of Commerce whose vision and sponsorship of the book brought it to its full fruition and the following outstanding organizations who endorsed its publication: Allegheny Conference on Community Development, County Commissioners, Mayor's Office, Convention and Visitors Bureau, Golden Triangle Association and the World Affairs Council of Pittsburgh. Most importantly, we thank the leadership and citizens of the Greater Pittsburgh Community who each day take part in advancing this remarkable city into the global frontier.

Thomas J. Foerster
Chairman
Allegheny County
Board of Commissioners

Charles A. Corry
Chairman
Greater Pittsburgh
Chamber of Commerce
Chairman & CEO
USX Corporation

Preface

When I started researching and writing the manuscript for *Passport to Pittsburgh*, I was fairly convinced that there was little about the city that I didn't already know. After all, I'd been promoting Pittsburgh for nearly all of my adult life and I knew the rote by heart:

Pittsburgh is safe, straightforward, friendly, affordable, honest, cultured, and clean. We have quaint, ethnic neighborhoods, a deep-seated work ethic, and all the pluses of Big City Life, minus the minuses.

As I traveled throughout the community, meeting with CEOs and university presidents, politicians, and neighborhood leaders, and archetypal Pittsburghers new and native, I was reawakened to the singularity of the place I call home and the people I call neighbors. The aforementioned characteristics aren't propaganda, they're the truth. And if you don't believe me, ask the 130 or so Pittsburghers I talked to in the course of writing the book. Some said it more or less eloquently, but all were nothing short of exuberant about the city that they, too, have come to love. To my delight, the most ardent were not the die-hard, longtime Pittsburghers, but the newcomers and the wandering natives who've recently returned.

For them, I hope the book makes them feel glad they live here. If you're not yet a Pittsburgher, I hope it makes you want to become one.

In the course of writing the book, I also came to realize the importance and extent of the public-private partnership approach to making things happen in Pittsburgh. Like all things in Pittsburgh, this book was a cooperative effort. All of the following individuals/organizations contributed in some fashion to shaping the manuscript. My deepest thanks to:

The Honorable Sophie Masloff; The Honorable Tom Foerster; The Honorable Jack Wagner.

Kenny Scholter; Tony Martin/Aero Club; Al Speak/Southwestern Pa. Regional Planning Commission; Don Riggs; Emery Sedlak; Scott O'Donnell, Pat Boyle, George Gamrod/Dept. of Aviation; Seth Schofield/USAir; Henry Nutbrown/PennDOT; Bill Millar/Port Authority of Allegheny County; Tasso Katselas/Tasso Katselas Associates; Don Morine/Allegheny Development Corp.; Ken Service/Duquesne Light; Mark Knight/BAA; Michael Berger.

Carol Brown/Cultural Trust; Robin Kaye; Lorene Vinski, Elisa Behnk, Jenny Preber/The Carnegie; Susan Neszpaul/American Wind Symphony; David Stock/New Music Ensemble; Marc Masterson/City Theatre Co.; Mark Taylor/Dance Alloy; Sylvia Turner/Pittsburgh Symphony Society; Barbara Luderowski/Mattress Factory; Mark Francis, Megan Shay/Andy Warhol Museum; Marty Ashby/Manchester Craftsmen's Guild; Alison Cordray/Pittsburgh Ballet Theatre; Pat

DiCesare/DiCesare-Engler Productions; Carolelinda Dickey/Pittsburgh Dance Council; Dan Fallon/Pittsburgh Public Theatre; Anita Gob/808 Penn Modern; Susan Peterson/Business Volunteers for the Arts; Pete Shovlin/Allegheny County Bureau of Cultural Programs; Ann Wardrop.

John Herbst, Carolyn Sutcher Schumacher, Ann Fortescue, Bart Roselli/Historical Society of Western Pa.; Brian O'Connor/Point Park College; Dr. Michael Weber/Duquesne University.

Jack Robinette, Lynne Robinson, Patricia Jurczak/Hospital Council of Western Pa.; Eugene Barone, John McDermott/Blue Cross of Western Pa.; Tom Chakurda/Allegheny General Hospital; Jeff Romoff, Jane Duffield/University of Pittsburgh Medical Center;

Howard Baldwin, Phil Langan/Pittsburgh Penguins; Scott Bender/Seven Springs Mountain Resort; John Connelly/J.Edward Connelly Associates; Myron Cope, Bruce Keidan/WTAE; Dennis Darak/Tri-State

Section PGA; Sean Parees/Quicksilver Golf Club; Andy Quinn/Kennywood; Dan Rooney, Lynne Balkovec/Pittsburgh Steelers; Mark Sauer, Rick Cerrone/Pittsburgh Pirates; Jay McCann/Diamond Club.

Vince Sarni, Art Morino/PPG Industries; Paul O'Neill, Dick Fischer, Vince Scorsone, Worth Hobbs, Anna Mae Litman/ALCOA; Helge Wehmeier, Barry Cohen, Sande Deitch/Miles, Inc.; Iwao Takahashi/Sony; Charles Corry, Bill Keslar/USX Corporation; Frank Cahouet, Sandra McLaughlin, Tom Butch/Mellon Bank; Bill Roemer, Betsy Fitzpatrick/Integra Bank; Roy Morris/PNC Financial Corp.; Herb Ellis/Contraves USA; Randall Harper, Elizabeth Harper/American Micrographics Co.; Barbara Moore/Anderson Transfer; Roger Fairfax, Fairfax Communications.

Dr. Mack Kingsmore, Dr. David Griffin, Dr. Diane Colbert/CCAC; Dr. John Murray, Tom Murrin/Duquesne University; Dr. Esther Barazzone/Chatham College; Louise Brennen, Pat Crawford/Pittsburgh Public

Schools; Dr. Dennis O'Connor, Dr. Burkart Holzner, Dr. Jerry Zoffer, Bill Young, Oval Jaynes/University of Pittsburgh; Dr. Robert Mehrabian, Peggy McCormick Barron, Don Hale, Ben Fischer/Carnegie Mellon University; Monsignor William Kerr, Patrician Green Cotman/La Roche College; Linda Croushore/Mon Valley Education Consortium; Hope Tauch/Allegheny County Assoc. of Public Schools; Chip Burke/Grable Foundation; Jane Burger/Frick Educational Commission; Doreen Boyce/Buhl Foundation; Mark Bibro/Louise Child Care; Dr. Jo-Ann Sipple/Robert Morris College; Nancy Bunt/Education Fund.

Bill Lafe/Emerging International Cities Project; Ninamary Langsdale/KPMG Peat Marwick; Dennis Unkovic/Meyer, Unkovic and Scott; John McCartney/U.S. Dept. of Commerce; Jack Midgley/Ronald Reagan Center for Public Affairs; Clay Deutsch/McKinsey & Company; George Oehmler, Judith Nees/World Affairs Council; Rebecca Ranich.

Rick Stafford/Allegheny Conference on Community Development; Justin Horan, Lance Schaeffer, Susan Wells/Chamber of Commerce, Earl Hord/Minority Enterprise Corporation; Ray Christman/Technology Development and Education Corp.; Joe McGrath/Convention and Visitors Bureau; Jay Aldridge/Penn's Southwest; Tim Parks/Pittsburgh High Technology Council; Jack Robin/Urban Redevelopment Authority; Kelly O'Toole/Office of Promotion; Frank Brooks Robinson/RIDC.

Mina Gerall, Tamara Dudukovich, Mary Ann Miller, Marla Meyer, Sally Wiggin, Tim Wesley, Brad Hemstreet, Bill Hulley, and Bill Metzger.

PASSPORT TO

The New Airport, The International City

PITTSBURGH

Light Up Night in Pittsburgh is an annual event that marks the beginning of the holiday shopping season.

CHAPTER

Have Wings, Will Travel

ONE

Pittsburgh was *almost* the birthplace of aviation. The experiments that led to the world's *first* unmanned engine-powered heavier-than-air flights were conducted in Pittsburgh by Samuel Pierpont Langley, and Langley would have preceded the Wright Brothers as the father of aviation by nine days if his first manned flight had been successful.

Samuel Langley came to Pittsburgh in 1867 at the age of 33 to teach astronomy and physics at the University of Pittsburgh and direct the Allegheny Observatory, which the university owned. A civil engineer by profession and an astronomer at heart, Langley made a name for himself and the observatory by developing tools and measurements for recording the sun's temperature. He also created and sold "standard time" to the railroads by transmitting the time on the observatory clock by telegraph.

■ *Aerobatic antics have been a common sight in Pittsburgh since 1910 when Pittsburghers saw their first air show on Brunot's Island. Photo by Roy Engelbrecht.*

Intensely curious, Langley also studied the principles of aerodynamics and aviation. He concluded that heavier-than-air flight was possible through a set of experiments with a "whirling table," a contraption made from two 30-foot wooden arms that rotated above an 8-foot-high axle. Powered by a 10-horsepower steam engine, the table whirled at a speed of 70 to 100 miles per hour. For three years, Langley studied the effects of air density, pressure, and temperature on his invention and gauged how much engine power he needed to lift the flying table, then published the results in 1890 in a document called *Experiments in Aerodynamics.*

■ *The experiments that led to the world's first unmanned engine-powered flights were conducted in Pittsburgh by Samuel Pierpont Langley. Photo courtesy of the Carnegie Library.*

Langley's *Experiments in Aerodynamics* inspired and guided Orville and Wilbur Wright. The study also caught the attention of the Smithsonian Institution, which hired Langley a year later. While the Wright brothers were tinkering in their bicycle shop in Dayton, Ohio, Langley set out at the Smithsonian to prove that heavier-than-air flight was possible by building and testing the world's first flying machines. His "aerodrome" was a wood and paper craft with a pair of tandem wings, a rudder, elevator, and engine. In 1896, from a houseboat on the Potomac River in Virginia, Langley successfully launched the airplane from a rail that acted as a slingshot. The world's first unmanned flight travelled about 3,000 feet, remained airborne for about 90 seconds, and demonstrated the probability of sustained flight.

Spits and Sputters

Regarded today among aviation's foremost pioneers, Langley inspired many of the first aviators and airplane makers and, according to Wilbur Wright, has the strongest claim on proving the practicality of flight.

Langley positioned Pittsburgh at the forefront of aviation, and throughout aviation history, Pittsburgh has been a leader in the industry. The nation's first Aero Club was founded here. A Pittsburgher, Calbraith

Perry Rodgers, made the world's first transcontinental flight. Many of the government's experiments with all-metal aircraft and new aircraft paints, varnishes, and dope, a shellac-like coating for aircraft wings, in preparation for World War I, were conducted in Pittsburgh. A division of Westinghouse Air Brake was an important manufacturer of airplane engines used to win World War I. The first all-steel propeller, the type featured on Lindbergh's *Spirit of St. Louis*, was designed and manufactured here. When Allegheny County Airport and the Greater Pittsburgh International Airport opened, both were the most modern facilities of their day. Three major airlines—United, TWA, and USAir—have historical connections to Pittsburgh.

Pittsburghers saw their first airplane in 1910, when the newly formed Aero Club of Pittsburgh sponsored a three-day air show on Brunot's Island in the Ohio River. But Pittsburghers didn't have an official airport until businessman Casper Mayer opened Mayer Field in Bridgeville in 1919. Mayer Field was only a grass strip, but it gave aviation buffs a place to congregate, putter, and dream. The field also gave many Pittsburghers their first look at an airborne airplane and aerobatic antics. The "Human Fly," a wingwalker who did headstands while the pilot "looped the loop," became a familiar weekend sight in the sky over Bridgeville.

In 1925, the Pittsburgh Aero Club developed what became the area's first municipal airfield and government air reserve base. Named for Pittsburgh pilot Calbraith Perry Rodgers who made the first transcontinental flight, Rodgers Field opened on 41 acres of land in Aspinwall that the Aero Club bought and then sold to the City of Pittsburgh and Allegheny County, which agreed to operate it as an airfield under a joint contract. Despite its famous namesake, Rodgers Field never flourished as a general aviation facility, in part because of the adjacent country club. After a young and gutsy pilot flying a very noisy airplane landed short on a fairway, the club's serious golfers, tolerating no further disruptions to their game, stifled further development of the airfield.

By this time, flying had become popular, if not common, still largely an avocation of the rich or the foolhardy. Few took the sport seriously or predicted its value beyond recreation, so sightings of men in their flying machines were marvelous but rare events. Risk-takers, captivated by the thrill and romance of flying, built homemade airplanes and tested them everywhere there was open space, including the track in Schenley Park.

In fact, it was thanks to the Schenley "Oval" that Pittsburghers saw their first Ford trimotor. Henry Ford had agreed to display the plane in Pittsburgh's first aviation trade show. Since the closest airport was inconveniently located miles away at Bettis Field in Dravosburg, the Ford pilot landed in Schenley Park, where the plane was dismantled, hauled to Motor Square Garden in nearby East Liberty, and rebuilt for the show where it was awed by thousands. Getting home was more tedious, however. Full of fuel, the trimotor was too heavy to liftoff the oval's short runway. Calculating carefully, the pilot lightened the craft by draining all but enough gas to get him to Bettis Field, where he stopped to refuel before heading west.

Business Takes Off

By 1926, Bettis Field had become the nucleus of aviation activity in the region. Originally called the McKeesport-Pittsburgh Airfield, Bettis Field was renamed in memory of Cyrus K. Bettis, an Army Air Corps pilot who held several world speed records. Now the site of Westinghouse Electric Corporation's Bettis Atomic Power Laboratory, Bettis Field in Dravosburg became Pittsburgh's first commercial aviation center. Bettis was the playground of D. Barr Peat and Clifford Ball, two nonflying businessmen who built an early flight school where many of Pittsburgh's first homegrown pilots were trained.

Among them was Kenny Scholter, who glimpsed an airplane for the first time while playing basketball at a playground in nearby Duquesne. "I saw that plane and knew I had to see it land," Scholter recalls. He ran the five miles uphill to Bettis to see the plane and, "basically, never left," says Scholter, who later broke a world altitude record and developed the Butler County Airport into a successful general aviation facility.

Scholter's fondest aviation memory is of his chance meeting in 1927 with Charles Lindbergh, his hero. After Lindbergh's record-breaking nonstop solo flight from New York to Paris that May, President Coolidge, hoping to boost the country's morale, commissioned Lindbergh to tour the nation in the *Spirit of St. Louis*. About two weeks before Lindbergh made the official tour, he quietly visited each airport on the circuit to inspect conditions and runways. So, when the world renowned and recognized aviator landed unannounced at Bettis Field on an afternoon late in July, the only person on hand to greet him was 17-year-old Kenny Scholter, camera in tow. As wild for

■ *Charles Lindbergh (right), with Kenny Scholter who was one of Pittsburgh's first homegrown pilots. Photo courtesy of Kenny Scholter.*

■ *Cliff Ball, founder of Pennsylvania Air Lines, believed that aviation and airports were an economic magnet. Photo courtesy of Kenny Scholter.*

photography as he was for airplanes, Scholter was rarely without his camera, especially at the airport. He introduced himself, snapped a few shots, and pointed Lindbergh and his co-pilot in the direction of Cliff Ball's hot dog stand, where they all had lunch before Lindbergh took off for the next airfield.

The following afternoon, a horde of reporters with word of the visit descended on the airport, only to find themselves a day late. Instead of Lindbergh, they discovered a grinning teenager with an undeveloped roll of film that eventually made the front pages of both *The Pittsburgh Press* and *Sun-Telegraph*.

Scholter's mentor, Cliff Ball, was one of Pittsburgh's leading aviation promoters. His motto, "Build the Nest and the Birds Will Come," described his belief in the importance of aviation and airports as an economic magnet. Like many of the day's entrepreneurs who had begun to envision the potential of aviation, Ball and his partner D. Barr Peat were in search of high-earnings opportunities in the industry. They found their cash cow in airmail.

Airmail was the exclusive enterprise of the federal government until Clyde Kelly, a congressman from McKeesport, wrote the Kelly Mail Act of 1925, which privatized the business. By paying private contractors based on the amount of mail they carried, the Kelly Mail Act effectively subsidized the growth of aviation operations and stimulated the aircraft manufacturing and parts industries. As routes grew, so did the need for aircraft and airports.

Cliff Ball was awarded one of the first 11 Contract Air Mail routes the government assigned. Flying three Waco-9s, Ball's pilots collected and dropped mail in Cleveland, Youngstown, and at Bettis Field in Pittsburgh, a lucrative 121-mile route. One of the few to succeed in the business, Ball secured the highest per-pound payout the government would provide, earning, in 1927, $3 a pound for carrying 20,000 pounds of mail some 70,000 miles and making more than 95 percent of his scheduled stops. When he augmented his line with larger, roomier planes the following year, he began to take passengers. Tickets went for $20 a seat, but because he made more money on a pound of mail than a pound of flesh, Ball had little incentive to schedule or promote passenger service.

He changed his mind in 1930. Airmail had become a luxury for the depression-era poor, so when postal poundage declined,

■ *USAir had its beginning in western Pennsylvania as an airmail airline which later added passenger service. Photo by Roy Engelbrecht.*

passenger service became the next frontier. Ball bought a 12-passenger Ford trimotor, merged the passenger and mail operations, and formed an umbrella company called Pennsylvania Air Lines.

Pennsylvania Air Lines evolved through a series of corporate mergers and acquisitions as a forerunner of United Airlines, a process helped along by the Pittsburgh Aviation Industries Corporation (PAIC). Founded in 1928, PAIC was an aviation holding company established by a prominent group of wealthy Pittsburgh businessmen, including Taylor Allderdice, Arthur Braun, J.H. Hillman, Jr., Maurice Falk, H.H. Robertson, William L. Mellon, Richard B. Mellon, and Richard King Mellon. Five PAIC subsidiaries encompassed all aspects of aviation: sightseeing and charter flights, flight training, aerial photography and mapping, airplane and parts sales, a credit company that invested in aviation ventures, and a consulting arm that offered management and operations advice to fledgling aviation outfits. PAIC also dabbled in aircraft manufacturing and tried to establish a downtown

airport on the Monongahela River for amphibian aircraft. The river runway never took off because floating debris and abundant barge traffic made landing on the Mon a precarious event.

With headquarters at what is now the Butler County Airport, PAIC was "ahead of its time," according to Kenny Scholter. Like their competitor, Cliff Ball, the PAIC investors learned that the key to making money in aviation was passenger service, especially when combined with a profitable airmail contract. PAIC bought Ball's Pennsylvania Air Lines, which eventually merged with Central Air Lines and became an important regional carrier. (Central Air Lines also had Pittsburgh roots; its lineage was traced to Pittsburgh Airways, a company backed by Oliver Kaufmann, the department store owner.) The new Pennsylvania-Central Airlines moved its headquarters operation from Allegheny County Airport in the early 1940s to the National Airport in Washington, D.C., and was renamed the "Capital Airline." United Airlines bought Capital in 1961.

■ *Dr. Lytle Adams, an oral surgeon from Irwin, invented a hook and cable system for airmail pickup. Photo courtesy of USAir.*

Pennsylvania Air Lines (left) was a precursor of United Airlines. All American (center) and Allegheny Airlines (right) were both forerunners of USAir. Pennsylvania photo courtesy of Kenny Scholter. All American and Allegheny photos courtesy of USAir.

In addition to its connection to United Airlines, PAIC also had a hand in the 1930 merger of Transcontinental Air Transport and Western Air Express, which became TWA, the airline that initiated transcontinental passenger service. PAIC received a 5-percent share of the merger in exchange for a 50-percent interest in Pittsburgh-Butler Airport. Another major airline, USAir, also had its beginning in the 1930s in western Pennsylvania. Dr. Lytle Adams, an oral surgeon from Irwin, had invented a system for picking up airmail in remote rural or mountainous areas lacking airports. Pilots of planes outfitted with a hook and cable system would swoop down, snag a mail bag that was suspended between two poles, and pulley it up into the cabin. Richard du Pont, a businessman and glider pilot, saw Adams demonstrate his novel design at the Chicago World's Fair in 1934 and started All American Aviation based on the concept. All American eventually added passenger service, expanded its operation, changed its name to Allegheny Airlines in the 1950s, and became USAir in 1979.

The First Modern Airport

Although aviation interests were flourishing in Pittsburgh, the city still lacked a modern airport. After damaging her aircraft during a landing at the rough-hewn Rodgers Field in 1928, world famous aviatrix Amelia Earhart said that she wouldn't fly to Pittsburgh again until there were better facilities for planes. Commander Richard E. Byrd, who organized the first flight over the North Pole in 1926, also scolded Pittsburgh for its lack of a quality airport.

"Pittsburgh, as the center of the steel industry, already has contributed much to the success of aviation through research, and in the furnishing of raw materials used in the development and manufacture of our present-day efficient aircraft engines and other aviation steel products," Byrd wrote in a 1928 letter to the *Sun-Telegraph*. "Other centers that have contributed far less than Pittsburgh in the development of aviation have been quick to recognize the need of a suitable airport, and this would seem to be Pittsburgh's obligation towards aviation right now."

The aviation editor of the *Sun-Telegraph* picked up the lament in an editorial later that year. "Pittsburgh might be fourth in population, area, etc., and perhaps first in wealth, but it doesn't even receive honorable mention when airports are the topic of conversation. Among flying men, Pittsburgh is known … as the city without an airport, and flying Pittsburghers are forever apologizing for the lack of facilities within this district. True, Pittsburgh has three landing fields . . . but none . . . is an airport by any stretch of the imagination."

"If Pittsburgh wants to be the real fourth city of the United States, it must have an airport that can compare in some measure with the ports of New York, Chicago, and Philadelphia, the first three cities of the nation."

Pittsburghers met the challenge. The Allegheny County Commissioners Joseph G. Armstrong, Charles C. McGovern, and

Edward V. Babcock, and Pittsburgh Mayor Charles H. Kline, with advice from the Pittsburgh Aero Club, Chamber of Commerce, Planning Commission, and the

■ *When the Greater Pittsburgh Airport opened in 1952, visiting dignitaries and celebrities described it as the "model of the future." Photo courtesy of the Allegheny County Communications Department.*

Department of Commerce Aeronautics Branch, selected land along Lebanon Church Road in West Mifflin, just a few miles from Bettis Field, for development of Pittsburgh's first modern airport.

When Allegheny County Airport opened in 1931, it again placed Pittsburgh in the vanguard of aviation. For both pilots and passengers, the airport ranked among the nation's finest. It featured an elaborate art-deco terminal building with ticket offices, baggage and mail rooms, a spacious passenger waiting area, dormitories for both male and female pilots, a lounge, and hospital. It was the only hard-surfaced airport open at the time and had more and wider runways than other major airports. It also featured a control tower and lighting system with runway flares for the first night landings that was said to be unsurpassed.

The new airport attracted commercial carriers, which developed rapidly when the 21-seat Douglas DC-3 debuted in 1936, and served as western Pennsylvania's commercial aviation hub until the opening of the Greater Pittsburgh Airport 20 years later.

The Taj Mahal of Aviation

The advent of war hastened the development of what became the nation's largest commercial airport. On the eve of World War II, the War Department recognized the need to protect western Pennsylvania from enemy attack and asked the Allegheny County Commissioners to identify a parcel of land for a military airport. Eyes turned to the Bell dairy farm in Moon Township, a level pastoral sprawl that would require little site preparation. In addition to the topography, the relative lack of fog, smoke, and prevailing winds made the farmland an ideal location for the 24-hour operation the War Department wanted.

During the war, the government trained pilots at the base. But when war ended in 1945, and the government no longer needed exclusive use of the field, the Commissioners began eyeing the facility as a replacement for the already burgeoning Allegheny County Airport. The site was ideal, not only because the airport was partially developed, but also because the tract of land surrounding it was undeveloped. By acquiring this additional land, the Commissioners ensured that the airport would eventually be able to grow to meet the demand of an increasing reliance on air transport. This farsightedness is regarded today as the most important decision influencing Pittsburgh's place in the world economy.

When the county established an aviation department in 1946 and broke ground for the new airport, about 75 construction contracts were negotiated to build the terminal and the miles of parkway necessary to support it. The $33 million development was billed as a facility "built for Pittsburghers by Pittsburghers with Pittsburgh products." Dick Construction, for example, was the general contractor. Graybar Electric performed the electrical work. Pittsburgh Plate Glass provided three acres of Twindow Solex Glass, a green-tinted, advanced technology insulated window that eliminated noise, heat, cold, and glare. The U.S. Steel American Bridge Company supplied more than 4,000 tons of structural steel. Westinghouse Electric

Corporation equipped the new terminal with 14 air-conditioning and heating systems, four elevators, six escalators, and three dumb-waiters.

Two-and-a-half years before it opened, aviation director John Sweeney told the *Sun-Telegraph* the airport would include "everything that can be found in a small city." Plans called for "70 hotel rooms, a theater, cafeteria, cocktail lounge, 40 spaces for three-dimensional advertising, and maybe a bank, post office, grocery store, swimming pool, and bowling alley."

The show piece was the seven-story terminal building itself. The black granite exterior, buffed marble interior, and fancy terrazzo floors would make the terminal the "model of the future." The revolutionary finger-dock design was called "a masterpiece of planning functional architecture."

When the airport opened on May 31, 1952, it met with rave reviews from the local press: "No airport terminal anywhere can hold a candle to the shimmering $10 million building that serves as the hub for the sprawling network of runways and taxiways" one article said. "The semi-circular, ultra-modern building has more curves than Mae West, more glass than the new Alcoa and Mellon-U.S. Steel skyscrapers combined. It is a bold step into the World of Tomorrow and puts Pittsburgh out front in aviation."

A newspaper advertisement promised "Plenty to see and do. Take in a movie, visit dozens of shops, go to the beauty parlor, tour the biggest air-conditioned building in this part of the country. It will be a long walk because you'll be in the biggest air terminal in the entire world."

During the ribbon-cutting ceremony, a formation of Air Force F-86 Sabrejets soared overhead, a symbol of the jet age the airport would serve. Within 15 years, Greater Pittsburgh Airport would outgrow its space and begin a series of expansions that culminated in 1987, when ground was broken for a new midfield terminal. ▣

■ *Stunt pilots are still a familiar sight in the city that was almost the birthplace of aviation. Photo by Herb Ferguson.*

CHAPTER
The New Airport
TWO

Allegheny County Commissioner Tom Foerster awoke in the wee hours of morning on October 1, 1992. His first appointment: a 5:30 a.m. meeting at the new Pittsburgh International Airport, where he would greet the first flight, a USAir red-eye from Seattle.

Long-awaited, the day would be hectic and emotional, a day of beginnings and endings. The first of October would mark for Foerster the completion of a long crusade to build the airport and the start of what he firmly believes is Pittsburgh's future.

■ *Marking the beginning of Pittsburgh's third Renaissance, the new airport was essential to secure Pittsburgh's future in the 21st century. Alexander Calder's "Pittsburgh" mobile is suspended in the core of the new airside terminal. Photo by Roy Engelbrecht.*

On this morning, Foerster left his home in Troy Hill, a Northside neighborhood of rowhomes, storefronts, schools, and churches that retains the flavor of German immigrants who put down roots in the 1800s. He looked over a sleeping, peaceful Pittsburgh and pondered the past. It had taken him 25 years to make this 20-minute ride to the airport.

■ The USAir-British Airways alliance opened up nonstop flights from Pittsburgh to London which strengthed Pittsburgh's growing international business posture. Photo courtesy of USAir.

In 1967, at the onset of his first term in office, Commissioner Foerster attended a Greater Pittsburgh Chamber of Commerce dinner where the CEO of TWA delivered the keynote address. "Unless you begin planning now," says Foerster, remembering the warning of the airline executive, "planes will be flying over Pittsburgh." Over, as in by-passing.

The thought so troubled the commissioner, a proud lifelong Pittsburgher, that he immediately began a tireless, often unpopular campaign to make sure that the planes that flew above Pittsburgh would land here as well. He saw the airport as an economic engine, a magnet luring more jobs and new companies — international companies in particular — to the region.

With the support of fellow Commissioner Leonard Staisey, Foerster spent several years and more than $10 million acquiring 6,000 acres of land surrounding the airport, doubling the then-existing acreage. "If we don't get the land now, it may not be available later when we need it," the forward-thinking Foerster told his critics, who regarded the acquisitions as wasteful government spending. They pointed to the practically new Greater Pittsburgh Airport, the "Taj Mahal" of aviation that opened 15 years earlier, as airport enough. "Trust me," the commissioner said solicitously, repeatedly. "This is the future of Pittsburgh."

But it would take more than available land to launch the project. Foerster needed a groundswell of community support as well as a shipment of money. The support came first. The commissioner successfully articulated the benefits of a new international airport to the city's business leaders, and through the Allegheny Conference on Community Development, positioned the new airport at the top of "Strategy 21," a list of regional development projects earmarked for intensive lobbying that would carry Pittsburgh into the 21st century. Funding followed. The county raised $608 million from a municipal bond sale and contributed $42.5 million from the public coffers. Pennsylvania invested $85 million in the airport and more than $160 million from a state bond sale for the adjoining access highway. The Federal Aviation Administration allotted $111 million, and then gave the project an added boost when it funded Pittsburgh to receive one of four advanced airport runway lighting and signal systems.

The private sector contributed to the coffers as well. Twenty-seven construction trade unions, representing some 3,000 workers, signed a historic five-year no-strike agreement that would hold down construction costs and guarantee the airport's on-time opening. Allegheny Development Corporation invested $70 million in a lease-back arrangement unique to airport development. A subsidiary of DQE, the parent company of Duquesne Light, the region's largest electric utility, Allegheny Development designed, installed, and now operates the airport's heating, cooling, and power center. The third-party agreement with Allegheny Development reduced the capital and maintenance costs, and fixed the operating costs for 30 years.

and gates at the new terminal would be shorter, and because there would be room for one aircraft to pull into a gate while another backed out.

The prospective savings in time and money convinced USAir, the airport's prime tenant, to agree to invest $1 billion in rent and landing fees over 30 years, and the project took-off. Ground was broken in 1987, and by

■ *The three-million-square-foot facility consists of three buildings: landside, central services, and airside buildings. Photo by Roy Engelbrecht.*

But Foerster still needed the airlines to foot the bulk of the bill. "When we were ready," the commissioner recalls, "the airlines (reeling from deregulation) weren't." Eventually, nine carriers came aboard with leases worth $30 million a year when a fuel-efficiency study showed that the proposed midfield design of the new airport would save the airlines as much as $12 million annually in fuel costs. The design called for an X-shaped airside terminal positioned midfield between the main parallel runways that aircraft could approach from all sides. According to the study, planes would spend less idle time in the air and on the ground — not only in Pittsburgh, but also at other airports with flights departing for Pittsburgh — because the distance between the runways

opening day, Foerster, who was re-elected four times since the start of the project, had silenced the skeptics and built an airport that again placed Pittsburgh at the vanguard of aviation. Declaring the start of Pittsburgh's third Renaissance, the commissioner snipped the ribbon and, as a crowd of celebrants looked on, welcomed the first passengers into the new $800 million airport complex.

Room to Grow

"Bursting at the seams" is how Aviation Director Scott O'Donnell describes Greater Pitt, the old airport. Built for propeller aircraft, not jets, the old facility "served us well, but its time had passed," O'Donnell says. By 1992, Greater Pitt had doubled its intended lifespan and was supporting twice the annual traffic it

■ *On the following page: The Pittsburgh International Airport's state-of-the-art runway lighting system enhances safety and efficiency. Photo by Roy Engelbrecht.*

■ *The airport's unique X-shaped design saves the airlines time and money, and reduces the time that passengers wait in idle aircraft. Photo courtesy of USAir.*

■ *Tasso Katselas, the airport architect, analyzed approximately 200 solutions before the final modified X-design was adopted. Photo by Roy Engelbrecht.*

was designed to handle. Foerster had been right — a new airport was essential to secure Pittsburgh's future in the 21st century. It was also necessary to secure USAir's.

After deregulation in the 1970s, USAir, then called Allegheny Airlines, chose Pittsburgh as the site of its first major hub. Within an hour's flight of several major population centers, Pittsburgh's proximity made the city an ideal hub location. As one of the nation's largest corporate headquarters cities, Pittsburgh also offered a stable business-passenger base for a growing airline. Consequently, USAir became Pittsburgh's primary carrier, and the city became one of the five busiest airline hubs in the nation.

The hub "gives Pittsburgh tremendous access nationally and internationally," says Seth Schofield, USAir's chairman and CEO. In 1992, more than 600 nonstop flights to more than 120 cities departed daily from Pittsburgh International; more than 450 were USAir flights. "Connections drive the number of nonstop and direct flights, so the ultimate ben-

eficiary of a hub operation is the local customer. That puts Pittsburgh in a powerful position to attract business and establish business relationships with other cities," says Schofield.

Pittsburgh and USAir grew together, and outgrew the airport. To compete with the major airlines that were acquiring additional routes by buying up smaller carriers, USAir needed to expand beyond the $10 million it spent on a new terminal concourse at the old airport. "It was an absolute necessity that we grow," says Schofield. To Foerster's delight, that meant investing in a new Pittsburgh airport.

Since the vast majority of the new airport's passengers would be USAir customers, and since more than 60 percent of the USAir customers would simply change planes in Pittsburgh, the airline played a pivotal role in developing what would become the world's first airport built specifically as a connecting complex. USAir enabled the start of construction by leasing 50 of the new airport's 75 jet gates, 20 of the 25 commuter gates, and 3 of the 5 international gates. The airline also invested $34 million in a state-of-the-art automated baggage system, which uses bar coding and laser scanners to speed sorting and delivery. The goal is for baggage to arrive in the landside terminal when passengers do. "We wanted to build something we can be proud of," Schofield says of the airport, "and we're the envy of all the folks around us."

Dubbed the "airport of the future" for its user-friendly layout and advanced operational technology, the new Pittsburgh airport features a design unique to airport architecture. The three-million-square-foot facility consists of three buildings: a three-story landside building that serves as the center for passenger ticketing, baggage handling, and airport offices; an adjoining three-story central services building that features the airport's only security checkpoint, a transit station, the commuter terminal, and, behind-the-scenes, airport operations; and a two-story, four-level airside building that houses the jet gates, shops, restaurants, and airline clubs.

The building's beauty is instantly perceptible, but its real splendor lies in the hidden potential — built-in expansion capabilities. The arms of the X are extendable; when demand dictates, gates can be added easily. In fact, a build-out plan calls for an additional 25 jet gates, an increase from 75 to 100, by 2003. More important, there remains room at the airport for new runways and a second airside terminal, since the present facility occupies only half of the available 12,080 acres. The county is already planning an addition to the commuter terminal and a new runway for 1998. The proposed runway, the Southern Parallel, will make Pittsburgh one of a handful of airports around the globe with three independent approaches.

■ *Electric sidewalks make Pittsburgh's new terminal more "passenger-friendly" for the weary traveler. Photo by Roy Engelbrecht.*

Combined with the $30 million state-of-the-art runway lighting and signal system, the triple approach will enhance the safety and efficiency of flying in and out of Pittsburgh, and serve as a lure for international carriers wanting to avoid the congestion of the eastern seaboard.

The Leading Edge

Pittsburgh became a center for aviation innovation a century ago when Samuel Langley began experimenting at the city's observatory with the principles that led to the world's first heavier-than-air flight.

The opening of the midfield terminal further advanced the city's reputation as a pacesetter in the industry. The new airport's X-shaped design is unique in the world. So is the safe and simple system of separate roadways for private and commercial vehicles that are picking-up or dropping-off passengers.

Few airports feature separate landside and airside terminals connected by a state-of-the-art underground "people-mover" designed and built by Pittsburgh-based AEG Westinghouse Transportation Systems.

The USAir automated baggage system, the high-tech flight and gate display systems, and the security system use the world's most advanced technologies. An Airmall with competing retailers and competitive pricing is the nation's first.

Now referred to as "the Pittsburgh X," the revolutionary design for the new airport originally resembled the Greek letter H in the creative mind of Tasso Katselas, the airport architect. Katselas analyzed "some 200 solutions — 20 versions of 10 variations," before ending up with the modified X that formed the final design. "The X was unpopular at first," he says. "It was unique and required research. It wasn't the lazy man's solution."

Katselas didn't set out to break aviation or architectural ground when he began design. Innovation wasn't the intent, he says, simply the by-product of a desire to make the airport "passenger-friendly." The architects and design engineers toured and studied airports around the world to develop a drawing that incorporated the most efficient and convenient passenger features, and corrected the least. The beauty of the X-shape, for example, is that it not only saves the airlines time and money, it also reduces the time passengers waste in idle aircraft. "What's good for the passengers is usually good for the airlines," Katselas notes.

The architect determined that a straight-line design would be best for passengers.

"We designed the airport to give people as few choices as possible — to eliminate confusion, to minimize the decisions they

■ Using shades of blue and grey, the designers created a soothing atmosphere. Photo by Roy Engelbrecht.

have to make," Katselas says. "Everything's clearly marked and straight ahead."

Passengers departing Pittsburgh get tickets and check baggage in the landside building, then pass unencumbered through security to board the people-mover that whisks them the half mile underground to the airside terminal. Seventy-six seconds later they emerge in the airside building to ascend a set of escalators that deposits them at the core of the X. All that they need is at once visible: Straight ahead is the information desk. To the left and right are electronic bulletin boards that list the status and gate locations of arriving and departing flights. On the periphery are dozens of shops and restaurants, where passengers can sit for a full-course meal, grab a snack, pick up a newspaper or souvenir, or buy any number of items — books, compact discs, jewelry, ties and scarfs, a handbag — that can be worn or fitted easily into a carry-on bag.

Four well-marked entryways, color-coded and labeled simply A, B, C, and D, extend like the arms of an X from the core. Passengers to enplane at Gate A-20 are guided by a network of gently moving sidewalks

down the A aisle. Even the most distracted of passengers aren't likely to find themselves at the right gate on the wrong arm; to eliminate the potential for confusion, Katselas sequentially numbered the gates — A1-A25, B26-B50, and so on. Numerous public phones, restrooms, water fountains, newsstands, foodstands, and pubs are conveniently located on both sides along the way.

Passengers arriving in Pittsburgh are greeted with the same conveniences. Restless travellers can access the same phones, restrooms, fountains, shops, and foodstands that parallel the electric sidewalks moving toward the airside building's main rotunda. Easily readable signs point in the direction of the baggage pick-up and ground transportation areas located on the ground level of the landside building, a short ride away on the high-tech tram.

The relentless attention Katselas paid to the minutiae of the airport is evident in details passengers would notice only if the conveniences weren't there. "Everything is designed," says Katselas. "Form and content coincide." Take the passenger seating areas. Katselas ordered the supple leather-like seats

■ On the following page: Pittsburgh International is the first airport in which the art, like this mosaic tile path, was built-in during construction, rather than affixed afterward. Photo by Roy Engelbrecht.

■ *USAir chose Pittsburgh as its first major hub and later became Pittsburgh's primary carrier. USAir crew photo by Roy Engelbrecht.*

in three subtle shades of grey. Interspersed, the varying colors of chairs give a warm, inviting, and occupied look to the waiting areas, even when they're empty.

Doors on both sides of the people movers open consecutively, rather than simultaneously. The outside doors open first, allowing departing passengers to exit. Then the inside doors open to incoming travellers. "A simple, common-sense solution," says Katselas, yet it seems that no one thought of it before. In most airports with people movers, doors open on one side only, precipitating a jostled mangle of comers and goers.

Strict standards for quality and consistency were placed on the designers of storefront signs and billboard art. The results are easy on the eye; nothing shouts or competes for attention. The coin-operated newspaper

boxes are color-coordinated and strategically placed. Even the tone of the recorded messages on the public address system is friendly, calm, and reassuring.

Five new works of art in the airport are functional as well, designed to soothe and direct passengers, not distract them. Alan Saret's walkways, for example, elegantly reinforce the directional signs in the airside building. Four shades of blue mosaic tile extend from the centers of the four arms of the X leading into the airside rotunda, subliminally leading passengers toward baggage claim. "As you can see," Katselas says, "it works," watching from the mezzanine as travellers gravitate to the ceramic pathway as if pulled by a magical, magnetic force emanating from the sea of tiny squares. The ceramic tile paths of Jackie Ferrara, in hues of slate, terra cotta, and turquoise, lead landside passengers toward their destination in the same fashion.

The five artists featured at the airport were selected from 250 proposals for their talent and experience in "installation" or "environmental" art, according to Michael Berger, chairman of the all-volunteer Airport Art Committee. Pittsburgh International is the first airport, and one of the first buildings, in which the art was built-in during construction, rather than affixed afterward.

In the international wing of the airside terminal, Michael Morrill's etched-glass wall and ceramic tile floor in soft shades of sea greens and blues symbolize cultural exchange. The outdoor steam gardens of Robert Morris welcome and envelop passers-through.

The meditation room or chapel, some call it the "cloud room," on the mezzanine is the work of Maren Hassinger. Large ceramic tiles fit together like pieces of a jigsaw puzzle, creating a floor of fluffy cumulus clouds. Heavenward, the walls and ceiling are awash in soft blues and pearly whites. A chair sits here and there, respites for the weary or worried. The whisper of soft wind breezing about the room and a shaded, nearly sound-proof glass wall mute the cacophony of surrounding airport activity. "A womb with a view," says Berger.

Coach-class Prices, First-class Selection

The subtlety of the airport is also experienced in details passengers won't feel, at least not in their wallets. "Street-pricing" was introduced to U.S. airport consumers when Pittsburgh International opened. "We're the first airport not to gouge people," says Commissioner Foerster, proudly.

The airport's retail tenants are contractually obligated to keep the prices of products in their airport store as low as those in their traditional stores, says Aviation Director O'Donnell. The first passengers through the new airport thought the prices were "introductory specials," he says. "On subsequent

trips they've been surprised by the consistency of the pricing. The after-Christmas sales knocked their socks off. It's another reason for passengers who book connecting flights to connect in Pittsburgh."

In addition to street-pricing, the Airmall features retail competition and "name-branding" to a degree previously unknown among U.S. airports, says Mark Knight of BAA Pittsburgh. International travellers, however, may recognize some similarities between Pittsburgh and London's Heathrow, one of several airports that BAA owns and operates in the U.K. BAA Pittsburgh is a subsidiary of a British firm that Allegheny County hired to develop, lease, and manage the 10,000 square feet of retail space in the airport. Prior to the Pittsburgh opening, the trend in airport retailing had been to hire a sole concessionaire, which eliminates the opportunity for competition in selection or pricing, and results in price-gouging and offended passengers.

BAA designed the Pittsburgh Airmall to appeal primarily to connecting passengers with an hour or two to eat and shop. But the arrival of street-pricing and name-branding is luring Pittsburgh shoppers as well. One-third of the nearly 60 retailers or restauranteurs who set up shop in the airport's 100 storefronts are new to the Pittsburgh market, including the Tie Rack and Waterstones, a bookseller that chose the airport as its second U.S. site. Both are British retailers who followed BAA to Pittsburgh. The Airmall also sports a Bally's of Switzerland, a purveyor of shoes, purses, and executive leathergoods; The Nature Company, which sells environmentally correct jewelry, toys, and gifts; The Wall, a CD store; and Ethel M. Chocolates.

"I can usually tell whether they're browsers or travellers," says Katselas, people-watching over lunch from a window seat at T.G.I. Friday's in the airside terminal. One day he saw a group of people step from a chartered bus outside the airport. He asked them if they were travelling. "We're just here to shop," they said. He knew why — the year the airport opened, Katselas did all of his holiday shopping at the airport, too. O'Donnell admits a weakness for the PGA Tour Store.

Window on the World

The aviation director refers to the new airport as Pittsburgh's "window on the world." Looking out, Pittsburghers see tremendous opportunities for growth of their hometown as an international city. Looking in, passengers — prospects — see Pittsburgh in a whole new light.

Katselas says he received a letter from a Munich woman who had recently changed planes in Pittsburgh. The letter said she'd seriously consider living in Pittsburgh based on the airport. That's the kind of feedback the architect likes. It means he accomplished what he set out to do — to make a statement about Pittsburgh. The old airport, tired and congested, "looked as people expected Pittsburgh to look," says Katselas. Now he often detects surprise as passengers arrive — "This is Pittsburgh?!"

"Customers get a good first impression of the city, which gets our meeting off to a good start," say Herb Ellis of Contraves, the world's largest manufacturer of scientific telescopes. Customers from around the world come to Pittsburgh to visit the company.

Despite Rand McNally's Most Livable City rating in 1985 and two Renaissance periods that cleaned the air and rivers, and dramatically enhanced the skyline, Pittsburgh continues to suffer an image problem. Katselas designed the airport to reflect the true Pittsburgh and leave a favorable first impression on the 12 million or more connecting passengers who never leave the airport.

Like Pittsburgh, the airport has "dignity, imagination, creativity," the artist expounds. "The steel trusses are honest, tough. They make a rich, effective statement. The columns

■ *The airport atmosphere and the people who work in it leave a favorable impression on the 12 million or more connecting passengers who may never get into the city. Photo by Roy Engelbrecht.*

■ *USAir invested $34 million in a state-of-the-art automated baggage system, which uses bar coding and laser scanners to speed sorting and delivery. Photo by Roy Engelbrecht.*

■ *The landside building serves as the center for passenger ticketing, baggage handling, and airport offices. Photo by Roy Engelbrecht.*

and beams pretend to be nothing but what they are. The colors are warm: clay reds, sky blues."

And then there is light, natural light, the "most neglected and underused aspect of architecture," Katselas says. To counter the persistent image of Pittsburgh as smoky and overcast, the architect designed 60-foot-high vaulted glass ceilings that let blue sky and sunshine engulf the landside building. Even at night, starlight and moonbeams brighten the space. Although clean and contempo-

agencies: Dozens of business and community leaders who make up the Allegheny Conference, Chamber of Commerce, and Southwestern Regional Planning Commission. City, county, state, and federal officials. The principal contractors — Tasso Katselas Associates, the architects; Mellon Stuart/Dick Enterprises, the construction managers; and Michael Baker Corporation, the project engineers. The FAA, Pennsylvania Department of Transportation (PennDOT), Department of Environmental Resources, and Southwest

■ *Pittsburgh International introduced "street-pricing" to U.S. airport consumers. The retail tenants are obligated to keep their product prices as low as in their traditional stores. Photos by Roy Engelbrecht.*

rary, the arches recall the aura of the great turn-of-the-century railroad stations. Katselas says he didn't aim for imitation, but the happy coincidence goes a step farther in depicting the real Pittsburgh, a city that has so effectively preserved its past while forging the future.

The process of building the airport also reflected the cooperative spirit that has become the way of life in Pittsburgh.

"Now that success is at hand, it is important to remember that no individual did this," Foerster wrote in a special edition of *Executive Report* magazine commemorating the airport opening. "It had been my privilege to lead this effort. But it truly was the work of a community of people...."

The project required the altruism and cooperation of numerous individuals and

Regional Planning Commission. The artists, airlines, and labor unions. Thousands of employees who worked overnight to move the entire airport operation in the five hours between the last take-off and the first landing of the USAir red-eye.

Nor did the cooperation stop at the doors of the new building. The midfield design required a new access road to open simultaneously with the airport. The Airport Expressway involved not only an infusion of additional state and federal funds, but a high degree of diligence and cooperation to ensure an on-time opening. PennDOT "fast-tracked" the project and completed the highway in one-third of the time it would typically take to build a $200 million, 8.5 mile limited access road. As a testament to the effectiveness of "unprecedented cooperation,"

according to PennDOT's District Engineer
Henry Nutbrown, the road opened not only in
time to coincide with the airport opening, but
three weeks ahead of schedule and under
budget.

For Nutbrown, the project was more
about people than pavement. "It's my hope
that the people who ride on the new highway
will appreciate the beauty, overall design and
efficiency, and recognize the efforts of the
thousands of people who contributed," he
said in the October 1992 issue of *Baker
Magazine*, a publication of Michael Baker
Corporation, the project manager for the
expressway.

When he gave the interview, the name
of the Airport Expressway was still in discussion. "I just hope they call it smooth, pleasant,
and beautiful," he said.

Debate also surrounded the name of
the new airport itself. Some suggested nam-
ing it in honor of its strongest proponent, but
Commission Foerster promptly vetoed the
idea, suggesting instead the obvious title.
"Greater" was dropped from the name, and
the former Greater Pittsburgh International
Airport became, very simply, Pittsburgh
International Airport.

"Because," explains Foerster,
"Pittsburgh needs no enhancement." ▐

■ *To counter the old image of Pittsburgh as overcast
or smoky, the architect used vaulted ceilings to let the
blue sky and sunshine engulf the buildings. Photo by
Gene J. Puskar.*

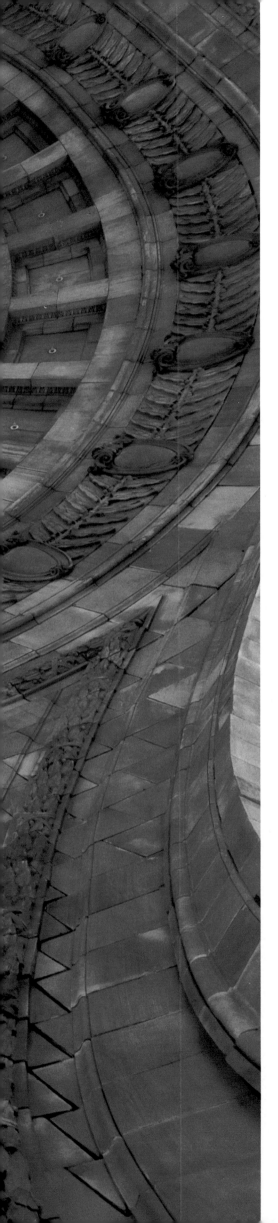

C H A P T E R

The Spirit of Pittsburgh Past

T H R E E

Pittsburgh was a place the world focused on in the 1890s. Pittsburghers were producing two-thirds of the nation's steel, half of its glass, and refining most of its oil. Some of the wealthiest industrialists—Carnegie, Heinz, Westinghouse, Frick, and Mellon, among them—lived and worked in Pittsburgh at the time.

So it was no wonder that Pittsburghers, literally on top of the world, were a bit putout when the U.S. Board of Geographic Names decided in 1891 that Pittsburgh should lose its "h" for the sake of consistency, along with the other cities and towns in the country whose names ended with burgh.

■ *In 1911, Pittsburghers petitioned to permanently preserve the original Pittsburgh spelling. This example of the 20 years of "Pittsburg" without the "H", can be seen in the rotunda of The Pennsylvanian. Photo by Roy Engelbrecht.*

efusing to conform, the citizenry retained the "h" on official documents and most correspondence, and consequently, for 20 years, Pittsburgh was Pittsburg everywhere but here. (As a result, few local examples of the Pittsburg spelling exist today.) In 1911, Pittsburghers decided to have it their way—officially. The city formally petitioned the board to reverse its decision, and the original spelling was permanently preserved.

The Pittsburgh Spirit

More than a historical aside, the story of Pittsburgh with an "h" is a symbol of the Pittsburgh spirit, says Bart Roselli, deputy director of the Western Pennsylvania Historical Society. Fate bestowed on Pittsburgh three rivers for transportation and the natural resources for industry that attracted those who would exploit them. But it was the gumption of great leaders and industrious laborers who gave Pittsburgh the spirit, identity, and resources that persist. A pride of place and self-determination are the legacies of the generations of risk-takers who settled and developed Pittsburgh.

There *is* a Pittsburgh spirit, a feeling of community pride, a we're-all-in-this-together attitude that is uniquely Pittsburgh's. It's the feeling that steals your breath at the end of the tunnels, puts a lump in your throat on Light-up Night, grips you with pride when you recognize a landmark or familiar face in a filmed-in-Pittsburgh movie. The late Mayor Richard Caliguiri used to say that the Pittsburgh spirit gave him goose pimples. It affects newcomers as well as natives, regardless of gender, age, heritage, or status.

The Pittsburgh feeling was there when Art Rooney died, when Chuck Noll retired, when Mario Lemieux circled the ice holding high the Stanley Cup it took the Penguins 26 years to earn. It is there during groundbreakings, ribbon-cuttings, and parades. It's a feeling of pride and ownership that makes every Pittsburgher a self-appointed ambassador.

Helge H. Wehmeier, the German-born CEO of Miles Inc. says he experienced the Pittsburgh spirit before he arrived here. He was introduced to Pittsburgh by

■ *Pittsburgh is a fascinating blend of historic and modern architecture. Photo by Herb Ferguson.*

■ *Nestled at the foothills of the Allegheny Mountains and at the confluence of three rivers, Pittsburgh is rich with natural resources. Photo by Herb Ferguson.*

■ *Pittsburgh has overcome many obstacles such as the floods of the 1930s. Photo courtesy of the Carnegie Library.*

FIFTH AVE. & MARKET ST.   MAR. 18, 1936

Pittsburghers on a ski lift in Colorado. "They were all champions," says Wehmeier, who moved to Pittsburgh in 1992 when he became Miles' president and CEO. "Now I'm an ambassador, too. I'm as much of a champion as the people I met in the chairlift."

"It's amazing how infectious Pittsburgh is," says Marty Ashby, a musician and director of performing arts at the Manchester Craftsmen's Guild. Ashby is a New Yorker who came to Pittsburgh by way of Cleveland. "I fell in love with the city the first day I was here."

Choreographer Mark Taylor, who moved to Pittsburgh in 1991, says he had "that magical thing happen" when he came through the Fort Pitt tunnels the first time. Like Wehmeier, Taylor is also a champion of Pittsburgh.

If Pittsburghers are fiercely loyal and unequivocally proud, it is because they feel they've earned the right to be. Pittsburghers have always had a will as strong as the steel that was made here. For, again and again, they have had to adapt, overcome obstacles, and work hard to make change happen.

Pittsburghers have rebuilt many times.

In 1845, when fire left one-third of the city in ashes, destroying nearly 1,000 buildings and leaving 12,000 homeless, pride of place inspired the immigrants and first-generation Pittsburghers to reconstruct. Pittsburghers repaired and rebuilt after floods through the 1930s, enacted smoke and flood control measures, and began the process of Renaissance in the 1940s, and responded with financial assistance, food banks, and job retraining programs when the steel industry began its decline in the 1970s. Pittsburgh is a leader in technology and health care industries today because Pittsburghers worked diligently to expand and diversify the city's industrial base.

"What brave people they were. What staunch faith they must have had in the old American concept that tomorrow can be made better than today," says author and historian David McCullough of Pittsburgh's early developers. McCullough, a native, was speaking at the first annual Historical Society's History Makers Dinner.

"If you were to take a prism and put it down someplace on the map of America and say, `This is where we might see the whole

story of our national life,' there is no better place than Pittsburgh. From the history of the Native American who lived in these magnificent valleys long before the coming of Europeans, through the French and Indian War, the Revolutionary War, the opening of the West, on through the Civil War, to the tumultuous change that began in 1869 when Andrew Carnegie literally saw the light of the Bessemer process, and on into our own time.''

The Great Industrialists

Pittsburgh was developed by entrepreneurs, inventors, visionaries, and trailblazers—immigrants who left all that was familiar to work for and realize the American Dream. They came from France, England, Germany, Italy, Ireland, Lithuania, Poland, Croatia, Serbia, Russia, and Africa. And not by accident. Ever since Major George Washington described the site that would be Pittsburgh in the mid-1700s as ''very well situated for a fort,'' the city's geographic location was hailed as superb. Nestled at the foothills of the Allegheny Mountains and at the confluence of three mighty rivers, Pittsburgh's environment was protected and pristine. Originally inhabited by Native Americans, Pittsburgh was settled by the French, who established Fort Duquesne at the Point. Wher the British took over the bastion and renamed it Fort Pitt, they called the surrounding area Pittsburgh in honor of the English prime minister William Pitt.

■ *The Pittsburgh inclines are an unusual form of mountain transportation. Photo by Tom Pollard.*

■ *George Westinghouse (left) and John Pitcairn (right) are two of the many legendary entrepreneurs who made their mark on Pittsburgh. Photos courtesy of the Carnegie Library.*

The location of Fort Pitt became a natural respite for the pioneers who lumbered in their Conestoga wagon trains over the mountains. Those early pioneers gave Pittsburgh's first merchants a steady source of patrons. Known as the "Gateway to the West," Pittsburgh was briefly a home away from home for many new Americans—at the turn of the 19th century, every third person on the streets in Pittsburgh was someone who didn't live here.

Besides the rivers, which carried goods and settlers down the Ohio to the Mississippi River and served as the impetus for the town's earliest industry, boat building and outfitting, Pittsburgh was rich with other natural resources that also attracted settlers and the future industrialists. There were forests for lumber to build homes, businesses, and factories as well as boats; vast quantities of coal for fuel (at one time the world's largest single deposit of coal was in Pittsburgh); iron-ore for nails, utensils, and tools; flax and cotton for textiles; clay-enriched soil for brickmaking; and deposits of limestone and sandstone for glassmaking. Pittsburgh's first industrialists were glass manufacturers. Major Isaac Craig and General James O'Hara, both militiamen in the British army that had established Fort Pitt on the present site of Point State Park, began making glass bottles in the late 1700s.

Pittsburgh grew steadily and prospered as the nation's workshop in the decades between 1870 and the First World War. What an exciting time to be in Pittsburgh! No city had as many industrial leaders and inventors, or the energy of Pittsburgh.

One of the most influential of Pittsburgh's shapers was Andrew Carnegie, a Scotsman who came to Pittsburgh with his parents in 1848. As a teen, Carnegie worked as a bobbin boy in the textile mill and then as a telegrapher. His ability to distinguish transmitted letters by sound caught the attention of J. Edgar Thompson, the president of the Pennsylvania Railroad, which had come to Pittsburgh in 1852. Carnegie became Thompson's personal secretary and, eventually, a line superintendent who introduced the use of sleeping cars. Described as an incomparable salesman, Carnegie's personal investment in sleeping cars was the start of his fortune. When he brought the Bessemer steelmaking process he discovered in England to Braddock, Pennsylvania, he named the mill the J. Edgar Thompson Works, after his largest prospective customer and former boss. J. Edgar Thompson was no slouch, either. He solved the problem of crossing the Alleghenies by building the Horseshoe Curve, still considered an engineering marvel.

While Carnegie advanced steelmaking, many other legendary entrepreneurs were making their mark on Pittsburgh and establishing Pittsburgh's reputation in the world. Sam Langley experimented with flight. Henry Clay Frick built the coke industry. Jones and Laughlin, who had preceded Carnegie in steelmaking in Pittsburgh, converted to Bessemer processing, becoming one of the area's largest steel manufacturers. George Westinghouse, who had already revolutionized the transportation industry by perfecting and patenting the air brake, formed the Westinghouse Electric Company, which manufactured equipment that generated and distributed electricity by alternating current. Michael Benedum helped advance Pittsburgh's stake in the oil industry. Charles Hall pioneered aluminum processing, a discovery he shared with Capt. Alfred Hunt who formed the Pittsburgh Reduction Company, the predecessor of the Aluminum Company of America (ALCOA). Henry Porter manufactured steam locomotives. John Pitcairn financed Pittsburgh Plate Glass, now PPG Industries. Mr. Boggs and Henry Buhl opened the Boggs and Buhl Department Store, competing with Isaac and Jacob

Kaufmann and Joseph Horne. Henry Heinz started the food processing and packaging industry 20 miles north of Pittsburgh in Sharpsburg with a crop of horseradish he prepared and sold in clear bottles to prove the purity of the product.

Thomas Mellon and his sons gave seed money to young industrialists, financing many of Pittsburgh's most successful business ventures. Mellon, an Irishman who was five years old when he came to Pittsburgh with his family, married Sarah Jane Negley, a daughter of one of the oldest families in Pittsburgh. Thomas and Sarah had eight children, including Andrew W. and Richard B., the two who most shared their father's uncanny knack for recognizing the potential of ideas. (Andrew went on to become secretary of the treasury under Presidents Harding, Coolidge, and Hoover, then the American ambassador to Great Britain, and Richard, the first president of ALCOA, raised a son, Richard King Mellon, who would become the private sector leader in Pittsburgh's Renaissance I.)

The Legacies

Pittsburgh continues to reflect the wealth and inspiration of these great industrialists as well as the generation of businessmen who came after them. Following in the footsteps of Carnegie, Frick, Heinz, Mellon, and the others were entrepreneurs like Willard Rockwell, Henry Hillman, and Alan Scaife. Pittsburgh offered them opportunities to amass wealth, and they repaid the city many times over. Their philanthropy has made Pittsburgh a resource-rich community. The Carnegie Institute, Carnegie Mellon University, Heinz Hall, Benedum Center for the Performing Arts, Hillman Library, and the Frick Art Museum represent just a few of their gifts. Additionally, the family and corporate foundations that bear their names continue to enhance the quality of life in Pittsburgh through investments in the arts, education, social services, and community and economic development.

■ *The philanthropy of men like Henry Clay Frick has enhanced the quality of life in Pittsburgh. Photo courtesy of the Carnegie Library.*

■ *The Mellon Bank Center is named for the Mellon family that has financed many of Pittsburgh's successful business ventures. Photo by Roy Engelbrecht.*

■ *Many Pittsburgh communities retain the architecture and flavor of their heritage like this church in Polish Hill. Photo by Roy Engelbrecht.*

For these men, the American Dream read like a rags-to-riches story. But for the average risk-takers who came on their heels, the American Dream was simply to build a home, a family, and a neighborhood. The magnetism of men like Andrew Carnegie to attract others is perhaps then their greatest legacy. For it was the mill workers and merchants, lured by the jobs the city's industrial base offered, who built the neighborhoods and lived the work ethic for which Pittsburgh is known. After laboring long hours in the factories, these workers went home to communities that retained a flavor of their heritage. In neighborhoods like Polish Hill, Bloomfield, Lawrenceville, Hazelwood, South Side, Coal Hill, McKeesport, Monongahela, and Homestead, they erected homes, businesses, churches, and community centers for themselves, their families, and neighbors. That Pittsburgh enjoys a wealth of 19th century architecture is a tribute to these laborers who cut no corners to ensure a good life for their families.

"One of the ironies of Pittsburgh is that many of the immigrant workers, particularly in the late age of steelmaking, came as temporary workers," says Brian O'Connor, a labor historian and associate professor at Point Park College, where he teaches a course in Pittsburgh history. "Their plan was to build a nest egg and go home. Of course, a lot of them didn't go home, and their primary concerns then became building homes and neighborhoods, and imparting to their kids that nothing came except by earning it. For good or ill, that's a Pittsburgh mores."

This work ethic was the basis of unionized labor, O'Connor says. Pittsburgh has partial claim to the origins of the nation's earliest iron and steel unions as well as the American Federation of Labor (AFL), which held one of its founding conventions here. Pittsburgh was also an important center in the birth of industrial unionism through the Congress of Industrial Organizations (CIO)

and the United Steelworkers of America. Pittsburgh workers "did not seek to overthrow America or the capitalist economy, they simply sought more for their labor," O'Connor says. "Unions weren't founded in the spirit of angry confrontation, but of collective bargaining."

The Past is the Present

As Pittsburgh moves toward the 21st century, the city remains a product of its past. Largely because of the topography of hills, valleys, and rivers that creates natural boundaries and distinct havens, neighborhoods continue to reflect the ethnic social, cultural, and religious diversity of the waves of immigrants who put down their roots.

The work ethic survives because Pittsburghers have achieved a great deal by working hard. Whether magnates or factory workers, Pittsburghers fostered a tradition of connectedness to the world: Pittsburgh is where the world's bridges were built, where steel for cars and battleships was forged, where atomic energy was harnessed, where the polio vaccine was discovered.

What brought people here in the past is what will bring people here in the future—a wealth of resources, this time not coal and rivers, but knowledge and ideas. What keeps people here is the legacy of the immigrants who developed Pittsburgh: a culture that embraces diversity, celebrates achievement, and encourages self-determination. ■

■ *Great leaders and industrious laborers have given Pittsburgh the spirit, identity, and resources that persist today. Carnegie Science Center photo by Herb Ferguson.*

C H A P T E R

Renaissance

F O U R

T he rise of the steel industry fueled Pittsburgh's rapid development in the latter half of the 19th century; ironically, it was
the decline of steel that brought growth in the last part of
the 20th century. The industrial heyday continued through World War I,
when Pittsburgh was a key shop in the arsenal of democracy. Then the
steel markets moved west, mills aged, and steelmakers discovered new
sources of coal and iron. Following World War II, a stressful time for
Pittsburghers with ties to Europe, the city embarked on an aggressive
rebuilding program to attract new industry and boost morale. It came to
be known as Renaissance I.

■ *Renaissance I and II resulted in dramatic capital improvements
to the city's infrastructure and skyline. Photo by Roy Engelbrecht.*

The word renaissance suggests romance, and, in retrospect, the period of rebuilding from 1945 through 1969 was a romantic time. Two "incredibly powerful people who couldn't have been more different," says urban historian Dr. Michael Weber, joined hands for a common cause. Mayor David Lawrence partnered with Richard King Mellon to save Pittsburgh—a staunch, working-class Irish-Catholic Democrat, and a Republican Protestant from a lineage of vast wealth.

To this day, Lawrence remains a local icon; his powers of persuasion are legendary. A Democratic party leader for more than 25 years, Lawrence campaigned for the Mayor's office in 1945 on what would have been a paradoxical platform for an ordinary democrat—he convinced working-class Pittsburghers that what was good for Big Business was good for them. "In 13 years as mayor, he never lost a vote in City Council," says Weber, author of a biography on Lawrence. Lawrence's muscle locally precipitated an illustrious political career. He later became Governor of Pennsylvania and widely respected at the national level, "a nice Mayor Daly," says Weber, comparing Lawrence to the famous Chicago politician.

Mellon's influence in the business sector was equally imposing. When Lawrence

■ *The USX Tower is the tallest building between New York and Chicago. Photo by Roy Engelbrecht.*

became mayor, Mellon, a fourth generation financier, not only controlled $3 billion in assets, but held controlling interests in many of Pittsburgh's major businesses as well. "Wherever he went, they went," says Weber, referring to the banker's magnetic appeal to corporate leaders. So when Mellon suggested that the CEOs of the top corporations form a conference to assist Mayor Lawrence, no one argued. What became the Allegheny Conference on Community Development provided the clout and capital (business outspent government six-to-one) for Renaissance I. "Mellon's number one rule was that no one could send an underling to a meeting of the conference," Weber says. "Decisions were made on the spot. No one had to go back and check with their boss."

The liaison of Lawrence and Mellon formed a "public-private partnership" that revolutionized the way things happen in Pittsburgh. Lawrence wooed the electorate while Mellon cajoled the CEOs, and government and industry came together to solve Pittsburgh's most pressing problems—persistent smoke, frequent floods, and a dilapidated downtown in which no new construction had occurred for nearly 15 years.

The public-private partnership cleaned the air and dammed the rivers. They built the Civic Arena, the 62-story U.S. Steel Building (now the USX Tower and tallest building between New York and Chicago), Oliver Plaza, and the highway known as the Parkway. They cleared land and removed and rebuilt two bridges to create Point State Park at the confluence of the Monongahela, Allegheny, and Ohio Rivers. A magnificent fountain at the tip of the triangle where the three rivers meet made the park a grand gateway to the city, and along with the development of Three Rivers Stadium, marked the beginning of the transformation of the riverfronts from industrial to recreational uses. Gateway Center, the nation's first privately funded urban renewal project, anchored the new "Golden Triangle."

The public-private partnership approach dictated that everyone share and

sacrifice for the good of the city. To secure federal funding for the dam essential to the flood control program, the leadership called in their chits with President Truman. To build the Gateway Center office complex, the Allegheny Conference guaranteed 80 percent of the occupancy.

To obliterate smoke pollution, the city enacted legislation to phase-out coal as a source of heat and power, forcing the railroads to convert from steam to diesel power. The citizenry bundled-up: before gas furnaces were popular, the 140,000 homeowners who depended on coal-burning stoves for heat converted to "disco coal," a part-rock substance that didn't heat well.

Renaissance II

Renaissance I resulted in dramatic capital improvements to the city's infrastructure and skyline. Equally important, the renaissance rallied the populace to new heights of pride and confidence.

This was the effect Mayor Richard Caliguiri hoped to duplicate when he launched Renaissance II in 1978, a time when Pittsburghers sorely needed hope and inspiration. The mills were closing, and Pittsburgh was settling into an emotional and economic depression. Within a few years, the region would lose 150,000 jobs to the decline of heavy industry and an era of mergers and acquisitions that stole several headquarters

■ *Gateway Center, a Renaissance I project, was the nation's first privately funded urban renewal development. Photo by Roy Engelbrecht.*

■ *On the following page: Three Rivers Stadium was one of the first developments which marked the beginning of the transformation of the riverfronts. Photo by Herb Ferguson.*

companies, including Gulf Oil, a prominent employer and generous benefactor. In Renaissance II, Mayor Caliguiri offered a plan for recovery—a building boom to create jobs and stimulate investment, not just downtown, but in the neighborhoods as well.

"It's remarkable that we've survived," says John (Jack) Robin, "let alone succeeded." Others have called the transformation "miraculous," "phenomenal," and "amazingly successful," but Robin's opinion, shaped by decades of insight, is, perhaps, the weightiest. In 1992, Robin celebrated his 80th birthday and nearly 50 years of public service, during which he served as right arm and political strategist for Mayor Lawrence. Throughout Renaissance II, Robin was a confidante of Mayor Caliguiri and chairman of the Urban Redevelopment Authority, the agency responsible for many programs that helped stimulate the economic recovery.

Following the precedent of Mayor Lawrence, Caliguiri looked to the Allegheny Conference for help. With Bob Pease, executive director of the conference, he redefined the public-private partnership for a new generation of corporate leaders. Bearing millions of dollars of incentives in the form of federal Urban Development Action Grants (UDAG), Caliguiri courted the corporations, urging them to work with him to make Pittsburgh a greater city.

They responded with a remarkable show of faith in the future of Pittsburgh. Global companies, no longer dependent on the region's natural resources, not only stayed in Pittsburgh, they made substantial financial investments as well. PPG Industries built a six-building headquarters kingdom, anchored by a stunning, 40-story, all-glass "castle." Mellon Bank invested in a new, 54-story headquarters on Grant Street. Numerous others, including Consolidated Natural Gas, Federated Investors, Duquesne Light, and Blue Cross of Western Pennsylvania, signed long-term lease agreements that ignited an explosion of building downtown. There were cranes in the skyline for nearly a decade as eight new office complexes and a convention center arose in the heart of the city.

■ *During Renaissance II, Pittsburgh invested in new land transportation systems to support the downtown building boom. Photo by Roy Engelbrecht.*

■ *The courtyard in PPG Place is a familiar meeting place for downtown Pittsburghers. Photo by Roy Engelbrecht.*

■ *Carnegie Mellon University is among the leading resources in robotics. This Ambler robot is a planetary exploration prototype. Photo courtesy of The Robotics Institute-Carnegie Mellon University.*

■ *Mayor Richard Caliguiri rallied the populace to a new sense of pride and confidence when he launched Renaissance II in 1978. Photo by Bill Metzger.*

"We did it just right. We didn't go overboard," says Robin. "We had no savings and loan scandals, no developers went belly-up, no glut of office space."

To support the downtown building boom, Pittsburgh invested in new land transportation systems during Renaissance II, building a light rail transit system between downtown and the southern suburbs, a downtown subway, urban busway, and the East Street Valley Expressway, a highway connecting downtown with the growing northern suburbs.

In addition, Caliguiri continued the riverfront redevelopment that Lawrence and Mellon started in Renaissance I. A historic railroad station along the Monongahela River became Station Square, a popular retail mall, restaurant, hotel, and office complex, and home to the Gateway Clipper Fleet. Roberto Clemente Park and an office complex were built on the north shore of the Allegheny.

On the north shore of the Monongahela, the Pittsburgh Technology Center replaced an abandoned mill, symbolizing the region's new economy. The Technology Center currently encompasses the University of Pittsburgh Center for Biotechnology and Bioengineering, and the Carnegie Mellon University Center for

Advanced Manufacturing and Software Engineering. The development set a precedent for riverfront projects throughout the region: Keystone Commons in Turtle Creek, City Center in Duquesne, and Industrial Center in McKeesport. All three of the former mill sites contain office, light manufacturing, and public recreational space.

Renaissance II also modernized the rivers as transportation arteries. In 1981, the Greater Pittsburgh Chamber of Commerce created the Association for the Development of Inland Navigation in America's Ohio Valley. Called DINAMO for short, the association is a multi-state partnership of government leaders, CEOs, and waterway shippers in western Pennsylvania, Ohio, Kentucky, and West Virginia who formed to more effectively lobby for federal and state dollars to improve the locks and dams on the Ohio River and its navigable tributaries. DINAMO secured funding for 10 new lock and dam facilities, and 3 more are under review, representing an investment in the region of more than $4 billion, according to Justin Horan, president of Pittsburgh's Chamber.

But Renaissance II didn't stop with infrastructure improvements. Government not only courted the corporate sector to enhance the Pittsburgh skyline, it looked inward as well, to reduce costs, increase efficiency, and improve service. One of the first major partnerships of the era was the Loaned Executive program sponsored by the Chamber of Commerce. The Chamber formed 11 Loaned Executive Task Forces, led by the CEOs of Pittsburgh's corporate conglomerates, who "brought economies and private sector know-how to City and County government," says Horan.

Through a project called the Committee for Progress in Allegheny County, or ComPAC, the loaned executives recommended more than 100 changes in county government. According to Horan, the county implemented 95 percent of the suggestions and realized a savings of more than $40 million for area taxpayers. A similar program called ComPEP, or Committee for Progress and Efficiency in Pittsburgh, analyzed city government operations and recommended improvements that saved city taxpayers nearly $3 million a year. During Renaissance II, the Chamber also developed COGNET, a computer network project that links the 132 municipalities of Allegheny County, and Leadership Pittsburgh, a program that cultivates young executives for service in government and community boards of directors.

A Neighborhood Renaissance

One of the prettiest skylines in the world is a fitting testament to the public-private partnership Caliguiri cultivated. But the Mayor's heart was in what he called "the heart of the city," its 88 ethnically diverse neighborhoods. A Pittsburgher of Italian descent who grew up in Bloomfield, Caliguiri

was more at home at a senior citizens center or community festival than in a corporate boardroom. He looked happiest when holding a festooned shovel or pair of scissors at an event celebrating the beginning of another neighborhood success story—the ribbon-cutting for a community center, opening of a parklet, or groundbreaking for townhomes.

The public part of the public-private partnership in the neighborhood renaissance was capitalized by the Community Development Block Grant Program, the community equivalent to the UDAG. Pittsburgh used the federal money for low-interest mortgages, home repair loans, facade improvement grants, and other incentives that made reinvestment financially enticing for homeowners and neighborhood merchants. The city also funded a full-time staff for community groups like the South Side Local Development Company, Manchester Citizens Corporation, and East Liberty Development, Inc. and established a new

■ *During Renaissance II, Pittsburgh's business leaders brought private sector know-how to City and County government through partnership programs. Allegheny County Courthouse photo by Roy Engelbrecht.*

organization called the Neighborhoods for Living Center to support neighborhood groups and market living and homebuying in city neighborhoods.

"By giving neighborhoods a hand in determining their future," says Mina Gerall, Caliguiri's neighborhood liaison, "the mayor created a resurgence of community pride and a feeling that the ordinary citizen could make a difference."

Neighborhood groups came into their own during Renaissance II. With staff and a budget, they formed their own partnerships with banks, foundations, real estate developers, and small business owners.

showcased the handiwork. Events like Paint Your Heart Out Pittsburgh, an annual paint-a-thon that attracts hundreds of volunteers, not only let older or disabled homeowners who couldn't afford to make improvements on their own be part of the renaissance, it reflected the community spirit that Renaissance II engendered. NeighborFair, a city-wide celebration of neighborhoods, was another annual event that symbolized the resurgence of the pride of place that Pittsburgh is known for.

All the activity attracted newcomers and had a positive effect on the economy. Gallery owners, antique dealers, and saloon

■ *Neighborhood renaissance created a resurgence of community pride. Restored home and window box photos by Roy Engelbrecht.*

Together, they built new homes, renovated older ones, attracted new business, put people to work, and made their neighborhoods prettier, safer, and more convenient places to live. Community-based development emerged as an industry. A coalition of lenders, foundations, and government leaders created the Pittsburgh Partnership for Neighborhood Development to continue community economic development.

Restoring and renovating were the vogue in Renaissance II. Across the city, homeowners scraped, sanded, stained, polyurethaned, plastered, and painted. They organized seminars on buying and renovating older homes. House tours in the Mexican War Streets, Allegheny West, and Shadyside

keepers gravitated to refurbished storefronts in the new, Historic South Side. First-time homebuyers settled down in Saybrook Court, Deutschtown Square, or Lookout Point, new townhome communities in South Oakland, East Allegheny, and Perry Hilltop. Apartment dwellers moved to renovations like The Pennsylvanian, a former railroad station downtown, or The School House, a former school on the Northside. Entrepreneurs started-up in business incubators like The Brewery, a former turn-of-the century German brew house.

Renaissance II also attracted the attention of the national media, and when Rand McNally named Pittsburgh the Most Livable City in 1985, it kicked-off a flurry of awards

■ *The Frick House Museum, Clayton, is an elaborate example of renovation at its foremost. Photo by Herb Ferguson.*

■ *The spirit of Pittsburgh renovation and renaissance is depicted in this bronze statue on the North Shore. Photo by Roy Engelbrecht.*

and recognition. Pittsburgh became a top 10 Healthiest City, according to *Health* magazine, the third Most Livable City for Women, according to *Savvy* magazine, and the eighth Best City for Business, according to *Fortune* magazine. The city also won an All-America City award for successful public-private partnerships and neighborhood redevelopment, and several Keep America Beautiful awards for the litter reduction work of the Pittsburgh Clean City Committee.

Few were happier with the applause than the staff of the Greater Pittsburgh Convention and Visitors Bureau, which has the job of attracting tourism and conventions to the city. Combined with the fresh face on downtown and the neighborhoods, and a new convention center and adjoining three star hotel, the positive publicity generated new interest in Pittsburgh from travel agents and tour promoters. With help from an Office of Promotion, the bureau established Pittsburgh's image as a destination city for the typical traveller—tourists in

groups, conventioneers, or families who spend three to four days in one location.

Those who can't picture Pittsburgh as a vacation get-away haven't talked with Joe McGrath, the bureau president. "Pittsburgh is a city where the reality exceeds the expectation," McGrath says. "Someone said that it's like going on a blind date that turns out to be Robert Redford."

"When I'm asked `what does Pittsburgh have that people want?' I say, what does Pittsburgh have that people don't want? In Europe, you visit castles; here we have Clayton (the historic mansion of Henry Frick) and Fallingwater (the Kaufmann mansion designed by Frank Lloyd Wright). In Hollywood, you drive by and look at expensive homes; here we have Shadyside. We have museums, the symphony, boating, golf courses, professional sports, skiing, shopping, restaurants—you name it, it's all here. Pittsburgh has it," McGrath says.

His sermonette is effective. In two years, the bureau charted a 30-percent

increase in the number of out-of-town tourists, nearly four million visitors. Tourism, one of the growing new industries in Pittsburgh, employs more than 42,000 people.

Rebuilding the Economy

Renaissance I and II began preparing Pittsburgh for the post-steel era—whether the city knew it or not. As downtown grew, so did job opportunities in the professions. New and growing businesses needed architects, designers, bankers, brokers, lawyers, accountants, and advertising specialists. Continuing education programs created employment for teachers. Research jobs flourished, as business looked to the universities for technology and training. Career opportunities in entertainment and the arts multiplied as corporate Pittsburgh made grants to the cultural community and as Hollywood identified the city as an alternative location for filmmaking. Jobs in health care developed as biomedical breakthroughs

advanced the city's reputation as a leading medical and bioresearch center.

In effect, Pittsburgh had quietly secured its future with new industries. So when steel production shut down, and job losses took over the headlines, the public and private partners (whose working relationships were by now indigenous to Pittsburgh) simply looked to the results of their labor. A redevelopment plan began to take shape—grow the existing industries, retrain the work force, and nurture entrepreneurship. Pittsburgh boasted 170 research and development (R&D) facilities, two of the nation's largest research universities, and the headquarters of 70 major national and multinational corporations, including 13 Fortune 500 firms—a ''reservoir of management, labor, talent, and capital to build on,'' according to Jack Robin.

A host of institutions sprang into action: Penn's Southwest to recruit new business and industry; the Chamber of Commerce, High Technology Council, Technology and Education Development Corporation, Small

Manufacturers Council, and Minority Enterprise Corporation, to name a few, to support existing and developing businesses, particularly in the areas of education and exporting; the Community College of Allegheny County and Private Industry Council to retrain the work force; the Urban Redevelopment Authority and Regional Industrial Development Corporation (RIDC) to connect burgeoning businesses with financing and real estate.

Together, they began to make a difference. The regional unemployment rate dropped steadily each year from a high of nearly 15 percent in 1983 to a low of 5 percent in 1991. The number of jobs grew by 27,000 between 1981 and 1990 within the city limits alone. The number of manufacturers in the region grew by 10 percent to 4,400 firms employing more than 250,000 people. More than 425 technology-intensive businesses were founded in the 1980s, swelling this segment of the economy to nearly 800 firms employing 70,000 workers. Many of the jobs lost to downsizing in manufacturing "were traded for new equipment and plant modernization," says John McCartney, district director of the U.S. Department of Commerce, "increasing productivity by 46 percent between 1982 and 1987, one of the highest rates in the country."

Service, technology, education, health care, and finance were identified as emerging industries, particularly in the areas of software, computers, industry automation, biotechnology, and bioengineering. The source of much of the growth was the "knowledge well," the term Jay Aldridge, president of Penn's Southwest, invokes to describe the region's universities and R&D laboratories. Both Richard Cyert and Wesley Posvar, the former heads of Carnegie Mellon University (CMU) and the University of Pittsburgh (Pitt), respectively, "committed their institutions in the early 1980s to the development of technology for the marketplace," Aldridge says. More than 30 of the 250 software firms in Pittsburgh in 1992 were spin-offs of CMU's School of Computer Science, including Duquesne Systems, the forerunner of the Legent Corp.

■ *Transplant surgeons Andreas Tzakis, M.D. (left) and John Fung, M.D. (right) perform the world's second baboon-to-human liver transplant at the University of Pittsburgh Medical Center on January 10, 1993. Photo courtesy of University of Pittsburgh Health Sciences News Bureau.*

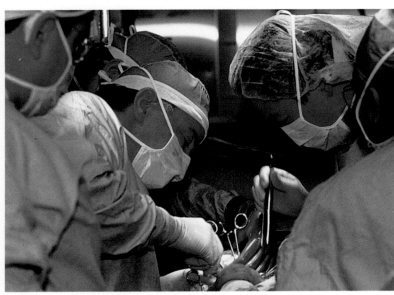

Carnegie Mellon is among the leading resources in robotics, information technology, and software development in the United States. With support from Westinghouse Electric Corporation in 1980, the university founded the nation's largest Robotics Institute, which brings together engineers and computer scientists who apply engineering and artificial intelligence principles to solve problems. Robotics researchers created an automated factory for Westinghouse. They are also developing a Mars rover for NASA and a driverless van that uses a special vision system to read the road for the U.S. Defense Advanced Research Projects Agency.

At CMU's Software Engineering Institute, the product of a $103 million award from the U.S. Defense Department in 1984, software engineers are developing software for the defense industry and training industry technicians to use it. At the Engineering Design Research Center and the Data Storage Systems Center, CMU researchers are advancing magnetic and magneto-optical recording technologies used to store data in computers and high-definition television, and creating technological systems to move products from design to production more rapidly. CMU is also a partner with Westinghouse and Pitt in the Pittsburgh Supercomputing Center, one of five national centers designated by the National Science Foundation. The center houses a Cray X-MP/832 and Cray-3, the fastest supercomputers in existence.

Similarly, both universities are leaders in biotechnology and bioengineering research. CMU supports a Science and Technology Center for Light Microscope Imaging and Biotechnology (one of 25 National Science Foundation Science and Technology Centers) as well as the Center for Fluorescence Research in the Biomedical Sciences. Pitt's Medical Center, which employs more than 12,000

people, is world renowned for biomedical advancements. Pitt researchers pioneered cardiopulmonary resuscitation (CPR), for example. Pitt is also developing a computerized archival system that will give physicians desktop access to patient information, advancing knowledge on the prevention and treatment of AIDS, cancer, and Alzheimer's disease, and creating artificial organ devices, including an artificial heart.

Pittsburgh is best known in the medical field, however, as the world leader in organ transplantation, thanks to Pitt's Dr. Thomas Starzl. According to Jeffrey Romoff, the head of the Medical Center, Starzl came to Pittsburgh as a result of Pitt's "deliberate effort to recruit the finest scientists and clinicians." Led by Starzl, the transplant research and surgical teams at Pitt have made single-organ transplantation commonplace. They are also advancing multi-organ and animal organ transplantation, and developing anti-rejection drugs and studying the immune system to identify the causes of organ rejection and serious illness. Pending breakthroughs in immune system research at Pitt "will make our heroic success in transplanting a liver seem somewhat small time by comparison," Romoff predicts.

According to the National Institutes of Health, Pittsburgh ranks among the top 10 U.S. cities for advanced medical research. In addition to the efforts at Pitt and CMU, the Allegheny Singer Research Institute, an affiliate of Allegheny General Hospital (AGH), has introduced several of the nation's firsts in cardiac surgery and sponsors one of the world's most comprehensive spina bifida centers. AGH surgeons were the first to perform an echocardiogram and use "cryosurgery" to freeze liver or prostate tumors.

More than a dozen teaching hospitals, and two medical schools—Pitt and the Medical College of Pennsylvania at AGH—place the city among the top 10 for medical resources as well. In 1992, more than 100,000 people worked in the region's 30-plus hospitals and biotech companies. To expand the health care and related industries in Pittsburgh, agencies like Pitt's Center for Biotechnology and Bioengineering, and the independent Pittsburgh Biomedical Development Corporation, are nurturing the transfer of medical technology to the market-place. Already, Pittsburgh is home to several dozen medical technology firms, including industry leaders like Respironics, Mylan Labs, Fisher Scientific, and Medrad.

"A local market for biotechnology already exists," says Aldridge, "because of the presence of large firms and major hospitals. Small firms can easily get a foothold in the local market."

Back to the Future

In the mid-1800s, a technological advancement called Bessemer processing made Pittsburgh the world leader in steel production. Today, technology is having a similar impact, not in one industry, but in many. Technology is not only creating new, technology-based businesses, it's strengthening the region's traditional metalworking manufacturers as well. Pittsburgh still produces 10 percent of the nation's steel and "remains one of the world's most successful industrial hubs, with economic output matching that of some small nations," according to the Commerce Department.

Pittsburgh also remains a fountain of entrepreneurship, the by-product of the grit and self-determination that set Pittsburgh's early industrialists apart from their peers. Of the 27,000 new jobs created in the City of Pittsburgh in the 1980s, one-third were at firms employing fewer than 150 people. Business management firms grew 118 percent, and 10 of the 15 largest were firms that didn't exist 10 years before. High-tech companies grew 97 percent, and 6 of the 14 largest didn't exist a decade earlier. These are indications that the seeds of the entrepreneurial spirit, planted by the likes of Langley, Carnegie, Westinghouse, and Heinz, are alive and well in Pittsburgh.

■ Pittsburgh pride and determination have stood the test of time. Town Crier photo by Roy Engelbrecht.

CHAPTER
Making International Connections
FIVE

Several years before the break up of the U.S.S.R. seemed imaginable, 200 Soviets came to Pittsburgh for *Chautauqua at Pitt*, an elaborate week-long cultural exchange sponsored by the Chautauqua Institute of New York. During their stay, the Soviets lived with Pittsburgh executives, met national leaders and celebrities, and were wined and dined in first-class fashion. The highlight of the visit, however, may have been the trip to Ross Park Mall, where each of the guests went shopping for Levi's, compliments of J.C. Penney's.

■ *St. John's Ukrainian Church is a beautiful example of the ethnic diversity of Pittsburgh. Photo by Herb Ferguson.*

When the Soviets couldn't find jeans in their sizes, the event took on major proportions. More than a shopping spree, it became a lesson in competitiveness. Although a resourceful host with a tape measure converted metric thinking into American inches and sent the Soviets home with the pants they longed for, the incident demonstrated how something as simple as a waistline measurement could sink an international sale. Shortly thereafter, a coalition of 50 organizations and experts in international relations formed the District Export Council to help small and mid-size manufacturers in Pittsburgh export their products. The Export Council became the catalyst for yet another Pittsburgh renaissance—the reconstruction of Pittsburgh's international image.

As in Renaissance I and II, Pittsburgh is employing the public-private partnership approach to chart its future. Business, government, and civic leaders created an Allegheny Conference-like group called the International Development Roundtable to develop a cohesive foreign policy for the region. "We're self-consciously developing an international focus," says Burkart Holzner, director of the Center for International Studies at the University of Pittsburgh. The goal of the 1990s is to turn individual strengths in the international arena into a regional international strategy, to build on Pittsburgh's considerable, but unconnected, international presence and network.

In fact, Pittsburgh has always been an international city. Beginning in 1800, immigrants from all parts of the globe made Pittsburgh one of the great melting pots of America. The ethnic fabric remains—there are few cities besides Pittsburgh where, at church, a wedding, or community festival, people still speak, dress, eat, play, sing, and dance as if they were in Germany, Italy, Poland, or Lithuania.

European ancestry is at the root of Pittsburgh's inclination to look outward, to stay connected to the world beyond the three rivers. The first generation born in Pittsburgh grew up speaking their parents' native

■ *Chautauqua at Pitt was an elaborate week-long cultural exchange with the Soviet Union. Photo courtesy of the University of Pittsburgh/Herb Ferguson.*

tongue, eating traditional ethnic food, and reading the newspapers their relatives sent from the old country. At the turn of the century, Europe wasn't a faraway place; it was home to Pittsburghers who still had aunts, uncles, cousins, and grandparents abroad. So it was natural for Pittsburghers to maintain the ties that are at the root of the city's international prominence in the arts, education, health care, and business.

Today, a cultural exchange in Pittsburgh is more like "old home" week, says Duquesne University's Tom Murrin.

"When we all get together," he says, referring to the city's education, government, business, and cultural communities, "it's like the United Nations."

Duquesne University's student body, for example, includes representatives of 81 nations. One of its biggest events of the year is a Nationality Dinner, featuring the native costumes, food, and dance from each of the nations represented. Duquesne also has joint research projects and transfer agreements with universities in several nations, including

China, Japan, and Spain. Point Park College offers graduate degrees in international business, attracts a large population of Middle Eastern students, and was among the first to institute an English as a Second Language program. Chatham College, a woman's college, features a multicultural curriculum that requires each junior-level student to study abroad at programs in Spain, England, Egypt, or the Galapagos Islands. Women from 22 nations study at Chatham, one of the few U.S. schools to give financial aid to foreign students. "We want to include women from Third World countries," Chatham's president, Esther Barazzone, explains.

The universities and colleges not only maintain many of Pittsburgh's current international relationships, they initiated many of the city's original international linkages as well. Pittsburgh's formal relationship with the government of Czechoslovakia, for instance, goes at least as far back as the end of the Second World War when the University of Pittsburgh (Pitt) was called upon to draft a constitution for the republic. More than 40

■ *The Duquesne University Tamburitzans preserve the music, dance, and customs of eastern Europe. Photo by Herb Ferguson.*

■ *The University of Pittsburgh is well known for its international expertise and ability to bring foreign dignitaries such as Nelson Mandela and Margaret Thatcher to Pittsburgh. Photos courtesy of University of Pittsburgh/Herb Ferguson.*

years later, Pitt established an International Management Center near Prague to help the Czechs create a free-market economy following the end of communism. Pitt (incidentally, the only university in the nation that teaches the Slovak language) graduated the first 30 Czech business managers from the school in 1992. In a similar program in Budapest, Pitt conferred the first 14 M.B.A. degrees ever awarded to Hungarians.

Pitt's dean of the Katz Graduate School of Business, Jerry Zoffer, says the business management center in Prague was "a new opportunity to demonstrate our international dimension and walk a pathway that hadn't yet been walked. The social responsibility to help a nation in transition was irresistible."

Much of Pittsburgh's international expertise resides in Pitt. "We can open doors internationally," says Pitt Chancellor Dennis O'Connor, noting that 14 of the 15 top officials in Indonesia in 1992 were Pitt alumni, for example. Pitt has student exchange programs, credit transfer agreements, or research collaboratives with 200 international universities, and attracts scholars, professors, physicians, and researchers from more than 50 nations. Future leaders of Third World countries come to Pitt for up to two years of study and immersion in the American (and Pittsburgh) experience under the H.J. Heinz Fellowship Program. The Pittsburgh Center for International Visitors, an independent nonprofit located on the Pitt campus, has helped acclimate tens of thousands of international visitors and new residents to Pittsburgh life. Patients come from all over the world to Pitt's medical center, a network of five major hospitals that together rank among the top 25 medical centers for specialized treatment. Pitt's Presbyterian-University Hospital is the world leader in organ transplantation.

The university's international studies program is also world renowned. Pitt confers degrees in Latin American, Asian, Russian/Eastern European, and Western European studies. Celebrated for their comprehensiveness, the Latin American, Asian,

and Russian/Eastern European programs are designated as national resource centers. To strengthen Pittsburgh's competitiveness in international trade, Pitt shares this international knowledge and expertise through the International Business Center. Business Center faculty offers consultation in international cultures, customs, languages, and business practices to local firms.

The university benefits from this exchange as well, says Pitt's Burkart Holzner. For example, since helping PPG executives establish a joint venture relationship with a Chinese firm, Pitt's consultative advice now includes research on how well the work force of a given nation can operate moving vehicles, like cranes and forklifts. Overlooking this factor, they learned, can lead to a lot of broken glass.

Pitt also brings numerous foreign dignitaries to Pittsburgh (Margaret Thatcher and Nelson Mandela visited in 1992) and sponsors cultural exchanges like the *Chautauqua at Pitt* event with the Soviets. In 1993, on the heels of the union of the European Community, Pitt was one of the local sponsors of the European Business Outlook Conference, which brought together national and international executives to discuss international trade opportunities in the new Europe. Pittsburgh competed successfully with seven U.S. cities, including Atlanta, Boston, and New Orleans, to host the U.S. Department of Commerce event, in part because of Pitt's international expertise and stature.

Applying its considerable expertise in international trade, the Greater Pittsburgh Chamber of Commerce also cosponsored the European conference. The Chamber established the Greater Pittsburgh World Trade Association in 1988, now the "largest world trade activity in the region," according to Justin Horan, Chamber president. Serving small and mid-size Pittsburgh businesses, the World Trade Association sponsors regular seminars, roundtables, and conferences with international business and political leaders, and maintains an extensive network of rela-

tionships with international Chambers of Commerce. The association also conducts trade missions. "The 1991 expedition to Eastern Europe and Russia resulted in several ongoing international business relationships for participants," Horan says.

International Culture

Pittsburgh is an international city when it comes to culture as well. Its international reputation in the arts was cultivated as early as 1896, when Andrew Carnegie instituted the esteemed Carnegie International, the world's second oldest international exhibition of contemporary art. Today, international regard is afforded to many of Pittsburgh's cultural institutions.

The symphony, ballet, and opera not only perform to consistent critical acclaim worldwide, but have world-class reputations that attract the finest musicians, dancers, and vocalists. The Mattress Factory, which

commissions and collects site-specific sculpture installations, is a one-of-a-kind museum. The New Music Ensemble and Pittsburgh Dance Council, organizations that present contemporary compositions and dance, are rarities in cities Pittsburgh's size. The International Poetry Forum publishes internationally and has presented poets from more than 25 foreign nations. The American Waterways Wind Orchestra, the first orchestra of its kind in the world, travels aboard a floating arts center to port cities throughout the United States, British Isles, Europe, Scandinavia, Russia, and the Mediterranean.

After the Carnegie International, the symphony was the first of Pittsburgh's cultural organizations to earn an international reputation. During its first international tour in 1947, the symphony travelled to Mexico City as the first major American orchestra invited to play at the Palacio de Bellas Artes. Since then, the symphony has completed 18 international

tours, including a Far East tour in 1987, when it became the third U.S. orchestra to visit China and the first to do so since diplomatic relations between the countries were established in 1979. The symphony's tours not only bring international acclaim to Pittsburgh, but offer Pittsburgh companies an opportunity to advertise abroad as well. During the 1992 European Tour, for example, USAir sponsored performances in Frankfurt, Paris, and London; AEG Westinghouse underwrote the cost of lodging in Frankfurt; and Mine Safety Appliances sponsored a concert in Madrid.

The cultural community both creates and reflects Pittsburgh's international connections. The popularity of the Duquesne University Tamburitzans, says Tom Murrin, is "an extraordinary manifestation" of the vibrancy of the city's Old World heritage. The Tamburitzans are like the Little League in Pittsburgh—youngsters begin at an early age as "junior tammies" and work their way up to the "varsity" team. Colorfully costumed, the Tamburitzans preserve the music, dance, and customs of eastern Europe, performing throughout the United States and Canada. "People are dumbfounded when they see them," Murrin says. "They can't believe they're American students."

Like the Tammies, the Nationality Rooms in Pitt's Cathedral of Learning keep Pittsburgh's ethnic heritage alive. A tour of the rooms, which reflect the origins of Pittsburgh's early settlers, offers a tour of the world, with stops in Italy, Germany, Poland, Hungary, Yugoslavia, Lithuania, Israel, China, and 15 other nations in Europe, Scandinavia, the Middle East, Asia, and Africa. A Nationality Committee maintains each of the rooms and also raises money for fellowships to send students abroad.

International Business

"Pittsburgh is as international as its people and activities," says Dick Fischer, who oversees international trade, licensing, and joint ventures for Pittsburgh-based ALCOA. By that, he means that Pittsburgh is "an extraordinarily international city." ALCOA, for example, "operates locally, but plans global-ly," Fischer says. No longer reliant on Pittsburgh's labor force or natural mineral deposits, a large percentage of ALCOA's business is in international trade, acquisitions, or joint venture manufacturing agreements. But the company remains in Pittsburgh because of the high quality of life and an atmosphere that's conducive to business.

The Fortune 500 companies with head-quarters in Pittsburgh operate globally, and almost all of the region's 4,400 manufacturers export internationally, creating a powerful international business network.

"Pittsburgh is a truly amazing city when it comes to global presence—there's repre-sentation from nearly every nation in the world among the major corporations," says Paul O'Neill, ALCOA chairman and CEO, about to embark on a tour of the firm's opera-tions in London, Budapest, Beijing, Shanghai, Tokyo, New York, and San Antonio.

"Globalization is a fact of life," says Vince Sarni, chairman and CEO of Pittsburgh-based PPG Industries. "PPG needs to participate in the global economy by locating our headquarters in a global city." Like ALCOA (and Westinghouse and USX, for that matter), PPG no longer relies on the region's natural resources, but remains in Pittsburgh because it's a good place to live and do business. With factories in Europe and the Far East, as well as in North America, more than 30 percent of PPG's sales and earnings came from outside the United States in 1992. The figure was up from 10 percent in 1983, and Sarni anticipates that the number will grow to 50 percent by 2000.

Homegrown companies account for only part of Pittsburgh's international busi-ness prestige, however. The region also hosts more than 250 foreign-owned firms, most of them new to Pittsburgh in the past 20 years. Contraves, a Swiss firm, is representa-tive of the type of foreign company that locates in Pittsburgh—it depends on technol-ogy, a highly-trained work force, international accessibility, and a quality of life that's attrac-tive to upper management.

How Contraves came to establish its U.S. headquarters in Pittsburgh is also typical of the region's foreign-owned firms—it found a lucrative acquisition opportunity in a Pittsburgh-based company. In 1974, Contraves bought the telescope manufactur-ing firm that Pittsburgh astronomer John Brashear, one of Samuel Pierpont Langley's contemporaries, started in the late 1800s. Contraves turned Brashear's firm into the world's leading producer of large scientific telescopes. Within a few years of the acquisi-tion, sales skyrocketed, from $10 million to $130 million, and so did the number of jobs. In 1992, the Contraves operation in Pittsburgh employed 850 people, most of them locals.

Like Contraves, many of the region's foreign-owned firms acquired an existing Pittsburgh company, but many were start-ups, preserving the city's reputation as an incubator for entrepreneurship. The majority manufacture durable goods, affirming Pittsburgh as an industrial hub despite the decline of traditional industries. Nearly 100 chose Pittsburgh as the site of their U.S. headquarters.

■ *Although a large percentage of ALCOA's business is in international trade, the quality of life keeps the com-pany based in Pittsburgh. ALCOA building photo by Roy Engelbrecht.*

■ *Contraves, with its U.S. headquarters in Pittsburgh, is the world's leading producer of large scientific tele-scopes. Photo courtesy of Contraves.*

"Proximity to a key supplier and markets is the overwhelming reason foreign companies locate here," says Ninamary Langsdale, of KPMG Peat Marwick, an accounting firm that conducts an annual survey of foreign-owned business in Pittsburgh. Other top reasons identified by the surveys include opportunities for acquisitions or joint ventures, the quality and cost of labor, the personal preferences of executives, and access to air transportation.

Location, Location, Location

Location, location, and location are the three mantras of the real estate industry, and the top reason firms choose Pittsburgh as a location or headquarters site. Ideally situated midway between New York and Chicago, and close to Toronto, Pittsburgh offers foreign and domestic firms convenient access to the major North American markets. Twenty metropolitan areas with more than one million people, 22 of the 35 top industrial markets in the United States, 51 percent of the U.S. population and purchasing power, are within a day's drive or hour's flight of Pittsburgh, as is 67 percent of the nation's manufacturing output.

Location was the main reason Sony chose western Pennsylvania in 1992 for its new U.S. manufacturing plant. "Pittsburgh has or is close to the source materials like glass, electrical components, and metal fabrication parts that we use to produce color TVs, projection TVs, and the picture tubes themselves," says Sony's Iwao Takahashi. For Sony and Contraves, Pittsburgh's location within hours of Corning, New York, a principal glass manufacturing center, made the region an ideal location. The glass Contraves uses to make telescope lenses is available in only two locations, Corning and Germany, and Sony uses Corning glass for TV picture screens.

Pittsburgh's location is enhanced by a comprehensive network of air, rail, highway, and water transportation systems that make it easy to receive and transport products and passengers. This transportation network

makes Pittsburgh an ideal location for a trucking company, says Barbara Moore, president of Anderson Transfer, a local and long distance trucker based in Washington, Pennsylvania. "Little" Washington, as Pittsburghers call it, is 20 minutes from Pittsburgh International Airport and 40 minutes from downtown Pittsburgh. "We're close to major centers of commerce—Philadelphia, Washington, D.C., Chicago. Boston is only 600 miles and Toronto is a straight run,"

■ *Israel Heritage Room (left) and the Ukrainian Room (right) are two of the more than 20 Nationality Rooms in Pitt's Cathedral of Learning. Photos courtesy of the University of Pittsburgh/Herb Ferguson.*

Moore says. She expects to see her business grow along with the anticipated increase in international flights that will result from the new airport. "Since it's so much easier to clear customs here than in New York, customers will be more likely to fly their goods into Pittsburgh, then truck them short-haul."

In 1992, close to 600 nonstop or direct flights to more than 120 U.S. and international cities departed daily from Pittsburgh International Airport. The number is expected to grow substantially—26 unreserved gates at the new airport are an invitation to airlines for whom there was no room at the former facility. "There's no question," says USAir CEO Seth Schofield, that the new airport will attract new carriers and destinations.

But every major city has an airport. What Pittsburgh's competitors lack are three rivers, natural resources that have spurred regional development since Native Americans fished from their shores in the

■ *The American Waterways Wind Orchestra travels aboard a floating arts center to port cities in the U.S., British Isles, Europe, Scandinavia, Russia, and the Mediterranean. Photo by Herb Ferguson.*

18th century. Today, the Port of Pittsburgh, which ships more than 34 million tons of products a year, is the largest and busiest inland port in the United States, in terms of originations and through-traffic as well as barge tonnage. The Monongahela, Allegheny, and Ohio Rivers, which converge downtown, connect Pittsburgh with inland ports on the Ohio-Mississippi system and trans-oceans ports in Baltimore and Philadelphia, enabling firms to ship goods to any port in the world. The viability of the waterways is ensured by two Pittsburgh-based groups, a multistate organization established in 1981 called DINAMO that has successfully lobbied for $4 billion in improvements to the Ohio River system, and the Port of Pittsburgh Commission, formed in 1992.

The Pittsburgh region also features an extensive mass transit network, seven major interstate highways and two major railroads, including CSX and Conrail.

Capital

Capital is as important to accessing markets as transportation is, and Pittsburgh

remains a significant and growing financial center. Three of the top 50 U.S. bank holding companies have headquarters in Pittsburgh—Mellon Bank Corp., PNC Financial Corp., and Integra Financial Corp. With combined assets of more than $60 billion, the banks are a major source of credit for domestic and foreign businesses locating in the region.

"You can't take it for granted anymore that a city will have financial institutions that are fiscally sound and well-capitalized," says Mellon Bank's chairman and CEO Frank Cahouet, pointing to states and cities where major financial institutions are failing and business is finding it hard to get credit. Thanks to "strong and highly competitive banks with broad product bases," he says, Pittsburgh is, financially speaking, well-off.

"We all have a different approach to lending," says Bill Roemer, chairman and CEO of Integra, which focuses on middle-market lending within the region. "We aren't strong in international finance, but Mellon and PNC are." PNC's international banking operations include "advising customers worldwide on financial strategies, offering foreign exchange services and conducting export financing on a large scale," says Tom O'Brien, chairman and CEO of PNC. ABN-AMRO Bank, one of the top 30 banks in the world, also offers international financing, handling all of its U.S. export financing from the Pittsburgh office.

In addition, some 15 venture capital firms with close to $500 million under management, 20 smaller commercial banks, 20 savings and loans, and 30 Pennsylvania economic development funds offer financing options for business. The Keystone Minority Capital Fund provides capital exclusively to growing minority-owned firms in western Pennsylvania. According to Earl Hord, president and CEO of the Minority Enterprise Corp., a nonprofit organization that supports the growth and creation of minority-owned business, the fund will raise $10 million. The average investment will range between $300,000 and $600,000.

Quality of Life

Quality of life in Pittsburgh has more to do with attitude than accommodations, although any executive will tell you that Pittsburgh's a great place to live and do business. Pittsburgh is manageable, comfortable, easy to navigate, cosmopolitan, and home-spun at the same time. Pittsburgh offers the business, cultural, educational, medical, and entertainment amenities of a major city, minus the crime and grime. There are urban, suburban, and rural neighborhoods within a reasonable commute of downtown.

More important, Pittsburghers are friendly, polite, caring, casual. It's often said that a Pittsburgher is someone who'll skip the directions and take you where you want to go. It's this kind of attitude that makes newcomers, especially foreign nationals, feel at home, according to McKinsey & Co. director Clay Deutsch, a newcomer several years ago. "Venturing outside national borders can be daunting, let alone relocating internationally," he says. "You care about two things: Is there a network of support? And, do you feel

comfortable? Pittsburgh scores high on both accounts. You can get your arms around Pittsburgh."

Numerous institutions, including the Pittsburgh Center for International Visitors and several dozen international consulates, trade organizations, and foreign Chambers of Commerce, help welcome and acclimate international newcomers.

Frank Brooks Robinson, president of the Regional Industrial Development Corp., which helps new businesses locate real estate, says a "caring service network, built on friendship and trust" makes it easy to do business. Newcomers who work with Robinson get first-hand exposure to the network. "When they have questions about utility bills, I walk them down to Don Moritz (CEO, Equitable Gas) and Wes von Schack (CEO, Duquesne Light). If they're concerned about finding the right kind of employees, I introduce them to other companies in their line of business."

"Pittsburgh is a small, big city," says Barbara Moore, "which means if you need help, there's a good chance that you'll know the person you need to talk to and can simply pick up the phone, or you'll know someone who knows who can help and can make the connection for you." As cofounder of PowerLink, a nonprofit organization that provides advisory boards of directors for fast-growing women-owned businesses, Moore has been overwhelmed by the "caring service network" Robinson refers to. "In the first year, we asked 40 CEOs and CFOs to be on boards of women-owned businesses. Only two said no, and one of them who couldn't commit the time turned around and gave us names of three of his friends," says Moore. "They do it for free for a year, and they love it—that's the great part."

Moore and Ilana Diamond formed PowerLink in 1991 after Moore won the Women's Business Advocate Award and became aware of women without M.B.A. degrees who owned businesses, but lacked the structural knowledge and business school contacts to make their companies

■ *This architectural detail found in Manchester reflects Pittsburgh's international connections. Photo by Roy Engelbrecht.*

grow. As an example, Moore points to Andrea Fitting, president of Printline, a graphic design and printing company that PowerLink helped. ''She has a Ph.D. in archaeology, but no M.B.A. Her confidantes are on a dig somewhere, and she needed to be linked with business experts here.''

''There's a feeling that you can make a difference here. Everyone cares and wants to chip in,''says Helge H. Wehmeier, the CEO of Miles who moved to Pittsburgh in 1992. ''One gets a receptive ear. It's easy to network. Very soon you know everyone. I tell other companies looking at Pittsburgh to consider how the community will treat you once you arrive, not just the deals they make to get you here. Pittsburgh treats you very well.''

■ *The Pittsburgh medical community has received international acclaim for genetic research. Pictured here is Urvashi Surti, PHD, Associate Professor of Pathology and Human Genetics at Magee-Womens Hospital and the University of Pittsburgh. Photo by Kenneth Love.*

Wehmeier says Pittsburgh is also comfortable because it reminds him of home in Germany and the other places he has lived in Europe, and he is not alone. Pittsburgh's European heritage, character, geography, and climate play a significant role in attracting reverse investment, according to the Peat Marwick studies, which show that Germany and the United Kingdom engender the most firms, followed by France, Sweden, and Japan.

''There is historical evidence that as Europeans came to this area, word of mouth attracted additional immigration,'' says Peat Marwick's Ninamary Langsdale. ''We felt that investment from foreign business would happen the same way, and the study confirms this. Germany and the United Kingdom have a significant and growing presence here, in start-ups, acquisitions, and joint ventures with local companies.''

Labor

''People are the Pittsburgh advantage,'' says Mellon Bank's Frank Cahouet. ''They're top notch, very professional, they make things happen. They're the best I've seen.''

A willingness and expectation to work hard have long been the trademarks of a Pittsburgher. Since the 1800s, when families from all over the world came to Pittsburgh to work for the American Dream, a work ethic, the belief that nothing comes except by earning it, has been ingrained in the cultural fabric. Both labor and management in Pittsburgh were brought up on the philosophy of ''an honest day's pay for an honest day's work,'' which translates to low turnover and high-productivity rates, some of the best in the nation.

Randy Harper, founder and chairman of American Micrographics Company, concurs. His records management business, with offices in Pittsburgh and Orlando, Florida, capitalizes on imaging, scanning, and microform technologies and requires ''detail-oriented, careful, and loyal individuals,'' Harper says. ''The difference in the work ethic here and in Orlando is like night and day.'' His Pittsburgh employees work for the company for 10 years, on average; turnover in Orlando is three times higher. ''If I had to close one of the facilities, I'd close the Florida office and stay here,'' says Harper, who used to dream of a headquarters in the warmer climate.

The notion of working hard is passed from parent to student, evidenced by the region's low drop-out rate and the number of colleges, universities, and proprietary schools. Miles' Helge Wehmeier says he's "impressed by the willingness of the labor force to continue their education." Twenty-nine educational institutions located throughout the region make continuing education accessible. They offer associate's, bachelor's, master's, and doctoral degrees in virtually every field of study, providing business with a source of technical and professional workers. Additionally, institutions like the Community College of Allegheny County and the Private Industry Council specialize in customized training programs for business. Heinz, for example, worked with Community College for two years to retrain about 500 employees to work in its newly automated food processing plant. The college not only

■ *The ethnic fabric can still be seen in places like this Hindu Temple in Monroeville. Photo by Herb Ferguson.*

trained the employees to operate the new equipment on-site at the plant, but offered basic refresher courses and computer instruction in the classroom as well.

The $100 million Heinz plant that opened on the Northside in the fall of 1992 also illustrates the ability of labor (less than 15 percent of the current work force is unionized) and management to come together in Pittsburgh. "We effectively had the opportunity to locate a new plant anywhere in the United States. This wasn't a decision we could make today and then in five years' time say, `Jeez, we were wrong, let's go home,' " Heinz CEO Anthony O'Reilly told *Executive Report* magazine in 1992.

"We sat down with the trade unions and discussed with them whether or not we would put this plant here. We were very open. We showed them our books . . . They taught us a lot about their ambitions and the security they sought for the work force, and we taught them a lot about the changing philosophy of the marketplace," reported O'Reilly.

The Heinz pact, the historic no-strike agreement between Allegheny County and the unions involved in building the new airport, and employee stock ownership plans at traditional factories like Weirton Steel are typical of the labor/management relationships in Pittsburgh, says Ben Fischer, professor of labor studies at Carnegie Mellon, "but they don't make the headlines." Fischer, who turned 79 in 1992, has worked for every president of the Steelworkers' union. "This is a place where you can do business with unions," he says.

Technology

But perhaps the most compelling reason for firms to locate in Pittsburgh is the availability of technology. Knowledge and ideas—intellectual capital—are the most important resources in an international city, says Dr. Jack Midgley, a consultant for companies adapting to the global marketplace, and director of the Ronald Reagan Center for Public Affairs. "The reason to be in Pittsburgh

■ *Pittsburgh has always been an international city. Photo by Roy Engelbrecht.*

■ *Known as "Computer U.", Carnegie Mellon University designs robots like this Trokobot that uses three arms in tandem to fulfill tasks. Photo courtesy of The Robotics Institute-Carnegie Mellon University.*

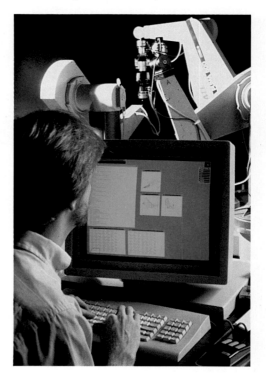

is to be close to ideas. Ideas equal wealth and stature in a global economy."

Pittsburgh is becoming a hub for idea-generation, "a magnet for scientists who are inventing and developing technologies that will be sold everywhere. These aren't blue or white-collar workers," says Midgley, "they're gold-collar workers, nobel prize material. They'll make the city a wealthier place to be."

With two major research universities, more than 170 commercial research and development facilities, and one of the nation's largest concentrations of scientists and engineers, Pittsburgh is expected to compete in the coming years with established technology meccas like Boston and the Silicon Valley. In addition to some 800 high-technology commercial enterprises, half of them formed in the 1980s, Pittsburgh is home to several major university research projects, including the Center for Biotechnology and Bioengineering, Center for Hazardous Waste Research, Supercomputing Center, Robotics Institute, and Center for Advanced Manufacturing and Software Engineering. Because the universities are committed to delivering knowledge and product to the marketplace, the technology advanced at these facilities will create the next generation of entrepreneurs and high-tech businesses. "Companies located near the technology

center will have a leading edge; they'll benefit first from the latest advancements," according to Midgley.

For example, known universally as "Computer U," Carnegie Mellon University, in partnership with IBM, Apple, NeXT, and Digital Equipment Corp., has pioneered the use of computers in education. The campus features 9,500 computers and workstations—one for almost every student, faculty member, and administrator—that can access other computer systems worldwide. This expertise has become an important resource for Pittsburgh's growing computer and software industry, and a lure for electronics companies like Sony. The university also operates an office in Japan, and in collaboration with Pitt, received a multimillion dollar grant to train American scientists and engineers in Japanese language and business skills.

"Cities that will be successful in the global marketplace will be able to create technology; communicate the information via data networks, fiberoptic links, and computer facilities; develop new products; have access to capital to finance new ventures; train and retrain the workers to deliver them to society; and have the transportation ability, like the airport, to export them," Midgley says, "and Pittsburgh has it all." ▯

■ *Pittsburgh is one of the great melting pots of America.*
Photo by Roy Engelbrecht.

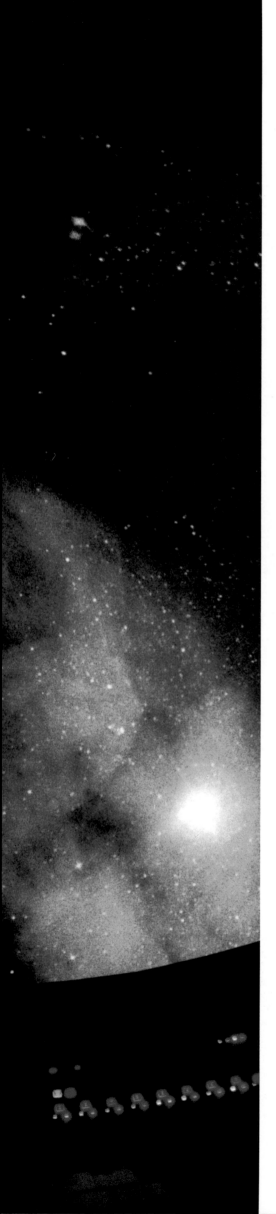

CHAPTER
Intellectual Capital
SIX

If intellectual capital is the financing of the future, Pittsburgh is vested for the 21st century. The region is endowed with world-class educational institutions, sophisticated retraining programs, state-of-the-art research facilities, and a work force that values scholarship, a legacy of the immigrants for whom education was part of the American Dream.

Parents instilled in their children the same industry for school work as they had for laboring in the mills and building neighborhoods. As a result, educational attainment rates are higher in Pittsburgh than the national average. Nearly every school district still graduates close to 100 percent of its students. In addition, the growing enrollments at regional colleges and universities illustrate the penchant for continuing education, and generous contributions from local corporations, foundations, and alumni to schools that traditionally meet or exceed their fund-raising goals indicate the community's regard for scholarship.

■ *The Carnegie Science Center offers four floors of displays designed to educate and inspire including the Buhl Planetaruim. Photo courtesy of Steve Savage, Sky-Skan, Inc. (All-sky: Anglo-Australian Board. Used with permission.)*

■ *Excellence in education begins early. Reading hour at the Carnegie Library. Photo by Roy Engelbrecht.*

Education is a fast-growing industry as well. The University of Pittsburgh, for example, is the region's 5th largest employer; Pittsburgh Public Schools are the 10th; there are 30 additional colleges and universities; more municipal school districts; and about 50 proprietary schools. But economic impact is just a clue to the relevance and relationship of education in the community. Doreen Boyce of the Buhl Foundation, which funds educational programs, talks about the richness and depth of the educational system: "We have an array of educational institutions and opportunities, from preschools through to the highest levels of doctoral and post-doctoral work. No matter what you're interested in, you're going to get a good fit."

In Pittsburgh, excellence in education begins at the preschool level, Boyce says. "Pittsburgh has a record of being alert and responsive in the area of child care." Louise Childcare, for example, is recognized nationally. A former orphanage founded in Pittsburgh in the early 1900s, Louise Childcare is also a local resource for parents who need day-care. Carnegie Mellon University (CMU) is home to a leading psychology-based child-care initiative. The University of Pittsburgh (Pitt) operates three nationally known child-care and education resources: the Office of Child Development, the Learning Research and Development Center, and Generations Together, which is pioneering intergenerational child care. "We created intergenerational child care here," says Boyce, "and it's spreading across the country."

One reason Pittsburgh maintains strong educational systems is "the willingness of foundations to fund experiments and cutting-edge innovations," she notes, "and the willingness to cooperate across interests." An example is a collaboration the Buhl

Foundation funded that brought together a college and university that essentially compete for local enrollment. Robert Morris College and CMU jointly developed the Writing Across the Curriculum Program that is now part of the Robert Morris experience. As a result of the partnership, the Public Broadcasting System (PBS) designated Robert Morris as the national expert in training business people to write and think clearly. Local colleges and universities also support cross registration programs, and, through the Pittsburgh Council on Higher Education, share ideas and resources to meet the needs of students and the community.

Collaborations

Monsignor William Kerr, president of La Roche College, and Esther Barazzone, president of Chatham College, were pleasantly astonished by the level of cooperation they discovered within the educational community when they arrived in Pittsburgh in 1992. "The inherent spirit of community here is something to celebrate," says Monsignor Kerr.

"People seek to be cooperative," says Barazzone. "My colleagues across the city really do sit down at the same table on a regular basis to find solutions to common problems." The proximity of some of the schools facilitates collaborations, she adds. The campuses of Pitt, CMU, Chatham, and Carlow College are located within walking distance in the adjoining neighborhoods of Oakland and Shadyside; Duquesne University, Point Park College, and a branch of Robert Morris are within walking distance downtown.

Reflecting Pittsburgh's bent toward public-private consortiums, partnerships are the underpinning of the local educational system. Partnerships between businesses and schools; foundations and schools; businesses, foundations, and schools; and institutions of higher education and schools sustain basic education in the public, private, and parochial school systems. The Pittsburgh Public Schools, which educates 40,000 city students, was one of the first districts in the United States to institute a formal partnering program in 1979. The Partnerships in Education Program, initiated with the help of the Greater Pittsburgh Chamber of Commerce and the Allegheny Conference, began by pairing major corporations with individual high schools. Today, the program also matches small businesses, foundations, universities, nonprofits, and neighborhood groups with elementary and middle schools. The activities vary, depending on the needs of the school.

One of the most extensive relationships is that of Westinghouse Electric Corporation with George Westinghouse High School. To encourage careers in science and engineering, and give workplace relevance to math and science courses, the company worked with the district to develop a curriculum for a four-year Math and Science Academy. Westinghouse scientists and engineers serve as mentors to the academy students who must complete a major research project to graduate. For each student who completes his or her project and has maintained a B-grade average throughout the program, Westinghouse grants a $2,000 college scholarship.

Other partnerships provide professional development opportunities for teachers; tutoring or shadowing for students; and financial or in-kind support for field trips, career-day experiences, or the school newspaper, for instance. Through Project Aspire, PPG Industries provides tutoring and an incentive program that helps Langley High School students save for college. Mellon Bankers tutor Perry High School students every Saturday morning. Miles Inc. works arm-in-arm with Reizenstein Middle School. The Frick Educational Commission, working with the Frick Art

■ *Frick International Studies Academy offers instruction in French, German, Spanish, and Japanese. Photo by Roy Engelbrecht.*

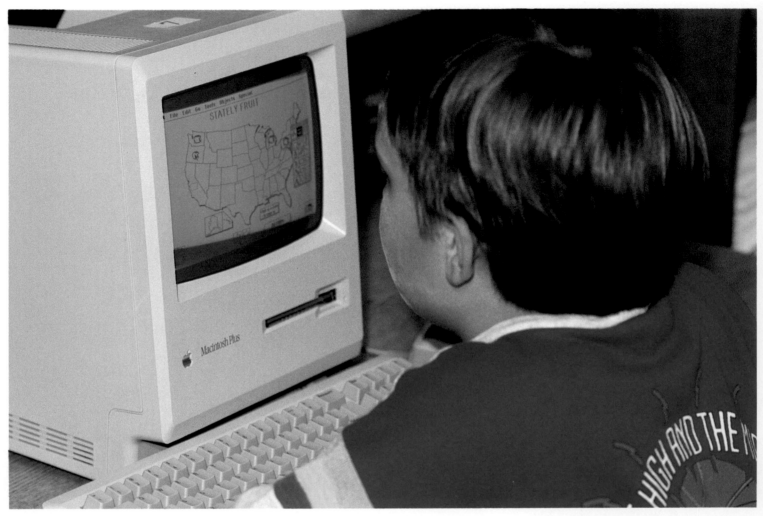

■ *Computer experience is an essential part of training the future work force to meet the needs of the community. Photo by Roy Engelbrecht.*

Museum, brings professional artists into the classroom as part of the multicultural track at the Frick International Studies Academy. The Giant Eagle supermarket chain provides work opportunities, on-the-job mentoring, and permanent positions for students of the Conroy Education Center, a school for students with learning disabilities. Carnegie Mellon University provides summer computer experiences for East End teachers and is applying for a grant to give stipends to 250 Carnegie Mellon students who will use computers to tutor public school students. Community groups, like the Brashear and Kingsley Associations, help kids after school with homework, or give after-school instruction in areas such as music, dance, or computers. Hospitals are even setting-up health centers in neighborhood schools.

At the onset of Renaissance II, the Allegheny Conference, recognizing the increasing importance of an educated, highly skilled work force to ensure global com-

petitiveness, established an Education Fund on the premise that it takes a whole community to educate a child. Until then, in Pittsburgh and elsewhere, the business of educating youth had been the sole domain of educators.

Through the Education Fund, local businesses began enhancing public schools. In addition to helping develop the Partnerships in Education Program, which links business with schools, the conference also created opportunities to link business with teachers. For instance, the Business Forum on Education, a series of seminars for teachers, brings "educational statesmen" to Pittsburgh, says Nancy Bunt, Education Fund director. Grant programs give stipends to teachers who propose innovative classroom or school-wide projects. The Mathematics Collaborative, cosponsored by the Ford Foundation, helps teachers apply business practices to math lessons. Similarly, a Principals Academy features monthly semi-

the leaders in town think that education is important."

Basic Education

One needs to look no further than the meticulously maintained elementary, middle, and high school buildings throughout the region to see that education is a priority in Pittsburgh. Tax dollars that provide for clean, safe, and architecturally-sound learning environments also afford teacher salaries that attract educators of the highest caliber.

Pittsburgh is blessed with dedicated, talented teachers who create "pockets of brilliance" in the classroom, according to parents. Teachers will sing, dance, act, mime, dress-up, stand on chairs, or pound on desks, if that's what it takes to help students learn. Some have been known to wear fairy costumes and wizard hats, sprinkle fairy dust around the classroom, and wave a magic wand to teach goal-setting to fourth and fifth graders. These accoutrements support a lesson called "I Am A Wizard Because . . .," which encourages students to use computer programs called DazzleDraw and Bankstreet Writer to draw and write about what they would do if they had magical powers. One teacher, who calls himself "a bit of an actor," turns his classroom into a Senate chamber to teach students the federal process of how a bill becomes a law. A loud and lively discussion inevitably ensues as the designated class Democrats and Republicans debate the merits of a fictitious bill that may affect their freedom of speech or expression, or a bill that mandates a high school dress code or bans books in the library, for instance.

Parents and students aren't the only ones who appreciate the efforts of teachers. International, national, and statewide institutions have recognized the abundant talent in the region's schools, which have mounted an impressive and growing list of honors, including: the world's best arts education

nars that expose principals to technical and philosophical developments in the business world.

The conference also created the Mon Valley Education Consortium to encourage collaboration among a group of "resource poor" school districts in the Mon Valley, the municipalities hardest hit by the decline of the steel industry. The consortium quickly developed a national reputation for innovation, competing successfully to host the 1992 National Drop-out Prevention Conference, which brought national acclaim to Pittsburgh area teachers and programs, as well as national leaders, including keynote speaker, Gen. Colin Powell. Director Linda Croushore says the consortium's success reflects Pittsburgh as a "resource rich" city with a "healthy foundation and corporate community that doesn't just give money to schools, but truly invests in school improvement issues."

Several additional coalitions have formed to strengthen school systems, includ-

ing the Extra Mile Foundation, a group of businesses led by PPG to support several Catholic schools; the Allegheny County Alliance for Public Schools, which fosters collaboration among Allegheny County's 41 school districts; and the Allegheny Policy Council for Youth and Workforce Development, a partnership of business, government, labor, education, and funders.

The Allegheny Conference formed the Policy Council in 1992 to implement the National Education Goals, advocate for public policy changes regarding education, and address education issues ranging from school readiness through lifelong learning. The creation of the Policy Council represents a "very clear indication that education is at the top of the community agenda," according to Jane Burger, executive director of both the Frick Educational Commission and the Grable Foundation, two foundations devoted to education. "It demonstrates publicly that the mayor, county commissioners, and all of program as chosen by *Newsweek* magazine, dozens of National Merit finalist awards, the Pennsylvania Teacher of the Year, U.S. Department of Education Blue Ribbon awards, Presidential Excellence in Education awards, the International Problem Solving Competition championship, Disney Corporation American Teacher award, and Gene Kelly Awards for Excellence in High School Musical Theater.

By creating school structures that give teachers flexibility and a stronger voice in designing curriculum, administrators inspire the creativity and high degree of teacher-student interaction that is not only prevalent, but widely regarded. Such novelty in the classroom is sparked by forward-thinking school superintendents and boards who have earned for Pittsburgh a reputation for being at the cutting-edge of educational advancements. For example, the two ideas that educators nationwide are looking to as models for improving the competitiveness of the U.S. educational system are already in place in Pittsburgh schools.

One idea is the concept of school "choice," which lets parents choose the school their children will attend based on curriculum rather than address. Without becoming mired in the national debate over vouchers and payment systems, Pittsburgh's schools have offered choice to parents and students. In the early 1980s, the city's schools introduced a "magnet" school program that not only lets parents choose in what neighborhood their child will go to school, but also what they'll study. The magnet schools offer intensive curriculums for students with special talents, interests, or career goals in such areas as science and mathematics, health technologies, or creative and performing arts. In the International Studies Academy, for instance, students can begin instruction in French, German, or Spanish in the first grade, or Japanese in the sixth grade, and continue through graduation. Parents throughout the region can also choose from an array of public, private, or parochial schools, or academic or vocational schools.

"Restructuring" is another popular strategy to prepare schools for the future, and several Pittsburgh school districts are already implementing restructuring programs. In a restructuring school, teachers work as design teams to tailor a particular school's curriculum to its particular student body. The results are "community schools" with "site-based management," says Louise Brennen, Pittsburgh Public Schools superintendent. "We're getting away from the central office dictating what each school should be like." Brennen sees restructuring as the most important educational movement of the 1990s because it involves the whole community in education. "Youngsters are coming to school today with different sets of demands on educators," she says, demands that public schools can't address alone. "We need parent and community involvement."

Community involvement in education is a way of life in Pittsburgh, perhaps because schools remain an integral part of the community. The classrooms where students read, write, and compute during the day are the meeting rooms for neighborhood groups or community college classes at night. The gyms and playgrounds where students exercise and recess five days a week host after-school bake sales, car washes, or summer carnivals. Auditoriums where students assemble for school-wide programs are also where many Pittsburghers vote for local, state, and national leaders. In these and other ways, the schools remain, as Brennen says, the "safe, familiar places in the community."

Educational Resources

While the schools support the community's social fabric, the community, likewise, supports the schools with a network of public

■ *Generations Together is a University of Pittsburgh program which is pioneering intergenerational learning and child care. Photo courtesy of the University of Pittsburgh/Herb Ferguson.*

■ *The Pittsburgh educational network also includes one of the nation's finest children's museums. Photo by Roy Engelbrecht.*

■ *Previous page: Fred Rogers, an educational television pioneer, is a proud Pittsburgher. Photo by Lynn Johnson.*

■ *The region's colleges and universities also provide the community with entertainment, cultural, and educational resources. Photo courtesy of Carnegie Mellon University.*

libraries, museums, resources, and educational institutions. "There's a learning culture here for children, because the whole community recognizes that learning goes on inside and outside the classroom," says the Buhl Foundation's Doreen Boyce. "We have great libraries—Carnegie initiated the whole library movement right here. Educational television (WQED-TV) started here. Fred Rogers (of Mr. Rogers' Neighborhood fame) is a Pittsburgher," Boyce says. "These things didn't just happen, they grew out of a sense that education is important."

Education is pervasive in Pittsburgh. Even institutions that aren't educational by intent sponsor educational programs that either visit students in the classroom or bring students into their institutional venue. For instance, through a multicultural program sponsored by the Pittsburgh Foundation, the Pittsburgh Council for International Visitors, which acclimates foreign nationals to Pittsburgh, lets students practice speaking a foreign language by giving tours to international visitors. Through the Poets-in-Person program, the International Poetry Forum takes visiting poets to area high schools to enliven literature, reading, and creative writing classes. The Pittsburgh Dance Council sponsors a similar program showcasing visiting dance troupes. When Grammy award winner Tito Puente came to town for the Manchester Craftsmen's Guild Living Masters of Jazz series, the Pittsburgh Fund for Arts Education sponsored an in-school jazz history lesson and student performance. The symphony takes music and musicians into the schools, and also conducts special performances and backstage tours for school students at Heinz Hall.

The educational network also includes a number of museums, including The Carnegie and one of the nation's finest children's museums, as well as a first-class zoo, conservatory, and aviary. Opening in 1994, the Regional History Center, which will detail the region's rich social, ethnic, and industrial history, will offer another educational resource for students, parents, and teachers.

The line of yellow school busses parked outside The Carnegie nearly every school day proves the educational value of the institution Andrew Carnegie bequeathed to Pittsburgh. The Carnegie complex includes the Museum of Art, Museum of Natural History, Science Center, library, music hall, and, opening in 1994, the Andy Warhol Museum. Located between the University of Pittsburgh and Carnegie Mellon University, the Carnegie's Oakland campus includes the art and natural history museums, the main branch of the library, and the music hall. "The building itself is a museum piece," says The Carnegie's Lorene Vinski. Andrew Carnegie, a believer in self-teaching, unveiled the "palace of culture" in 1895, offering Pittsburghers a place to educate themselves in art, music, science, and literature. The statues of Michelangelo, Bach, Galileo, and Shakespeare standing guard at the entry ways reflect Carnegie's intent.

"The whole mission is education," says Vinski of The Carnegie. Both museums and the Science Center have education departments, and the natural history museum, with more than 10,000 objects on display, is one of the world's largest natural history research facilities. The Carnegie also houses the nation's third largest collection of dinosaur artifacts, the main attraction for hundreds of thousands of youngsters who visit the museum each year. A Museum on the Move program takes The Carnegie to school children who can't come to Pittsburgh.

On the Northside, the Carnegie Science Center, designed to "educate, excite, entertain, and inspire" is "an amusement park for the mind," Vinski says. Opened in 1991, the Science Center offers four floors of displays where children (and parents) can learn about science and the environment by touching, moving, and talking back to the exhibits. The Science Center also houses a multi-sensory Omnimax Theatre (thanks to the generosity of John Rangos, the chairman of Pittsburgh-based Chambers Development Corp.) and the Buhl Planetarium, once a separate facility. The former planetarium is now

the Educational Annex, a science center exclusively for school children.

The World Affairs Council is another community institution with a purely educational mission. The council hosts ambassador-level or cabinet-level policymakers who discuss key global issues with corporate and civic leaders in nearly two dozen different formats, ranging from Ballroom Luncheons to Five O'clock Forums. The heart of its program, however, goes into the schools. Since 1966, the council's International Affairs Education Program has taken national and international leaders visiting Pittsburgh into high schools throughout the region. The purpose, says council president George Oehmler, "is to discuss major geopolitical, economic, national security, cultural, and social issues" with the future generation of world leaders. In a typical year, council speakers address some 11,000 students and teachers on more than 100 occasions. The council also sponsors the annual World Affairs Institute, an all-day think-tank held at the convention center for more than 300 students and teachers. At the institute, students tackle complex subjects, such as "The `New' Soviet Union" or "U.S Foreign Policy After

■ *Pittsburgh maintains one of the strongest technical education systems in the nation. Photo courtesy of the University of Pittsburgh/Herb Ferguson.*

the Cold War," then report the results to their classes at school.

Higher Education

The region's colleges and universities also have a role beyond academics. They not only provide the region with a skilled and knowledgeable work force, they are cultural resources and economic engines as well. In addition to the 11 institutions of higher learning in the city, another 20 throughout the region contribute irreplaceable services to the communities where they are based. Without them, there would be fewer theaters, concerts, lectures, libraries, newspapers, radio stations, and sports events. There would be tens of thousands of fewer student consumers and volunteers for community events. There would be fewer businesses and jobs that result from university spin-offs. Existing businesses would have fewer resources.

Three of the region's largest educational institutions—University of Pittsburgh (Pitt), Carnegie Mellon University (CMU), and the Community College of Allegheny County (CCAC)—led the transformation of Pittsburgh's economy from heavy manufac-

turing-based to service and technology-based.

To Pitt Chancellor Dennis O'Connor, Pitt and Pittsburgh are one and the same. A state-related university, Pitt historically has been a vehicle for "upward mobility" in the city, O'Connor notes. Today, the university is not only a primary supplier to the local work force (one of every three college graduates in Allegheny County holds a Pitt degree), but an economic generator as well. The University of Pittsburgh Applied Research Center, a 55-building research and development complex, generates technology jobs and serves as an incubator for several start-up ventures and spin-offs, and the Pitt medical center operates three area hospitals.

"Pitt offers expertise and assistance a phone call away. We want to be seen as a resource, and we've delivered," O'Connor says, summarizing the university's impact on the larger community. "If you look at the signature industries in Pittsburgh—education, health care, information technology, and biotechnology—Pitt is involved in every one. Together with CMU, we're responsible for pushing the envelope back. We're not just transplanting organs, but studying the

■ *Students from the Rogers School for Creative and Performing Arts present "P.J.'s High", a drug and alcohol prevention production. Photo by Roy Engelbrecht.*

■ *The University of Pittsburgh, a world-class educational institution, is the region's 5th largest employer. Photo courtesy of the University of Pittsburgh/Herb Ferguson.*

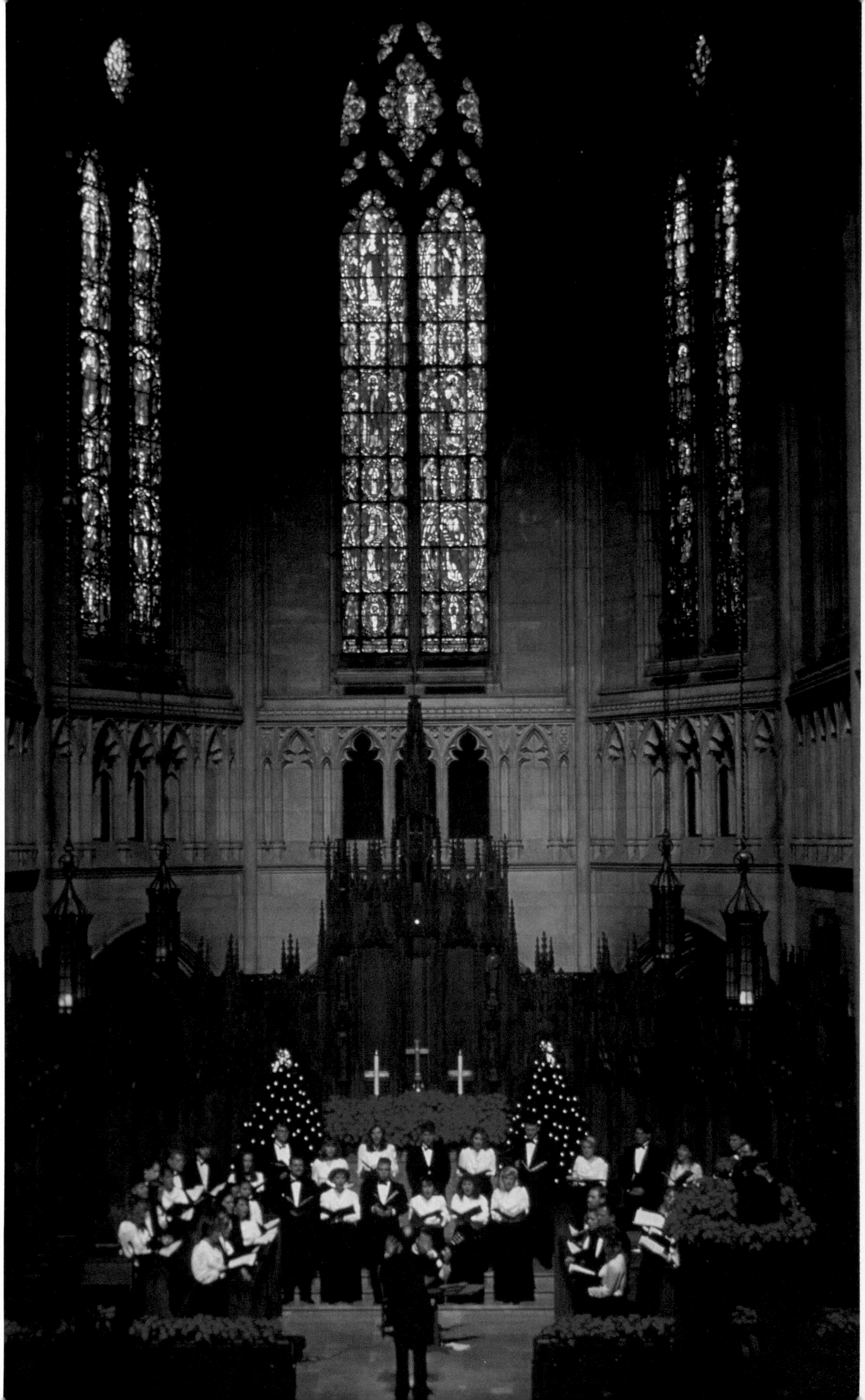

immune system, which will have a far greater impact on Pittsburgh and the world."

"We're training Pittsburgh's teachers and social workers; when the steel mills declined, Pitt's social workers put their knowledge to work in the Mon Valley, helping out-of-work families. Pitt did something tangible for those communities."

"When Senator Harris Wofford needed expertise on the issue of health care costs, he turned to Pitt, and we developed a white paper on health care cost containment."

Carnegie Mellon University is equally respected. Although half the size of Pitt in student enrollment, CMU rivals its next door neighbor in stature. The CMU drama department, which conferred the nation's first degree in drama in 1917 (when it was known as Carnegie Tech), continues to produce many of the "who's who" in Broadway and Hollywood. The university's H.J. Heinz III School of Public Policy and Management is also renowned, providing direction and expertise for present and future public leaders.

But technology is the area for which Carnegie Mellon is most highly regarded. "Carnegie Mellon is a very powerful engine for jump starting a lot of high-tech businesses in this region," says Robert Mehrabian, university president. By 1992, Carnegie Mellon researchers had generated more than 30 technology businesses, mostly software companies, and Mehrabian says the university will continue to spinoff companies, hopefully at a rate of three or four a year. But creating technology businesses isn't the primary role Mehrabian envisions for Carnegie Mellon, a private institution that receives less than one percent of its budget from state funds. Rather, he sees CMU as a resource for existing business.

Known as "Computer U," Carnegie Mellon's computer expertise helped ALCOA update its information system. At the Robotics Institute, the largest of its kind in the world, university engineers are advancing autonomous vehicles for hazardous waste clean-up; when hazardous waste spilled at Three Mile Island near Harrisburg,

Pennsylvania, Carnegie Mellon's robot was available for clean-up. The university's development of machine translation will help business translate manuals and documents in numerous languages at the touch of a keyboard, furthering the city's internationalization. To assist redevelopment of the city's riverfronts, CMU has developed a template to locate the areas along the rivers contaminated by former manufacturing processes.

Mehrabian feels strongly that "CMU must play an active role in helping the city grow" culturally as well as economically. Thus, he committed to make Pittsburgh the "most accessible city in the nation for people with disabilities." The result is a book called *Access to Pittsburgh* that lists the accessibility of parking, curbs, entrances, interiors, restrooms, telephones, and fountains of 600 buildings city-wide. It covers office buildings, educational institutions, attractions, restaurants, and stores. The university not only audited the buildings and computerized the information, but is developing electronic kiosks for placement throughout the city.

The Community College, though not a research institution, is just as important as Pitt and CMU as a community resource. The fourth largest higher education institution in Pennsylvania, CCAC instructs 24,000 full-time students at four major campuses and nine community locations throughout the region. Conferring two-year degrees, it views itself as a bridge to the community and to four-year schools. Half of its students go on to earn bachelor's degrees. The college's "bread and butter," says President John (Mack) Kingsmore, is an inexpensive, transferable education for the working class. CCAC's annual tuition is about 75-percent less than Pitt's, its closest competitor. "Our strengths are accessibility and flexibility. There's no time frame on learning. We're accessible to anyone at any age," Kingsmore says, "anyone who wants to make a change."

Although it banks on accessibility, CCAC's flexibility has made it one of the nation's most sophisticated schools when it comes to retraining. On a moment's notice in the early 1980s, CCAC developed a

■ *Researchers at the University of Pittsburgh study the three dimensional aspects of complex molecules. Photo by Roy Engelbrecht.*

■ *Heinz Chapel is a beautiful source of inspiration for many who visit or study at the University of Pittsburgh. Photo courtesy of the University of Pittsburgh/Herb Ferguson.*

■ *WDUQ, which broadcasts from the Duquesne campus, is just one example of the contribution of local educational institutions to the Pittsburgh quality of life. Photo by Roy Engelbrecht.*

comprehensive retraining program for Pittsburgh's unemployed. It offered free tuition, books, fees, and out-placement services to laid-off workers. "Within 24 hours of the advertisement," Kingsmore recalls, "we had thousands of calls." Between 1983 and 1990, the college awarded associate's degrees, many of them in the allied health professions, to 13,000 Pittsburghers. More than 80 percent of the students who started the program finished.

Based on this success, the college developed a retraining program for business and industry. Recognizing that future workers will change jobs seven or eight times in a lifetime, twice as often as in the past, the college creates on-site customized training curriculums for major corporations as well as small, emerging companies. The work site program is complemented by off-site classes at the college's Center for Professional Development downtown that features basic courses and computer classes.

Educational institutions with little direct involvement in economic development also contribute immensely to the quality of life in Pittsburgh. Duquesne University, for instance, is a leader in the arts. WDUQ-FM, Pittsburgh's National Public Radio affiliate, broadcasts from the Duquesne campus, and several major arts organizations, including the International Poetry Forum, Tamburitzans, New Music Ensemble and Opera Center, are based there.

The City Music Center, a project of Duquesne's School of Music, is an example of the university's charitable involvement. The center provides free music lessons to children whose parents can't afford professional instruction.

"A father told me the lessons changed his daughter's life," said Duquesne President John Murray, Jr., poignantly pointing to the impact of higher education in Pittsburgh.   ▣

■ *The Community College of Allegheny County (CCAC) helped lead the transformation of Pittsburgh's economy from heavy manufacturing-based to service and technology-based. Photo by Roy Engelbrecht.*

The Culture of Pittsburgh

When it comes to concerts, few names are as recognizable in Pittsburgh as Pat DiCesare's. A Pittsburgh
songwriter and musician, and one of the top concert
promoters in the nation, DiCesare, Sr. has been bringing the biggest

names in show business to Pittsburgh since 1963, when he booked The

Beatles at the then-new Civic Arena. Today, DiCesare-Engler productions is

one of many entertainment organizations in Pittsburgh, but in the 1970s,

DiCesare recalls, it was him and the symphony and not much else.

When DiCesare and his partner Rich Engler bought the Stanley

Theatre in 1978, they wanted to reopen the concert hall with a series of

performances by Frank Sinatra and Dean Martin. According to Sinatra's

agent, Pat remembers, Frank liked DiCesare's proposal, but said he didn't

know what he'd do in Pittsburgh for a whole week. DiCesare back-

pedaled: "New York is an hour away."

■ *Built in 1928 as the Stanley Theatre, the Benedum Center is believed to be the third largest stagehouse in the world. Photo courtesy of the Pittsburgh Cultural Trust.*

Alot has happened since 1978. New York is still an hour away (via the new airport), but there is now a lot more of New York in Pittsburgh. The Golden Triangle has become a mecca for the New York brand of artistic talent. "You're not anonymous here," says Mark Taylor, a New York choreographer.

"I was feeling more and more that the artistic future of the country would not be directed by a group of artists sequestered in one area of the country talking to themselves. As artists, we need to get out and articulate what we do," Taylor says. He came to Pittsburgh in 1991 to be the artistic director of the Dance Alloy, a dance company that commissions and debuts contemporary works.

The preeminent conductor of the Pittsburgh Symphony Orchestra, Lorin Maazel, Pittsburgh Opera Maestro Tito Capobianco, and Patricia Wilde, the former Balanchine dancer who directs the Pittsburgh Ballet Theatre ("When you want to learn ballet, you come to see Patricia Wilde...") were also newcomers to Pittsburgh in the 1980s, attracted by the city's growing cultural reputation.

"We have many more opportunities here as artists than we did in New York," says Carolelinda Dickey, the head of the Pittsburgh Dance Council who arrived in Pittsburgh in the late 1980s. "For a city our size," Dickey says, (note the *our*), "it's not unusual to have a symphony, opera, and ballet. It *is* unusual to have a Dance Council," which features contemporary dance productions from around the world.

"We're somewhat of an anomaly. Our contemporaries are in Paris, London, Rome, New York,

■ *The Pittsburgh Symphony Orchestra, one of the oldest in the nation, often features guest conductors. Photo by Herb Ferguson.*

■ *As a result of the symphony's early formation, Pittsburghers are a musically literate audience. Photo by Ben Spiegel.*

Chicago, San Francisco. It says something quite special about Pittsburgh that we exist here and flourish. People who live here have no idea of the cultural reputation the city has," she says. She had recently spoken to a cultural group in Caracas about the success of the arts in Pittsburgh.

"I'm a demon concert-goer, and I can't keep up with it all," says David Stock, the founder, director, and conductor of the Pittsburgh New Music Ensemble "I've lived all over the country and am not just being a Pittsburgh chauvinist when I say that we're one of the richest cities imaginable," culturally speaking. The New Music Ensemble is a resident company that performs contemporary chamber music and also sponsors an international music festival that attracts musicians and attendance from around the world.

A Pittsburgher, Stock left the city after finishing his first master's degree because the "climate was not conducive at the time" for performing the kind of music he wanted to perform. "Because not all composers died a hundred years ago in Germany," Stock quips, his New Music Ensemble plays "the music of our time," that of living and primarily American composers. He says he's participated in an "explosion of artists doing alternative work" in Pittsburgh since returning from London and establishing the New Music Ensemble in 1975. "Pittsburgh isn't New York or Toronto, and we can't pretend that it is," says Stock. "Let's be us, and what us is, is pretty darn good!"

A 1992 directory of arts organizations published by the Pittsburgh Cultural Trust lists more than 200 music, dance, theater, musical theater, folk art, visual art, literature and poetry organizations, museums, and galleries in Pittsburgh. "There's a mix in the tapestry," says Carol Brown, president of the Cultural Trust. "Lively mid-sized and smaller arts organizations are nipping at the heels of the bigger groups."

■ *The Pittsburgh Civic Arena attracts the biggest names in show business and the world of sports. Photo by Herb Ferguson.*

The Cultural Trust attributes the growth of the arts to a 100-year history of support of the philanthropic community. Pittsburgh corporations and foundations traditionally have given generously to the arts, not only to support growth, but to enhance the quality of the arts as well. They donate their time and expertise in addition to money. A program called Business Volunteers for the Arts, sponsored by the Greater Pittsburgh Chamber of Commerce, pairs executive-level managers with arts organizations that need a high-caliber of pro bono expertise. According to Susan Peterson, who runs the program, there are always more volunteers than she has slots to train them.

Local government is also a strong advocate of the arts. An annual Independence Day celebration at Point State Park featuring an outdoor symphony performance (the 1812 Overture is traditional) and fireworks is typical of the city's extensive arts and cultural repertoire. A variety of music, dance, and theater is performed at Hartwood Acres, a beautifully secluded outdoor performance arena owned by Allegheny County.

The city and county were also among the public and private sector interests that formed the Cultural Trust in 1984 to stimulate economic development by encouraging the growth of the arts. The trust is currently developing a 12-block "Cultural District" in what used to be a "red light" district downtown. At the heart of the development is a new 17-story auditorium, office and retail building designed by the renowned architect Michael Graves. When the building opens, the 800-seat theater will become the

permanent home of the Pittsburgh Public
Theatre, joining the Benedum Center for the
Performing Arts, Heinz Hall, and the Fulton
Theatre as the fourth performing arts venue
in the Cultural District.

The Benedum Center is the home of
the Pittsburgh Opera, Pittsburgh Ballet
Theatre, Civic Light Opera ("where
Broadway spends the summer"), and the
Dance Council. Built in 1928 as the Stanley
Theatre — the same Stanley Theatre where
Pat DiCesare hoped to host Frank Sinatra —
the dazzling 2,800-seat auditorium was once
called a "movie palace version of
Versailles." The Howard Heinz Endowment
bought the historic landmark from DiCesare-
Engler in the early 1980s, and simultaneously
helped establish the Cultural Trust to over-
see its renovation. With additional funding
from the Claude Worthington Benedum
Foundation, the Cultural Trust managed the
$42 million meticulous refurbishment and
reopened the theater as the Benedum
Center in 1987.

Believed to be the third largest stagehouse in the world (the stagehouse is the
performing and equipment area), the
Benedum is a perfect theater for artists to try
out new work, according to Carolelinda
Dickey. "In all of my years of touring, I'd be
hard-pressed to come up with a theater that's
better than the Benedum. It stands up against
any European opera house and surpasses
most of them."

Two blocks from the Benedum is the
equally opulent Heinz Hall, the home of the
Mendelssohn Choir and the Pittsburgh
Symphony Orchestra, which owns and operates it. Dubbed the "Temple of the Cinema"
when it was built in 1927, Heinz Hall was
restored in 1970, also with funding from the
Heinz Endowment. The partially renovated
Fulton Theatre is "a rare example of a turn-
of-the-century American vaudeville house,"
according to the Cultural Trust. More than 20
arts organizations, including Filmmakers at
the Fulton, which presents art and foreign
films, the Three Rivers Lecture Series and
the Dance Alloy, reside at the Fulton.

■ *Civic Light Opera's production of The Pirates of
Penzance. Photo courtesy of Civic Light Opera.*

■ *Hundreds of jazz musicians got their start in Pittsburgh at one of the many popular jazz clubs. Photo by Roy Engelbrecht.*

The Performing Arts

As a testament to the tradition of philanthropic support, The Carnegie and Symphony, two of Pittsburgh's most distinguished cultural organizations, are, in 1992, approaching their centennial anniversaries. George Westinghouse helped establish the Pittsburgh Symphony Orchestra in 1895, which makes it one of the oldest orchestras in the nation. Westinghouse persuaded 25 of his peers, including steel magnates Frick and Laughlin, to donate to the cause. Henry Heinz made a substantial donation a few years later, beginning a tradition of Heinz family and corporate support for the orchestra that continues today.

Andrew Carnegie was also a symphony supporter. While Westinghouse was passing his hat, Carnegie unveiled the magnificent Music Hall at the Carnegie (rhymes with "leggy") Institute, which the symphony called home for many years. Carnegie's generosity was also responsible for the symphony's first tour, a performance at Carnegie (rhymes with barnaby) Hall in New York in 1900. Since then, the orchestra has performed frequently at Carnegie Hall and, by 1992, had completed 18 international tours.

"International endorsements make the hometown audience appreciate you even more," says the symphony's Sylvia Turner. "They're like winning the World Series or Super Bowl. This kind of recognition inspires musicians, and they come home and play in a very strong fashion." The same can be said for the resident performers of the ballet and opera, which have also earned praise from around the world.

As a result of the symphony's early formation, Pittsburghers are a musically literate audience. Ballet subscribers, for instance, are as interested in the scores as they are in the dance. The first orchestrations for wind symphonies and the world's first wind orchestra also resulted from Pittsburgh's enthusiasm for new music. Robert Boudreau came to Pittsburgh in the 1950s with an idea for a symphony without strings that captured the interest of Mayor David Lawrence and Jack Heinz. But, in order to create a stringless symphony, Boudreau would have to compose or commission compositions for only winds, brasses, and percussions. Heinz funded the experiment and Lawrence married it with a plan to draw Pittsburghers back to the rivers and, in 1957, launched the American Waterways Wind Orchestra, a symphony minus the strings. Today, the orchestra, under Boudreau's direction, has commissioned more than 400 stringless scores and continues to perform free concerts from a floating barge on the banks of the Allegheny River at Point State Park.

Pittsburghers also have an affinity for jazz that dates back to the earliest days of the genre. "There were so many jazz artists in Pittsburgh in the 1940s that big bands would

■ *Heinz Hall was restored in 1970 with funding from the Heinz Endowment. Heinz Hall garden photo by Herb Ferguson.*

come through here when they needed musicians,'' says Marty Ashby, a musician and the director of performing arts at the Manchester Craftsmen's Guild.

The Craftsmen's Guild sponsors the Living Masters of Jazz concerts, a series that features premier jazz artists. Along with the annual week-long Mellon Jazz Festival and weekly Jazz Society concerts, the Craftsmen's Guild is reviving the jazz tradition in Pittsburgh. "Hundreds of jazz musicians," including George Benson, Errol Garner, Billy Eckstein, Billy Strayhorn, Mary Lou Williams, Amal Jamal, and Roger Humphries, "got their start in Pittsburgh, at the Hurricane, Encore, or Crawford's Grill, three hot clubs on the jazz circuit," says Ashby.

Pittsburgh has a long history of producing talented artists, but until the 1980s, many of the homegrown performers had to leave the city to find work in their fields. Thanks to the growth of the arts and the movie industry, "there is less of a need for people who want a career in the arts to leave," says Dan Fallon. The city established a film bureau to recruit filmmakers, and between 1990 and 1992, nearly 30 feature films and television movies were filmed in the city, employing thousands of actors, producers, directors, editors, set designers, casting crews, technicians, extras, and the like.

Pittsburgh has come full circle, Fallon says. "The arts are growing because the talent is staying, and the talent is staying because the arts have grown." And then

■ *One of Pittsburgh's great strengths is the number of grass roots theater and arts organizations that showcase local artists. Shakespeare Fest photo by Herb Ferguson.*

there are those, like Fallon, who are returning. (Carolelinda Dickey says that Pittsburgh should be named the "Most Returned-to City." She gets more than 100 resumes a year from Pittsburgh dancers who want to come home.)

As managing director of the Pittsburgh Public Theatre, Fallon has the distinction of being the only theater manager in the country lucky enough to be running a major theater in the town of his birth. Dan graduated from Carnegie-Mellon University with degrees in mechanical engineering and psychology, left town for his graduate degree in business, and worked for General Dynamics and General Motors. He was involved in theater all along as a hobby and decided, in 1982, to return to Pittsburgh and begin a

tory companies as increasing competition, but Fallon's philosophy is "the more the better. The smaller companies raise the level of interest in theater, and that's good for all of us."

The City Theatre, for example, is evidence of a growing theater audience. Established in 1974 as a program of the University of Pittsburgh, the now independent City Theatre company moved in 1991 from a tiny, on-campus stage in Oakland to a renovated church in the South Side. The audience doubled in size during the company's first season in the new neighborhood, largely due to the expanded seating capacity of the new theater. But attendance had been growing at a rate of 35 percent a year for the previous six years. "There aren't a lot of places in the

■ The Frick Art Museum is one of the many established private galleries and institutions in Pittsburgh. Photo by Roy Engelbrecht.

career in the arts by working as a stage manager with the Civic Light Opera. His plan: make some contacts and go off to New York to be successful. He didn't count on "falling in love again" with his hometown.

Fallon started in community theater and established a musical theater company in Pittsburgh before joining The Public. One of the city's great strengths, he says, is the number of grassroots theater and arts organizations that support and showcase local artists. Some view the proliferation of smaller repertory companies as increasing competition,

country that could support this kind of growth in theater, especially during a recession," says Director Marc Masterson.

The Visual Arts

Like the performing arts, the visual arts are enjoying growth in Pittsburgh as well. New art venues are popping up in the Cultural District and in neighborhoods throughout the city, joining the established private galleries and institutions, such as the Carnegie Museum of Art, the Pittsburgh

■ On the following page: Phipps Conservatory is a breathtaking collection of flora for Pittsburghers and visitors to enjoy. Photo by Roy Engelbrecht.

■ *The Carnegie is probably best known locally for its collection of rare dinosaur artifacts. Photo by Roy Engelbrecht.*

Center for the Arts, and the Frick Art Museum. The opening of the Andy Warhol Museum in 1994 is expected to further elevate Pittsburgh's reputation in the visual arts world.

The Andy Warhol Museum is a project of The Carnegie, the Andy Warhol Foundation for the Visual Arts, which inherited Warhol's estate, and the Dia Center for the Arts, a New York-based cultural institution that collects the works of contemporary artists, including Warhol. The Andy Warhol Foundation and Dia Center have donated their extensive Warhol collections to the Carnegie, making their gifts among the largest in both quantity and financial value ever given to a U.S. museum.

According to Curator Mark Francis, the Warhol Museum will be the first large single-artist museum in the United States. He compares it in scale to the Picasso Museum in Paris and the Van Gogh Museum in Amsterdam. "I hope the museum will become a great pilgrimage place," Francis says. "If you want to know about America, you'll come to the Warhol Museum."

The museum's opening will represent a homecoming of sorts for the late Pittsburgh native. The third of three boys of immigrant parents who came to Pittsburgh at the time of World War I, Andy Warhol took his first art classes on Saturday mornings at the Carnegie Museum of Art, graduated from Carnegie Mellon University's design program, and worked as a window-dresser at Horne's department store. Eventually, the artist realized the American Dream of his parents by becoming rich and famous. His portraits of consumer products (Campbell's soup cans, Heinz, and Brillo boxes), icons (Marilyn, Elvis, and the Kennedy's), car crashes, and electric chairs capture the essence of the 1950s and 1960s and achieved instant celebrity.

Warhol's beginning at The Carnegie offers "a kind of clue to the cultural role the museum plays in Pittsburgh," Francis says. Best known locally for its collection of rare dinosaur artifacts, The Carnegie is respected

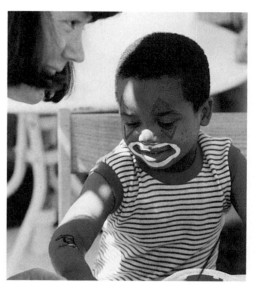

■ *Pittsburghers have an opportunity to celebrate the creative side of life at a variety of arts related functions. Photo by Roy Engelbrecht.*

■ *Children of all ages look forward to the Pittsburgh Children's Festival of Performing Arts. Photo by Roy Engelbrecht.*

■ *The Carnegie is respected globally for the art museum's International exhibition and collection of Impressionist paintings. Photo by Roy Engelbrecht.*

globally for the art museum's International exhibition and collection of Impressionist paintings. An acclaimed contemporary show that features the work of select international artists every three years, the Carnegie International is among the largest sources of the art museum's permanent collection. First held in 1896, the International is the second oldest exhibition of its kind, preceded by the Venice Biennale by only a year.

The genesis of the International began when Andrew Carnegie exhibited 25 paintings of contemporary artists during the opening events of The Institute a year earlier. His interest in contemporary art further set the great industrialist/philanthropist apart from his peers, says Ann Wardrop, a trustee of The Carnegie and a docent at both the Carnegie and Frick art museums. "Because (Thomas) Mellon and (Henry) Frick were collecting the old masters, Carnegie said he would collect the old masters of tomorrow."

Contemporary art is also the forte of the Mattress Factory, an "alternative museum." The Mattress Factory in the Mexican War Streets, a historic area in the Northside, commissions, presents, and collects site-specific installations. "Not everything is beautiful" at the Mattress Factory, says Barbara Luderowski, who founded the museum in a six-story warehouse that was a mattress mill at the turn-of-the-century. The museum is unique in approach as well as appearance. The purpose of the Mattress Factory is to foster contemporary art and artists, and it does so by giving artists money for materials, travel, publicity, and living expenses while they install their work. Luderowski also gives them complete freedom — artists are not required to commit to the exact nature of their creations when they're commissioned. The results are often a bedlam of "stuff." Artists have been known to cut through walls and ceilings, and have used materials as diverse as 6,600 beer cans, 5,632 shoe boxes, live birds, hay stacks, four pounds of phosphorous, garbage bags of human hair, and 150 bundles of wood lath in their installments.

The Mattress Factory "is one of the great undiscovered cultural resources in America," said John Caldwell in the *Wall Street Journal*. Caldwell was curator at the Carnegie, then the San Francisco Museum of Art. "The art you see there usually can't be seen anywhere else except New York, and often not even there."

The Art of Football

The same CEOs who sit in the front row of Heinz Hall on Saturday night can be found on the 50-yard line of Three Rivers Stadium on Sunday afternoon, for football is as much a part of the culture of Pittsburgh as the century-old symphony. There are some, in fact, who attribute the growth of the arts in the 1980s to the success of the Steelers in the 1970s. The team brought recognition to the city, which stimulated the economy and attracted new companies, which, in turn, increased the contributions to the arts.

Pittsburgh's reputation as a great football town developed in the 1970s when the Pittsburgh Steelers began the drive to win four Super Bowls, the first team to do so. A stadium full of zealous fans dressed in black-and-gold and waving Terrible Towels cheered them to victory, year after year after year after year. Steeler games have been sold-out ever since.

"People got caught up in the Steelers' winning, because Pittsburgh was being perceived in a positive way," says Bruce Keidan, a sports reporter and broadcaster. "The image of being a winner was important and people responded to it. The City of Champions had a better ring to it than the Smoky City."

But Steelers President Dan Rooney politely disagrees with Keidan's perspective on the genesis of Pittsburgh fan-itis. Pittsburgh's reputation is one thing, says Rooney, how we see ourselves is something else altogether. "The support the Steelers receive is second to none, but it's not because we won the Super Bowl," he says. "Pittsburgh is a great football town because of its heritage."

The roots of professional football are in Pittsburgh, in the topography that separates ethnic neighborhoods and engendered community-based football teams. Mill-based teams developed later as an employee relations strategy and became so competitive that management would pay ringers to play for their team; hence, the professional football athlete.

"Football was part of the real fiber of the community," says Rooney. "It was the center of activity on a Friday night, and every young man was expected to play. The game was played with a passion because of the neighborhood and mill rivalries," hence, the passionate Pittsburgh football fan. "Pittsburgh fans are recognized as being the most

■ *This "tightrope walker" can be found in the Scaife Gallery of The Carnegie. Photo by Roy Engelbrecht.*

■ *The Vintage Grand Prix is an annual event held at Schenley Park. Photo by Craig DiSanti.*

■ *The Pittsburgh Pirates have produced a long list of "Hall of Famers" and seven world championships. Photo courtesy of Pittsburgh Pirates/Andrea Hawk.*

knowledgeable when it comes to football. I've been to other cities where the fans cheer at the wrong times. Here, they know what's happening."

Dan's father, the legendary Art Rooney Sr., founded the Pittsburgh Steelers football franchise in 1933, the year after Dan was born. According to Myron Cope, a sports reporter and broadcaster in Pittsburgh for more than 40 years, Art Rooney used to say that Pittsburgh fans were "tougher" than the fans in other cities. It's a theory Cope applies to help explain the success of the Pittsburgh Pirates and Penguins as well: "The fans demand more; therefore, the teams produce more."

Cope also attributes the success of Pittsburgh's professional sports teams to "good managers, like the Rooneys, and good first-round draft picks, like Steeler quarterback Terry Bradshaw and Penguin center Mario Lemieux." A true Pittsburgher, Cope is known for telling it like it is: "Of course, you had to have been pretty lousy to get the first-round draft pick." The ability of the teams to come-from-behind, and the willingness of the

fans to help them along, is, perhaps, a further reflection of the Pittsburgh heritage.

The Golden Girls majorettes, the late Tiger Paul, the Pitt band at half-time, the crazy Panther, the way the Greeks line-up outside the dugout at Pitt Stadium to usher in the team at the start of the game — these are football traditions that are part of the culture of Pittsburgh as well, according to Oval Jaynes, University of Pittsburgh (Pitt) athletic director. Pitt football has been part of the Pittsburgh landscape for more than a century.

The athletic director attributes the Pitt football tradition and the university's nine national football championships to the "fine young athletes" Pittsburgh produces. Every Friday night in fall and winter at high school stadiums throughout the region, varsity football is met with the same enthusiasm the players and fans had for the community-based teams at the turn-of-the-century. "When I think of Pittsburgh football, I think of Beaver Falls, Monessen, Donora, Charleroi, Johnstown, Altoona, Uniontown, Blairsville," says Jaynes, his voice trailing off. "It's hard to think of a town in western Pennsylvania that

■ *Football is an important part of the culture of*
Pittsburgh. The Pittsburgh Steelers were the first to win
four Super Bowls. Photo courtesy of Pittsburgh
Steelers/Michael F. Fabus.

hasn't turned out great athletes." In the 1980s, Pitt turned out more professional football players — hometown heros such as Tony Dorsett and Dan Marino — than any other school, he says.

Jaynes moved to Pittsburgh in 1991, but had recruited here throughout his 30-year career as a high school and college football coach and athletic director. He feels he was destined to turn up at Pitt. A native of North Carolina, Jaynes says he grew up with a "certain reverance for Pitt and the Pitt football tradition," thanks to the stories of his father and grandfather who both played football for Duke University. Their favorite tale was of the game when Duke upset Pitt the year that Pitt would have went undefeated.

Basketball, Baseball, and Hockey

If the number of fans on hand to cheer for Pitt or Duquesne University basketball, Penguins hockey, and Pirates baseball at any given game are an indication, then Pittsburgh is not only a great football town, it's a great sports town in general. A member of the Big East basketball conference, the Pitt Panthers routinely sellout Fitzgerald Field House, but the biggest basketball event of the year is the annual shoot-out with crosstown rival, the Duquesne Dukes at the Civic Arena.

The Penguins and Pirates have the same loyal following of fans as the Steelers. "Each team has had an extraordinary track record of success and support from both the community and corporate sectors," says Howard Baldwin, Penguins president and owner. "The fans are very enthusiastic, and since the cost of a ticket to a sporting event can be pretty high, you've got to love it, and Pittsburghers do."

Although Penguins tickets are hard to come by now, hockey hasn't enjoyed the long history of widespread patronage in Pittsburgh that football has. Until Mario Lemieux joined the team in 1984, and led the Penguins to back-to-back Stanley Cup championships in 1991 and 1992, hockey was a "cult sport" here, says Keidan. Having Mario "was like having Babe Ruth in your town. He's

■ *The Party Liner is one of the seven ships in the Gateway Clipper Fleet which features historical tours, dance cruises and romantic moonlight sails. Photo by Roy Engelbrecht.*

■ *On the following page: The Pittsburgh Penguins hockey team won back-to-back Stanley Cup championships in 1991 and 1992. Photo by Herb Ferguson.*

the greatest that ever was and suddenly he's playing in your own backyard. You didn't have to be a rocket scientist to recognize that you were watching something special.''

Thanks to Lemieux and the success of the Penguins, the number of school and children's hockey leagues in Pittsburgh is growing so rapidly that perhaps when history is written in 2100, it will be community-based hockey teams instead of football teams that will have defined the city's sports culture.

Baseball, on the other hand, is as Pittsburgh as chipped ham and Klondikes. Rooting for a club called the Alleghenies, the name of the team that preceded the Pirates, Pittsburghers began a love affair with baseball in 1876. Like most lasting relationships, the team of Pittsburgh and the Pirates has weathered good and bad seasons, and gen-

erated a mountain of memories. Say ''Forbes Field,'' ''Babushka Power,'' ''Bob Prince,'' or ''We had 'em allllll the way!'' to any Pittsburgher over 30, and you'll evoke a rush of nostalgia.

The ''Buccos'' have produced a long list of venerated Hall of Famers, including Honus Wagner, Pie Traynor, Ralph Kiner, Danny Murtaugh, Roberto Clemente, and Willie Stargell, and won seven world championships — the first in 1903, the most recent in 1979.

But perhaps the 1985 season best reflects the tenacity of the relationship between the franchise and the fans. That was the year when the team was for sale and appeared about to leave Pittsburgh. Pittsburghers wouldn't sit for it, however. ''I remember 40,000 people coming out one night to watch a dreadful Pirates team play

■ *The Mattress Factory is an alternative museum which gives artists a great deal of creative freedom in the pursuit of contemporary art. Photo courtesy of the Mattress Factory.*

the Chicago Cubs in a meaningless game simply to demonstrate their love for the franchise," says Bruce Keidan.

Responding to the public plea, a group of business leaders formed a partnership and bought the club, ensuring the continuation of professional baseball in the city. Led by the late Mayor Richard Caliguiri and James Roddey, a recently transplanted Pittsburgher from Atlanta who recognized the team's importance in the community, the group of new owners included ALCOA, Carnegie Mellon University, Eugene and Raymond Litman, John McConnell, Harvey Walken, Mellon Bank, PNC Corporation, PPG Industries, USX Corportion, and Westinghouse Electric Corporation.

The following year, 13 avid Pirate fans formed the Diamond Club to boost attendance. In 1986, the all-volunteer club sold 60,000 tickets; in 1992, 35 members sold more than 500,000 tickets worth more than $1 million. Jay McCann, one of the founders of the Diamond Club, says the group came together to contribute to keeping the Pirates in Pittsburgh. "We enjoy going to the ball game," he says matter-of-factly. To sell his share of tickets, he and a friend formed an informal production company that sponsors pre- and post-game parties. Invitations go to a database of 2,200 of their "closest" friends, McCann says.

Inspired by the staunch support of the hometown fans, the Pirates have performed phenomenally since the buyout. Between 1986 and 1992, the Pirates won three divisional titles and sold more than three million tickets for three consecutive years. "That's a terrific record," says Mark Sauer, who joined the team as president and CEO in 1991. "There's no question that the Pirates will be staying in Pittsburgh."

■ *Three Rivers Arts Festival is an annual celebration of the arts held at Gateway Center. Photo by Herb Ferguson.*

CHAPTER

City of Neighborhoods

EIGHT

"On balance, Pittsburgh's the best place I've lived by far," says

Barry Cohen, a Chicago native. "It combines the best of the

Midwest in terms of attitudes, values, and a service-orienta-

tion, yet offers all of the attractions of a big city. But here, they're more

affordable and accessible. The shopping, parking, theater are great.

People are polite and friendly. We joined The Carnegie, my kids love the

Regatta. Station Square is wonderful, really neat. "

■ *West Park is one of the many peaceful spots throughout the city that Pittsburghers can enjoy. Photo by Roy Engelbrecht.*

■ From peanuts and parades to weddings in the park, Pittsburgh is a great place to have a family and enjoy a real sense of community. Photos by Roy Engelbrecht.

"There are bigger cities, but we don't have the fall-out, the downside of bigness," says J. David Griffin, dean of the Community College of Allegheny County. "I haven't seen the combination and consistency in other cities of all of the entities that represent quality of life here — education, business, culture, recreation, health care, morals. And people. People are our strength as a city. Pittsburgh is responsive to the broadest population — young and old and in-between, white and black, advantaged and disadvantaged. When the die is cast, Pittsburgh will always work in favor of the people. "

"In Pittsburgh, it's accepted that your emotional energy will be split between your job and family," says Mark Taylor, who moved from New York. "There's a wholeness, a balance of life here. Pittsburgh is a conservative community, but that doesn't mean we're closed to new ideas. There are good things that go into being conservative — traditional values, for instance. It's a great place to have a family. "

"Conservative? People have always told me that Pittsburgh was conservative. I haven't found that to be true. Pittsburghers aren't real quick to change, but that doesn't mean they're conservative. They can adhere to a radical point of view, but they'll stick to it," says Carolelinda Dickey, who calls herself a transplanted Pittsburgher. "I sometimes think Pittsburgh is better appreciated by people who grew up elsewhere and moved here. There's a real sense of community. "

The common thread that runs through the fabric of Pittsburgh is a sense of place, "a sense of community." No matter where you live in Pittsburgh— in the city, suburbs, country or mountains— you live in a neighborhood first. To others, we're from Pittsburgh. But to Pittsburghers, we're from Bloomfield, Butler, the Hill, Cranberry, Bethel Park, Edgewood, Thornburg, Overbrook, or Ligonier.

Though defined by the pattern of hills, valleys, and rivers, a neighborhood of Pittsburgh is more than a geographical designation. Neighborhoods are personified by housing styles, the corner butcher who knows you by name, schools, places of worship, the crossing guard you routinely wave to every weekday, the shortcuts. Neighborhoods have personalities you grow attached

to and come to love, a source of pride mysterious only to those who haven't lived here.

The neighborhood culture inspires a generosity that makes the city a safe and clean environment. The annual KDKA Children's Hospital fund drive offers a telling snapshot of the inherent benevolence of Pittsburghers. Each December, KDKA radio broadcasts from windows of downtown department stores while Pittsburghers, clad in wool and mittens, line-up in the chill of winter to present an offering on-the-air and wish the children well. "Hi, I'm Susie Miller from Yough High School. My friends and I collected $50 for the kids at Children's Hospital. Merry Christmas." Kindergartners who save up $2.50 in nickels from their allowances receive the same warm acknowledgment from station personalities as do the small

■ *Pittsburgh offers all the attractions of a big city with the attitudes and values of a smaller community. Photo by Roy Engelbrecht.*

business owners who match the contributions of employees and present a check for $2,500. Each holiday season, Pittsburghers bring forth hundreds of thousands of dollars "for the kids."

More than money, though, it's the personal involvement in causes for the common good that sets Pittsburghers apart. Pittsburghers don't simply write a check and send it in, they get in their car or board a bus and hand-deliver their donation, along with a word of encouragement. Pittsburghers will spontaneously form a group to collect food and clothes for families who lose their homes and belongings to fire or flood. They'll volunteer through their church or community to start food banks and soup kitchens for laid-off workers. They'll shop for new coats for Project Bundle-up, an annual event sponsored by WTAE-TV and the Salvation Army. They'll donate gently-worn business suits so women on welfare can put their best feet forward on job interviews.

Neighborliness is also the secret to Pittsburgh's safety record, says Pittsburgh Public Safety Director Lou DiNardo. Close-knit neighbors who "keep an eye out" for each other, DiNardo says, are a safeguard against lawbreakers. As a result of attentive neighbors and active community groups, Pittsburgh traditionally ranks among the safest cities in the nation. In 1992, Pittsburgh was safer than 44 of the 48 U.S. cities with populations greater than 300,000, according to a Federal Bureau of Investigation report.

Actually, the city may be safer than the numbers imply. Some cities manipulate their statistics to present the safest possible record, but not Pittsburgh, DiNardo says. "We tell it like it is. A car theft is a car theft, even if we recover the vehicle within 48 hours, which is typically the case." In some cities, though, a stolen car recovered in the same time frame is referred to as "missing," he says, a category the FBI doesn't consider. "It's not a crime to lose your car."

The abundance and high quality of health care institutions in Pittsburgh are the product of the neighborhood culture as well.

"Hospitals everywhere began as voluntary, nonprofit community institutions, but the concept of charity has prevailed more strongly in Pittsburgh than in other areas of the country," says Jack Robinette, president of the Hospital Council of Western Pennsylvania. "You'll rarely, if ever, hear of someone who is turned away from a local hospital because they can't pay."

The Hospital Council is an umbrella organization of area health care institutions that celebrated 50 years of service in 1992. Its membership includes more than 85 acute-care inpatient hospitals in the 30-county western region, which reaches to State College, Pennsylvania, near the middle of the state. More than 30 of the hospitals are located within Allegheny County, and half of those are within the heart of the city.

In an effort to "keep up with the Joneses" during the 1980s, when government cutbacks in health care subsidies forced community hospitals to become more competitive, many developed specialty niches and acquired state-of-the-art equipment. The results make Pittsburgh one of the best places in the world to live when you're in need of medical attention. "And eventually, we all are," says Robinette. "For most maladies, excellent care is as close as your community hospital, and for rare or difficult to treat illnesses, the expertise is available at the hospitals in the city."

Emergency health care is also top-shelf. There are two emergency helicopter services that serve the region, and city residents benefit from one of the nation's most highly ranked Emergency Medical Service (EMS) bureaus. The formal title of "paramedic," the highest degree of prehospital training attainable in this field, is mandatory for every member of Pittsburgh's force. (In fact, the paramedic profession was started in Pittsburgh.) This service is enhanced by the city's First Responder system, which deploys specially trained firefighters who administer basic life support until paramedics arrive, ensuring the fastest possible response time.

■ More than 30 hospitals are located within Allegheny County. Allegheny General Hospital photo by Roy Engelbrecht.

■ *Pittsburgh is a showcase for a wide variety of architectural designs including Falling Water, the Kaufmann mansion designed by Frank Lloyd Wright. Photo by Roy Engelbrecht.*

Hospitals provide more than quality health care. They also give back jobs as well as community services. "The hospitals are the steel mills of the 1990s," says Tom Chakurda of Allegheny General Hospital (AGH), which has a written agreement with 14 surrounding neighborhoods outlining seven ways the hospital will support the community. For example, AGH established a scholarship program through the Community College of Allegheny County for neighborhood residents pursuing careers in nursing or the allied health professions. Working with Integra Bank, AGH also developed a low-interest mortgage program for employees who buy a home in one of the neighborhoods near the hospital. Employees can also borrow up to half of the downpayment from the hospital credit union.

A House to Call Home

Even for buyers who don't use a special financing package like the one AGH offers, buying a home in Pittsburgh is remarkably affordable. Newcomers, especially those from cities of the same size or larger than Pittsburgh, are overwhelmed by the low cost of Pittsburgh real estate. In 1992, Pittsburgh ranked fifth among U.S. cities for most affordable housing costs. The average sales price of a house in Pittsburgh is $100,000 less than in Boston, for instance, and $70,000 less than in Seattle. Simply put, buyers get more house for their money in Pittsburgh than elsewhere.

Cultural pride and diversity is evident in the fastidiousness and variety of the region's architecture. Even rural farmland is available within an easy commute of downtown. Forty-five minutes north of the city is the middle of nowhere and all of the serenity seclusion offers. Closer in, the 132 municipalities of Allegheny County reflect an array of

■ *No matter where you live in Pittsburgh, you live in a neighborhood first. Photo by Roy Engelbrecht.*

housing styles — spacious tudors on mani-cured lawns in suburban Mt. Lebanon, new split-levels in the developing North Hills, secluded family estates in Fox Chapel and Sewickley.

Within the city itself, 90 distinct neigh-borhoods are distinguished by a collection of homes that range from the post-war ranch styles that sit on expansive front lawns in Oakwood, to the cliffhanger that offers unpar-alleled views of the downtown skyline in Fineview, to the quaint and sturdy front-stooped frame rowhome in South Side or Lawrenceville, to the two-and-a-half-story brick with box gutters, lots of gingerbread, and a big front porch in neighborhoods everywhere, the quintessential "Pittsburgh" house.

The neighborhoods of Pittsburgh are endowed with an abundance of turn-of-the-century styles, built when homes were built to last forever. More than 60 percent of the

■ *Visiting the Pittsburgh Zoo is a favorite family activity.*
African habitat photo by Roy Engelbrecht.

homes in the city were built before World War II and reflect the craftsmanship of a bygone era. It's not unusual to find a house with brick walls a foot thick that's been handed down through several generations of the same family. The wood used to lay floors and carve mantels came from trees shaped hard and strong by a century of growing, a supply all but exhausted today. Sound-proof, energy-efficient plaster formed the walls and ceilings. Details that would cost a fortune to duplicate today, such as 12-inch oak baseboards, mahogany doors, parquet floors, and bevelled or stained glass windows, are common among the treasures of Pittsburgh.

Nature's Blessings

All this evidence of community mindedness sits on a backdrop of nature's blessings — mountains and valleys, rivers and lakes, and gently rolling, verdant acreage that change like scenes in a play as the season's colors mark the passing of time. Emerald in spring, kelly in summer, golden and crimson in autumn, ivory in win-

ter. Each season brings new hope and opportunity, and the rite of community traditions tied to the climate — the first robin, mowing the lawn, the onset of football, changing the snow tires. The effect is a sort of mental Renaissance for Pittsburghers: Four times a year, we get to start over.

The ever-changing scenery is a never-ending playground. Downhill skiing, cross-country skiing, water skiing, powerboating, sailing, kayaking, rowing, white water rafting, windsurfing, fishing, hunting, spelunking, golfing, running, and biking — all are sports the landscape and seasons support.

The first of December through the end of March is the official ski season in western Pennsylvania. Located an hour's drive from downtown, nestled in the Laurel Highlands of the Allegheny Mountains, the Seven Springs Mountain Resort and its neighbor, Hidden Valley, are the region's premier ski areas. Established in the era of Bing Crosby and *White Christmas*, the picturesque Seven Springs offers rustic charm for those who prefer sipping brandy by the fire. For serious skiers, however, the resort features more than 500 skiable acres, a 900-foot vertical drop on the North Face and "superior" snow-making and lift capabilities, says Seven Springs' Scott Bender. "Once we get temperatures low enough to make snow, we have

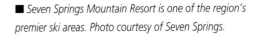

■ *Seven Springs Mountain Resort is one of the region's*
premier ski areas. Photo courtesy of Seven Springs.

■ *Three Rivers Regatta is an annual event founded by John E. Connelly in the late 1970s. Photo by Herb Ferguson.*

skiing all season." Hidden Valley features cross-country skiing as well, as do several parks in the heart of the city. Boyce Park in suburban Pittsburgh offers lessons and slopes for beginning skiers.

"The skiing is every bit as good in western Pennsylvania as it is in New England," says Bender. National recognition proves his point: *Ski and Snow Country* magazines have ranked Seven Springs among the top 10 best ski resorts in the eastern United States.

When the snow melts, Pittsburghers become avid golfers. Golf season typically runs from the first of April through October, although the weather is often conducive for golfing through Thanksgiving. Called one of America's most golfable cities because of the quantity of courses, "Pittsburgh is lucky," says Dennis Darak, executive director of the Tri-State PGA, "to have championship-quality facilities, a good mix of country clubs, golfing communities and resorts, and a variety of very nice public courses. The natural terrain is rolling and hilly, and golf courses use that to their advantage." One would expect nothing less from the hometown of Arnold Palmer.

Pittsburgh's championship-caliber clubs include the courses at Oakmont, Quicksilver Laurel Valley, and Sunnehanna, Darak says. Oakmont, the site of the Women's U.S. Open in 1992, will host the Men's U.S. Open in 1994. Quicksilver, an "absolutely breathtaking" public facility,

■ *On the following page: Oakmont Country Club, the site of the Women's U.S. Open in 1992, will host the Men's U.S. Open in 1994. Photo by Roy Engelbrecht.*

■ "Anything That Floats" parade is one of the highlights of the four-day Three Rivers Regatta. Photo by Herb Ferguson.

according to Darak, hosts the Senior PGA Tour.

Named among the top 15 courses and the best public course in Pennsylvania by *Golf Week* magazine, Quicksilver is the product of Bob Murphy, a local CEO who saw opportunity in the sparsity of upscale public courses in the area. Murphy redesigned the course of the former country club (adding 74 bunkers, new greens, five new tees, and hard fescue grass to give it a "links-look"), revamped the club house and changed the

name. "Anyone can come to golf and entertain. There is no membership," says Sean Parees, golf director.

Most cities have good golfing; however, most don't have the three rivers that make Pittsburgh a "recreational panacea in this part of the country," says John E. Connelly, riverman extraordinaire. According to the Census Bureau, 87 percent of the nation's population equate recreation with water, Connelly says, and Pittsburgh has water in triplicate, in the form of the Allegheny,

Connelly's interest in the rivers began in the 1950s during Renaissance I, when he joined the board of the then-new Allegheny County Sanitary Authority, which spent $100 million to develop waste water treatment plants and clean-up the rivers. "For generations, people turned their backs on the rivers and developed inward," he says. "In the 1950s, we turned that around."

Launched in 1958, the Gateway Clipper Fleet played a key role in the transformation of the rivers. Connelly wanted the

Monongahela, and Ohio Rivers that converge at Point State Park downtown. Today, boaters, skiers, and other fans of the water share the rivers with the towboats and barges that have long served as a primary mode of transportation for the city's manufacturers.

Think of the three rivers, and Pittsburghers think of Connelly's Gateway Clipper Fleet and the annual Three Rivers Regatta, an event the riverman founded in the late 1970s with his brother Eugene.

public to experience the beauty of the city's newly cleaned rivers and growing skyline, so he purchased a 100-passenger sternwheeler and began selling rides up and down the Allegheny, Monongahela, and Ohio. Host to informative historical tours, entertaining dance cruises and romantic moonlit sails, the Clipper rides grew in popularity. The following year, Connelly added a second Clipper and the first Good Ship Lollipop. Not much bigger than a first grade classroom, the Good Ship Lollipop predates Chuck E. Cheese's as the preferred birthday party place and reward for good report cards for young Pittsburghers. Today, crowned by the 1,000-passenger Majestic, the Gateway Clipper Fleet of seven ships carries more than 800,000 tourists and party-goers annually.

■ *Renovations in and around downtown Pittsburgh have made it a warm and friendly location for businesses, or simply to shop and browse. Station Square photo by Roy Engelbrecht.*

■ *On the following page: Northside Farmers Market is a place where Pittsburghers enjoy a "neighborhood" feeling when purchasing home-grown fruits and vegetables. Photo by Roy Engelbrecht.*

Aboard Connelly's boats, amidst the dreamy reflection of the city skyline and the tranquil splash-splash of the swells, Pittsburghers developed an affection for the rivers that has led to a wave of waterfront development. Three Rivers Stadium, Station Square, the Carnegie Science Center and submarine, Sandcastle water amusement park, the Boardwalk, Washington's Landing — all are popular entertainment venues along the shores of the rivers that followed the launch of the Gateway Clipper, and more are planned.

Pittsburghers themselves took to the water as well, in droves. In 1992, there were 30,000 boats registered in Allegheny County. From early spring through late fall, and on

■ *There is a broad spectrum of events to enjoy at the Pittsburgh Marathon, which has become part of the culture of Pittsburgh. Photo by Roy Engelbrecht.*

many days in between, when the sun is shining and the temperature warm, the rivers become a buzz of power boaters, water-skiers, and jet-skiers. (An occasional sailboat or sailboard will slide by, but serious sailors head north to Moraine State Park or Lake Erie, one of the nation's five Great Lakes three hours away.)

The highlight of boating season is the Three Rivers Regatta, a free four-day extravaganza held on the shores of Point State Park the first weekend of August. The Regatta features a variety of water entertainment, including Formula One boat racing and the traditional Anything That Floats parade, as well as an airshow, hot air balloon launch, outdoor concerts, and fireworks.

■ *Water sports and facilities are abundant in Pittsburgh including Sandcastle, a water amusement park. Photo courtesy of Kennywood Park.*

■ *The neighborhoods of Pittsburgh have personalities you grow attached to and come to love. The Priory courtyard photo by Roy Engelbrecht.*

According to Connelly, the purpose of the Regatta is to recognize the rivers as the city's most valuable asset — not only for recreation, but also for sustenance. The rivers flow from two separate water sheds in New York and in West Virginia. Reaching Pittsburgh, the sources provide an ample supply of water that virtually protects Pittsburghers from the threat of drought or shortages, another reason businesses choose Pittsburgh as a manufacturing location.

A Pittsburgh Paradigm

Like the symphony and the Steelers, the Regatta is part of the culture of Pittsburgh. So is the Marathon in May, the Arts Festival in June, and the Independence Day celebration. To Pittsburghers, they're not just events, they're part of our makeup —like Kennywood Park.

■ *The Children's Festival represents Pittsburgh's belief that the future generation is the strength of the city. Photo by Roy Engelbrecht.*

Perhaps there is nothing as quintessentially Pittsburgh as Kennywood Park. "America's finest traditional amusement park" has been a Pittsburgh tradition since 1898. In many ways, the park serves as a microcosm of Pittsburgh. Like Pittsburgh, Kennywood is green and quaint, a blend of the old and new. It's fun and family, ethnic and reliable. A product of the past, yet progressive. Like Pittsburgh, Kennywood has

had to adapt to the decline of the steel industry to survive and succeed.

People who grew up in Pittsburgh grew up with Kennywood. They went to Kennywood, at least once a year, on the day of their school picnic, probably in May or June. School picnics were the brainchild of Christopher Magee, a Pittsburgh politician and contemporary of Andrew Carnegie. To win votes from parents, Magee treated their offspring to an annual outing at a city park. In 1906, one of Kennywood's original owners convinced Magee to bring the brood to Kennywood, and thus began the tradition that continues today. Once a year, every school district within a 90-mile radius of Pittsburgh comes to Kennywood for a day-long picnic.

Kennywood is located near the banks of the Monongahela River in Duquesne, Pennsylvania, a few miles upstream from Pittsburgh, on a parcel of land originally owned by Anthony Kenny. Before the turn-of-the-century, Kenny leased the land to the Monongahela Street Railroad, a company owned by Andrew Mellon. Mellon wanted to develop the beautifully wooded tract into an end-of-the-line trolley park. Kenny's Wood, as Mellon called it, was one of 13 end-of-the-line amusement parks designed by the railroads to attract passengers.

There were various owners, all with connections to the railroad, until 1906, when Magee established the park's bread-and-butter business, and Kennywood became the privately owned family operation it remains today. Community, ethnic, church, school, and company picnics are still the "mainstay of the park's business," says Andy Quinn, director of community relations. Quinn's great-great-grandfather was one of Kennywood's original owners. Irish Day, Italian Day, Polish Day, Westinghouse Electric Day, Heinz Day, St. Bart's Day, Brookline Day. "These are the events that endear us to Pittsburghers," says Quinn. "People come every year of their life on that day."

In the 1920s, Kennywood added the Jack Rabbit, Racer, and Pippin (which

predated the Thunderbolt), the three rides that would eventually make the park internationally famous as the Roller Coaster Capital of the World. The Steel Phantom, the world's fastest and longest vertical drop roller coaster, debuted in the 1991 season. The youth of Pittsburgh pine for the day when they measure up to the statue of Kenny Kangaroo, the park mascot, and graduate from Kiddieland to the coasters.

Like Pittsburgh, Kennywood reflects the melting pot influence of the city's ethnic immigrants. One of six national historic landmarks in Allegheny County, Kennywood maintains several of the park's original buildings, including the Merry-Go-Round, as well as the traditional wooden coasters. The architecture is a lively blend of oriental, colonial, and art deco motifs, and "whatever was the vogue at the time," says Quinn.

"Change at Kennywood can be very painful," he says, a fact that thrills the natives. Generational ties are strengthened at Kennywood, where families can still bring a picnic and lunch by the trees, where parents and grandparents can mentally revisit their first ride on the Thunderbolt or kiss in the Old Mill. Among the evidence of modernization, the past is preserved, and the park remains the Kennywood they remember.

And in spite of the decline of steel, the rise of technology, and the changes involved in remaking an international city, the community spirit that defines and safeguards the Pittsburgh we grew up with remains intact as well.

■ A day on the water is a way of life for many Pittsburghers. Photo by Herb Ferguson.

Charting the Future

AFTERWARD

Pittsburghers are relentlessly honest and self-critical: everyone said "Don't just write the good things—no one will believe it."

Like every city charting its post-Cold War future in a global economy, Pittsburgh faces challenges and opportunities. Yes, Pittsburgh is not a perfect place—we're not finished yet.

In 1994, the city will enter a new era in government leadership. The retirement of Mayor Sophie Masloff, who served five years as Mayor and 12 in City Council, brings to a close an administration begun in 1977 by Mayor Richard Caliguiri, who died in office. The times were tumultuous: between 1978 and 1993, Pittsburgh withstood the devastating decline of the steel industry; retrained and placed thousands of unemployed mill workers; developed new health care, technology, and service businesses to reverse the economy; and masterminded a building boom that dramatically altered the city's skyline and stimulated neighborhood reinvestment.

Despite the decline in federal support for cities during the 1980s, under Masloff's watch, Pittsburgh maintained a balanced budget and still managed to reduce the wage tax to attract new residents. Sustaining fiscal viability and expanding the tax base will be among the challenges that confront the new mayor.

Leadership roles in the business and community sectors are changing as well. The Fortune 500 companies native to Pittsburgh have grown into international conglomerates. Their loyalties are divided among all of the communities in which they do business. Consequently, there is a tapering of the corporate support Pittsburgh relied on for nearly a century, and smaller emerging companies are stepping up to fill the void. Colleges, universities, and foundations are also playing a larger role in shaping public policy and supporting social services, education, and the arts. A growing number of women and minority-owned business leaders are changing the dynamics of a city founded on male-dominated manufacturing enterprises.

The new cadre of leaders will become responsible for safeguarding Pittsburgh's reputation for quality of life in a nation where "urban" and "violence" are often synonymous. They will decide how to allocate shrinking resources among wide-ranging groups of financially needy arts, education, and human service organizations.

They will care for a growing elderly population and address the impact of a national health care policy on the city's medical businesses and institutions. They will strive for a more efficient and cost-effective local government. They will tackle the complex issues inherent in regionalization and internationalization.

The new leadership will also engineer another Renaissance, a third building boom that already began with the opening of the airport. On the agenda: More downtown and waterfront housing. Six proposed downtown office complexes. The rejuvenation of downtown as a major shopping center, anchored with the reopening of the former Gimbel's department store building. Continuing development of the Cultural District. A new office building, hotel, and public park at Station Square. Reuse of former mill sites along the rivers. The new bridge across the Mon. A subway connecting the Northside with Oakland. An extension of Point State Park. The Mon Valley Expressway and Southern Beltway. The development of 10,000 acres along the Airport Corridor. The Airport Busway. Maybe Maglev.

They will also open the new Pittsburgh Regional History Center, Andy Warhol

Museum, and, perhaps, a Smithsonian aviation museum in the halls of the former airport.

These tasks are no more daunting than cleaning the air, damming the rivers, or rebuilding the economy—successes accomplished by working together.

When it comes to problem-solving, the Pittsburgh advantage is experience, will and spunk, and the partnerships in place to effect change: the International Development Roundtable, Allegheny Conference on Community Development, Pittsburgh Partnership for Neighborhood Development, Greater Pittsburgh Chamber of Commerce, Southwest Pennsylvania

Growth Alliance, the Regional Transportation Partnership, and so on.

To quote Margaret Mead: "Never doubt that a small group of thoughtful, committed citizens can change the world. Indeed, it is the only thing that ever has."

Working together, generations of thoughtful, committed Pittsburghers have improved this international city, and, in turn, have changed the world. Never doubt that Pittsburghers, native and new, will continue to do so.   ◰

■ *A new cadre of leaders will become responsible for safeguarding Pittsburgh's reputation for quality of life. Photo by Roy Engelbrecht.*

PASSPORT TO
Pittsburgh's Enterprises
PITTSBURGH

CHAPTER

Networks

NINE

Bell of Pennsylvania,
164-165

Port Authority of Allegheny
County, 166-167

Columbia Gas of
Pennsylvania, 168-169

Corporate Jets, Inc.,
170-171

USAir, 172-173

Consolidated Natural Gas
Company & People's Natural
Gas Company, 174-177

Duquesne Light, 178-179

British Airways, 180-181

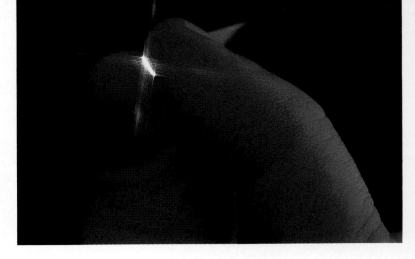

Bell Atlantic: Positioning Pittsburgh on the Forefront of Telecommunications Technology

It was not so long ago that having a single-party telephone line meant a Pittsburgher had the latest in telecommunications technology.

Today, Bell of Pennsylvania's residence and business subscribers can avail themselves of telecommunications options that introduce new levels of ease, convenience, and security to their homes and businesses.

These same customers can count on a feature-rich network that's among the most efficiently operated in the world, backed by advanced computer switches, with unmatched reliability and prices that are among the lowest in the country.

Bell of Pennsylvania

At the same time, customers can be assured that Bell of Pennsylvania continues to explore new ways to enhance the quality of life in Pittsburgh.

Communicating with Light

Many of those advances are made possible by Bell of Pennsylvania's investment in fiber-optic technology. Fiber-optic cable transmits signals as bursts of light, powered by lasers, over hair-thin strands of glass.

The technology offers the ability to carry vast amounts of voice, data, and video signals at speeds and capacities never before possible. It's the key to a vast array of services for business and residence customers alike.

Bell of Pennsylvania continues to construct new fiber routes between its switching centers. Its fiber rings already circle the Pittsburgh metropolitan area. Called SMARTnet, they offer the most fiber-intense, advanced applications networks anywhere.

With SMARTnet, Bell of Pennsylvania provides business

■ *Bell of Pennsylvania is a subsidiary of Philadelphia-based Bell Atlantic Corporation.*

■ *Fiber-optic cable transmits signals as bursts of light.*

customers with leading-edge services and reliability they need to meet their most stringent communications requirements.

Through SMARTnet and diverse fiber routing, the network is protected from failures and can restore itself in minutes.

Bell of Pennsylvania continues to meet the increasingly complex and sophisticated communications needs of its large business customers with a growing list of services.

Those services include Switched Megabit Data Service, which allows businesses to transport data more efficiently and at high speeds. Switched Redirect Service gives customers the ability to redirect their incoming calls for load control or in the event of an emergency.

Centrex Extend Service allows Centrex customers with multiple locations to communicate and interact as though they are at the same location.

Bell of Pennsylvania designed and installed a unique communications system to serve the new Midfield Terminal at Pittsburgh International Airport. The system incorporates the latest design in "intelligent network" technology. It offers flexibility, diverse fiber routing, protection from failures, and the ability to restore itself in an emergency.

Fully Computerized

Thanks to its investment in state-of-the-art equipment, Bell of Pennsylvania serves 100 percent of its customers with computer-controlled switching machines. They allow customers to take advantage of information-age options that add new levels of convenience and security to their lives.

These personal call-management "I.Q. Services" include features that allow customers to automatically redial a busy number (Repeat Call), trace a call (Call Trace),and block numbers from which they do not wish to receive calls (Call Block).

Customers with Call Forwarding service activate the service from any touch-tone phone with Ultra Forward service. The company also offers Answer Call service, which turns the telephone into an answering machine without the need to purchase one, and Home Intercom service, which lets you use the telephone to communicate within the home without the need to purchase additional equipment.

Connecting You to the Future

Even as Bell of Pennsylvania continues to move ahead with its fiber-optic "Network of the Future," the network's possibilities continue to emerge, with applications benefiting health care, education, economic

■ *State-of-the-art equipment allows Bell of Pennsylvania customers to take advantage of information-age options.*

development, and the quality of life for older citizens.

For example, imagine an educational network for job skills and retraining that every citizen of the commonwealth can access from their home, office, or school.

Imagine easy access to up-to-the-minute results of research from around the nation or the world that affect manufacturing processes and product composition.

Imagine a sophisticated communications network that enables state-of-the-art inventory and distribution systems for businesses already in Pittsburgh or those looking to relocate.

Imagine anyone being able to work from their home full time or several days a week, bringing jobs to Pittsburgh and to every corner of the state and skilled workers to every business.

Imagine shopping from your home, browsing through video "stores" offering a wide variety of products from groceries and clothing to cars and houses.

Imagine a "video house call" over the network, talking with your doctor face-to-face without traveling to a hospital, clinic, or the doctor's office.

Bell of Pennsylvania's Network of the Future holds the key to these and many more services that benefit every aspect of life.

Bell Atlantic Family

Bell of Pennsylvania is a wholly owned subsidiary of Philadelphia-based Bell Atlantic Corporation, which also is the parent company of New Jersey Bell, Diamond State Telephone (Delaware), and the Chesapeake and Potomac Telephone Companies of Maryland, Virginia, West Virginia, and Washington, D.C.

Bell Atlantic also is the parent of one of the nation's largest cellular carriers and of companies that provide business systems for customer-based information technology, including software, systems integration, hardware and software services and support, and financial services throughout the United States and internationally.

In addition, Bell Atlantic International offers network services and consulting to telephone authorities throughout the world and in conjunction with Ameritech owns a majority interest in Telecom Corporation of New Zealand.

Quality and Service

Bell of Pennsylvania employees are committed to being leaders in the promising

landscape of services offered by communications advances.

With their focus on quality, employees are dedicated to making Pittsburgh a better place to live and work by applying the most advanced telecommunications technology and the highest standards of service.

■ *Bell of Pennsylvania designed and installed a unique communications system to serve the new Midfield Terminal at Pittsburgh International Airport.*

P ublic transportation has played a crucial role in the economic development and vitality of Allegheny County and its many municipalities. Directly or indirectly, Port Authority of Allegheny County, or PAT, affects the life of every local resident and is essential to the health and economic well-being of the region.

Japanese, German, and English language brochures to help residents and visitors explore Downtown Pittsburgh using the PAT system. PAT also stays in touch with ideas through regular meetings with the Allegheny County Transit Council. ACTC is a voluntary consumer advocacy/citizens advisory group comprised of Allegheny County residents

PAT opened the South Busway in 1977 in order to bypass the congested Fort Pitt Bridge, Green Tree Hill, and Liberty Tunnels. The two-lane roadway, which connects Downtown and the Overbrook section of the city, became the nation's first roadway reserved exclusively for buses and other transit vehicles. The Busway shares right-of-way with the "T" rail system, a unique and highly efficient arrangement. The Busway's success was quickly realized as bus ridership topped 20,000 daily passengers.

PAT opened the Martin Luther King, Jr. East Busway from Downtown to Wilkinsburg in 1983. Located within a narrow railroad corridor through densely populated neighborhoods, ridership on the Busway has grown steadily. By 1993, more than 30,000 riders were using the Busway daily. Customer satisfaction and system accessibility are two of Port Authority's main goals, and PAT continues striving to provide safe, efficient, and user-friendly public transportation services for the citizens of Allegheny County.

PAT is planning four major capital projects which are expected to substantially increase mobility for thousands of area residents. Projects include construction of the Airport Busway/Wabash High Occupancy Vehicle (HOV) facility; the extension of the Martin Luther King, Jr. East Busway to the Swissvale-Rankin border and possible future

Port Authority of Allegheny County

The numerous streetcars and freight and passenger inclines that provided essential service and stimulated economic growth in a once-teeming steel town live as memories of the area's past. Yet public transportation, even though vastly transformed from what it was a century ago, remains crucial to the economic vitality and livability of Pittsburgh, and continues to play an active role in its development as the city enters the 21st century.

Today, PAT provides a network of public transportation services to persons traveling within a 730-square-mile area including the City of Pittsburgh and Allegheny County.

By operating a fleet of approximately 900 buses, 55 light rail vehicles, 16 rehabilitated trolleys and the historic Monongahela and Duquesne Inclines, and by sponsoring ACCESS, the nation's largest paratransit program for elderly and disabled persons, PAT has become one of the nation's largest, most diversified and innovative public transit agencies.

In 1986, PAT became the first transit property in the country to introduce recorded classical music into its subway system. "The Sounds of Pittsburgh: Classical Underground" became an instant hit with commuters and has remained popular. Other efforts to serve its ever-changing, diversified customer base include the introduction of

who are regular Port Authority Transit riders and are interested in improving transit services.

PAT provides public transportation services to nearly 285,000 riders daily and 80 million riders annually. Among its facilities, PAT owns and operates two exclusive busways — the 4.3-mile South Busway and the 6.8-mile Martin Luther King, Jr. East Busway. PAT's 22.5-mile Light Rail System, the "T", includes the popular Downtown subway. In the spring of 1993, PAT reopened the Arlington/Warrington section of its rail route.

The challenge to provide efficient public transit service requires continued action and commitment from PAT and local officials. One of the finest examples of this is the development and implementation of busway technology. While relatively simple in concept, the development of exclusive roadways for transit totally separate from other highway projects had never before been accomplished in the United States.

extensions to the Mon and Turtle Creek valleys; the rehabilitation of the remaining 12 miles of aging trolley lines (Stage II); and the extension of the Downtown subway to the North Side and to Oakland and Squirrel Hill (Spine Line).

Building upon the success of the South Busway and Martin Luther King, Jr. East Busway, PAT firmly established itself as a transportation leader both locally and nationally. The Airport Busway/Wabash HOV project is part of PAT's Busway System Expansion Program and is seen as a crucial element in future economic development, traffic mitigation, improved mobility, and better air quality in Allegheny County.

The first phase of the Airport Busway will link the Golden Triangle with the Borough of Carnegie, providing a quick and efficient bypass to the Fort Pitt Bridge and Tunnel, and Green Tree Hill. The Busway is projected to provide transportation to approximately 53,000 daily riders, removing thousands of cars from the area's congested roadways, improving access to communities, reducing air pollution, and saving energy.

The Martin Luther King, Jr. East Busway was originally planned to extend to Swissvale, but due to community concerns at the time, the Busway was built only as far as Wilkinsburg. Since the Busway's successful opening in 1983, much interest has been expressed in extending it. The project is expected to be completed in 1996, with daily

■ *The Martin Luther King, Jr. East Busway enables thousands of PAT daily riders to bypass congested roadways throughout the city.*

ridership projected to increase from 30,000 to 48,000 by the year 2005.

Each of these projects have the potential to considerably enhance mobility for the residents of Allegheny County. However, the projects are only part of the overall solution that is needed if we are to solve Allegheny County's mounting transportation problems and provide access to new and existing economic opportunities.

The business climate and demographics of the area have undergone many changes over the years, and Port Authority is preparing to meet the formidable challenge of tailoring its services to meet new demands.

Since 1970, Allegheny County's population has declined by more than a quarter of a million people, many of those leaving the city of Pittsburgh — with population down approximately 29 percent. Allegheny County experienced a resurgence in population growth, particularly in the county's outer suburbs, in the opening years of the 1990s.

Such growth, increased population and employment opportunities are expected to continue through the next decade for communities in neighboring Butler County; in northern Allegheny Country and its eastern suburbs; and in areas surrounding the new Pittsburgh International Airport as job opportunities and economic development become more prevalent.

With that in mind, PAT continues to monitor service levels and invest in its facilities and carefully planned capital projects to serve the community and stimulate economic growth.

New busways and light rail system improvements can help provide efficient main-line service into concentrated employment centers. The major task, however, is finding a way for public transit to efficiently serve sparsely populated neighborhoods or scattered and relatively small employment centers that are becoming increasingly commonplace in many suburban communities. PAT's challenge for today and for the future is to work closely with community leaders, businesses, residents, and others to continue to find new, innovative, and efficient ways to meet the changing needs of its customers. ▣

■ *The historic Monongahela Incline continues to offer tourists and commuters a spectacular view of the city.*

In the quest for a cleaner environment and more profitable economy, Columbia Gas of Pennsylvania offers its customers innovative ways to breathe a little easier and save money.

While Columbia continues to provide safe, reliable, and competitively priced natural gas service to customers for traditional uses, the company also promotes new uses that highlight additional economic and environmental benefits for the increasingly popular, clean-burning fuel.

In the home, Americans enjoy the comfort and economy of advanced natural gas heating systems, gas water heaters, gas ranges, gas fireplace logs, and outdoor gas security lighting.

■ *A Columbia Gas of Pennsylvania employee fills up his natural gas-powered car at Columbia's public access natural gas fueling station at the company's Bethel Park facility. The station is open 24 hours a day, seven days a week.*

same line that brings gas into the home.

Natural gas has been proven to be efficient and is produced in abundance in the United States, which has a supply sufficient to last an estimated 200 years.

Columbia Gas of Pennsylvania

Gas appliances such as compact natural gas space heaters (garage, patio, deck, and pool heaters) and natural gas generators that automatically produce electricity during emergency power outages offer customers even more comforts.

To help clean up the air, natural gas-powered vehicles are available that can be refueled in the driveway. A compact compressor system fills the vehicle overnight from the

■ *A visually impaired customer receives instructions from a Columbia Gas of Pennsylvania serviceman on how to operate dials on her gas range that are specially marked with larger numbers for easier visibility. Called the ServicePlus program, Columbia also offers specially marked thermostats to serve customers with special needs.*

More than 90 percent of the natural gas used in this country is produced in the United States. That helps save jobs and reduce the nation's trade deficit by decreasing the need for imported oil.

Across the United States, nearly one million new customers chose natural gas for their homes in 1992, and electric-to-gas conversions were at an all-time high.

The growing demand for gas service is driven largely by cost savings. Annual utility bills for homes heated and cooled by gas are roughly one-third to one-half lower than for a comparable all-electric home.

Columbia has made significant efforts to respond to the marketing opportunities available to the natural gas industry brought about by the Clean Air Act Amendments of 1990 and the Energy Policy Act of 1992.

Environmentalists agree that clean-burning natural gas will play a major role in reducing atmospheric pollution.

Columbia's goal is to assist customers by identifying their environmental needs and

doing what it can to market natural gas technologies to meet those needs.

Natural gas is the lowest emitter of the three main contributors to smog, including carbon monoxide, nitrogen oxides — chemicals created during combustion — and volatile organic chemicals, which are compounds of hydrogen and carbon that come mostly from products derived from oil, including gasoline, paints, and solvents.

Columbia is actively promoting environmental marketing opportunities such as natural gas vehicles and forklifts, natural gas public fueling stations, natural gas cooling and air-conditioning, natural gas incinerators, electric-power generation and cogeneration. Cogeneration is a process that produces electricity and steam simultaneously from natural gas.

Columbia Gas is a leader in the move to increase the use of natural gas vehicles. They reduce pollution by 90 percent compared with gasoline-powered vehicles. Natural gas-powered vehicles also save money, because the fuel costs about one-third less than an equivalent measure of gasoline. Studies also have shown that the fueling system on natural gas vehicles is safer than gasoline vehicles.

Some of Columbia's natural gas vehicle activities include:

— The introduction in 1992 of five National Park Service natural gas-powered pickup trucks at the Gettysburg National Military Park, Gettysburg, Pennsylvania, to help preserve the famous battlefield.

---The loan of the "Columbia," the nation's first transit bus built from the ground up to run on natural gas, to the transit authority in York, Pennsylvania, to promote natural gas-powered transportation.

— The official presentation of a natural gas bus to The Pennsylvania State University, the first vehicle powered by compressed natural gas in the University's fleet of some 700 vehicles. The bus is used to transport prospective students and their parents and new students on orientation tours of the campus.

— The installation of one of the Pittsburgh area's first natural gas public fueling stations at its service center in Bethel Park. Company fleet owners or private citizens are able to fill their natural gas vehicles 24 hours a day.

In addition to sponsoring natural gas vehicle promotional events to help the environment, Columbia has initiated state legislation on environmental issues, including bills to provide grants for retrofitting vehicles to run on alternative fuels and to provide for research and development of exhaust emissions reduction technologies.

Columbia prides itself in providing excellent service to its customers. Columbia employees focus on meeting the needs of customers, especially those with special needs. The company provides both educational materials and special programs targeted to specific audiences such as the economically disadvantaged, customers with disabilities, and older adults.

One Columbia program offers the visually-impaired the opportunity to have heating thermostats and appliance dials specially marked for ease of use.

The company makes individually tailored payment arrangements available to customers who fall behind in their bills and directs these customers to agencies offering

■ *A crew from Columbia Gas of Pennsylvania installs plastic pipe into the ground. Columbia's ongoing investment in its infrastructure system ensures that customers will receive the best quality natural gas service.*

financial assistance. Company-matching fuel funds provide last-resort help to ensure that low-income customers can keep their heat on

Columbia also takes pride in being active in economic development and corporate citizenship.

The company is a major role player in efforts to attract business to the area and throughout the state. Columbia officials work closely with city and state economic groups, local and state chambers of commerce, and other entities to aggressively pursue new business for the region.

Columbia recognizes the importance of reliable energy supplies and service to prospective businesses, and has proven experience and success in fulfilling the energy requirement of new industry.

The company understands the significance of being an active corporate citizen. Company representatives play a key part in many area civic efforts and campaigns, such as the United Way, Junior Achievement, United Negro College Fund, March of Dimes, and the many locally based service organizations, chambers of commerce, the arts, education and other organizations.

Columbia has been a leader in the business sector in encouraging advancements in education in the communities it serves.

Its Education 2000 program is based on the idea that today's youth are tomorrow's work force. This program is designed to improve education for children at home and in the community and focuses on parental involvement and building partnerships between schools and businesses.

Columbia has established several partner schools, including Pittsburgh city school, Carrick High, and encourages its employees to volunteer at these schools. Employee volunteers spend several hours a month at the partner schools in activities such as mentoring and classroom speaking.

Columbia believes a better educated work force will attract and keep good business in the community and contribute to the economic revival of the country.

In looking to the future, Columbia will continue to demonstrate the economical and environmental advantages of clean-burning natural gas as a better energy to use in many residential, commercial, and industrial applications to produce a finer quality of life for all Pennsylvanians....and help us all breathe a little easier.

Columbia Gas of Pennsylvania, with corporate offices in Pittsburgh, is the largest investor-owned natural gas utility in the state and serves nearly 362,000 customers in 450 communities in 26 counties. Employing nearly 950 people, Columbia of Pennsylvania invests more than $25 million for capital improvements each year. The company is one of five natural gas distribution companies of the Columbia Gas Distribution Companies, headquartered in Columbus, Ohio, which serves a total of more than 1.8 million customers. ▪

■ *A Columbia Gas of Pennsylvania employee discusses the environmental advantages of natural gas-powered vehicles and natural gas air conditioning at an energy and environmental exposition in Pittsburgh.*

■ *In the past 25 years, Corporate Jets, Inc. has grown from a charter service of a single aircraft and helicopter to an enterprise with a fleet of 100 aircraft.*

Corporate Jets, Inc.

To get a good idea of how much the aviation industry has changed during the past 25 years, look at the history of Corporate Jets, Inc. From a charter service sporting a single aircraft and helicopter, to an $80 million international enterprise with more than 625 employees and a fleet of 100 aircraft, Corporate Jets is riding out a turbulent economy on the strength of its diversity.

The headquarters for Corporate Jets' far-reaching operations is a fixed-base operation (FBO) at the Allegheny County Airport, seven miles from downtown Pittsburgh—and 70 miles from the heart of Pennsylvania coal country and the company's first home in Somerset, Pa. Coal industry executive Fred S. Shaulis founded Corporate Jets in 1969 to provide aircraft services for local corporations.

In fact, charters still supply Corporate Jets with some of its most high-profile customers. On a given day, a Learjet flying from Pittsburgh or Corporate Jets' Scottsdale, Arizona FBO could be carrying a former U.S. president, a movie star or a corporate mover and shaker to their destination. Corporate Jets has built its reputation on high quality, executive aviation services. In a poll conducted by Aviation International News, Corporate Jets was named one of the top 15 full-service companies in North America.

"That's a distinction we're very proud of, because we strive to provide top-notch, reliable service to all our customers, with a safety record second to none," said Corporate Jets President Richard Ryan, who, like most of the company's top executives, is a certified pilot with extensive military flying experience.

As Corporate Jets began to grow through the 70s and early 80s, maintenance became a logical area for diversification. The need for reliable maintenance was critical, yet Corporate Jets was dissatisfied with the services it was receiving from outside contractors.

"We were frustrated maintenance customers," Ryan said. "We couldn't continue to function with work that was improperly completed or aircraft sitting idle because parts were on order. So we created our own maintenance division and we have always kept our focus on 'doing it right.' At Corporate Jets, we pride ourselves on very low technician turnaround and our $2 million parts inventory. We've learned from experience that maintenance customers demand service from experienced personnel...and they also expect minimal downtime."

While customer service propelled Corporate Jets' expansion, changes in the business climate drove the company to diversify. With the oil industry collapse in the 80s, the need for pilots and helicopters decreased. Looking at the bigger picture, more and more corporate travel was being replaced with the fax machine or the tele-conference.

"If we wanted to continue to grow...and we did...we realized that we had to seek opportunities in other areas," Ryan said. One of the most important growth areas, air medical services, grew out of the military med-evac programs first used in Korea, then refined in Vietnam.

The concept of combining life-saving medical procedures with rapid helicopter evaluation to civilian hospitals was in its infancy when Corporate Jets entered the health care field in the 1980s. Early on, Corporate Jets provided fixed-wing transport of organ procurement teams for most of the medical centers in Pittsburgh.

As Corporate Jets became more heavily involved, the company developed a national air medical services network, managing operations in 18 cities, from Cheyenne, Wyoming to Tampa, Florida.

In its medical division, the company provides pilots, maintenance and all-around logistical support for a total of 35 aircraft, both helicopters and fixed-wing. Organ transport is still a critical part of the program. On alert around the clock, Corporate Jets dispatches aircraft to fly surgical teams and transplant organs with life-support equipment anywhere in the continental United States. Corporate Jets supplies jet transportation for the Center for Organ Retrieval and Education (CORE), located in Pittsburgh, as well as for the University of Arizona Medical Center. Corporate Jets is also the backup carrier for the New England Donor Bank of Boston.

■ *Corporate Jets' headquarters is a fixed base operation (FBO), seven miles from downtown Pittsburgh.*

However, most of the company's air medical clients contract with Corporate Jets for medically-equipped helicopters. For example, the MedSTAR Program at Washington Hospital Center in Washington, D.C., uses two American Eurocopter BK-117's. For this program, Corporate Jets has assigned eight pilots and two mechanics.

In Western Pennsylvania, the company manages the STAT MedEvac program. STAT MedEvac is a service of the Center for Emergency Medicine, a consortium of Pittsburgh-area hospitals. Corporate Jets provides the pilots and maintenance for the program's four helicopters and one turbo prop advanced life-support fixed-wing aircraft. Helicopters are based in Pittsburgh, Greensburg, Butler County and at the Allegheny County Airport.

"There continues to be strong growth potential in air medical services," Ryan explained. "It's a $250-million-per-year industry which should experience real growth over the next decade." In the early 1990s, Corporate Jets acquired the helicopter operations of U.S. Jet, Inc., in Washington, D.C. and a Dallas-based helicopter modification and service facility, Heli-Dyne Systems, Inc. to capitalize on the air medical industry's potential.

Much like the creation of the maintenance division twenty years ago, the Heli-Dyne/U.S. Jet acquisitions allow Corporate Jets to more fully serve its customers. At Heli-Dyne Systems, employees provide component overhaul, engineering and electronics completion services, as well as design and installation of custom medical interiors. Heli-Dyne is also a factory-authorized service center for most major helicopter manufacturers.

"The Heli-Dyne acquisition provides a support facility for our rapidly growing helicopter business and gives us a profitable, new dimension. Typically, a hospital buys a 'green' helicopter and it specifies how the interior should be completed. With Heli-Dyne, we can now compete favorably in the entire helicopter completion marketplace," Ryan said.

A fully-outfitted helicopter costs between $2-4 million, with completion costs representing $200,000-$500,000 of the total, depending upon individual specifications. From an economics standpoint, the Heli-Dyne acquisition should make a positive impact on Corporate Jets. And the division's Dallas location doesn't hurt, either.

"Several American helicopter manufacturers, including Bell Helicopter Textron and American Eurocopter, are located nearby. And our presence in the area allows us to intensify service to hospital programs that we manage in the South and Southwest," Ryan explained.

As analysts continue to pinpoint air medical services as a growth area, Corporate Jets has taken full advantage of its window of opportunity to become an industry leader. In the meantime, the newest window of opportunity for the company has opened in the government sector.

Several federal agencies have called upon Corporate Jets' services as early as the mid 1980s. The company has provided a variety of aviation support services for the department of State, Defense, Justice and Transportation.

Air Force fighter training is one example of Corporate Jets' many government contracts. Recently, the company's dart tow operation, based out of the Scottsdale FBO, has relocated two F-86 aircraft and personnel from Sardinia, Italy to Soesterberg, The Netherlands to participate in live gunnery practice.

And in February 1993, Corporate Jets was awarded a contract by the Department of Transportation to maintain two FAA-operated Hawker 800s at the Rhein Main Air Base in Frankfurt, Germany.

The State and Justice Departments have chosen Corporate Jets for one of the company's largest government projects to date: the worldwide maintenance contract for all Drug Enforcement Administration airplanes and helicopters. Once again, Corporate Jets' diversity has created new opportunities for growth.

"The government business is a $4 billion-a-year business overall, of which selective projects should be very profitable to us," Ryan said. "We've also talked to other governments about providing similar services."

It's a source of pride for founder Fred S. Shaulis, Rich Ryan and all Corporate Jets employees that the company has come so far in such a short time. Yet as diverse as the company and the industry have become, there are some basic principles about aviation that haven't changed since the Somerset days.

"We're committed to safety, reliability and to quality customer service," Ryan said. "Excellence in the air begins with excellence on the ground."   ▣

■ *Corporate Jets was named one of the top 15 full-service companies in North America. Pictured here is Corporate Jets' Scottsdale, Arizona FBO.*

Glance up at the sky over Pittsburgh at almost any time of day and chances are you'll see a USAir plane skimming above the horizon toward the Pittsburgh International Airport. It's a sight that many consider part of the scenery, but those airplanes represent the region's vital link to the rest of the world—from Franklin, Pa., to Frankfurt, Germany.

Ever since All American Aviation, the forerunner of Allegheny Airlines and later USAir, began carrying passengers in 1949, Pittsburgh has been a key part of the system. It became even more so when Allegheny created a "hub" here in the 1970s, putting Pittsburgh at the center of an ever-expanding

USAir

system of "spoke" cities, which feed their passengers to the central collection point for connections to fly elsewhere.

USAir's Pittsburgh hub is one of the nation's largest. More than 450 jet and commuter flights leave every day to over 100 nonstop destinations. The activity created more than 12,000 local jobs by the early 1990s. The level of local air service is a selling point for economic development leaders to attract new business—and more jobs—to the area.

As an Allegheny County official once said, "If your airport is not a hub, you're in deep weeds."

The advantages to living in a hub city become immediately apparent with a glance at the USAir flight schedule. The local market alone could not support, for example, multiple daily nonstops to places like Seattle, San Francisco, Chicago or Philadelphia. But by collecting passengers from spoke cities for connections here, frequent flights become feasible, and Pittsburgh travelers and shippers are able to take advantage of them.

On Oct. 1, 1992, USAir and western Pennsylvania embarked on a new era in their long-standing partnership. On that day, the new Pittsburgh International Airport terminal opened and overnight made traveling to and through the city a world-class experience.

■ *When a bag passes through the 360-degree laser scanning array of USAir's state-of-the-art automated baggage system (ABS), the system's computers route it to the proper conveyor by signaling a pusher unit that physically moves the bag from one belt to another.*

"This is a venture that promises to shape the future of both the airline and the region for years to come," says USAir Chairman and President Seth Schofield. "It is a tangible example of the kind of public-private cooperation that sets Pittsburgh apart from many other cities."

USAir made substantial investments to make the new airport a reality, starting with its 30-year agreement to lease 53 of the airport's 75 jet gates and 20 of its 25 commuter spaces. That long-term commitment was the key to obtaining bond financing for the $750-million project.

Pittsburgh International has since become a high-technology showcase of USAir's efforts to improve passenger service. New systems and software have automated myriad airport functions—from assigning jets to their gates to handling baggage.

USAir's $31-million automated baggage sorting system is a six-mile maze of tunnels, bridges, belts and motors. Using laser beams to "read" bar-coded luggage tags, the system automatically routes bags via high-speed conveyors to aircraft loading zones or to baggage carrousels for passengers ending their trips in Pittsburgh. Skycaps use touch-screen computers at curbside to issue bar-coded bag tags for departing passengers.

Inside, more than 600 personal computers, linked by a fiber optic network, are used by USAir agents, giving them a single, accurate and instantaneous source of information to better serve passengers.

High above the airport in the USAir control tower, an internal information system with artificial intelligence capabilities assists personnel in juggling the availability of gates,

■ *The recently approved agreement between USAir and British Airways will provide many USAir communities with direct, "seamless" service between British Airways' vast worldwide route system and USAir's strong domestic U.S. system.*

■ *USAir Chairman, President, and CEO Seth E. Schofield.*
flight crews, maintenance teams and the like to maintain the on-time integrity of the airline.

Unseen to passengers, but vital to shippers and the U.S. Postal Service are new and expanded USAir facilities for handling cargo and mail. Both buildings feature computerized sorting systems similar to the one used to process passenger bags.

While the new Pittsburgh Airport is a bricks-and-mortar testament to USAir's vision of the future, there are many other examples. And perhaps none is so far-reaching as the alliance with British Airways designed to position USAir as a global player for the 21st century.

In 1993, USAir and British Airways embarked on the first phase of a relationship that ultimately aims to connect some 340 destinations in more than 70 nations. The alliance links USAir's vast domestic system with British Airways' world network in what has been described as "the dawning of a new era in air travel."

For Pittsburgh, the alliance in June 1993 brought a long-sought nonstop flight to London. The service is operated under British Airways' route authority, but flown using a leased USAir aircraft and crews. A number of USAir flights from such cities as Columbus, Indianapolis and Nashville are timed to connect to the London service from Pittsburgh, thereby funneling more customers through the new airport's international terminal.

For the passenger, the association between USAir and British Airways offers seamless service when traveling on either of the airlines' networks. This means that mak-

ing reservations, checking in for flights, baggage transfer and so on is handled as if it is occurring on a single airline.

For USAir, the ability to feed and receive passengers from British Airways' extensive international system provides a powerful marketing opportunity that strengthens USAir on the domestic scene. The relationship also includes an equity investment that helps solidify USAir's financial status and its role as a corporate citizen in the many communities it serves.

"USAir is broadening its perspective. It has become obvious that to be a competitive player in this industry, you must by able to compete globally," says Schofield. "Our alliance with British Airways ensures USAir a role on the world stage as airline networks begin to span the entire globe."

USAir has been looking to the future in many other ways as well. While it continues to link the many small communities it grew up in, USAir has become a major player in the coast-to-coast and Florida markets. In fact, USAir is the largest airline to and within Florida.

To better serve both its traditional and newest markets, the airline has added new jets to its fleet.

USAir was the U.S. launch customer for the Fokker 100, a 100-passenger aircraft especially suited for short-haul trips. The F-100 is an extremely quiet, fuel-efficient airplane equipped with the latest computer equipment. In its "glass cockpit," the numerous round dials and gauges of the traditional environment have been replaced by video screens that alert the pilots only when a system needs attention.

For transcontinental trips and in those markets with high traffic volumes, USAir is now flying the Boeing 757, a 190-seat aircraft that is equally efficient on short trips like Pittsburgh to Washington or longer

hauls, such as Philadelphia-San Francisco. Surveys have shown that passengers like the 757, with its "club-like" sections created by mid-cabin lavatories, extra-large overhead bins and in-flight entertainment systems.

USAir was the first airline to begin equipping its jets with a new safety system called TCAS, which scans a "bubble" around an aircraft, warns of any approaching traffic and gives aural and visual avoidance commands. Likewise, USAir was also the first to install FlightLink, a radically new approach to air-to-ground communications for passengers developed by In-flight Phone Corp. The system consists of an interactive video screen in every seat back and a telephone handset and key pad under every arm rest. FlightLink offers digital, static-free phone calls or the ability to link laptop computers to the ground as well as onboard video games and a variety of other services. By 1994, USAir plans to have FlightLink installed on over 400 aircraft.

"USAir has its eye firmly on the future. Everything we do, we want to do well," says Schofield, "because our goal is to provide our customers with value for their money with safe, dependable, and convenient air transportation." ℗

■ *USAir begins with you--its customers. This is the company's commitment to provide safe and reliable air transportation, offer excellent service, and provide added value for its customers.*

Three things are guaranteed to cause nightmares among gas company executives: economic recession, ever-changing government regulations, and unseasonably warm weather.

Every one of those hobgoblins has haunted Consolidated Natural Gas in recent years. Yet they haven't stopped the company from carrying out the most aggressive expansion program in its 50-year history as one of the country's largest gas producers, transporters, and distributors.

"CNG is accustomed to coping with a tough business environment and succeeding," says Chairman and Chief Executive Officer George A. Davidson, Jr.

sharply reduced demand for gas to heat homes, schools, and businesses.

But where its competitors have faltered, CNG has succeeded by streamlining operations, by maintaining its status as one of the largest gas producers in the country, and at the same time extending its area of operations far beyond its traditional base. Where CNG for most of its 50 years has served customers primarily in Ohio, Pennsylvania, West Virginia, and upstate New York, the reach of its operations now stretches along the East Coast from the Carolinas northward.

Its initiatives have positioned CNG for continued strong growth as the economy

■ *More than a half billion dollars of new construction has helped CNG widen its markets to include much of the East Coast.*

In gas distribution alone, CNG is among the largest gas utilities in the country, serving directly about 1.7 million customers in the mid-Atlantic region and Ohio. It is most familiar to consumers by the names of its local utility companies.

In Pittsburgh, The Peoples Natural Gas Company has provided gas to homes, offices, and factories since before the turn of the century. In nearby states, five other distributors — The East Ohio Gas Company in Cleveland, Ohio; West Ohio Gas Company in Lima, Ohio; The River Gas Company in Marietta, Ohio; Hope Gas, Inc. of Clarksburg, West Virginia; and Virginia Natural Gas, Inc. of Norfolk, Virginia — all play important roles in the growth and development of their service areas.

CNG Transmission Corp. operates a network of interstate gas pipelines and storage fields, delivering gas to CNG's distribution utilities and to more than 20 major non-affiliated utilities in New York and along the East Coast. Much of the company's recent growth has resulted from expansion of the pipeline network to serve the East Coast areas.

The decline of heavy industry over the past two decades in CNG's traditional territories in Ohio, Pennsylvania, West Virginia, and upstate New York left the company with two options: stand pat and watch its business shrivel or expand into more diversified and faster-growing markets. Accordingly, CNG has spent the past decade pushing out the boundaries of its territory. With its heavy dependence on imported oil to heat residences and provide energy for factories and electric power plants, the East Coast became CNG's target of opportunity.

Consolidated Natural Gas Company

■ *CNG is the largest independent gas and oil driller in the Gulf of Mexico.*

And that's just what CNG has done. The company has grown during a time when the economy hurt its industrial customers and restricted new business development, when new government rules are drastically changing the face of interstate natural gas transmission, and when a series of warm winters has

strengthens and as demand for environmentally sound energy continues to expand.

CNG is a $5 billion holding company whose operating subsidiaries include six gas distribution utilities, one exploration and production company, and an interstate natural gas transmission company.

■ *A key facet of CNG's operations is its network of underground natural gas storage fields, the largest in the county.*

CNG's regional grid of pipelines is a complex web of several hundred receipt and delivery points and more than two dozen storage fields instead of a simple stovepipe configuration where gas enters one end and leaves the other. And the company has used this asset to begin serving utilities in Virginia, Maryland, Washington, D.C., New York, New Jersey, and the New England states.

"We were ahead of the rest of the natural gas industry in preparing to serve markets in the East, and that just adds to our opportunities for growth there," Davidson says.

To the south, CNG acquired the fast-growing Virginia Natural Gas utility in 1990 and completed the construction of a 135-mile pipeline into that state. The expansion gave the company access to a region of unusual economic vitality, including the "Golden Crescent" from the Washington suburbs south through Richmond to Norfolk.

CNG has expanded its markets even further south by signing a 20-year agreement to provide gas to Public Service Company of North Carolina, Inc., which supplies much of that state, including the Research Triangle cities of Raleigh, Durham, and Chapel Hill. When service begins, it will represent CNG's first long-term service in the Carolinas.

In 1992, CNG completed much of its largest pipeline project, a $240 million project to double its capacity to transport gas from western Ohio, where it connects with several pipelines, to the Leidy storage complex in central Pennsylvania. At Leidy, CNG delivers gas to pipelines that serve New York, New Jersey, and New England.

The company also has acquired partial ownership interests in two new lines — the Niagara Import Point project and the Iroquois pipeline — which bring Canadian gas into the United States.

All in all, the new pipeline projects and expansion will help increase Consolidated's transmission throughput, the volume of gas carried by its transmission operations, from recent levels of 425 billion cubic feet as recently as 1987 to more than 750 billion cubic feet.

Affecting all of CNG's operations are sweeping changes enacted by federal government regulators that are intended to increase competition in the gas industry by requiring interstate transmission companies to, in effect, become just transporters of gas rather than merchants of gas. Essentially, the new regulations will change the role of interstate transmission companies from that of a wholesale merchant to one more akin to that of a trucking company or a railroad.

Under the new system, customers — such as gas distribution utilities, power plants, and big industries — who used to purchase all or most of their gas from an interstate transmission company now will purchase supplies directly from producers and then contract with transmission companies for transportation, storage, and delivery services.

Not all customers want to take responsibility for doing all of that however. So for those who want help in this new environment, CNG in 1993 formed a new subsidiary — CNG Gas Services Corporation — which can arrange supplies, transportation, and storage for customers.

One of CNG's most valuable assets during this time of growth is its complex of underground gas storage fields — the largest such complex in the world.

Twenty-seven old gas fields in the porous rock beneath the Appalachians, with a whopping 885 billion cubic feet of storage capacity, enable CNG and its customers to buy gas at the best prices year-round, store it in summer when demand is low, and pump it into

■ *CNG's utilities provide natural gas service to more than 1000 communities in Ohio, Pennsylvania, West Virginia and Virginia.*

the pipelines for use when demand increases during the heating season. If it weren't for its ability to store gas, CNG wouldn't be able to meet peak demand in winter months efficiently.

CNG has also begun to expand its exploration and production operations recently. Already the largest independent gas and oil producer in the offshore Gulf of Mexico, CNG Producing Company has recently teamed up with Shell, Mobil, and British Petroleum to develop the deep-water "Popeye" field. This new field — 140 miles south of New Orleans and in 2000 feet of water — is the deepest deep-water gas field in the Gulf of Mexico to date.

CNG's other exploration and production operations extend to the Rocky Mountains, the mid-Continent area, the onshore Gulf of Mexico region, the Appalachians, and Canada.

Consolidated Natural Gas began operating as an independent company in 1943, but its history dates back nearly a century to the Standard Oil Company of John D. Rockefeller and the origins of the natural gas industry.

Standard Oil grew its integrated natural gas business from exploration to distribution by creating companies and taking over others throughout the Appalachian region. Among those companies were the anchor utilities of today's CNG: Peoples, East Ohio, Hope, and River.

In assembling the system, Standard Oil also helped develop commercial markets for natural gas and developed the first pipelines, no easy task 100 years ago when markets were separated by rivers, forests, and mountains.

When the government ordered Rockefeller to break up his Standard Oil monopoly, the gas operations became the dominion of Standard Oil (New Jersey), Rockefeller's flagship company. There they remained until 50 years ago, when new laws regarding public utilities required Standard to spin off its gas companies unless it wanted to come under the regulators' control. Thus, Consolidated Natural Gas Company was created as a completely independent entity.

CNG carried on its aggressive program of expanding service areas and developing new customer bases. After World War II, the natural gas industry grew exponentially as homeowners switched from coal- or oil-fired furnaces to cleaner, more efficient gas furnaces. In Allegheny County surrounding Pittsburgh, efforts to shed the "Smoky City" image led to nearly universal use of gas heat.

While developing new customers always has been an important facet of CNG's marketing efforts, tough economic times have required even more creative approaches to market development.

One way to build new markets is to make it easy for customers to try natural gas. Consolidated's local utilities, for example, sometimes help finance the cost of first-of-a-kind equipment installations. In return, customers agree to share data and let other prospective customers tour their plants to see the new technology in action.

This kind of investment pays off. For example, CNG's East Ohio Gas utility helped a printing company develop an incinerator to burn off noxious fumes from the drying ink. Now, similar technology is being applied at two auto plants in CNG's territory to incinerate paint fumes.

Such cooperation also has helped the company preserve business in mature industries. Customers may draw on the skills of teams of engineers and technical experts at CNG's local utilities. Recruited from the steel, chemicals, plastics and glass industries, the experts advise companies how to become more competitive through innovation. One outgrowth of this initiative involves a technique for using natural gas in blast furnaces in steel mills. It allows the steelmaker better control and productivity.

CNG also is working with mass transit agencies, trucking companies, automakers, and government agencies to broaden the use of natural gas-powered vehicles.

In the years to come, CNG expects the market for natural gas to expand in ways no one can now visualize. That means that its basic marketing approach—helping the customer with the latest and best natural gas technologies—will be as important in the future as it has been for the past century. ■

■ *The state of Virginia provides CNG one of its best growth markets. This is Colonial Williamsburg, served by CNG's Virginia Natural Gas Company subsidiary.*

■ *A high level of performance in customer relations and customer service is a key goal at Peoples Natural Gas.*

Some things never change. Among them is the emphasis that The Peoples Natural Gas Company places on customer satisfaction.

As Roger E. Wright, president of Peoples Gas, said, "Our efforts to provide a high level of performance in the area of customer relations and customer service will continue."

Other things seem to change continuously, government regulations among them. Even so, "Peoples is well positioned to maintain competitive gas prices and a steady supply amidst the latest regulatory changes," Wright said.

Regulatory change in the 1990s has major implications on both ends of the natural gas pipeline.

For customers, statewide implementation of Clean Air Act amendments serve to further emphasize the benefits of natural gas as a fuel.

"Environmentally clean natural gas remains the fuel of choice in helping commercial and industrial customers meet strict new standards," Wright said.

New technologies that take advantage of clean-burning natural gas make it the fuel of choice in responding to the new regulations, according to Raymond M. Smith, vice president for marketing.

"This is particularly true in the case of natural gas vehicles," Smith said. "Natural gas is cleaner than gasoline and diesel, it costs less, and there is an abundant supply."

By early 1993, Peoples Gas was operating 270 natural gas-powered trucks and vans in its own fleet. Across the United States, more than 30,000 vehicles were running on natural gas.

Natural gas has also proved its worth in helping reduce air pollution in energy production.

Firing natural gas in combination with coal in electric generating stations improves efficiency and reduces harmful emissions. Three electric utility coal boilers in Peoples' service area had been equipped to cofire with natural gas by 1993.

In addition, drying coal with natural gas was found to raise the efficiency of coal cleaning operations and to reduce refuse.

Peoples will continue to work along with the rest of the industry to develop and promote new technology that helps reduce pollutants and improve efficiency through the use of natural gas, Smith said.

For utility companies, Federal Energy Regulatory Commission Order 636 was a landmark, a major restructuring of the natural gas industry designed to increase competition. The order uncouples the sale of natural gas by interstate pipeline companies and the sale of pipeline capacity and storage service.

When Pew discovered how to compress natural gas, he made possible the transmission of natural gas over long distances and under controlled conditions.

A half century later, Peoples Gas provided the fuel that replaced coal as a source of heat, especially in the homes of Pittsburgh and surrounding Allegheny County. The switch enabled the city to remake its image from the smoke-shrouded workshop of World War II America into a national corporate center under bright, clean skies. ▣

Peoples Natural Gas Company

One result of the order is that Peoples Gas and other local distribution companies took on more responsibility for obtaining gas supplies and arranging delivery of the gas from the producing zone to the market.

Peoples' established methods of supplying gas, which include greater production and purchases of Pennsylvania gas than any other distribution company in the state, and capital investments that enhance Peoples' flexibility and efficiency "will help to assure that customers will continue to have safe and reliable service," Wright said.

The 1,240 employees of Peoples Gas deliver natural gas to 336,000 residential, commercial, and industrial customers through 7,500 miles of Peoples Gas pipeline.

The company has been a force for economic development since its founding in 1885 by Joseph Newton Pew and Edward O. Emerson. By 1929, the company's service area accounted for one-eighth of the natural gas consumption in the country.

Peoples Gas, which became part of Consolidated Natural Gas Company in 1943, made profound contributions to energy availability across the country and in the character of Pittsburgh.

■ *Peoples is promoting the use of vehicles powered by clean-burning natural gas. Here, Ray Smith, a Peoples executive, fuels his natural gas-powered Ford at home.*

Less than ten years after the company lost more than 20 percent of its sales following the collapse of the steel industry, Duquesne Light had progressed to being named Electric Utility of the Year by Electric Light & Power (EL&P) magazine. The company achieved this dramatic turnaround through a combination of reorganization, financial restructuring, cost cutting, strategic planning and a forward looking approach to meeting the challenges of a changing electric utility industry.

In making the award, EL&P cited the "superior results" that had been achieved for customers, employees and shareholders, and stated that "the company embodies what

Duquesne Light

we look for in strong corporate citizenship."

"The crisis of the 1980s forced us to take steps that might not have been necessary under easier circumstances, but because we took them early, we are now able to deal more effectively with a changing business environment," said Wesley W. von Schack, chairman, president and chief executive officer.

One of the steps that Duquesne Light took was to increase its emphasis on delivering customer value. The company has upgraded its electricity distribution system, making it one of the most advanced in the country. A combination of computer operated monitoring and switching devices now provide the ability to remotely switch customers' electric service to other circuits during storm related outages. Under most conditions, more than two-thirds of the customers on a typical 23 kilovolt distribution circuit can be restored to service within five minutes. This technology improves circuit reliability, reduces outage time, decreases operating costs and limits the number of circuits required.

In the famous "Blizzard of '93," Duquesne Light customers got to see firsthand just how good the electric system is, when the Pittsburgh area was hit with the most severe blizzard this century. In little more than 24 hours, the storm dumped more than two feet of snow on the region. The snow, accompanied by high winds, caused widespread

power outages. But Duquesne Light and its people proved more than equal to the test.

From the receipt of the first customer's telephone call through to the last line to be repaired, Duquesne Light people responded promptly and professionally to the extreme blizzard conditions. For some this meant staying at their work stations throughout the night; for others it meant working in chest-high snow drifts to make repairs. But this extra effort paid off for the customers. More than 40% of the 100,000 customers whose power was interrupted by the blizzard had their lights back on within 15 minutes, and a full 75% had their power restored in two hours or less. Most of the remaining customers were restored within six hours.

These efforts did not go unappreciated. Customers and local government officials took time to call or write to express their thanks for a job well done. In a letter to Duquesne Light Chairman Wesley von Schack, Allegheny County Emergency Management Coordinator Robert Kroner wrote: "It was certainly impressive that your workers were able to battle the elements and still maintain such a high level of performance in restoring power to your customers. Thank you for being there when we needed you the most and for doing such an outstanding job."

And Dr. Bruce Dixon, director of the Allegheny County Health Department, wrote: "On behalf of your many customers in Allegheny County, I am writing to express our thanks for your company's prompt and efficient actions to restore power supplies during our worst snowstorm in many decades. Because of the untiring efforts of your employees, many of our residents were spared an additional hardship caused by extended power outages."

■ *The Brunot Island Wildlife Habitat was one of the first sites in the United States to be selected for certification in an international registry of the non-profit Wildlife Habitat Enhancement Council. The habitat, which is adjacent to one of the company's power stations, demonstrates that industry and nature can coexist in harmony.*

■ *Duquesne Light has been among the environmental leaders in the greater Pittsburgh region. The people living here enjoy some of the best air and water quality in the United States.*

While maintaining a safe and reliable supply of electric power for its customers is a top priority for Duquesne Light, it is not the only way it serves the community. Stimulating economic growth in the region also has been an ongoing emphasis for the company. Since 1987, the company's economic development efforts have helped add or retain more than 15,500 jobs for the region. Andrew Greenberg, Pennsylvania Secretary of Commerce, recently called Duquesne Light's results "a leading example of electric utility involvement in regeneration of its region through their marketing, service and pricing."

Duquesne Light's concern for the region it serves also can be seen in the company's environmental record. The people of Duquesne Light understandably are proud of their company's strong environmental

■ *During the famous "Blizzard of '93," Duquesne Light people demonstrated their commitment to quality service as they promptly restored power following outages caused by the most severe blizzard this century. Aiding in their efforts was the company's distribution system, which is one of the most advanced in the nation.*

accomplishments. Air quality achievements began in the early 1970s, when the company became the first utility in the United States to install and operate plant-wide sulfur dioxide scrubbers.

Over the years the company has invested more than $600 million in environmental control equipment, which has positioned the company well to meet the requirements of the Clean Air Act Amendments of 1990 without the need for major capital investments. Duquesne Light's Pennsylvania coal-fired plants are among the cleanest in the nation, and they already reduce sulfur dioxide emissions to a rate 50 percent less than the 1995 Clean Air Act Phase I standard.

"This is just one example of how our company's environmental commitment exceeds what is required," von Schack said. "We have developed a strategic plan that underscores our commitment to deliver environmental value. At its core is a charter that conveys the guiding principles for the company's management of environmental matters: sound resource management, full compliance with existing regulations, protection of the health of our employees and the public, and the fostering of environmental awareness."

One way the company promotes environmental awareness is through the area schools. In cooperation with the Western Pennsylvania Conservancy and the Audubon Society of Western Pennsylvania's Beechwood Farms Nature Reserve, Duquesne Light has developed an environ-

mental education program which focuses on the theme of the Western Pennsylvania Conservancy's annual calendar. The program uses the theme as the basis for a variety of interdisciplinary lesson plans about the environment for students in kindergarten through high school.

The company also sponsors the Famous & Historic Trees Program, in conjunction with American Forests. In this program, authenticated descendants of notable American trees—including trees planted by George Washington and Abraham Lincoln, and trees from the woods at Walden Pond—are being offered to all of the 59 school districts in the company's service territory. In addition to the trees, the schools receive corresponding educational materials on the environment and the wise use of energy.

The company's other environmental activities include clean-coal technology, testing electric vehicles under actual usage conditions, and maintaining a wildlife habitat adjacent to one of its power stations. In 1992, this Brunot Island Wildlife Habitat Enhancement Project was one of the first sites to be selected for certification in an international registry of the non-profit Wildlife Habitat Enhancement Council.

But working to protect and improve the physical environment is not the only way that Duquesne Light helps

the people in its service territory. The company also works to improve the quality of life in the community through a variety of community relations initiatives. These include partnerships with area schools, support for human service and cultural organizations, and the Employee Community Action Committee (ECAC), a group that encourages and coordinates the volunteer activities of the people of Duquesne Light. Through the ECAC and individual efforts, Duquesne Light people have become known throughout the region for their community involvement. And in 1990, the company was recognized for having the best overall community relations program of any corporation in the United States.

"All that we do is aimed at delivering value to our shareholders, customers and the community we serve," von Schack said. "While we have made tremendous progress, the job is not finished. But I am confident that the women and men of Duquesne Light can meet the growing challenges of an increasingly competitive energy services marketplace with the same competence and dedication that have been the foundation of our success." ▣

■ *The people of Duquesne Light are actively involved as volunteers in improving the quality of life in the community.*

Pittsburgh is growing in importance for British Airways.

In June 1993, the airline further improved its service to Pittsburgh residents with the introduction of daily nonstop flights to London Gatwick.

The nonstop service is a key step in the implementation of the world's first truly global alliance, between British Airways and USAir. The service uses a USAir Boeing 767 in British Airways livery and USAir crews in British Airways' uniforms, under a wet-lease arrangement.

British Airways

June also marked the start of the second phase of code-sharing, with USAir flights linking five more cities with the new British Airways Pittsburgh service—Cincinnati, Columbus, Dayton, Indianapolis and Nashville. Milwaukee and Phoenix came on-line August 1st.

■ *British Airways provides daily nonstop 767 service from Pittsburgh to London Gatwick Airport.*

The launch of codeshare services in May connecting Rochester, Syracuse and Cleveland over Philadelphia with London marked the successful first step in British Airways' important alliance with USAir, the dominant domestic carrier in and out of Pittsburgh International Airport.

In March 1993, British Airways received approval from the U.S. Department of Transportation to proceed with the arrangement and, by summer 1993, had invested $400 million in USAir in return for a 24.6 percent equity stake in the airline.

The arrangement bolstered the financial condition of USAir, which has endured the recession of the early 1990s and served to secure USAir's position at the new Pittsburgh Airport facility, and the thousands of jobs it provides.

British Airways also planned at press time to invest an additional $450 million in USAir, if current U.S. law was changed to increase the

■ *(Left) Sir Colin Marshall, Chairman of British Airways (Right) Robert Ayling, Group Managing Director of British Airways.*

level of foreign investment in U.S. airlines, so that additional funding could be made available to USAir.

The alliance has allowed USAir to share its airline codes with British Airways on flights to designated cities. Passengers check in once and fly to any city in the world served by USAir or British Airways, and never have to recheck their luggage as they would if connecting with other airlines.

It opens up a new world for travelers from the Pittsburgh region, offering connections at London into one of the world's most extensive route systems.

More than 25 million people choose to fly with British Airways every year. That is the equivalent of a passenger boarding one of the company's jets every second, around the clock, all year long.

Almost three out of four of the passengers flies on one of the airline's international scheduled services. This makes British Airways almost a third again as big as the second-largest international carrier.

The British Airways route network stretches an unduplicated 363,000 miles—just short of the distance from Earth to the Moon and back. It features some 150 destinations in 71 countries, serving more of the world's leading international markets than any other airline.

It's no coincidence that the main base of British Airways—London's Heathrow Airport—is still the crossroads of the airline world and the busiest international airport anywhere. And the North Atlantic air traffic corridor—the routes served by British Airways between the United States and Great Britain—is the busiest long-haul business air traffic corridor in the world.

British Airways' leading role in the international airline industry dates back to 1919, when one of its forerunners launched the world's first scheduled daily international air service.

The service was established by a British company with the no-frills name Aircraft Transport and Travel, using converted Royal Air Force bombers and pilots fresh from the victory in World War I.

The first regularly scheduled flight linked London's Hounslow Field, a military airbase, with Le Bourget, an airfield near Paris. Aboard was one passenger, some mail, and a cargo that included newspapers, Devonshire cream, and some grouse. It took off at 9:10 a.m. and arrived two and a half hours later.

But competitors soon sprang up, and in order to survive, the airlines merged to form Imperial Airways in 1924. With a healthy subsidy from the British government, Imperial served as the air link between the far-flung outposts of the British Empire.

By 1936, a company called British Airways was formed, but it merged a year later with Imperial to form the government-owned British Overseas Airways Corporation (BOAC).

During the next 50 years, BOAC broke new ground in international routes and service, a period highlighted by the introduction in 1976 of Concorde, the supersonic transport. Concorde was developed jointly by the British and the French.

British Airways became a private company in 1987, and today it is the only airline in Europe owned by private shareholders. In fact, 27 percent of British Airways stock is owned by U.S. citizens.

Today, British Airways views itself as an important global player in the international airline travel industry.

"Our agreement with USAir and our commitment to Pittsburgh exemplify our approach to meeting the needs of the flying public," said Sir Colin Marshall, chairman of British Airways. "We believe that with our seamless service around the world and our unsurpassed dedication to service, we can satisfy the most demanding passenger. In that lies our promise for the future."

The agreement between British Airways and USAir also permits the lease by British Airways of three USAir jets to date, for nonstop trans-Atlantic flights from Pittsburgh and Baltimore/Washington International airports to London's Gatwick airport.

That leasing arrangement provided the key to the second important impact of British Airways' alliance with USAir in Pittsburgh. It opened up nonstop flights from Pittsburgh to London—a move seen by many in the local economic development community as having a positive impact not only on the Pittsburgh region's employee base at USAir, but on the city's growing international posture as well.

Economic development experts took the view that if international business travelers had easier and faster access to Pittsburgh, they would be more apt to strengthen their business ties with the region. The USAir-British Airways pact could do that, they said.

Sir Colin Marshall, chairman of British Airways, made it clear at the time that he expected to follow through with future agreements and investment with USAir.

"We believe that our investment in USAir has strengthened that carrier and given confidence to its management, work force, and the communities it serves," he said. In time, the agreement will provide customers with seamless service across the route networks of both carriers which combined, cover 339 destinations in 71 countries.

■ *British Airways flys to 150 cities in more than 71 countries around the world from its London Hub.*

■ *"The strength of British Airways is its people."*

Manufacturing and Distribution
CHAPTER
TEN

84 Lumber Company,
184-185

Miles, Inc., 186-187

USX Corporation, 188-189

Mine Safety Appliances
Company, 190

Westinghcuse Electric
Corporation, 191

LEGENT Corporation,
192-193

Cameron Coca-Cola
Bottling Company, 194

GENCO Distribution
System, 195

Bacharach, Inc., 196-197

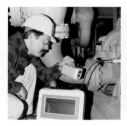

Kennametal, Inc., 198-199

Pittsburgh Annealing Box
Co., 200-201

Calgon Carbon
Corporation, 202

■ *Joe Hardy and his daughter Maggie, who is now the executive vice president of 84 Lumber.*

The story of 84 Lumber is the story of the American Dream. The company's dramatic growth from a single lumberyard in the town of 84, Pennsylvania, to the nation's largest privately owned building materials retailer, with almost 400 stores in 31 states, is testimony to the fact that the entrepreneurial spirit is alive and well in Pittsburgh.

In the last four decades, Joe Hardy has gone from selling homegrown vegetables door-to-door while a student at the University of Pittsburgh to overseeing a $1 billion-a-year company.

Today the company's familiar red "84 lollipop" signs can be seen on country roads

84 Lumber Company

and major highways from coast to coast. A "regular" on the Forbes 400 lists of the nation's richest people and the country's largest privately owned companies, Hardy attributes his phenomenal success to several factors: "work hard, believe that nothing is impossible, and marry someone whose father will lend you the money to get started."

Hardy continually pays tribute to the memory of Robin Pierce, father of his wife, Dorothy. Pierce lent the young Hardy $27,000 to launch the first 84 Lumber store in 1956. That check is now prominently displayed in the library of Nemacolin Woodlands, the posh resort in Farmington, Pennsylvania, that Hardy purchased in 1988.

Nemacolin, operated by Joe's 27-year-old daughter, Maggie, is another rags-to-riches tale. In the four years after 1988, Nemacolin Woodlands was transformed from a down-at-the-heels country inn to Pennsylvania's highest-ranked resort and world class spa.

Both 84 Lumber and Nemacolin Woodlands demonstrate Hardy's ability to define the market and deliver the product in the most cost-effective way. While the target audiences for Hardy's two enterprises are obviously different, the commitment to delivering the best value for the dollar is the key to success for both operations.

In the case of the lumber company, Hardy decided early on that its niche would be "the lowest-cost provider of lumber and building materials, a no-frills, cash-and-carry operation."

That was the philosophy when Hardy opened that first store in 1956, and that is the philosophy today. Timing was also a major

factor in Hardy's success, as he entered the market just as the construction business nationwide was taking off.

"The company took off like a rocket," he recalls. "We couldn't grow fast enough." At one point in the company's history, more than 50 new stores opened in one year.

Today growth has leveled off, with about 20 stores opening each year. The company has recently streamlined its inventory in an effort to remain lean, again focusing on the commodity items.

To accomplish the "no frills" approach that is its hallmark, the company keeps a tight rein on spending. No one, not even top-level officers, has an expense account, a fancy office, a company car, or even a designated parking space. Stores are not heated or air-conditioned.

A vigilant pricing department constantly monitors competitors' activity, and an aggressive purchasing division continually works to improve the company's "power buying" position.

Hardy also believes in limiting the number of products sold, and keeping the store operations simple.

"Every time we varied from that approach—like selling grass seed and birdhouses—we got into trouble. We have constantly reminded ourselves of what we are. We deal in commodities, basic building products, nothing fancy," he says.

That simple approach also applies to the company's finances. Hardy pays cash for the stores he opens. If they don't make a profit, he closes them, a move he describes as "very, very painful, but sometimes necessary."

To ensure profitability, Hardy places great emphasis on training and development of the company's 3,500 associates. They are not called employees. Every management person is a graduate of "84

■ *84 Lumber, which was once a single lumberyard in 84, Pennsylvania, is now the nation's largest privately owned building materials retailer.*

University," a 25-year-old annual training program that keeps associates sharp in product knowledge and selling skills.

The company operates on a "team" basis, with associates sharing commissions and not competing against each other.

Hardy generously rewards both performance and loyalty, with cash bonuses and weekends at Nemacolin Woodlands for top performers. He has established a $1 million endowment fund to help associates' children with college expenses. Hardy also gives scholarship money to children whose parents have worked at the company at least 20 years.

84 Lumber is known as a place where talented people can climb the ladder quickly. Everyone starts in the lumber yard, selling to customers and learning the inventory. But it is not unusual for those in their 20's to join upper-level management within a few years. Even Joe's daughter Maggie, now executive vice president of 84 Lumber, started in the

stores, hauling lumber and stocking shelves, before moving into the company's executive development program. Training programs are held at the company's beautiful new training center and dormitory complex in 84, Pennsylvania.

In 1992, 84 Lumber launched a program that has catapulted the company into the national spotlight — Affordable Homes Across America. The program offers quality homes ranging from $39,900 to $69,000, which includes virtually everything but the lot.

Hardy considers the new program a logical extension of the company's commitment to be the nation's low-cost provider of basic commodities. With 84 Lumber's broad distribution base, its commitment to providing quality goods at the lowest possible cost, and the nation's critical need for affordable housing, the program is expected to double the size of the company within the next five years.

Hardy plans to "move the basics ahead" in the 1990s and promises record growth for 84 Lumber, not only through Affordable Homes, but also by adding new stores, truss plants and house panel manufacturing plants throughout the nation in the next few years.

The driving force that has propelled both 84 Lumber and Nemacolin Woodlands to the forefront has been Hardy's indomitable spirit of entrepreneurship. In that spirit, he has established the Department of Entrepreneurial Studies at Washington & Jefferson College in Washington, Pennsylvania, to promote the concept among young people.

In just a few short years, W&J's Entrepreneurial Studies Department has become widely recognized for offering one of the nation's leading programs for preparing young people to go into business for themselves.

Hardy believes that encouragement of entrepreneurship is essential for the future economic health and welfare of the Pittsburgh community and of the nation.

"We need to help young people try out their ideas." he said. "We need to provide an environment where they can make mistakes and learn from those mistakes. We need to encourage young people to follow their dreams and to believe that nothing is impossible."

■ *The familiar red "84 lollipop" signs can be seen on country roads and major highways from coast to coast. Photo by Scott Goldsmith.*

New companies form in Pittsburgh seemingly every day, but when a new corporation springs full-blown into the world, boasting $6.5 billion in annual sales and approximately 23,000 employees, people pay attention.

That's how it was on January 1, 1992, when the new Miles Inc. was created through the merger of three sister companies — Pittsburgh-based Mobay Corp., a chemical company; Agfa Corp., an imaging technologies company; and the health care company Miles — with their Pittsburgh-based holding company.

Although the Miles name may not have been familiar to Pittsburghers, many quickly learned they had been using Miles products

Miles Inc.

for years. They discovered that the company's products included such name brands as One-A-Day vitamins, Alka-Seltzer, S.O.S pads,and Agfa film, as well as prescription pharmaceuticals, diagnostic test systems, pigments for colored roofing tiles, dyes for coloring textiles and paper, coatings and polymers for cars, polycarbonate resins for compact discs, and rubber for tires.

■ *At Miles Inc.'s optical disc laboratory in Pittsburgh, company researchers employ the same equipment used by customers in the compact disc and optical memory industries to test new polycarbonate formulations -- the plastic resin from which the majority of discs are made.*

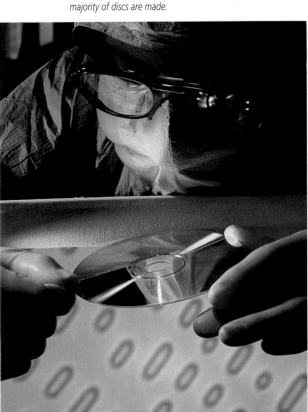

Among the key objectives of the reorganization was the development of a common corporate identity and culture. The company is well on the way towards establishing a strong identity as a leading research-based chemicals, health care and imaging technologies company. Attention is now being focused on Miles' culture.

To make certain everyone at Miles recognizes the path that must be traveled together, the company has developed a "Vision and Values" statement. The Miles vision is:

"...to be a leader in the markets we serve and to be a major contributor to our worldwide parent company. We will achieve our vision through a diversified, highly motivated workforce; by satisfying and retaining loyalties of our external and internal customers; with an organization that fosters teamwork and is unencumbered by bureaucracy; by being environmentally responsible and by being good corporate citizens in the communities in which we work."

Each Miles employee received a copy of the Vision and Values statement along with a message from Helge H. Wehmeier, president and chief executive officer, explaining the development and purpose of the document.

"Like a catalyst in the chemical process, the one element that's essential to achieving our objectives and thus making us more competitive is communication," said Wehmeier.

"Each of our employees must know where we're going, why, and how we're going to get there. They need to understand they have a common goal, that everyone has a personal stake in the success of Miles."

"The holding company was good in bringing about some uniformity in this organization here in North America, but it was insufficient in making us one company vis-a-vis our customers and vis-a-vis our own people," Wehmeier said. "That was our prime purpose in bringing about one operating company."

Being one large company also has benefits in developing current Miles employees and attracting new people.

■ *President and Chief Executive Officer Helge H. Wehmeier says Miles' success in Pittsburgh makes the city more attractive to companies seeking locations for R&D and service operations.*

"When you break down a large organization into several compartments, you make it very difficult for the development of people, because you limit them to small ponds," explained Wehmeier.

To address this limitation, the company has implemented a Job Opportunities Program, under which interested employees can apply for selected job openings that are posted. In the case of senior professional and senior manager positions, employees at any Miles site in the country can respond.

In addition, says Wehmeier, Miles can now hire talented people from outside and give them opportunities to find their specialized fields of interest.

"Under the new organization, the person coming to Miles doesn't have to decide whether to join the imaging business, or whether to join the health care business, or whether to join the chemical operations," he said. "They join Miles, one company. And they will be developed within one company."

Operating as one company also promotes the sharing of ideas, programs, and systems to better serve Miles' various customers, Wehmeier said.

Today, Miles Inc. is made up of eight divisions: Agfa, Agriculture, Diagnostics, Industrial Chemicals, Organic Products, Pharmaceutical, Polymers, and Polysar Rubber. Three of the divisions and about 1,700 of the company's employees are based in Pittsburgh, although no more than 100 of them work at headquarters downtown, since many in administrative and support functions remain at division sites.

■ *Miles is a major provider of health care products, with an over-the-counter line that includes the well-known* **Alka-Seltzer** *brand, prescription pharmaceuticals and, shown here, diagnostic tests and equipment.*

Located in One Mellon Center, Miles selected Pittsburgh for several reasons. Not the least of those reasons was Pittsburgh's newly expanded airport. It is centrally located for access to Miles' divisions and major research and manufacturing operations in West Haven, Connecticut; Tarrytown, New York; Ridgefield Park, New Jersey; Bushy Park, South Carolina; Elkhart, Indiana; Kansas City, Missouri; Houston, Texas; and Sarnia, Ontario in Canada.

The city's proximity to the numerous sites became even more important to Miles because the reorganization into a single operating company increased the need for interaction and communication.

"Locating the headquarters of our company in Pittsburgh was one of the best decisions we ever made," Wehmeier said. "Of course, we had the advantage because our chemical divisions (Mobay) had been at our Parkway site for so long. So it was similar to asking a family member for advice. The city was a good fit for the Mobay culture and since we had the same parents, we knew it would suit us as well."

Wehmeier believes that companies like Miles represent the very future of Pittsburgh.

"Whereas the city was once dominated by heavy manufacturing, it is now a services and brain center," he said. "Our being here — and being successful here — makes Pittsburgh more attractive to companies with operations similar to those of Miles and other Pittsburgh companies. In a sense, we've blazed the trail for them."

The fact that Pittsburgh already is home to several large and well-respected international companies offers Wehmeier and everyone at Miles the opportunity to share ideas and experiences with people who have a similar base of experience and face similar challenges.

"We can benefit from what they learn, and vice versa," he said.

Miles managers have discovered what Mobay managers have known for 30 years, that Pittsburghers come to their jobs with a strong work ethic and commitment to excellence.

"These are the very values that are important to our company, so the Pittsburgh-area employees who join us are already in synch with our culture," Wehmeier said. "This makes the transition to our company much smoother. This also makes it easier for us to sustain these values at Miles because they are woven into the fabric of day-to-day life in Pittsburgh."

Wehmeier also praises Pittsburgh's tendency for directness and informality, characteristics that promote open and honest communications.

"This is important to a company like ours because we need the best thinking and ideas from everyone at Miles to move the organization forward," he said.

Miles' commitment to the future runs deep and manifests itself in the company's willingness to spend money on developing new products and growing new markets. In 1993, Miles is spending nearly $500 million on research and development, part of it in the laboratories housed in the 14-building complex on the Parkway West.

Projects under development in Pittsburgh and other locations now include development of low volatile organic compound polyurethane-based coatings for the auto industry, new recycling technolo-

gies for polyurethanes, a drug to reduce harmful cholesterol, and a number of new diagnostic systems.

The company also strives to make important contributions to the community beyond just being a good employer. It has sponsored the Carnegie International art exhibition, its financial support helped build new studios at WQED-FM, and it has donated to the Fresh Air Camp and Rainbow Kitchen, programs which benefit the city's socially and economically disadvantaged. Also, Miles has created a partnership which links educators to industry, and whose mission will be to promote a more dynamic and relevant learning environment in science and technology in the elementary schools. As a further indication of its commitment to Pittsburgh, Miles assumed the landmark sign on Mt. Washington when Alcoa decided not to renew the lease it had for more than 25 years.

"While Miles benefits from being in Pittsburgh, we like to think Pittsburgh is a better place to live because we're here," Wehmeier said. "Clearly, we do much more than work here. We live here." ▣

■ *Elsie Sankar (left) and Cheryl Williams were among 25 Miles employees who donated their personal time to paint and repair buildings and recreation equipment at the Fresh Air Camp in Mars, Pa. Previously, Miles financial resources and employee volunteers helped construct an arts and science building at the camp, which is for economically disadvantaged children.*

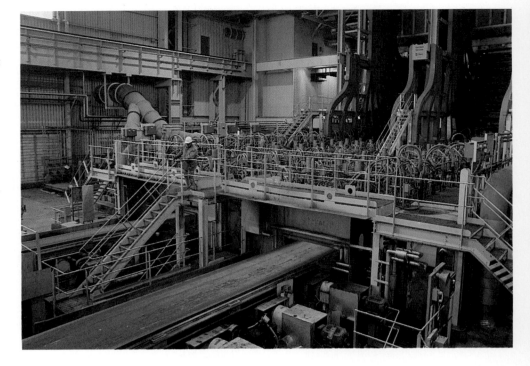

■ *U. S. Steel produces 100 percent of its steel from continuous casters, including this facility at the Edgar Thompson plant in Pittsburgh's Mon Valley.*

USX Corporation, headquartered in Pittsburgh, is a major worldwide producer of energy — oil and gas — and is also the nation's leading producer of steel products and a key participant in the domestic gas gathering business. The corporation has separated its common stock into three distinct classes — USX-Marathon Group, USX-U. S. Steel Group and USX-Delhi Group. Each of these stock issues reflects the financial performance of the individual line of business.

The USX-Marathon Group, headquartered in Houston, is involved in global crude oil and natural gas exploration, production and transportation. It is also involved in the domestic refining, marketing and

USX Corporation

transportation of crude oil and petroleum products.

Internationally, Marathon's exploration and production activities have extended to five continents, with production flowing from such varied locations as the United Kingdom, Ireland, Tunisia, Egypt and Indonesia. The centerpiece of Marathon's international operations is the Brae Field complex in the U.K. North Sea, off the northeast coast of Scotland. Marathon has been producing liquid hydrocarbons there on a major scale since the mid-1980s and continues to develop substantial reserves.

On the domestic front, Marathon is operator and holds a 49.4 percent interest in the Yates Field in west Texas. The field, which Marathon discovered in 1926, is one of the most prolific oilfields in U.S. history and still among the leading fields in production and reserves, outside of Alaska.

Marathon is also very active in the Gulf of Mexico, where it operates more than 30 offshore platforms and maintains a substantial exploration program. In addition, Marathon is a significant producer in the Rocky Mountains and Alaska's Cook Inlet. The company also conducts a wide range of onshore production activity in the Southwest and Central regions of the U.S.

Marathon continues to pursue attractive opportunities to find and produce oil and gas worldwide. Many of today's best prospects are in the international sphere. A major area of focus for future activity is the former Soviet Union.

In the United States, Marathon's refining, marketing and transportation system is one of the most efficient in the industry. Five refineries, located at Detroit; Garyville, Louisiana; Indianapolis; Robinson, Illinois; and Texas City, Texas, give Marathon a rated refining capacity of more than 600,000 barrels of oil per day.

The company, mainly through its Marathon Pipe Line (MPL) subsidiary, operates or holds an interest in more than 6,000 miles of crude oil and refined-product pipelines. MPL is also the largest interest owner in LOOP INC., operator of the Louisiana Offshore Oil Port. This is the nation's only U.S. deepwater port capable of handling the world's largest crude oil tankers. From an environmental standpoint, it is the nation's preferred facility for receiving large international crude shipments. Marathon also operates more than 50 petroleum-product terminals and a related fleet of tanker trucks.

The company markets gasoline through approximately 2,200 independent Marathon-brand service stations in the Midwest and some 1,500 gasoline/convenience-store outlets in the Midwest and Southeast. These units — chiefly under the Speedway and Starvin' Marvin names — are owned and operated by Marathon's Emro Marketing subsidiary. Emro also has its own retail propane business. Marathon's wholesale operations market product inventories not moved through retail. In addition to gasoline, diesel and heating fuel, wholesale products include asphalt, heavy fuel oil and commercial jet fuel.

Another company product is liquefied natural gas (LNG). In a joint venture, Marathon operates two cryogenic LNG

■ *Marathon production from the rugged waters of the U.K. North Sea has flowed from the Brae Field since the mid-1980s.*

tankers that take gas liquefied at a plant on Alaska's Kenai Peninsula and transport it, under U.S. export license, to two large utilities in Japan.

The USX-U. S. Steel Group manufactures and sells a wide variety of steel mill products, coke and taconite pellets. Primary steel operations include the Gary (Indiana) Works, the Fairfield (Alabama) Works near Birmingham and the Pittsburgh-based Mon Valley Works. The Mon Valley Works includes the Edgar Thomson steelmaking and Irvin finishing operations on the Monongahela River and the Fairless finishing plant near Philadelphia.

U. S. Steel coke production takes place at the Clairton Works — also on the Mon River — and at Gary Works. At Minntac, on northern Minnesota's Mesabi Iron Range, iron ore mining and taconite pellet operations support the steelmaking effort.

Heavy investment in advanced technology has kept the company in the forefront among American integrated steelmakers. U. S. Steel now produces 100 percent of its steel via continuous casters and has reduced manhours per ton of output to historically low levels that place the company in a leading position worldwide.

Not only in quantity but in quality is U. S. Steel a top player. Major customers — Ford, Chrysler, Delco Chassis, General Electric, American National Can and many others — have presented specific U.S. Steel facilities with a host of awards and honors recognizing consistently outstanding performance in meeting product and delivery needs.

U. S. Steel's steep capital investment reflects a strong commitment to environmental enhancement. State-of-the-art technology controls more than 95 percent of emissions from company production facilities. While U. S. Steel continues to improve its control technology, it focuses increasingly on outright prevention of pollution at the source.

Innovative programs have come to the fore. Near the Fairfield Works, U. S. Steel has worked with government agencies to design and build a wetlands system of ponds to neutralize acid mine drainage and stockpile runoff. This has restored normal aquatic life to creek waters previously affected by the drainage.

U. S. Steel's Clairton facility is the most environmentally advanced coke plant in the country. A program developed at Clairton called CITE (Continuous Improvement to the Environment) has given intensive training to all employees on the efficient and effective operation of their facilities and their responsibility to the environment. CITE has proven so successful that U. S. Steel has expanded it to other plants.

In addition to primary steel mill operations, U. S. Steel participates in several steel joint ventures. The major ones include USS-POSCO, Pittsburg, California; USS-Kobe, Lorain, Ohio; Pro-Tec Coating Company, Leipsic, Ohio; Worthington Specialty Processing, Jackson, Michigan, and Double Eagle Steel Coating Company, Detroit.

U. S. Steel is also involved in a number of other businesses, among them coal mining, mineral resources management, real estate development, engineering and consulting services, technology licensing, and leasing and financial services.

The USX-Delhi Group, based in Dallas, is a major intrastate gas gatherer. Its 8,000-mile pipeline network connects 4,400 natural gas supply points. This network is integrated with processing facilities that enable Delhi to condition suppliers' gas to pipeline quality, and extract natural gas liquids when market conditions are favorable.

Delhi has long been involved in the premium-customer end of the market, successfully serving Southwestern local gas distribution companies and electric utilities tied directly into the Delhi pipeline system. Delhi's superior record serving such customers stems from its ability to provide extreme swing capacity, based on seasonal demand, and emergency standby service.

Another strength is Delhi's many connections with interstate and intrastate pipelines. These provide access to markets throughout the U.S., which enables Delhi to switch supplies on an immediate basis to take advantage of regional price differentials.

As a corporation, USX is no longer primarily the steel company that arose out of the 1901 formation of United States Steel Corporation. USX today is really three separate businesses, each with its own management, operating under the USX Board of Directors. ◰

■ *Serving local gas distribution companies is a key element of Delhi's strategy, as exemplified by this pipeline – shown during construction – at Tyler, Texas.*

When men and women go to work in dangerous places, it's a safe bet that MSA (Mine Safety Appliances Company) products go with them.

Founded early in the 20th century by two engineers who had seen too many lives lost in mining accidents, MSA became the United State's largest company dedicated solely to the development and manufacture of safety equipment.

In 1914, two young U.S. Bureau of Mines' engineers, John Thomas Ryan and George Herman Deike, were working thousands of miles apart when they had the same idea. They concluded that for more miners to survive the dangers of their work, better equipment was needed.

Mine Safety Appliances Company

On June 15, 1914, Ryan and Deike put up a small sign outside a single office in a downtown Pittsburgh office building declaring that MSA was open for business. Their first goal was to give miners a safe way of finding their way in the dark.

Since the earliest days of underground coal mining, miners used lamps with open flames to see. The flames frequently ignited the explosive gases that accumulated underground.

Electric lighting was brought to mining when Ryan and Deike convinced Thomas A. Edison to reduce the size of his nickel-iron alkaline battery so miners' helmets could be fitted with battery-powered electric lamps.

"Within a few years, that first cap lamp was used in mines around the world. It saved thousands of lives and started a revolution in

■ *Confined spaces present many hazards for workers and the Passport™ Personal Alarm, the world's smallest, lightest five-gas portable alarm, allows fast evaluation of atmospheres for oxygen deficiency, combustible gas and certain toxic gases.*

the development of innovative personal protective equipment from MSA," said John T. Ryan III, MSA president, chairman, and chief executive officer. He is the grandson of the co-founder.

By the early 1990s, MSA's contribution to workplace safety included over 4,000 products including protective helmets, self-contained breathing apparatus, air-purifying respirators, eye and face protection, industrial clothing, and hearing protectors. The company also manufactures a variety of portable and continuous instruments for detecting dangerous gases. MSA products are used in general manufacturing, firefighting, chemical and petroleum production, asbestos abatement, hazardous materials cleanup, public utilities, nuclear power generation, construction, and the armed services. As an example of MSA's reach in the market, U.S. forces in the Persian Gulf War were protected by MSA-made masks. A specially designed mask for Apache helicopter pilots was delivered so quickly MSA was given a U.S. Army commendation.

MSA's 5,300 employees are stationed in offices located in 17 states and 24 international operating companies touching every continent. Headquarters and research facilities are based in Pittsburgh. The Safety Products Division develops, manufactures, and markets personal protective devices such as respirators, hardhats, and clothing, among other items. The Instrument Division produces sophisticated portable and permanently-installed environmental monitoring gear for the workplace along with instrumentation for

■ *For firefighter rescue, the Quick-Fill System from MSA lets a firefighter transfill, or equalize, his air supply with a fellow firefighter who may be down and running out of air from his self-contained breathing apparatus. The system is an MSA exclusive.*

hospitals. The Callery Chemical Division produces a variety of specialty chemicals related to the production of pharmaceuticals and for use in automobile air bag systems.

MSA also has major groups of research and development engineers, both at the Pittsburgh headquarters and in offices around the globe.

After the products are made and sales transactions are completed, MSA continues to work with customers through an extensive network of service centers staffed with certified specialists and stocked with spare parts and diagnostic equipment for customer support.

MSA believes that safety equipment can do the job it is designed for only if the manufacturer understands the customer's needs and problems. To that end, MSA has made a hallmark of producing training aids, including instruction manuals and audio-visual programs.

Thanks to two engineers who believed that it was good business to manufacture devices to shield workers against the hazards of mining, the men and women who put themselves in harm's way in service to industry do so with greater protection and greater confidence in their personal safety.

The Westinghouse Electric Corporation is a company with more than a century-old association with the city of Pittsburgh.

Chartered on January 8, 1886, Westinghouse started operations with 200 employees in a rented plant at Garrison Alley and Fayette Street in Pittsburgh, the city that still serves as the home for the corporation's headquarters and a number of its businesses.

From those early days when George Westinghouse and his fledgling company pioneered the alternating current transformer, whose basic features remain standard today, Westinghouse has been recognized as a leader in engineering and technology.

Few companies can point to achievements over such a long period that have contributed so significantly to the industrial might of the United States and the world. From building the first generators at Niagara Falls to developing the first fully automatic electric range for the home to demonstrating the first electronic television camera tube to important firsts in nuclear power and radar, Westinghouse has established a name over the years for product excellence.

Today, Westinghouse has locations around the world and continues to build on its outstanding international reputation for the development of advanced products and services for governmental, industrial, and commercial applications. The corporation's activities center on three technology-based businesses—power systems, electronic systems, and environmental services—as well as on its historically successful businesses in transport temperature control and broadcasting.

Major Westinghouse products and services in power systems include fossil and nuclear power systems and plants, nuclear fuel, process control systems, superconducting magnets, alternative energy systems, and naval nuclear power systems. More than 40 percent of the operating nuclear power plants in the world are based on Westinghouse pressurized-water reactor technology. Westinghouse, which built the world's first utility-grade turbine generator in 1903, now has turbine generators operating in more than 45 countries.

■ *The headquarters building of the Westinghouse Electric Corporation at Gateway Center in downtown Pittsburgh.*

In electronic systems, the corporation produces military and commercial electronic systems, including airborne and ground-surveillance radar, as well as systems for electronic warfare, anti-submarine warfare, space sensors, information services, logistics and support, home security, and postal applications. Westinghouse has provided military radar systems to the United States and its allies for more than 50 years.

Westinghouse's environmental services involve the handling and treatment of hazardous waste, emissions monitoring and control, management of government-owned facilities, and waste-to-energy plants. Westinghouse owns and operates the only incinerator in the United States permitted to burn low-level radioactive waste. In 1992, the corporation reached important milestones in its environmental businesses, including the start up of a 70,000 ton-per-year hazardous waste incinerator near Salt Lake City, Utah, which when combined with its existing incinerator in Kansas, gives the corporation the capacity to process almost 15 percent of the contaminated bulk solids and soils that must be incinerated each year in the United States.

The Westinghouse Thermo King business unit is the world's foremost supplier of mobile temperature control for trailers, trucks, shipboard containers, and railway cars. This includes refrigeration for trailers, trucks, railcars, and sea-going containers, as well as bus and railcar air-conditioning, and vehicle and cargo heating.

Westinghouse pioneered commercial radio by making the first such broadcast at Pittsburgh's KDKA in 1920. Today, the corporation has the largest non-network radio

group in the country with 16 stations. It also owns 5 television stations, which together reach 10 million homes a week. Other related businesses include television production and syndication, cable programming and distribution, and satellite and telecommunications services.

For more than a century now, Westinghouse has been recognized as a pro-

Westinghouse Electric Corporation

ducer of world-class products and services. But its primary identity has been with Pittsburgh and its people. Westinghouse and its employees are seen in all phases of community life, from helping in local education to health and welfare to culture and the arts. Whether it's volunteerism for the good of community projects or grants for civic and social programs, Westinghouse is a company dedicated to building for the future. ⓦ

■ *The Westinghouse Science and Technology Center just outside of Pittsburgh is one of the largest industrial R&D complexes in the United States.*

The computer industry has evolved so rapidly that businesses often find the hardware affordable, but the systems and their components sometimes unmanageable.

LEGENT Corp. became a major presence in the computer industry by recognizing those needs and filling them for the business community.

Its specialized software, designed specifically for managing corporate computing environments, performs a wide variety of functions, including evaluating the performance of computer systems, conducting cost accounting, transferring files, automating operations, managing software development,

LEGENT Corporation

analyzing computing requirements, and predicting future needs for computing capacity.

LEGENT also produces software that detects system problems and points the way toward more effective service to end users by identifying deficiencies such as inefficient or inappropriate storage of data and slowdowns in processing or accessing data.

In short, LEGENT's products enable computer systems to operate more efficiently.

Although LEGENT was formed in the late 1980s, the roots of its predecessor companies date to the early days of computing, when IBM mainframes dominated the marketplace.

■ *LEGENT's automation products allow data center operators to monitor system activity.*

LEGENT's predecessors provided software solutions to IBM users to make their applications—the programs which told the computers what to do—operate faster and more efficiently. When customers found that the solutions could save them money and make them more competitive, the early LEGENT companies took off.

One of those early firms was Pittsburgh-based Duquesne Systems, which merged with Morino, Inc. of Vienna, Virginia, to form LEGENT in 1989.

While LEGENT's headquarters are located in Virginia, the company's largest office is in Pittsburgh, which serves as the seat of LEGENT's finance and administrative activities and is the site of one of the firm's major labs for product development and client services.

The Pittsburgh location also houses the central computing center that serves all of LEGENT's development labs, the corporation's business applications, and LEGENT's management information systems.

The company made a firm commitment to maintain a significant presence in Pittsburgh when it announced plans to build a new $40 million, seven-story office building near the Pittsburgh International Airport. LEGENT planned to occupy the new building by late 1993, moving from its previous location on the city's North Side.

The introduction of personal computers in the early 1980s spawned a new generation of high-technology giants such as Lotus and Microsoft. Individual programmers created a boom in new applications based on spreadsheet and word processing programs.

Other hardware companies emerged to challenge IBM's market dominance, creating a free-for-all among large and small players in the computing industry. Recognizing the opportunities presented by an evolving industry, LEGENT broadened its areas of expertise to meet the new demand.

■ *Home of LEGENT's Pittsburgh operations, Fall 1993.*

As desktop computers became more sophisticated and the software more responsive to the needs of individual industries and companies, computer users chose to connect their PCs to other PCs. That allowed them to share applications and data through what are known as local area networks. With that development, yet another LEGENT market had evolved.

The local area networks, or LANs, allowed organizations to combine the computing power of all their machines and in doing so allowed workers to better communicate with one another. Local area networks incorporate everything from office information systems to automatic teller machines.

The development of LANs meant that many companies lessened their dependence on large mainframe computers, relying instead on smaller systems to store such data as customer, credit, and inventory information, that was accessible from any of the PCs on the network.

But companies using LANs soon discovered that their PC networks were becoming increasingly difficult to manage. As a consequence, the efficiency of the software and the employees was being lost.

Technology continued to evolve and created countless new opportunities to address those problems, but still they needed software solutions to prevent the advancing technology from going to waste.

LEGENT already did business with more than 10,000 companies, including more than a quarter of the world's largest corporations, and it was poised to help with the newest generation of computer dilemmas.

For example, one LEGENT product, known as PARAMOUNT ™, collects information on all computers in a network and feeds it all to one computer screen, where a spe-

■ *Data retrieval and migration is a perpetual function of the data center, often managed by LEGENT products.*

cialist can monitor usage and immediately respond to any problems which might arise anywhere in the network. This provides the ability to manage far-flung computers from a central location.

Another example is LEGENT's XCOM 6.2 product line, the industry's leading system for transferring data files from computer to computer. In computer networks, information must be transferred seamlessly, and XCOM addresses that need. Sales of the product line have been growing at a rate of more than 100 percent a year.

LEGENT offers more than 130 products and has strived not to become overly dependent on a single product or market. For example, last year's most popular product represented only 11.5 percent of total new license sales.

"We have always felt that it was essential to serve all our markets—and all our customers—equally," said Joe Henson, LEGENT chairman since 1989. "That way you can be constantly aware of the new trends and adapt to new markets."

LEGENT's ability to adapt to those new markets and respond quickly to customer needs has brought it a rate of growth which is enviable, even in an industry where overnight success has become commonplace.

LEGENT's sales grew by more than 30 percent over its first few years, making it a $430 million company by the early 1990s with some 2,400 employees in 14 countries around the globe.

Despite its rapid growth, the company has not sacrificed service. LEGENT, which had no debt and approximately $180 million in cash at the end of 1992, was recognized in a Gartner Group survey of computer users for providing the best customer support among

broad-based systems software vendors, as well as for being the group's technology leader.

Expansion also has come about through a successful strategy of mergers and acquisitions. Shortly after the 1989 merger which created LEGENT, the company acquired Business Software Technology, Inc., a Massachusetts software firm, for $42 million in stock.

LEGENT's largest and most significant acquisition came in 1992 when it merged with another software maker, Goal Systems International, Inc. of Columbus, Ohio, in a stock swap valued at $400 million.

The Goal acquisition made LEGENT the second-largest provider of systems management software and positioned it to better compete for the top spot in the industry. Analysts applauded the move, because it expanded LEGENT's product line and market area.

"We've grown to serve these new markets, and companies turn to us because we understand computing from the mainframe down to the desktop," said John Burton, a cofounder of BST who was named LEGENT's president and chief executive officer in 1992.

The two former top officers at LEGENT—Glen F. Chatfield, former chairman of Duquesne Systems and former CEO of LEGENT, and Mario Morino, who headed Morino and was chairman of LEGENT—brought in Henson and Burton with the goal of building LEGENT into a $1 billion company.

Henson, who retired as president and CEO of Prime Computer after building that company from $300 million

to $1.7 billion in his seven-year tenure, said he would like to become perhaps the first executive to build both a hardware and a software firm into billion-dollar businesses.

"It's doable. It is not irrational, but it's not a piece of cake," the chairman said.

That goal is achievable, Burton believes, by maintaining a 20 percent annual growth rate—not out of line with LEGENT'S past performance. But he insists that the company not pursue a course of growth-at-all-costs.

Growth must be managed . . . " without sacrificing the quality of the company as viewed by customers, employees, and the investing public, but also not without sacrificing profitability," said the president and CEO.

Because of the strong relationship between the company and the city, LEGENT expects to share its future with Pittsburgh.

"Pittsburgh is an excellent place to live and work," Henson said. "We need what Pittsburgh has to offer in the way of talent and energy and entrepreneurship every bit as much as Pittsburgh needs LEGENT." ■

■ *Magnetic tapes provide the necessary data and backup for end users as well as for maintaining operating systems.*

■ *The families of Cameron Coca-Cola celebrate the Grand Opening of 112,000 sq.ft. Sales and Distribution Facility in Houston, PA. The new facility will service the Pittsburgh Metropolitan Market as well as parts of West Virginia and Ohio.*

The family that has quenched the thirsts of Western Pennsylvanians for more than a century is known for quality, service and corporate citizenship in the way that Coca-Cola is synonymous for refreshment.

The Cameron Coca-Cola Bottling Co., Inc., besides bottling some of the region's most proular soft drinks, has thrown its support behind a variety of highlight attractions including the Coca-Cola Star Lake Amphitheatre.

Along with its popular Coca-Cola products, Cameron uses its state-of-the-art distribution system to supply a variety of other drinks rapidly gaining in popularity, including Nestea Iced Tea, PowerAde and Ameron Water.

Cameron Coca-Cola also has forged partnerships with the city's three major sports teams: The Steelers, the Pirates and the Penguins.

Whether it's printing special cans to commemorate winning seasons or sponsoring promotional events, Cameron's involvement has sparked marketing opportunities.

Founded in Washington, Pennsylvania in 1889 by Wilfred Cameron, a native of New Castle, the company started out delivering its own brand of soft drinks by horse and buggy.

In 1919, the Camerons acquired the Coca-Cola franchise. Beginning in the 1970's, the company expanded it's market area by acquiring bottling companies in Wheeling and Sisterville, West Virginia, as well as in Steubenville and Cambridge, Ohio.

In 1983, the company took the major step of acquiring the Pittsburgh, Beaver and Uniontown, Pennsylvania and the Canton, Ohio Coca-Cola bottling franchise and unifying its many holdings under the Cameron Coca-Cola name.

"We have worked hard to strengthen the Coca-Cola image in our market", Cameron said.

Today, 12 members of the Cameron Family operate the company, which now employs about 350 people serving more than three million customers in parts of Pennsylvania, Ohio, and West Virginia.

Increasing the level of recycling and the use of recycled materials in soft drink containers remain important goals for the company. "In 1992, the Soft Drink Industry recycled 60% of all soft drink containers", said Wendy Cameron.

Cameron Coca-Cola Bottling Company

■ *The home of the Cameron Coca-Cola Bottling Co., Inc. from 1889 to 1953.*

"Our goal has been to integrate ourselves into the community, not only by selling our products and our name, but by helping improve the quality of life in our area", said Jim Cameron, V.P. of Sales. "Hopefully we have contributed toward making Western Pennsylvania the fantastic place that it is for everyone to live and work."

"Our company has benefited through the publicity and the goodwill the partnership has generated", Cameron said.

The company also has been a major contributor to local charitable organizations. Cameron Coca-Cola's generosity and community involvement earned it the title of Outstanding Philanthropic Organization of the Year in 1992.

"We have supported cultural programs, sports activities, ethnic programs, neighborhood events, and we've actively supported our local school system", said Wendy Cameron, who manages community relations. "We have tried to touch all aspects of the community. We're a family business, and we're proud to have our products be a part of everyone's family here in Western Pennsylvania."

That dedication to family is the essence of Cameron Coca-Cola's success.

As the 21st Century approaches, Cameron Coca-Cola continues to seek new ways to package, market and distribute its products and to contribute to the region's prosperity.

■ *Genco's recently completed, 200,000 sq. ft. warehouse facility and corporate headquarters in Cheswick, PA was designed and built by its development division.*

Headquartered in the northern Pittsburgh suburb of Cheswick and nearly 100 years old, family-owned Genco provides customized distribution, product reclamation, and warehouse construction. Genco's mission is to study the needs of each of its customers and provide the highest level of service, said James M. Schwartz, general manager of Genco Development, one of the company's four operating units.

"We enable our customers to concentrate on what they do best, whether it's manufacturing, retailing, or whatever," he said. "And we'll take care of what for them is a headache." Using Genco, companies can avoid the direct costs and complications of building and equipment maintenance, under-utilized space and employees, and inventory management.

Genco's customer list includes H.J. Heinz, Calgon, Kraft, the Pennsylvania Liquor Control Board, Hershey, Chesebrough-Ponds, and scores of others. The company operates two million square feet of distribution center space in Pittsburgh and Harrisburg, Pennsylvania; Gainesville, Georgia; and Jacksonville, Florida. Other Genco facilities are located in Oregon, North Carolina, Ohio, and Indiana.

Genco's Distribution Services group can handle goods by the pallet, case, or even piece. Genco not only provides distribution services in its own buildings, but also can supply the management and labor in facilities owned by its clients. In addition to basic services, Genco provides shrink-wrap packaging, labor-intensive product manipulation, and light-assembly services.

"We are basically customer demand-driven," Schwartz said. "If a customer comes to us with a request for an unusual service, we go the extra mile to provide that service. If we accepted only conventional distribution requests, we would be limiting ourselves and our opportunities for growth."

Genco's Scanning Solutions unit utilizes computer scanning technology to solve product reclamation problems for their customers. Scanning Solutions software saves Genco clients millions of dollars through the centralized processing of returned and damaged merchandise. Previously, returned goods rarely found their way back to store shelves. Instead, they were left in a forgotten corner of the warehouse. Genco's network of return centers for retailers such as K-Mart, Sears Roebuck, and Wal Mart maximizes revenues received from returned goods.

Another business unit, Genco Development offers complete warehouse design and construction expertise for customers that are building or renovating their own facility. In fact, Genco is able to manage all phases of warehouse construction, including site selection, design, financing, and permitting. "By analyzing the customer's distribution needs, we can determine the layout that will maximize labor efficiency and space utilization," Schwartz said.

Genco's Transportation Division provides complete transportation services with a private warehouse fleet and freight management group. Genco's warehouse fleet operates 30 trucks that service warehouse customers. The freight management group offers access to more than 100 carriers nationwide and also provides transportation consulting services.

Recognized as a visionary and progressive company within the distribution industry, Genco consistently employs new technologies to improve efficiency and customer service, such as the implementation of radio frequency (RF) and bar-code systems in its warehouses that increase productivity and reduce paperwork. Genco also utilizes elec-

tronic data interchange (EDI) networks that provide real-time processing and inventory information.

Genco has a long tradition in the distribution industry. In 1898, Hyman Shear began a drayage company known as the H. Shear Trucking Company with a blind horse and a wagon delivering to the Pittsburgh area. In 1917, the company purchased its first gas-powered truck. By 1940, under Sam Shear's leadership, Genco had entered the public warehousing business and it's fleet had grown to over 40 trucks. Since 1970, Herb Shear, the third generation of the family, has led Genco's expansion that provides customers with the complete array of integrated logistics services that is offered today.

GENCO Distribution System

While nearly a century has passed since Hyman Shear began the Genco tradition, the company still adheres to the philosophy of service and reliability. "Although we have progressed from a blind horse and wagon to diesel-powered tractors and computers, some things do not change," Schwartz said. "We still maintain our tradition of hard work, dependability, and our deep commitment to the needs and satisfaction of our customers. That will never change." *P*

■ *Genco's material handling capabilities include pallet, case, and piece handling, labor-intense services, product reclamation, nationwide transportation services, and customized computer and EDI technologies.*

■ *Bacharach's Sentinel® 44 multi-gas personal monitor.*

Bacharach Inc. was born in the mines, mills and factories of Pittsburgh and has grown into a leading manufacturer of instruments used for measuring, calibrating and testing in a wide variety of industries.

Founded in 1909 to fulfill a need for ventilation and gas measuring devices, Bacharach today serves markets around the United States and the world, helping technicians and researchers in mills, laboratories, refineries and scores of other industrial settings.

Since it was purchased in January 1986 by Paul M. Zito, Bacharach has followed a path of climbing sales and market expansion with more growth expected in the years ahead.

Bacharach, Inc.

The company has grown by developing new products, such as a portable combustion analyzer for determining the efficiency and safety of boilers or furnaces. It also has grown by acquiring products from other companies, including the acquisition of a line of analytical lab instruments from Perkin-Elmer Corp.

■ *The Bacharach Specialist 9000 diesel fuel injection system analyzer.*

"Our growth during the last several years and the strategic position we hold in today's marketplace are directly attributable to the emphasis we place on delivering quality products to our customers," Zito said.

"An experienced and dedicated workforce, backed by extensive service and distribution networks, makes Bacharach a formidable competitor in each of its markets."

Bacharach is divided into four operating groups: Gas Detection Products, Testing & Measurement Products, Diesel Systems, and Analytical Instruments.

The company has been manufacturing instrumentation for gas detection longer than any other. Bacharach is recognized as a leading producer of both fixed systems and portable instruments for protection against the hazards of combustible and toxic gases.

These products have a variety of applications in a number of major markets, including petrochemical, oil and gas, utilities, municipal systems, government and the armed services.

Bacharach has always been a pioneer in the industry, producing the first practical electronic sensors and instruments for the detection of combustible gases and vapors in 1927.

Demand for gas detection instruments to safeguard workers is driven by the ever-increasing concern for employee safety and by specific government regulations from agencies such as the Occupational Safety & Health Administration.

New, stricter environmental regulations at the federal, state and local levels also are boosting orders for Bacharach's monitors. These markets are expected to increase at rates of 20-25 percent per year.

Bacharach's Gas Detection Group is also responsible for marketing the instruments of GMD Systems Inc. This affiliate company manufacturers monitors of acutely toxic

gases encountered in chemicals manufacture and other industries.

Since the 1930s, testing and measurement instruments for the heating/ventilation/air conditioning (HVAC) industry have been an integral part of Bacharach's business. Portable instruments for measuring and recording temperature, relative humidity and air velocity are still an important part of this business.

Today the Testing & Measurement Group has grown to include a family of portable combustion and environmental analyzers, which are used to "set up" boilers and furnaces for optimum efficiency and minimum stack emissions. These analyzers are used in a wide variety of applications, from indoor air quality studies to environmental compliance by large power plants.

For over 35 years Bacharach's Diesel Systems group has been designing and building high quality calibration equipment, testers and tools for diesel engine service. No other American manufacturer provides all the products and services required to successfully operate a diesel service center.

The market outlook for Bacharach's diesel systems is positive, the result of increasing concern for improved fuel efficiency and performance on the part of the fleet owners and original equipment manufacturers. Prospects are further boosted by the award of a multi-year contract by the U.S Army for fuel pump calibration stands.

Produced for the Army, Bacharach's computerized calibration stands are used at military installations around the world for servicing and maintaining diesel fuel injection systems on tanks, trucks, generator sets, and other support vehicles and engine applications.

In 1988, the company entered the analytical laboratory instrument market with the purchase of the complete line of Coleman products and a high performance liquid chromatography system from Perkin-Elmer. This was the first major acquisition by Bacharach since the company was purchased from United Technologies by Zito.

The acquisition placed Bacharach in markets in which it had not previously competed, and it entered those markets with brand names that already were highly regarded and strongly positioned. Continued product development, particularly new environmental analyzers, is making this product group even stronger.

As strong as the domestic market has been, the international market looks even stronger. The company has established itself as a player in the global marketplace. Twenty-five percent of Bacharach's total sales are outside the United States, and international growth in both sales and operations is in an expansion mode.

An established distributor network is in place in each country where the company's products are marketed. Bacharach Instruments International S/A, a Danish subsidiary, further supports Bacharach's European customers.

With establishment of the European Economic Community, Bacharach is proceeding with plans to expand manufacturing operations in Europe through acquisition and merger.

By the early 1990s, the company's strongest markets included Canada, Europe, Asia, Latin America and Australia. Significant contracts for diesel systems were secured in Taiwan, Mexico and Korea. The gas detection portion of the business was steadily increasing in the Middle East and Asia, and the company continued to pursue several avenues designed to initiate business in the People's Republic of China.

Since its early years, Bacharach has been committed to research & development and product innovation. In its mission statement, the company pledges to "provide customers with high quality, cost-effective products and services, to place an emphasis on quality in every area of operation, to be a company recognized for technological advancements in all of its markets, to maintain a high regard for the environment and to be a good corporate citizen in every community where Bacharach facilities are located."

In the past couple years, the company has earned a half dozen U.S. patents, and two foreign patents. Several other applications or disclosures are now in progress. As a group, Bacharach engineers have been recorded as inventors on nearly 50 patents.

As part of its approach to customer service, Bacharach is one of the few companies in its market sector to maintain a nationwide network of factory owned and operated Service Centers to provide after-market support and service.

Bacharach Service Centers provide customers, whatever their location, with local warranty service, product training and technical support, spare parts inventories and preventative maintenance programs.

The company has experienced strong growth in this sector with the recent opening of two new regional service centers and another is scheduled to open in 1993. Bacharach is also adding innovative services such as on-site service through the use of mobile service vans, flexible training programs and equipment rentals.

While the company has enjoyed success as it grows in sales and market penetration, owner Zito recognizes that the hard work is never finished.

"The challenge now is to continue to strengthen Bacharach's position as a market-driven, quality conscious manufacturing and service organization," he said.

"As a dynamic company, with a young and aggressive management team firmly in place, we confidently look forward to meeting that challenge." *P*

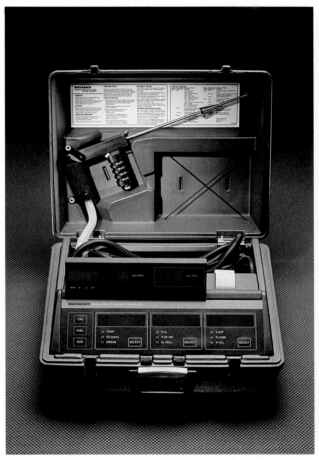

■ *Bacharach's model 300 portable combustion analyzer for setting up boilers and furnaces for optimum efficiency.*

■ *Bacharach's corporate headquarters in Pittsburgh.*

■ *The Corporate Technology Center is a product innovation and engineering resource for Kennametal customers worldwide.*

I t is more than a metaphor to say that Kennametal Inc. is on the cutting edge.

Founded in 1938 in Latrobe, Pa., on metallurgist Philip M. McKenna's invention of the first commercially successfully tungsten-titanium-carbide alloy used for cutting steel, Kennametal today is a global manufacturer and distributor of tools, tooling systems, supplies and services to a variety of industries. Kennametal products and services are found almost anywhere metal is being turned, milled, or drilled, coal is being mined, or highway pavement is being milled or cut.

From its worldwide corporate headquarters, 40 miles east of Pittsburgh in Latrobe, Kennametal holds the largest share of the North American metalworking products

Kennametal Inc.

■ *Carbide-tipped construction tools from Kennametal contribute to highway construction, repair, and renovation.*

market, leads mining and construction markets worldwide, and is evolving as an increasingly important global player. International markets generated nearly 30 percent of Kennametal's $600 million 1992 sales, and about one fifth of the company's 4,900 employees work outside of the United States. The company is pursuing a number of ways to bolster its international presence, including product, service and acquisition strategies.

By 1993, Kennametal had plants at nine locations in the United States and manufacturing facilities in Canada, the United Kingdom, France and Germany. Through subsidiaries, affiliates, distributors and agents, Kennametal markets products around the world.

Metalworking products account for about 80 percent of annual sales. The company provides tooling systems—components for precision cutting of metals under demanding conditions—for the majority of manufacturing industries. Beyond its traditional offering of carbide tooling, Kennametal develops and markets other advanced tool materials including ceramics, cermets and polycrystalline diamonds. The company also provides a full line of tool holders, milling cutters, and other cutting tools and supplies, as well as a broad range of productivity consulting services.

In addition to serving metalworking customers worldwide, Kennametal is also the world's leading producer of carbide-tipped tools for mining and construction. Mining products include drums, blocks, bits, carbide "compacts" for drilling tools, and accessories. Construction tools include blocks, bits, grader blades, and snowplow blades.

Metallurgical products represent Kennametal's third major business segment. The company produces proprietary metallurgical powders for use in its metalworking, mining and construction products. It also provides a variety of powders for specialized markets. By producing its own metallurgical powders and conducting its own research and development, Kennametal maintains full control over the quality and direction of the products it manufactures.

Although it does business far from the limelight that envelops other high-tech industries, Kennametal is one of the strong hands driving productivity and quality through manufacturing industries. "Kennametal is in the business of helping its customers increase their productivity," said Robert L. McGeehan, president and chief executive officer. "For

example, in metalcutting or in mining and construction, the performance of a cutting tool is critical. A relatively inexpensive metalcutting insert or conical bit can determine the productivity of a $3 million manufacturing cell, or $300,000 road planer," McGeehan said.

Kennametal creates tooling systems to meet specific customer needs. The KM® quick-change tooling system is one such offering; it was developed to address customer concerns over "downtime" lost while tools were changed between metalcutting operations. KM tooling enables users to change tools quickly and with the level of accuracy needed for high-precision machining operations. Less time spent changing tools means more time spent productively cutting, and more cost-efficient use of high-overhead machining systems.

Another typical customer-needs-driven product line, Kennametal's selection of RPF™ ramping, plunging and face milling cutters, is a response to manufacturers' desire to reduce the number of machining operations necessary to produce cavities and dies in metal workpieces. A single RPF cutter can replace a number of separate tools and operations in the cavity production process. The system offers considerable gains in productivity; in a typical operation on a horizontal mill, use of the RPF cutter reduced machining time from 14 hours to two and cut machining costs per part by seven-fold.

Such advances illustrate Kennametal's evolution from tooling manufacturer to full-service productivity resource for its customers. That evolution began when Philip McKenna's metallurgical breakthrough instantly created a demand for his cost-saving new tools. The competitive advantages of tungsten-carbide swept the machine tool industry and sparked Kennametal's initial success. With only one domestic competitor, Kennametal grew rapidly, reaching $4 million in annual sales by 1943.

As a cutting tool industry grew up around it, the company sought new applications for its technology. The early 50s saw Kennametal's pioneering efforts as a tooling supplier to the mining and, later, the construction industries. High quality products and aggressive marketing have made the company the global leader of those markets.

Subsequently, Kennametal also began to offer additional metalworking products, such as tool holders, drills, and milling cutters, that took advantage of its presence on the factory floor and its sales and distribution network. Kennametal's purchase of the Erickson Tool Co. in 1980 was its first acquisition toward this end.

Today Kennametal continually seeks new ways to fulfill customer needs. The company has devoted itself to increasing the value it delivers to its customers, and does so by providing a continuing stream of innovative products and by sharing its expertise through productivity consultation services.

"We feel our expertise is on the shop floor, where it's always been. Many of the people at Kennametal, myself included, came up from the shop floor," McGeehan said. "Since we're already there in the shop, it's good for us and good for our customers if we extend our influence and share more of our expertise."

■ *Expert field sales engineers solve customer's machining problems on the shop floor.*

"Not only do we know how to use carbide, but we also know how to use the drills, cutters, and other tools used throughout metalworking operations. Today, through partnerships with some of the top tooling manufacturers, Kennametal can offer its customers a majority of the tools and accessories they use in their shops, in addition to our traditional line of Kennametal core products," McGeehan said.

Kennametal's application assistance to its customers goes beyond tooling; in today's competitive manufacturing arena, success involves cutting costs as much as cutting metal. "The trend in manufacturing is to reduce the number of suppliers and become more dependent on them, thereby reducing the indirect labor component of manufacturing costs. Tool engineering, for instance, has become the province of the supplier. Kennametal is perfectly willing to take on the role," McGeehan said.

Customers are showing their willingness to let Kennametal do just that. General Motors chose Kennametal over 49 other companies to be the exclusive supplier of tooling for engine and drive train production at the automaker's Saturn Corporation subsidiary. "We showed Saturn that Kennametal knows its way around the shop floor. Saturn wanted to make the most competitive automobile possible, so we began working together," McGeehan said.

Cummins Engine, a global manufacturer of diesel engines and power systems, selected Kennametal to be its primary tooling supplier of turning and boring products in North America.

Likewise, judging by quality, on-time delivery and customer satisfaction, among other criteria, Industry Week magazine named Kennametal's Cleveland, Ohio, toolholding products facility to its "Ten Best Plants" list for United States manufacturing operations.

The future path for Kennametal's evolution is reflected in the Corporate Technology Center it

■ *Kennametal metalcutting tools, like this ceramic-coated insert shown cutting steel, boost productivity in nearly every manufacturing industry.*

opened in late 1991. Six Kennametal research and development operations in the company's corporate headquarters area were consolidated in the 150,000 square-foot CTC to form a single, synergistic unit. Not simply an attractive new location where Kennametal engineers conduct research and development, the $27 million facility is offered as a resource to customers worldwide. It was built in the belief that being first with innovations gives customers a competitive edge.

Beyond eliminating the movement of people, products, and ideas among the scattered sites, the CTC streamlines and accelerates Kennametal's R&D efforts. It combines under one roof all phases of the development process, including the genesis and evaluation of ideas, the creation of new products, the development of manufacturing processes, and the build-up to full-scale commercial applications. The CTC enables Kennametal to greatly decrease the amount of time necessary to develop a new product and get it to the marketplace.

"Customers recognize the value we've created in our new research center. That's what we do: create and deliver value. Philip McKenna's invention in 1938 was the force that started this company moving," said McGeehan. "He created value then. We're doing the same thing today and we're doing it not only in the Pittsburgh area but for customers around the world." ■

Pittsburgh Annealing Box Company (PABCO) acquired a world of metal working expertise during a century of continuous service to the steel industry as a leading maker of annealing covers and furnace components used in heat treating sheet steel.

Today, it applies that expertise in a variety of industrial and consumer markets through a family of interrelated companies.

PABCO remains the dominant manufacturer of components for annealing furnaces, used for processing flat-rolled steels. Units of the PABCO network also produce special-purpose industrial cylinders and pipe, fabricate structural steel and provide maintenance

From its roots in steelmaking, which has overcome challenges as great as any faced by modern industry, PABCO has grown and prospered by cultivating strengths that are watchwords among successful companies, market leadership, benchmark quality and technical sophistication that enable PABCO companies to be leaders in their market niches.

"Although ours are relatively small companies, they are all dominant players in their respective fields. That is the position we would expect to be in wherever we look for newer, more innovative ways of serving our customers," said Sam Michaels, chairman of PABCO and its subsidiaries.

formability of the metal after it has been rolled flat for use in auto bodies, appliances, office furniture and a variety of other products. Inexperience in an annealing equipment vendor can cripple productivity and undermine product quality.

Steel operators throughout the world recognize PABCO as the leader in manufacturing durable, reliable annealing equipment. The company has introduced more innovations in annealing equipment than any other manufacturer and is the source of most of the annealing covers in use in the steel industry today. The quality and design of its products are the international benchmark.

PABCO's Specialty Products Division carries on one of the company's more traditional activities. From its base in McKees Rocks, Pennsylvania, the division produces industrial cylinders and heavy-wall pipe for special applications in the chemical, steel and nuclear power industries.

Pittsburgh Annealing Box Co.

services for industrial equipment. Other PABCO companies manufacture the only U.S. government-approved mobile bomb disposal equipment, specialize in rolling bonded metal, manufacture some of the world's most sophisticated cookware, and finance industrial equipment.

Pittsburgh Annealing Box Company was founded in 1893 on the north shore of the Ohio River across from The Point in Pittsburgh, the cradle of the American steel industry.

Annealing, one of many steps involved in producing flat-rolled steels, restores the

As a leader in its field, the division welds and press-forms pipe from carbon and stainless steels, aluminum, copper and nickel alloys in wall thicknesses up to three inches, to specifications that are impossible to achieve in conventional rolled pipe.

The other PABCO companies stand out in similar ways.

Inland Metal Fabricators, which was acquired by PABCO in 1971, represents another area of service to industry. The Indiana-based subsidiary is a leading fabricator of access steel and miscellaneous structural steel for utilities and power plants, chemical plants, refineries, and steel mills.

PABCO gained a leading position in mechanical maintenance and repair when it acquired Daman Industries in 1979. Daman, founded in 1953, specializes in repairing and rebuilding pumps, compressors, large fans and other heavy industrial equipment. Its experience in developing and carrying out maintenance programs has helped manufacturers increase their efficiency and competitiveness.

Also significant is Daman's development of Ceramaloy®, a ceramic-powder coating for metals that are subject to high abrasion and corrosion. Today, marine propulsion shafts,

■ *Pittsburgh Annealing Box products being manufactured in Brazil.*

many of which are made by Daman, are commonly treated with this product.

Several years ago, Daman introduced its vibration analysis service, which is prominent as one of the preventative maintenance practices that enable manufacturers to avoid unplanned downtime. It can detect early warning symptoms in the rotating parts of costly industrial machinery.

Another PABCO company of particular relevance today—in light of the alarming rise of terrorism in the world is NABCO. Acquired in the mid-eighties, the company developed a new total-containment bomb disposal unit that is utilized currently by the FBI, the U.S. Army, U.S. Navy, police departments of New York City, Los Angeles, and other American cities. Security organizations around the world use NABCO equipment.

■ *A technician conducts vibration analysis of a high-pressure pump; one of various maintenance services provided by Daman Industries.*

In 1988, PABCO acquired Clad Metals, Inc., of Canonsburg, Pennsylvania, one of the world's leading suppliers of specialty bonded metals. The company produces a variety of combinations of stainless steel, aluminum and copper.

Clad Metal's products spring form proprietary processes for bonding stainless steel, with its highly stable, non-reactive properties, to the other metals with entirely different properties. The development of the bonding processes contributed to an era of dramatic progress in the specialty metals industry. These bonded metals are used in applications for the aerospace, pharmaceutical, automotive, and cookware industries.

All-Clad Metalcrafters Inc., a division of Clad Metals Inc. was also acquired in 1988. The cookware business was a natural outgrowth of PABCO's Clad Metals Inc. By taking advantage of the bonded metals developed by Clad, All-Clad produced a unique and superior product and is recognized as the maker of some of the world's finest cookware.

Its four lines of cookware are sold in the finest department and specialty stores across the United States.

All-Clad cookware features a tri-metal process that imparts even heating characteristics sought by chefs in the world's best restaurants, from the River Cafe in Brooklyn to Harry's Bar in Venice, Italy, from New York's Le Cirque and Little Nell's in Aspen to Wolfgang Puck's restaurants in California.

Chef instructors of the Culinary Institute of America have packed off All-Clad cookware to win medals at the International Culinary Olympus in Frankfurt, Germany. The Culinary Institute also features All-Clad in its American Bounty restaurant and throughout the institute's book, The New Professional Chef.

■ *NABCO Bomb containment vessels staged for shipment to the Far East.*

Industrial customers rely on PABCO for financial service as well as products, equipment and expertise. PABCO owns Capital Resource Group Inc., an equipment leasing and financial service company.

As it ushers in its second century of existence, Pittsburgh Annealing Box Company is poised for continued growth and achievements.

"We're very proud of our company's history and our reputation as leaders in so many fields," says Michaels. "By remaining true to our orientation in metallurgy, we have amassed a network of products, services and experts that no single company in the group could support on its own."

■ *All-Clad Metalcrafters cookware from four product lines.*

Few companies go about their business as quietly as Calgon Carbon Corporation while touching the lives of so many people around the world in so many beneficial ways.

The Pittsburgh-based firm specializes in an environmentally friendly chemical material called granular activated carbon, a harmless black product made from coal.

Roasting and toasting the coal creates vast networks of microscopic pores within the coal. In fact, one pound of activated carbon has a total inner surface area of approximately 100 acres. When impurities pass through a bed of activated carbon, they are attracted and retained within the internal structure.

"The largest application that's likely ever to exist for activated carbon is in the treatment of drinking water," said Thomas A. McConomy, president and chief executive officer of Calgon Carbon.

The company supplies some of the biggest municipal water treatment plants in the world and its granular activated carbon is used in twice as many water treatment plants as any other activated carbon supplier in the world.

"But we haven't lost sight of the fact that activated carbon can be applied in a wide variety of processes, and we're continually looking for new ones. Most people don't realize how many ways their lives are enhanced by the use of activated carbon."

■ *"Through an adsorption process, hydrophobic contaminants present in drinking water are attracted to the porous internal structure of activated carbon granules and physically bonded by electrostatic forces. Organic compounds are greatly attracted, and can be readily adsorbed onto activated carbon."*

Calgon Carbon Corporation

Activated carbon captures a wide variety of unwanted substances from ingredients in the foods we eat, the water and beverages we drink, the air we breathe, the pharmaceuticals that cure us of disease, the gasoline that powers our cars and the odors that crinkle our noses when we drive on smoggy urban highways or open the door of a neglected refrigerator.

Those are only a few of the ways in which the engineers and scientists of Calgon Carbon use environmental technology to improve the quality of life for millions of people around the globe.

At more than double the size of its nearest competitor, Calgon Carbon is recognized as the world leader in sales of activated carbon, for which there are more than 700 consumer, environmental and industrial applications.

■ *Abatement operator monitors pollution control equipment at Calgon Carbon Corporation's Neville Island plant.*

Some examples: Activated carbon is essential in the natural, water process used to decaffeinate coffee and tea. It is the heart of the charcoal filters on cigarettes. It freshens the air on submarines and in industrial settings. It purifies food sweeteners, both natural and artificial. It sucks odors from sewers. It captures gasoline fumes inside our cars' fuel tanks and the odors in our refrigerator. It eases the task of collecting specks of gold from low-quality ore, and it renews the solvents used in dry cleaning clothes.

In addition to cleaning the water that comes out of the household faucet, activated carbon purifies the water used to make beer and soft drinks and scores of other food and beverage products.

Calgon Carbon, which had annual sales in 1992 of about $300 million, is the sole supplier to the U.S. Military of activated carbon used in gas masks, and the company supplies about half the activated carbon used by troops of the North Atlantic Treaty Organization (NATO).

Another one of the many benefits of granular activated carbon is that it can be used again and again, thanks to a reactivation process that can recover about 90 percent of the material. That reduces the problem of disposing of used materials common to other filtration and purification processes.

The recovery rate for granular activated carbon, the form in which Calgon Carbon is the world leader, is much greater than for powdered activated carbon.

Calgon Carbon manufactures and reactivates activated carbon and also produces equipment that utilizes activated carbon.

The origins of Calgon Carbon date to 1942 and the Pittsburgh Coke & Iron Company's Activated Carbon Division. The division became part of Calgon Corporation which was subsequently acquired by Merck & Co., Inc. Management purchased the assets of Calgon Carbon in 1985 and opened the company to public stock ownership in 1987.

Under the visionary, even-handed leadership of Tom McConomy and his down-to-earth, no-frills management team, Calgon Carbon's employees serve customers in more than 60 countries on six continents. In Pittsburgh, the company operates an equipment and assembly plant and the industry's largest research and development facility.

It also operates eight activated carbon manufacturing plants and five reactivation facilities in the United States, Germany, Belgium and the United Kingdom.

"This is a product that can make things better for all of us," McConomy said. "We are proud of the fact that our future lies in the pursuit of cleaner water, cleaner air and a healthier life for people around the world."

■ *Photo at right by Roy Engelbrecht.*

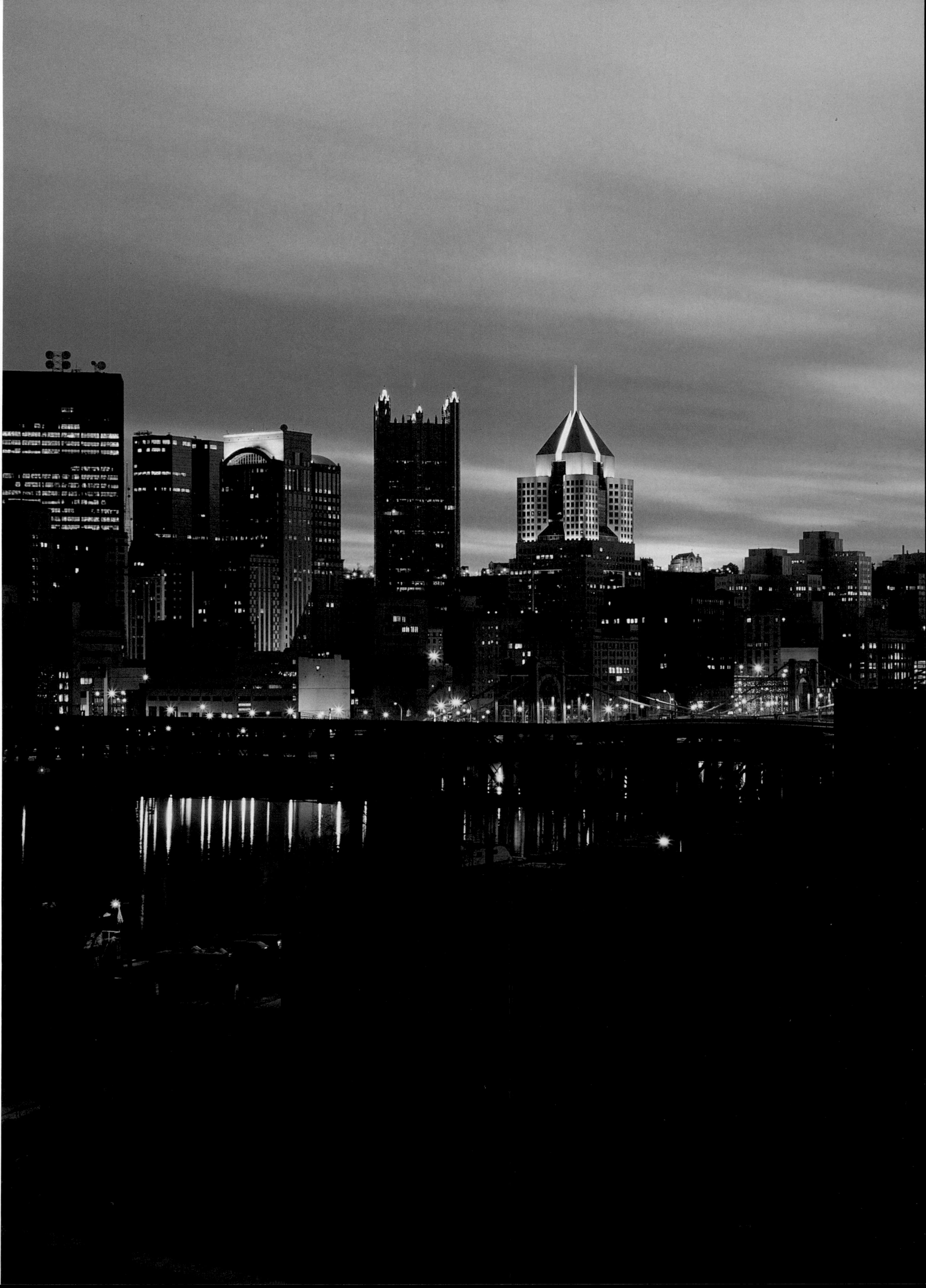

CHAPTER
Business
and
Finance
ELEVEN

Mellon Bank Corporation, 206-209

PNC Bank Corp., 210-213

Federated Investors, 214

Executive Report, 215

ABN AMRO Bank N.V., 216-217

The Travelers Companies, 218-219

Allegheny Business Machines, 220-221

David L. Lawrence Convention Center, 222

Parker/Hunter Incorporated, 223

Integra Financial Corporation, 224-225

Todd Pittsburgh Group, 226-227

Greater Pittsburgh Chamber of Commerce, 228-229

■ *This two-story, 20-foot by 60-foot building in downtown Pittsburgh was Mellon's first banking location.*

Mellon Bank Corporation & Pittsburgh
A Joint Legacy, A Bright Future

With a legacy of innovation and banking leadership, and a clear vision for the future, Mellon Bank Corporation is looking ahead confidently as one of the institutions that will lead the U.S. banking industry into the 21st century.

Formed in Pittsburgh as T. Mellon & Sons' Bank in 1869, Mellon today ranks among the 25 largest bank holding companies in the United States. But it is not size alone that distinguishes Mellon. Through prudent and opportunistic growth, Mellon has broadened its geographic reach as well as its range of financial services businesses and products. In

Mellon Bank Corporation

■ *Through the sophisticated technology on its Capital Markets trading floor, Mellon provides customers with access to financial markets throughout the world.*

doing so, Mellon has created a uniquely diversified banking institution.

Mellon's diversity—in the geographic areas it serves, the products it offers, and the businesses in which it engages—provides strategic balance that reduces risk and provides the flexibility necessary to respond effectively and quickly to the volatile, ever-changing banking environment that is likely to prevail through the balance of this decade and into the next. And, while its growth has

taken it across the United States and around the globe, Mellon remains rooted firmly—and proudly—in Pittsburgh.

Redefining Banking

Today, Mellon retains its historical place among the leading lenders to large businesses and mid-sized companies in the Central Atlantic region, and is a major competitor in consumer and small business lending and deposit services in that region.

At the same time, it has attained leading national positions in businesses such as trust and investment, through which it administers and/or manages the investment of hundreds of billions of dollars in pension and other assets of companies, foundations and individuals; cash management, through which it helps companies manage their cash flows; and mutual fund services, through which it provides recordkeeping and administrative services for hundreds of mutual funds.

By augmenting its traditional lending and deposit services with a broad array of non-lending financial services, Mellon has, in essence, redefined banking.

And history indicates that, for Mellon, this is nothing new.

Where It Started

What today is one of the nation's most important financial institutions began as a private banking house on the first floor of a two-story, 20-foot by 60-foot building in downtown Pittsburgh, whose population at that time had swelled to 86,000.

Its founder was a retired judge and former farm boy from Tyrone County, Ireland. Thomas Mellon was well thought of by the business leaders in the city. They respected and trusted him and, when T. Mellon and Sons opened, were eager to do business with him. By 1872, profits had reached $800,000 and were increasing steadily. Shortly thereafter the bank began financing many of the fledgling companies that eventually would fuel America's Industrial Revolution, thus positioning Pittsburgh as its crucible. People

with imaginative business ideas knew the Judge and sons Andrew and Richard would listen attentively to their plans and give fair consideration to any request for financing.

Before the end of the 19th century, countless companies came into being with financing from Mellon. Among them were the Pittsburgh Reduction Company—which today is known as ALCOA, the world's largest producer of aluminum—and many steel companies which were predecessors of today's leading steel producers. This tradition would endure over time, as Mellon eventually went on to finance key companies in the energy and, later, the airframe industries.

Into The 20th Century

The turn of the century also brought Mellon's conversion from a private bank to a national bank. The result was Mellon National Bank, an institution that, even then, resembled today's modern and more diversified banking companies. Around that same time, the Mellons exchanged an interest in Mellon Bank for shares in the Union Trust Company, which was particularly active in securities underwriting.

In 1923, after 47 years in banking, Andrew Mellon was appointed to serve as Secretary of the Treasury under President

■ *The corporation's signature event, the Mellon Jazz Festival highlights Pittsburgh's rich jazz heritage and provides entertainment for thousands of Pittsburgh area residents.*

Woodrow Wilson, and dedicated the rest of his life to public service. Richard B. Mellon assumed the bank's presidency and, with him at the helm, Mellon continued to grow throughout the 1920's. In 1929, Richard formed Mellbank Corporation, a bank holding company for many western Pennsylvania banks. His foresight in taking this step proved invaluable, as Mellon and the Mellbanks survived the economic crises of the Great Depression era. In fact, even when the governor of Pennsylvania declared a banking holiday on March 4, 1933—and many banks did not open that day or ever again—Mellon remained open for business as usual, quelling fears and serving some 10,000 customers in just over three hours.

After the Depression, the third generation of Mellons took command, as Richard B. Mellon's son, Richard King Mellon, took Mellon's reins and moved it into the modern era of banking.

In 1946, Mellon merged with the Union Trust Company to form Mellon National Bank and Trust Company. It also entered consumer banking by expanding its office locations and merging with the Mellbanks. Mellon's pioneering efforts went on to include the first known installation of a computer by a bank in the mid-1950's; in the 1960's, the creation of branches in London and Tokyo; and its becoming one of the first banks to offer its own credit card.

In 1967, Richard King Mellon retired, and for the first time, someone outside the Mellon family began overseeing the daily operations of the bank. To this day, however, the Mellon family continues to be represented on the

Mellon Bank Corporation board of directors.

In 1972, Mellon National Corporation was formed as a one-bank holding company, and, in 1984, its name was changed to the current Mellon Bank Corporation.

The 1980's

The 1980s was a period of rapid expansion for Mellon, as changes in Pennsylvania banking law enabled it and other Pennsylvania bank holding companies, for the first time, to acquire bank holding companies in other regions of the Commonwealth. Mellon acquired The Girard Company, based in Philadelphia, and CCB Bancorp, based in State College, in 1983; and

Northwest Pennsylvania Corporation, based in Oil City, in 1984. Because The Girard Company owned a bank in Delaware, the acquisition of Girard also gave Mellon its first branch banking presence outside Pennsylvania. In 1986, Mellon acquired the failed Community Savings and Loan of Bethesda, Maryland, providing entry into a third state. Then, capping three busy years on the acquisition front, Mellon acquired Harrisburg-based Commonwealth National Financial Corporation in 1986.

In the late 1980s, Mellon proved itself adept at surmounting the problems that affected virtually every major U.S. banking company at that time.

Under the direction of Chairman Frank V. Cahouet, Mellon rebounded from its first-ever loss in 1987, partly by undertaking a historic transaction through which it shed a substantial portion of its problem loans and recapitalized with the issuance of new stock. This action, and the restructuring of Mellon's businesses, enabled the corporation to resume its growth with the purchase of 54 Philadelphia branch offices in 1990.

Mellon's tradition of innovation continued in 1991, when it introduced supermarket

■ *A national historic landmark, the banking floor of Mellon's main office in downtown Pittsburgh is one of Pennsylvania's busiest banks.*

■ In 1984, Mellon moved its corporate headquarters into this modern 54-story office tower at One Mellon Bank Center in Pittsburgh.

Then, in 1992, Mellon undertook two of the most highly regarded acquisitions in banking that year, announcing its acquisitions of The Boston Company and of the deposits, branches, and most of the assets of Meritor Savings Bank.

The Boston Company, a trust and money-management subsidiary of Shearson Lehman Brothers, furthered Mellon's push into the fee-based trust and investment businesses. Like Mellon, The Boston Company had been a long-standing leader in these businesses, and its merger into Mellon created a position of sustainable leadership in this important area.

The acquisition of the branches of Meritor, which did business in Philadelphia as "Philadelphia Savings Fund Society" put Mellon at the top of the Philadelphia banking market and ensured its ongoing prominence there regardless of future market developments.

Community Commitment

Throughout its history, Mellon Bank Corporation's commitment to the communities it has served has extended beyond the financial products and services it offers. As a responsible corporate citizen, Mellon takes seriously its role in shaping and building strong, prosperous communities in which to live, raise families and do business. Today, Mellon remains firm in this commitment.

Mellon stresses a "total resources" approach to community support, which draws on a balanced mix of cash contributions, employee volunteer time and in-kind donations of goods and services. Included in that approach is Mellon's Gift Program, through which Mellon matches employee's donations to cultural organizations, secondary schools, and colleges and universities; the Mellon Volunteer Professionals (MVPs), an organization of retired Mellon employees who perform thousands of hours of community service; and employee volunteer efforts and contributions to the United Way through payroll deductions. Mellon also sponsors fund-raising and other informational seminars to enable nonprofit organizations to help themselves more effectively.

Mellon carries its total resources philosophy into its sponsorship of community activities and events. Among the most visible is Mellon's annual signature event, the Mellon

banking to western Pennsylvania. The program, which since has spread to other Pennsylvania markets, enables consumers to do their banking seven days a week, on an extended-hours basis, in the convenience of their own supermarket.

That same year Mellon purchased United Penn Bank, based in Wilkes-Barre, and gained a strong presence in northeastern Pennsylvania, one of only two remaining major population centers in the state that it had not served previously.

■ *Retired Judge Thomas Mellon, who was well respected by Pittsburgh business leaders, founded T.Mellon & Sons' Bank in 1869.*

■ *Chairman Frank V. Cahouet led the Mellon turnaround in the late 1980s creating what today is one of the most powerful financial institutions in the nation.*

Jazz Festival. Held in June, the Mellon Jazz Festival brings to the region a multitude of free and ticketed jazz concerts held in public places and venues throughout downtown Pittsburgh and in the surrounding communities.

Mellon also concentrates its corporate support on several primary causes, namely literacy, and housing and business development initiatives in low- to moderate-income neighborhoods.

Mellon's Community Development Corporation (CDC), one of only a handful of bank CDCs nationwide, is continually involved in housing projects with neighbor-

hood community development organizations. In addition to providing technical and management assistance to small businesses, community organizations and public agencies that serve the low- to moderate-income sector, the Mellon CDC also provides credit enhancements which enable organizations and small businesses to secure funding that would not be available through traditional loan products.

Mellon's support of housing and economic development enterprises was established long before the Community Reinvestment Act (CRA) was enacted in 1987. Through Mellon's CRA calling program, branch per-

sonnel are active in meeting with community groups and organizations to assess the needs of the community and develop products and services to meet those needs. In addition, Mellon makes grants to community groups and economic development organizations that promote job creation, urban revitalization and housing development in low- to moderate-income areas.

Into the Future

Strong and growing, Mellon Bank Corporation is in firm control of its destiny and positioned well for the changes that are likely to dominate banking into the next century. Mellon Bank is proud to have played a role in shaping the city's past and looks forward to its continuing community role in defining the city's future.

Like Pittsburgh, Mellon has met the many challenges that have come its way throughout its history and has emerged stronger and more competitive.

In that joint legacy lies bright promise for the future. ◪

■ *Always an innovator, Mellon launched its supermarket banking program in 1990, providing consumers with banking services in high traffic grocery stores seven days a week.*

Banking and watchmaking may be as different as two industries can be, but Thomas H. O'Brien cites an example about watchmakers in which he sees a lesson for bankers.

As the chairman and chief executive officer of PNC Bank Corp. tells it, the Swiss accounted for more than two-thirds of the world's production of watches in the mid-1960s.

Then the Swiss developed quartz technology. It turned out to be one of the biggest breakthroughs in time-keeping since the invention of the mainspring and balance wheel.

Because of the traditional way in which they viewed the making of a watch, the Swiss determined that quartz technology would

PNC Bank Corp.

■ *Thomas H. O'Brien, Chairman and CEO of PNC Bank Corp.*

never sell, "not because it didn't work, but because they wanted to focus on fine-tuning the existing technology," he said.

The Swiss share of the watch market shrunk to around 10 percent.

"They still make very fine watches. They just make fewer of them," O'Brien said.

The relevance of the story stems from the explosion of technology and the deregulation of the financial services industry. Those forces have combined to put banks in competition with stock and bond brokerages. A variety of other forces have combined to put banks in competition with credit unions, finance companies, credit card companies, and even manufacturing companies that issue credit cards.

The moral of the story reverberates through much of what PNC Bank accomplished during its first decade as a bank holding company, and it will undoubtedly echo throughout the organization for years to come.

PNC Bank's chief executive is not one for "blind adherence to the traditional manner in which we look at our problems and conduct our business."

In large part, that explains the level of energy and resources that PNC Bank has devoted to continuously streamlining its organization, developing new services that meet the needs of segmented customer groups and seizing opportunities in the financial services world not only as it exists now, but as it will come to exist in this era of rapid change.

With the rapid consolidation of the nation's 13,000 banks and a frenzy of competition for customers, "Fewer banks will be competing in certain areas of our businesses, but they will become extraordinary competitors with great efficiencies of operations, significantly sharpened marketing skills and the ability to provide consumers with high quality at lower cost," O'Brien said.

Regardless of what the financial services industry looks like in the years ahead, "The benefits will be there only for those institutions positioned to take full advantage of the structural changes in the industry," O'Brien said.

PNC Bank plans to be well positioned.

How it will accomplish that might be gleaned from what PNC Bank is and what it has been doing.

PNC Bank is one of the nation's largest bank holding companies with more than $51 billion in assets. It operates retail, investment management and trust and investment banking businesses in Pennsylvania, Delaware, Ohio, Kentucky and Indiana, and provides corporate banking services to customers across the nation.

Retail banking—traditional checking and savings accounts, car loans and mortgages—is only one part of PNC Bank's business, although an important one.

■ *According to Chairman and CEO Thomas H. O'Brien, bankers can learn a valuable lesson from the Swiss watchmaking industry.*

Headed by A. William Schenck III, executive vice president, PNC Bank's retail line of business serves more than 2 million households and operates more than 550 offices in PNC Bank's five-state region. It also provides banking services to 70,000 small companies.

Five areas within retail banking are being cultivated for significant growth: student loans, credit cards, mortgage banking, credit insurance and securities distribution.

PNC Bank is the retail banking leader in seven of the 14 regional markets in which it operates in those five states.

Corporate banking may be unfamiliar to the general public, but the proprietor of any small business and the chief executive of any major corporation know how crucial a bank can be to a business' success.

Through its corporate banking business, PNC Bank provides financing, investment, administrative and financial advisory services to businesses and government agencies throughout the United States and Canada.

James E. Rohr, president of PNC Bank Corp., heads corporate banking, whose customers include approximately one-third of the 9,000 mid-sized companies in its service area, dominating market share.

■ *PNC Bank's downtown Pittsburgh headquarters.*

■ *Retail banking is only one part of PNC Bank's business.*

Among numerous corporate banking services, PNC Bank is a leader in helping companies manage their cash. PNC Corporate Services, which includes electronic payments and information processing, is a major strength for PNC Bank and an area expected to grow substantially.

A top priority in corporate banking has been careful and systematic attention to credit quality, which encompasses the credit worthiness of corporate borrowers, the viability of the projects and ventures being financed, and the bank's level of exposure in industries that experience boom/bust cycles.

Through its investment management and trust business, headed by Richard C. Caldwell, executive vice president, PNC Bank provides asset management, trust and administrative services to individuals, mutual funds, corporations, municipalities and non-profit institutions. It administers more than $170 billion in assets and has discretionary authority to invest $58 billion of that amount.

PNC Bank is the sixth-largest bank money manager in the U.S., one of the largest trustees for individuals, and is the largest U.S. bank manager of mutual funds.

Some 300 mutual funds with 2.6 million shareholders and assets exceeding $70 billion rely on PNC Bank for mutual fund services. It leads the industry in encouraging corporations to use mutual funds to manage liquid assets.

PNC Bank also sells its economic and investment research to more than 225 institutions, including other banks, brokerage firms, insurance companies and pension funds.

PNC Bank's objective is to leverage its size and capabilities to become the leading provider of investment management services among all U.S. banks.

PNC Bank's fourth major line of business is investment banking, which includes PNC Securities, PNC Corporate Finance, PNC Equity Management Corp. and the management of the bank's own funds.

The business is led by Joe R. Irwin, executive vice president and chief investment officer.

Through its broker/dealer subsidiary, PNC Securities, the bank was one of the first holding companies in the country authorized to participate in origination, trading and distribution of various securities. It is one of the largest bank underwriters of revenue bonds for education and the health care industry.

It also provides full service retail brokerage services through 10 offices in Delaware, Kentucky, Ohio and Pennsylvania, and operates one of the nation's largest low-cost brokerage services.

Most recently, PNC Securities launched the PNC Family of Funds, 16 mutual funds offering a diverse range of investment opportunities.

PNC Corporate Finance provides loan syndication, acquisition financing, private placements, mergers and acquisition advisory services, and structured financing to corporate customers.

Of the elements that make up the investment banking line, asset and liability management—or management of PNC Bank's investment portfolio and its attendant interest rate risk—is by far the largest part.

The link that bonds the four lines of business described above is PNC Bank's determination for finding ways to deliver financial services of the highest possible quality to individuals, corporations—even other banks, at the lowest possible cost.

That's hard to do for any company unless management can reliably estimate its costs in providing any one service, which bankers like to call "products."

"You can't manage what you can't measure, and the banking industry has never been able to measure the performance of its products or businesses to our satisfaction," O'Brien said.

Surprising as it may seem, most banks cannot describe in accurate detail how much money, if any, they make in providing checking accounts to retail customers.

The reasons have to do with the web of complex relationships between the costs of acquiring funds, processing data, handling paper checks, and building, maintaining, and staffing branch offices, among other things.

A company such as PNC Bank that operates in diverse communities and multiple states must be able to quantify information about market conditions and customers in order to deliver its products and services with maximum effect.

■ *Chartered in 1864, The First National Bank of Pittsburgh was formerly on the PNC Bank building site.*

With that awareness, PNC Bank set out in the mid-1980s to design and build a computer system that can drill down through massive layers of data to pinpoint costs, identify trends, and thereby serve in designing low-cost, high-quality banking services.

The system is driven from a single, state-of-the-art data processing center that PNC Bank built in the airport corridor west of its downtown Pittsburgh headquarters.

Not only does the new center allow PNC Bank to consolidate data processing centers that came with its acquisition of other banks, but it was also built to support a bank of twice PNC Bank's current size, giving an indication of the bank's ambitions.The resources that the center provides have played a major role in supporting PNC Bank's pioneering shift from geographic organization to that of line-of-business, and in quantifying a management profitability system that has brought the bank's "best practices" to the fore throughout its service area.

These initiatives represent fundamental changes in the way PNC Bank will conduct its business in the "slow-growth, highly competitive banking environment we foresee through the balance of this decade," O'Brien said.

More important, they give PNC Bank what it believes are the means and the vision to succeed in a turbulent era of regulatory change and fierce competition. That view is more than just fodder for annual reports. It carries considerable weight with customers,

for whom financial strength and stability are major criteria in choosing a bank.

Such achievements promise to strengthen what is already one of the leanest, most efficient banking organizations in the country.

While asset size ranked PNC Bank the 10th-largest banking company in the United States by the end of 1992, its performance by almost every significant measure exceeded that of many of its much larger competitors.

The company has historically had a profit margin nearly double that of the industry (20.5 cents compared with 13.8). That kind of performance gives PNC Bank greater flexibility to grow its lines of business and undertake long-term initiatives to bolster not only its profitability but also the quality and value of the financial services it brings to customers.

"This comparative advantage puts us in a very attractive position," O'Brien said.

Flexibility has also allowed PNC Bank to continually fine-tune the services it provides, as well as create new ones.

In corporate banking, for example, the company introduced "Working Cash," an electronic cash management service that gives small businesses quick access to financial information directly from the bank's computers, and a trust-related 401(k) program for mid-sized companies.

To date, it has launched a total of 11 regional banking centers offering services previously available only at bank headquarters. Among them are small business services, trust, securities and private banking. More than 40 such regional banking centers are planned across the bank's service area.

Robinson Town Banking Centre was the first of its kind in the Pittsburgh region. Its quick success spawned a second regional center in the North Hills, where the striking architecture and full-service banking features were replicated on McKnight Road.

PNC Bank's automated office at Pittsburgh International Airport is another result of the company's internally driven technology. A showcase of banking technology, it quickly became a magnet for travelers who enjoy, among other things, the convenience of the bank's new ATMs, which can cash checks to the penny.

■ *PNC Bank designed the Airport Banking Center with customers from all its markets in mind.*

■ *Robinson Town Banking Centre offers services previously available only at bank headquarters.*

■ *PNC Bank's computer system is driven from a single state-of-the-art data processing center.*

Customers can call up stock quotes and news stories on a computer-based data system, open accounts, transact business and apply for a car loan or a mortgage. Instead of dealing with traditional teller lines or platform officers, customers at the Airport branch deal with Financial Services Advisors who offer assistance to customers, guiding them through the electronic transactions. The use of advanced technology permits the bank to be staffed 80 hours a week—twice the usual branch hours—which would not be economical for a traditional branch.

Because the Airport is designed as a hub, with Pittsburgh as a transfer point for 65 percent of the traffic, PNC Bank designed the Airport Banking Center with customers from all its markets in mind. And, because USAir is the major carrier in many PNC Bank markets, the unique Airport branch serves existing customers from Louisville to Philadelphia and attracts potential customers, who may encounter for the first time at the Airport the capabilities of PNC Bank.

Throughout the PNC Bank organization, technology has given rise to a network of personal computers that puts information at the fingertips of the company's bankers for the convenience of customers.

Under its line-of-business management, PNC Bank took a function that was performed within its retail banking operations—the processing of automated teller machines (ATM)

and point-of-sale (POS) transactions—and spun it off into a new source of revenue.

The new venture, Electronic Payment Systems, Inc., is one of the nation's largest processors of ATM and POS transactions. The company is a joint venture among PNC Bank and three other banking companies: Banc One, CoreStates and Society.

The joint venture represents about 1,400 financial institutions with 13,000 ATMs serving 26 million cardholders in 16 states, primarily in the Mid-Atlantic and Midwest.

The configuration of PNC Bank and the direction it is taking have put it a long way from the world of banking that existed in 1852 when two giants of the steel industry, B.F. Jones and James Laughlin, joined with other investors in founding the Pittsburgh Trust and Savings Company.

Two years later, the organization moved into quarters at Fifth Avenue and Wood Street, where PNC Bank is based to this day.

Pittsburgh Trust was chartered as the First National Bank of Pittsburgh in 1864. A number of bank combinations and name changes occurred between then and 1959, when Pittsburgh National Bank was created in the merger of Peoples First National Bank and Trust Company and Fidelity Trust Company.

Pittsburgh National began with 52 offices and less than $1 billion in assets.

PNC Bank's predecessor, PNC Financial Corp, was born in 1983 with the merger of Pittsburgh National Corporation and Provident National Corporation in Philadelphia.

The new bank holding company quickly earned a reputation among investors as an engine of profitability, and in the marketplace, as a leader in banking technology and customer service.

Since then, the opportunities for growth through acquisition have proliferated and PNC Bank has participated on an active, but disciplined basis.

"I know that the years ahead will continue to present us with increasing economic, competitive, and regulatory pressures," O'Brien said. "But I believe that we are positioned to respond to these pressures."

By 1993, PNC Bank had so efficiently integrated the operations of its growing family of affiliate banks that the decision was made to deliver the resources of the $51 billion organization under a single, unified name. Hence, the holding company as well as its affiliates became known as PNC Bank.

"I've told our employees I believe we have a unique opportunity to create something special here—for them, for our customers, and for our shareholders," O'Brien said. "I'm excited about the future."

Federated Investors

Many may believe that New York is the financial capital of the Western world, but the founders of Federated Investors know better.

From headquarters in an office tower in downtown Pittsburgh, Federated's 1,400 employees comprise one of the largest money management organizations in the nation, with more than $70 billion in assets under management. As a major supplier of mutual funds and other related investment products to financial intermediaries, chances are good that many people who have invested money through a bank or a broker have done business with Federated.

"Being located in Pittsburgh is a plus. I can assure you, no one in New York can compete with us. You cannot find better employees than the people of the Pittsburgh area to entrust with the management of major financial assets or to provide the services that we offer," said Glen R. Johnson, President of Federated's MultiTrust® Systems.

Two-thirds of Federated's business comes from supplying investment products—U.S. government, municipal, corporate bond, money market, and equity funds—to bank trust departments. Those institutions, in turn, are able to provide additional services to their customers with efficiencies unachievable on their own.

"We simplify the lives of the institutions that use our funds. We improve their performance and greatly increase their profitability," Johnson said. "While we started in the 1970s by just managing their cash, now trust departments can rely on us to handle most of their investments and to do it much more efficiently than they ever could on their own."

Federated rose rapidly from humble beginnings. John F. Donahue started the firm in 1955 by selling mutual funds person to person. He and his partner, Richard B. Fisher, distributed prospectuses on the streets of downtown Pittsburgh and sold stock mutual funds to individual investors across kitchen tables.

"Jack's dream was that everybody ought to own a piece of corporate America," Johnson said. Both Donahue and Fisher still actively run the firm, and Federated now serves individual investors across the nation through its relationships with more than 3,500 financial institutions around the country.

Many of Federated's responses to investment opportunities have shaped the financial services industry. In 1969, for example, Federated created the first mutual fund to give individual investors access to U.S. government securities. In 1974, it helped lead the way in developing money market mutual funds.

Federated created the first tax-free money market fund in 1979, and, in 1986, introduced the first fund to invest primarily in variable rate demand notes. Always the pioneer, Federated also developed the amortized cost method of accounting, which enables money market mutual fund shares to maintain a $1.00 per share value.

While Federated has made a name for itself serving bank trust departments, a large portion of its business also comes from providing investment products and services to broker/dealers and from helping to manage pension funds, including components of 401(k) plans, for some of the country's largest corporations.

Contributing to the company's success is the latest in data technology, much of which Federated developed to meet its special needs. Federated introduced the mutual fund industry's first on-line order entry system and is a leader in supplying advanced systems that support the growing 401(k) retirement market.

Federated views the future as one rich in opportunity. "Mutual funds are the wave of the future," said Johnson. "Right now, about one out of every four households owns a mutual fund in an industry that is soon to exceed $1.3 trillion. By the year 2000, mutual funds will be owned by one out of two households. Right there you have a doubling effect. It's the place to be."

But product and computer software aside, Federated considers its main advantage over the competition to be its people.

"Compare the people in New York and those who work in Pittsburgh, and we have a whole set of different circumstances," said Johnson. "We have people who care."

Federated Investors, headquartered in downtown Pittsburgh, is one of the largest money management organizations in the nation.

Executive Report magazine is celebrating its 12th anniversary covering the business scene in the Pittsburgh region. The magazine, under the auspices of its current publisher and president, Linda A. Dickerson, who took full ownership of the publication in 1986, has developed into the leader of local business publications with more than 80,000 business readers monthly. This represents more than double the number of subscribers of any other area business publication.

The editorial focus includes profiles of Pittsburgh corporations and the individuals that shape and shake the business community along with updates which target specific industries. Among the key issues analyzed and investigated have been leadership, metropolitanism, education, and high-performance manufacturing.

In addition to award-winning hardcore business journalism, the pages of Executive Report also feature many of the lifestyle aspects of its executive readers. The Pittsburgh Golf section, featured monthly between March and October, covers the rich tradition of the game in southwestern Pennsylvania.

The magazine's readers are primarily comprised of middle-and upper-level managers of corporations and business owners. More than 80% of Executive Report's sub-

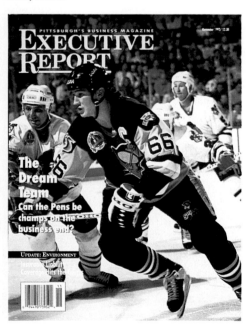

■ Features such as the business side of the local sports teams keeps **Executive Report** fresh and interesting to its 80,000 monthly readers.

scribers are in the these categories. This targeted, affluent, managerial audience is obtained through a rigid, quality controlled circulation process audited annually by the Business Publications Audit (BPA).

But don't be deceived by the name Executive Report. Sixty percent of the magazines subscribers are from companies with less than 100 employees. The editors are quite cognizant of this fact and small business coverage receives special and regular attention in the magazine.

Some results of this attentiveness are that in 1986 the magazine's publisher, Linda Dickerson, was elected as a delegate to the White House Conference on Small Business. In 1989 she was named the Small Business Administration's (SBA) Media Advocate of the Year in the district, state and Mid-Atlantic Region. Also in 1989, Linda was named the NAWBO/YWCA Woman Entrepreneur Honoree. The magazine has co-sponsored the SBA Awards since 1991 and publishes an annual section devoted to the winners.

To meet the needs of the region Executive Report has begun to diversify through contract publishing ventures. In 1992, in conjunction with the Allegheny County Commissioner's office, the magazine published The Pittsburgh International Airport Commemorative Book, an 80-page book celebrating the new airport's opening. In 1993 the magazine's expert staff will continue these efforts by publishing the Westinghouse-Family House Golf Invitational Program. This tournament is the richest charity event in the nation with over $700,000 in prize money attracting the PGA's top professionals to Pittsburgh.

Community service is a major component of the Executive Report infrastructure. Linda Dickerson holds more than 20 board directorships and chairs or co-chairs as many as seven of those at one time. The boards include The United Way, Junior Achievement, The Pittsburgh Ballet, Community College of Allegheny County and Point Park College to name a few. The magazine contributes more than $65,000 per year in gratuitous advertising for non-profit organizations.

Executive Report also publishes several supplements on behalf of charitable organizations including The United Way, A Case for Involvement, Junior Achievement's Business

■ Strong corporate profiles have been a trademark for **Executive Report.**

Executive Report

Hall of Fame, Public Relations Society of America (Pittsburgh chapter) Renaissance Awards, and in 1993 will introduce the Performing Arts Preview.

The magazine co-produces the Pittsburgh Best Deal Awards with Price Waterhouse honoring the deals and dealmakers that have had a significant impact on the Pittsburgh region. Executive Report also produces the ER Live for Literacy events which benefit organizations involved with literacy awareness including The Greater Pittsburgh Literacy Council and The United Way, the Carnegie Library/Point Park College Library development fund, and in 1993 the Community College of Allegheny County.

Executive Report is committed to providing the finest business journalism in a high quality environment for its readers. The magazine will continue to forge ahead as the leader in local business journalism and service to the Pittsburgh community. An integral part of our mission will always be to promote the economic vitality and development of this region. Executive Report is published for Pittsburghers by Pittsburghers.

Like their predecessors, who three centuries ago projected Dutch commercial power around the world from a base in Amsterdam, the bankers in the Pittsburgh office of ABN AMRO support regional corporations with the resources of a $250 billion institution that encircles the globe.

"We've found that one of the factors that distinguishes ABN AMRO is our ability to work simultaneously with U.S.-based companies and their overseas subsidiaries, partners, and customers," said Lee D. Cutrone, Jr., senior vice president and manager of ABN AMRO's banking center at One PPG Place, Downtown.

ABN AMRO Bank N.V.

ABN AMRO is one of the world's oldest and largest banks. With assets exceeding $250 billion in 1993, the Amsterdam-based organization ranked among the world's top 20 banks.

The bank has 50,000 employees among its more than 1,850 locations in 55 countries. Capital of $18 billion and an Aa1 credit rating give ABN AMRO strength and stability that few banks can match.

Through a strong presence in Europe, North America, Central and South America, the Middle East, the Far East, and Australia, ABN AMRO delivers extensive services, including lending, foreign exchange and risk management, access to capital markets, international corporate finance and consulting, syndication, trade finance, cash management, corporate trust, investment management, private banking, and leasing.

"We can make all of those capabilities work for our corporate customers through our Pittsburgh branch," Cutrone said.

The flagship of Dutch banking also stands apart in other ways that matter, especially to corporations that take a long-term approach to international business opportunities.

■ *Lee D. Cutrone, Jr.*
Senior Vice President and Manager
ABN AMRO Bank N.V.
Pittsburgh Branch.

"Many international banks have been consolidating their overseas operations. The reasons vary, but include difficulties they've encountered in one place or another," Cutrone said. "We've continued to expand and strengthen ABN AMRO's global network in step with the needs of the major corporations that are our customers."

That distinction reflects ABN AMRO's approach to global banking.

U.S. banks, with the exception of a few money center banks, pursue international banking through divisions that emerged as separate entities from the core organization.

"In a number of cases the international divisions could be turned on and turned off and a number of banks did that, in fact, over the past decade," Cutrone said.

But, global banking is part and parcel of ABN AMRO.

The bank can trace its antecedents to the Dutch East India Company some 300 years ago. The origins of the bank itself date to 1824 when the Dutch King Willem I founded the Nederlandsche Handel-Maatschappij, a trading company that was the forerunner of Algemene Bank Nederland, or ABN.

ABN AMRO Bank N.V. was formed on September 22, 1991, as the result of a merger between two of the Netherlands' largest banks, ABN Bank and Amsterdam-Rotterdam Bank, or AMRO.

Entering the merger, ABN and AMRO were both major international financial institutions with strong reputations in both the Dutch domestic market and international markets.

The bank has 10 U.S. branch offices: Atlanta, Boston, Chicago, Houston, Los Angeles, Miami, New York, Pittsburgh, San Francisco, and Seattle. Chicago is ABN AMRO's North American Headquarters with treasury and other specialty services centered primarily there or in New York.

Other major U.S. subsidiaries and affiliates are LaSalle National Corp. in Chicago, LaSalle Trust, European American Bank in Uniondale, New York, and ABN AMRO Securities (USA), Inc. of New York.

The U.S. operation alone, with $37 billion in assets and approximately 8,000 employees, ranks as one of the largest banks in the country.

ABN AMRO began banking in the United States in 1941, before most European banks became active in North America.

Although it has offices in the nation's most prominent corporate centers, ABN AMRO's character is more like that of the Midwest, where its U.S. operations are directed.

"The United States is like ABN AMRO's second home, and in the United States, the Midwest has always been the center of our growth. Pittsburgh's business culture also tends to be more similar to that of the Midwest than the East," Cutrone said.

ABN AMRO opened its Pittsburgh office in 1978, just in time for the wrenching shift in the region's economic base from heavy manufacturing to diversified industries with a much broader, service-oriented segment.

"The bank looked at what Pittsburgh was experiencing and said, 'We'll stay,' " said Cutrone.

"ABN AMRO is well into its second century, and we've been in the U.S. for more than half a century. This organization has always been reluctant to make decisions based on short-term considerations."

Having stood by its customers through the economic transition of the 1980s, the Pittsburgh organization sees solid prospects for continued growth in its market area, which reaches from Pennsylvania into Ohio, West Virginia, and Kentucky.

The city's location, within a brief plane ride of approximately half of the nation's population, is also a major benefit, he said. The opening of a new terminal complex at Pittsburgh International Airport will only enhance the advantage of Pittsburgh's position on the U.S. map.

Another fundamental strength of the region is the university community that has contributed to growth in a number of areas, especially in medical sciences and high technology.

"We think this area will continue to experience strong stability and growth that is slow to moderate, but controlled," Cutrone said. "We don't expect to see the boom-bust cycles that are applauded one day and bemoaned the next. Pittsburgh is fortunate in that regard. We no longer get pneumonia when the national economy gets a cold."

"The region's economic diversity has arrived in part on the back of companies that have grown their businesses in the global market, an initiative that ABN AMRO is particularly well equipped to support," Cutrone said.

■ ABN AMRO Pittsburgh's management team. Back row, left to right: Roy D. Hasbrook, Lee D. Cutrone, Jr., Dennis F. Lennon Front row, left to right: Shirley K. Kersten, Kathryn C. Toth, James M. Janovsky.

In fact, ABN AMRO's export finance services for North America are conducted through the Pittsburgh office.

"Our specialty is not the everyday brand of trade finance, like the standard letter of credit business. Of course we do that through any of our branches. Our strengths in export finance include structuring the export of large-ticket capital goods that range anywhere from several million dollars to several hundred million dollars," Cutrone said. "The market served by the Pittsburgh office includes some of the largest capital goods exporters in the entire United States."

The primary thrust of ABN AMRO in the United States is corporate banking services for Fortune 1000 companies. ABN AMRO also works with companies with annual sales of at least $200 million wherever there is a good match between the client's needs and the bank's capabilities.

"We want to understand where the client is going as a company, how they are structured, and whether or not we can bring to bear new ideas to improve performance. We are solution oriented. Does the balance sheet need restructuring? With support of our capital markets teams located in the U.S. and worldwide, we may offer attractive alternatives appropriate for your particular situation," Cutrone said.

ABN AMRO also expects the Pittsburgh region to continue attracting smaller businesses than the behemoths that dominated the economy in the past but whose diversity strengthens the regional economy.

"Although a lot of banks make the claim, ABN AMRO truly operates from the basis of client relationships. Our primary mission is not to make loans. Strong, ongoing relationships are the pillar of our business," Cutrone remarked.

■ *The Taking Care program is one of several award-winning wellness programs being used as models for the nation.*

When The Travelers began introducing the Taking Care employee wellness program, skeptical companies demanded proof that the young program worked and would cut health care costs.

That was yesterday. Today, the benefits of being "under The Travelers' umbrella" are apparent and abundant.

With Taking Care in place at numerous companies in Pittsburgh and around the country, human resources professionals are sold on the benefits of encouraging better health and informed use of health care services among employees.

The program is a key element in The Travelers' system of managed care, the benefits of which are enjoyed by more than 16,000 members in the Greater Pittsburgh area employed by dozens of local companies, both large and small.

The Travelers, which opened a full-service office serving western Pennsylvania in the 1950s, has been a leader in fulfilling the insurance needs of area residents since the time of the Civil War.

It wasn't long ago that the term "managed care" was as unfamiliar to people as "glasnost," "aerobics," and "cablevision."

Nevertheless, forces have been at work for years that would bring the term into wide-

The Travelers Companies

A cost-benefit analysis showed that in its own use of Taking Care, The Travelers achieved a return of $3.40 for every dollar it spent on the program. The savings totaled $7.8 million in one year.

The Taking Care program, recipient of the first annual C. Everett Koop National Health Award, is one of several award-winning wellness programs being used as models for the nation, helping make U.S. health care resources more cost-efficient and effective and health improvement programs more available.

■ *The Travelers' system of managed care help make U.S. health care resources more cost-efficient and effective.*

spread use among the business, medical, and insurance communities. Managed care has evolved into a force of its own, and those who understand it are in a position to revolutionize the health and productivity of the American worker.

Until fairly recently, American medicine was almost entirely a cottage industry. Thousands of practitioners served a steadily growing, increasingly affluent market. Yet few patients knew much about the services they used. People tended to accept the decisions of their doctors without question.

In the 1940s, health maintenance organizations, or HMOs, arrived on the scene. For a fixed price, HMOs provided groups of employees or private individuals with a specified set of health services. Attention was paid to controlling costs of individual treatments, but it wasn't until recently that they concentrated on when and how treatments were administered and how patients and their dependents could make the best use of the system.

The next step towards managed care came about in the early 1980s. Employers and insurance companies focused on clamping down on escalating hospital costs through a process known as utilization review. It required that employees have their medical needs reviewed by the insurer before the costs of treatment would be approved.

Once again, employers saw certain costs decline. But they also saw others start rising while employee morale went down. Standing on its own, utilization review frequently gave employees the impression that their access to health care was being blocked by their employer's concerns with the bottom line. Disputes abounded.

The Travelers recognized that something was missing from all these plans. HMOs and utilization review seemed most effective for controlling certain narrow sets of costs. They did little for other costs, such as those stemming from low worker morale and high benefits administration costs.

"In the 1980s, we began to see that we'd only been chipping away at the problem," said Paul Glover, who was at that time senior vice president for The Travelers Managed Care & Employee Benefits Operations. "We had been working in the right direction, but we needed a more comprehensive solution."

Comprehensive solutions start with broader visions. Travelers set about designing a "win-win" system to satisfy each segment of the health care equation: the doctors and hospitals on the supply side and employers, employees and their families on the demand side.

Employers needed to start getting more for their benefit plan investments to control skyrocketing expenses and satisfy employees and dependents.

"We realized focusing on costs alone wasn't enough. The real goal, the one that would benefit everyone concerned, was improving the health and the productivity of the workers and their families," Glover said.

For employees, The Travelers developed a wide-ranging, flexible package of programs, going far beyond calculating the risks and paying the costs of medical bills. Included are the educational programs designed to help people lead healthier, more productive lives, and services to help them differentiate between times they need to seek professional medical help and times when they could effectively care for themselves. Other programs turn them into more knowledgeable consumers of health care so that they can make better decisions in partnership with their physicians.

Still other Travelers' programs work to speed recovery, so that employees can more quickly begin enjoying the fruits of restored health and productivity. To see that the quality care is needed, the company works with carefully selected networks of physicians, hospitals, and other treatment facilities in hundreds of communities across the country. Supporting and supervising those networks on a local basis are Travelers' own team of physicians, nurses, and other certified medical professionals.

In western Pennsylvania, nearly two dozen hospitals participate in The Travelers managed-care system, including Children's, Mercy, Magee-Womens, Forbes Regional Health Center, St. Clair, and Washington. Employees of dozens of local companies under The Travelers' red umbrella receive care at lower cost if they go to one of the network hospitals or one of the hundreds of participating physicians.

■ *The Travelers' goal is to improve the health and the productivity of the workers and their families.*

"The supply side of the equation needs just as much TLC as the demand side," Glover said. "We want the best professionals and institutions within our system, and we work hard to attract them and keep them with Travelers."

Beyond the large numbers of employees and dependents Travelers steers toward its networks, the company also makes it easier for network members to treat patients and to be paid for their work.

Travelers, a multibillion dollar company based in Hartford, Connecticut, providing employee benefits and managed care to millions of Americans, has its own staff of medical professionals around the country who work with the local networks. The company is developing ways to help physicians and hospitals learn more about the costs and effectiveness of their treatment strategies and to compare their approaches with other professionals.

The benefits employers enjoy from managed care extend beyond the bottom line. First, workers who spend less time worrying about their health and that of their dependents are more productive. They see their benefits plans as true benefits; something that enhances the quality of their lives. Companies spend less time dealing with questions and complaints, thanks to quality networks, smoothly operating reimbursement systems and responsive, local medical management teams.

■ *The benefits of being "under The Travelers' umbrella" are abundant.*

For the future, people in the managed-care field see technology leading to new linkages and even higher levels of service. "We can't stand still," said Glover. "The competitive pressures on American companies are multiplying."

Many business leaders are concerned about the way demographics and declining educational levels are shrinking the American talent pool. Smarter, more motivated employees will be in greater demand.

In that kind of environment, comprehensive managed-care systems like the one offered by The Travelers promise to bring the benefits of better health and productivity to the American work force and to their employers as well.

■ *The Cornerstone of ABM —On-Site Service Training Facility.*

Allegheny Business Machines was founded on the belief that the future of the office machine industry belonged to those who offered the best technology and supported their customers with the highest-quality service.

That principle served the company well as it blazed a trail on the way to becoming the Pittsburgh region's leading source of office equipment. And if ABM's growth and success in the early 1990s are any measure, that founding principle will prove to be very durable as the company rolls out enhanced services, such as facilities management, and new technology, such as multifunction office machines, to meet the evolving needs of the regional business community.

and train them and their employees."

It was by design, then, that Allegheny Business Machines pioneered new levels of service through full-time customer support personnel.

What started as a good idea became a tradition that continues to drive ABM in new directions to deliver greater value in technology and service.

ABM was founded in 1975 as a branch operation of Canon USA. Mattola purchased the company in 1981 and applied his insight and innovation in ground-breaking areas

America's best selling lines of photocopiers and facsimile equipment, including plain paper laser technology. Canon is also the world leader in laser printer technology.

Alco Standard operates North America's largest network of office equipment dealers. It is one of the largest service companies on the Fortune 500. Alco Standard has more than 25,000 employees worldwide and sales of 6 billion. Its Office Products Division, whose employees number in excess of 10,000, places tens of thousands of photocopiers annually and generates sales in excess of $2 billion per year.

Allegheny Business Machines

ABM's philosophy has its roots in the experiences of its president, Guy Mattola, more than 30 years ago. As a young technician servicing office equipment, Mattola realized that many of the problems he was fixing stemmed from a lack of training and understanding on the part of the people operating the machines.

"I vowed that if I ever got my own business, I'd hire someone to follow up with customers after the sale, answer their questions,

■ *The ABM Commitment — People...Product...Performance.*

such as customer service and support. ABM has grown substantially through the years and is widely recognized as the authority in the sales and service of photocopying, color graphics, micrographics and optical disk, facsimile, and related products in the Canon family of technologically advanced office equipment.

By the early 1990s, ABM, now a division of Alco Standard Corp., employed 140 individuals as annual sales were rising by double-digit percentages.

Canon USA was growing, too. From a small office in New York City, staffed by just five people in 1955, the organization became a family of companies with more than 8,500 employees and an extensive network of sales offices, dealers, and manufacturing facilities spanning North America.

The Canon-ABM-Alco Standard connection represents a powerful resource for the business community.

Named "Manufacturer of the Year" for two years running by the National Office Machine Dealers Association, Canon manufactures what is widely recognized as

ABM combines the Canon heritage for high-quality, cost-effective technology and the financial strength and market reach of Alco Standard, supported locally by the service-oriented members of the ABM team who know best the needs of companies in the Pittsburgh region.

ABM's relationship with Alco Standard is cemented with the shared expertise of the more than 50 companies that are part of the Office Products Division. Through monthly statistical compilations, periodic technical seminars, and other links, every operating unit is able to deliver the service excellence of the nationwide network.

"Our customers come back again and again because we provide solutions and comprehensive service. We're able to do that in part because our customers trust our products and our advice, and when they talk to us, we listen," Mattola said.

Those principles underlie nearly every aspect of ABM, including employee attitudes.

"We involve all of our employees in team-building sessions that help improve our effectiveness in our relationships as fellow employees and as members of a unified team working for our customers," said Steve Fedell, vice president of Allegheny Business Machines.

Training is the cornerstone of employee performance at ABM. In 1992, for example, the company invested two man-years of training in service personnel alone.

"I'd venture to say there's not another dealership that comes near that level of investment in training its personnel, and that translates into unparalleled service and customer satisfaction," said Controller Bob Scheer.

Unlike other dealers, ABM has two full-time, factory-certified instructors on its staff to assure that ABM technicians have access to continuous on-site training.

"Typically, dealerships will send one or two technicians out for factory training and have them come back and attempt to train the rest of the staff," Mattola said. "That's okay for as far as it goes. The expertise that we've obtained through on-site, factory-authorized training for every technician has enabled ABM to deliver a level of service that has allowed us to place more equipment as well as attract and retain more customers than any other dealer in the area."

It's no surprise then that while the national average service life for a business copier is under three and a half years, the equipment of ABM's customers has a demonstrated working life that exceeds six years on average.

"As we start our 19th year in business, we have equipment that's been in use at customers' sites for 8, 10, 11 years, producing millions of copies. That's unheard of in this business," Mattola said.

"With few exceptions, there are not many companies that can claim to have a machine with millions of copies on it. We have scores

of them. That's a testament as much to the service we provide and the attention we give to our customers as it is to the quality of Canon equipment."

Proof of ABM's preeminence is its relationships with more major corporations than any other dealer in the Pittsburgh region. In a continuation of its leadership role in improving office productivity, ABM is introducing these corporations as well as other business entities to the concept of facilities management, or the outsourcing of noncore business operations.

"Corporations are asking themselves why they should lock up their resources, their people, their money, and their equipment operating a business in which they are not experts," Fedell said.

Increasingly, major customers find that it pays to have the specialists at ABM run their copy centers.

For companies that need on-site capability, ABM helps contain costs by improving equipment up-time and utilization rates.

"In most cases, we can do the work faster. Equally important, by managing their facilities for them, we

■ *ABM Headquarters— Strategically located in the Pittsburgh metro area.*

■ *Canon Technology in Review ... A demonstration of high end productivity.*

provide the customer with almost unlimited flexibility in rapidly adjusting to changes in the size, configuration, and staffing of their organization," Fedell said.

For the 1990s and beyond, Allegheny Business Machines is leading the way with multifaceted machines such as copier/laser printers that connect to office computer networks, receive data from personal computers, and print, collate, staple, and copy. Technology will find photocopiers evolving into equipment that scans prototype documents, from hard copy or from computer files, and duplicates on demand.

Because ABM recognizes that not all customers need the same level of service and shouldn't have to pay for more than they need, an array of service packages is available.

Rather than leave the utilization of equipment to chance, ABM developed systems that analyze customers' needs and allow ABM to recommend changes that will fill their needs precisely without waste.

"It all goes back to understanding your product and listening to your customer," Mattola said. "That's one aspect of our business that will never change no matter how fast the technology advances."

Imagine planning a dinner party for thousands of guests, preparing for a visit from the President of the United States, supervising the building of a two-story, landscaped house in just three days, arranging the setup of a full-court basketball tournament, or coordinating the details of several meetings being held simultaneously. This and much more is all in a day's work at the David L. Lawrence Convention Center.

Versatility is a key feature at the center, which has the capacity to accommodate a variety of events ranging from an intimate meeting for 10 to a grand banquet for 4,000 to a general session for 8,600. The exhibit area has 131,000 square feet of exhibit

The mission of the center is to serve as a catalyst for attracting national, regional, and local events to Pittsburgh for the purpose of strengthening Allegheny County's economy. As a mid-sized facility, the center traditionally

■ *The Lawrence Convention Center is conveniently connected to the Vista International Hotel via a glass-enclosed skywalk. The marquee displays information about upcoming and current events being held in the building. Photo by Gene J. Puskar.*

David L. Lawrence Convention Center

space, providing the perfect setting for public shows, conventions, trade shows, and banquets.

When most people think of a convention center they often think of large scale events. But, that is not always the case. In addition to the exhibit area, the center has 25 comfortable, soundproof function rooms which are suitable for virtually any business meeting or social event, large or small. Other features include in-house catering, sophisticated audiovisual equipment and services, teleconferencing, ample indoor parking, and a convenient downtown Pittsburgh location.

■ *North Meeting Room 1*
Some of the third level meeting rooms provide spectacular views of Pittsburgh's Northside, rivers, and bridges. Photo by Gene J. Puskar.

has been most successful at attracting national religious meetings and conferences focusing on the steel, glass, and aluminum industries. Local public shows are also key revenue-generators for Allegheny County.

"The center's success can be attributed to the energy and commitment of the staff," said Executive Director James M. Kiesel. "Most people see only the finished product of an event and don't realize the scope and magnitude of details that need to be meticulously coordinated to insure its success. Our staff knows how to pull it all together and that is why they are by far our biggest asset."

The center was named after David Leo Lawrence, one of Pittsburgh's most powerful and prominent urban politicians. Known as the "people's politician," Lawrence devoted his 50-year career to uniting Pittsburgh's business community to bring about the much acclaimed Pittsburgh Renaissance, one of America's most successful urban projects. It is only fitting that a facility which was built to serve the Pittsburgh community should bear the name of this legendary politician. Lawrence would be pleased to know that his namesake has served the community in

many ways, not only as an economic engine, but also by opening its doors to blood drives, food banks, and disaster relief programs.

In operation since 1981, the center is governed by the Public Auditorium Authority, a five-person board comprised of officials who are appointed jointly by the Mayor of Pittsburgh and the Allegheny County Commissioners. The board is responsible for setting policy and overseeing the center's operating procedures.

The Greater Pittsburgh Convention and Visitors Bureau serves as the center's national and regional marketing agent, while the center's staff focuses on promoting the facility locally. "This system eliminates duplication of efforts and enables the center's staff to concentrate on client relations, local marketing, and operations," said Kiesel.

The center has made great strides in recent years, and consistently strives to stay progressive and make improvements. For instance, plans are underway to extensively renovate the meeting rooms and common areas of the facility. Additionally, a newly installed energy management system will more efficiently control the building's operations.

"We are continually reviewing existing policies, expanding services, and developing more innovative marketing packages," said Kiesel. "We believe this will give us the edge we will need to stay on top in this competitive industry." ▣

■ *"At Parker/Hunter, we all work towards a common goal, which is to create and preserve wealth for our clients by responding promptly and professionally to their financial needs and objectives," says Robert W. Kampmeinert-Chairman and Chief Executive Officer.*

Investing and managing money wisely requires skill, knowledge of the financial markets, and most importantly, an understanding of the individual or business whose funds are being invested.

For almost a quarter of a century, Parker/Hunter Incorporated has been working with individual and corporate clients, providing them with a full range of investment products and services.

The firm is engaged in the business of investment banking and stockbrokerage, including the underwriting of corporate and municipal securities, corporate and municipal finance, venture capital financing, equity research, portfolio evaluation and management, trading and market making, mutual funds, corporate and government fixed income securities, and the handling of stock and bond transactions on most exchanges and in over-the-counter markets.

"One of the reasons that Parker/Hunter has been successful is our commitment to our corporate philosophy" says Robert W. Kampmeinert, Chairman and Chief Executive Officer. "We all work towards a common goal, which is to create and preserve wealth for our clients by responding promptly and professionally to their financial needs and objectives."

Parker/Hunter was established in 1969 by the merger of two Pittsburgh stockbrokerage firms, Kay, Richards & Company and McKelvy & Company, founded in 1902 and 1928, respectively.

Since that time, Parker/Hunter has grown to become the largest independently owned full service stockbrokerage and investment banking firm in Pennsylvania. A member of the New York Stock Exchange, the firm has approximately 280 employees in sixteen offices in Pennsylvania, Ohio and West Virginia.

Parker/Hunter's support departments are located at the firm's headquarters in the USX Tower in Pittsburgh. These departments, which include Equity Research, Portfolio Management, Mutual Funds, Retirement Planning, Public Finance, Insurance and Annuities, Syndicate, Taxable and Tax-Exempt Fixed Income securities and Equity Trading, are staffed by professionals who work closely with the firm's Investment Executives and their clients. Parker/Hunter's offices are located within 200 miles of the firm's headquarters, which facilitates these close working relationships.

The Equity Research Department provides clients with high quality, timely research reports, with special emphasis placed on small and medium-size companies. They also publish a Recommended Stock List, *Market Notes*, a monthly market and economic commentary, *Investor's Quarterly*, a newsletter for Parker/Hunter clients, and an annual publication on investing.

Professional investment management for individuals and institutions is offered by the firm's Portfolio Management Department. Each portfolio is individually crafted, paying close attention to a client's financial objectives. The Department periodically reviews a client's portfolio and makes appropriate recommendations. Parker/Hunter offers its portfolio management services without a fee, and all clients are eligible, regardless of the size of their portfolio.

The firm's Public Finance Department acts as financial advisor and consultant to municipalities, authorities and hospitals. They assist in raising capital to meet their client's financing requirements, usually through the public underwriting or private placement of long-term debt.

Parker/Hunter Incorporated

Parker/Hunter's Investment Banking Department, also headed by Mr. Kampmeinert, serves as financial advisor to companies seeking to raise long-term capital for growth and expansion. The Department is also involved in all aspects of merger, acquisition and divestiture work, valuations of common stock and venture capital.

The firm's underwritten public offerings and private placements of common stock have proven to be excellent investments for clients. Parker/Hunter has acted as investment banker to some well known regional companies including Respironics, Medrad, Tuscarora, Amsco and Legent (formerly Duquesne Systems).

Being a regional firm means that Parker/Hunter people live and work in the same communities as their clients. This familiarity helps them to better understand the needs of their clients, whether they are individuals, businesses or institutions, and to provide them with service of the highest quality.

A t Integra Financial Corporation, the whole truly is greater than the sum of its parts.

In four short years, Integra strategically assembled the most extensive community banking network of any financial institution in western Pennsylvania. Integra's dedication to customer and community service makes it the bank to watch in western Pennsylvania.

With assets of $13.5 billion, Integra is the region's third largest bank holding company and one of the country's top 50.

Serving in excess of one million customers through 260 branch offices, Integra operates three banks—Integra Bank/South headquartered in Uniontown, Integra Bank/North in Titusville and Integra Bank/Pittsburgh—with

■ *Integra Bank serves customers through 260 branch offices — the most extensive community banking network in western Pennsylvania.*

Integra Financial Corporation

offices throughout 22 counties in western Pennsylvania.

Tracing its young history to nine regional banks and three thrift institutions, Integra Financial Corporation is now parent to three super community banks as well as trust, mortgage, investment and insurance subsidiaries.

Integra's roots date back to January 1989, when two bank holding companies—Pennbancorp and Union National Corporation—joined together in what was

■ *Integra Chairman and Chief Executive Officer William Roemer (left) and Integra President and Chief Operating Officer Len Carroll look ahead to a bright future for Integra. Photo by David Farmerie.*

termed a "merger of equals." Integra began as a collection of seven western Pennsylvania banks—Union National, First Seneca, Keystone National, McDowell National, Pennbank, Gallatin National and First National of Washington, PA. Over the next three years, Integra successfully realigned these banks into three affiliates—Integra Bank/South, Integra Bank/Pittsburgh and Integra Bank/North—each with its own marketing area.

Integra's growth continued in 1990 with the addition and consolidation of 16 Horizon Financial offices, and a year later with the purchase of insured deposits of ten branches of Atlantic Financial Savings.

The acquisitions of two larger institutions—Landmark Savings Association in June 1992 and Equimark Corporation in January 1993—capped this exciting period and vaulted Integra into the role of a major player on the local banking scene.

Over the years, Integra has established a track record of quickly reaping the fruits of its aggressive growth program. While the addition of Horizon and Atlantic Financial offices, and the Landmark and Equimark acquisitions, have more than doubled Integra's asset size, the total number of full-time employees rose only 25 percent.

Each time Integra has grown through a merger or acquisition, the customers and the investment community have challenged the

company's management to deliver on promised economies and service benefits.

In 1989, Integra management's blueprint for the future called for an aggressive "in-market" growth strategy that, based on deposits, would make Integra banks either first or second in their respective markets, or at least give them 15 percent of the deposits in each county. By 1993, that goal had been achieved in 14 counties.

Also by 1993, Integra had more than tripled its asset base and market presence in customer-rich Allegheny County, bringing Integra Bank/Pittsburgh's retail penetration more in line with its sister banks to the north and south.

In 1991, Integra Trust Company was formed by combining the banks' trust departments into a single subsidiary with more than $7 billion in trust assets under centralized administration. The company operates the largest and most comprehensive network of branches delivering trust services in western Pennsylvania.

Integra announced the formation of Integra Mortgage Company in 1992, bringing together the mortgage operations of Integra, Landmark and Equimark. This subsidiary conducts retail mortgage banking operations in Pennsylvania and Virginia, and wholesale operations throughout the mid-Atlantic states.

One of Integra's major growth strategies has been to increase the number of banking relationships with our existing customers.

Classic Choice, introduced in 1990, is a nationally recognized program, offering a range of superior traditional and non-tradi-

■ *Integra Chairman and Chief Executive Officer William Roemer (left) and Pittsburgh Steelers All-Pro running back Barry Foster (right) greet students and officials from South Vo Tech High School — The 1993 Know the Score School Of The Year. Integra, The Pittsburgh Steelers and WTAE Radio sponsor Know the Score - A nationally acclaimed drug and alcohol awareness program for western Pennsylvania schools.*

tional banking services, including certificate of deposit bonuses, no-service-charge checking, educational seminars and travel opportunities.

Another relationship program is IntegraMax, which provides customer access to a wide array of services packaged to address personal financial needs—both immediate and over the long term.

IntegraMax, which debuted in 1992, offers qualified customers reduced rates on a variety of loan products, including home mortgages, installment loans and lines of credit. It includes electronic banking and credit card services and discounted brokerage and travelers check transactions.

Integra s drive to increase the level of quality consumer and business loan volumes has paid off, allowing the banks to record significant loan increases during a time when national loan volume trends were on the decline.

Integra s commitment to customer service was underscored in July 1992 when Governor Robert P. Casey signed the Interaffiliate Banking Bill, which allows customers to conduct business at all branches of Pennsylvania banks and savings & loan institutions owned by the same holding company. Integra was instrumental in securing adoption of this law, which greatly enhances the convenience of its banking franchise in the region.

This commitment to superior customer service is the basis of Integra's super community banking philosophy. "We are committed to delivering the kinds of products and the level of personal customer service and responsiveness that our market needs," explains William F. Roemer, Integra's Chairman and Chief Executive Officer. "We are large enough to provide outstanding resources and small enough to keep the decision-making that affects the customer as close to the customer as possible."

The result, Roemer emphasizes, is that customers, investors and employees get what they expect from Integra—"the genuine bonding of a personal relationship with the best banking team in western Pennsylvania."

The Integra team cares not only about the quality of service provided to the community, but also about the quality of life in the communities served. Many of our employees serve on civic and charitable boards and are active participants in various fund raising campaigns.

In conjunction with the Pittsburgh Steelers, Integra sponsors "Know The Score on Alcohol and Other Drugs," a nationally acclaimed program that recognizes the efforts of local schools to educate students about the dangers of substance abuse. Integra has also been recognized for its leadership in supporting the Scouting For Food campaign, March of Dimes WalkAmerica, Junior Achievement Bowl-a-thon, and American Heart Association Heart Walk.

Looking back over the past four years, Bill Roemer concludes, "I firmly believe we have created a banking gem in western Pennsylvania. Our challenge going forward will be to make it glisten." ▣

■ *Minutes before takeoff at the Pittsburgh International Airport, these Classic Choice members anticipate an exciting trip to the Carribean Islands. Integra customers who are Classic Choice members enjoy a wide range of superior traditional and non-traditional banking services, including educational seminars and travel opportunities. Photo by Harry Giglio.*

The mission of the Todd Pittsburgh Group is to satisfy the financial security needs of their clients by providing the highest quality plans, products, service and personal talent. The Todd Pittsburgh Group is comprised of:

Todd Organization of Pittsburgh, Inc., Executive Benefit Services; Todd Benefit Services of Pittsburgh, Inc., Employee Benefit Services; International Settlement Design, Inc., Structured Settlement Services.

The Todd Organization of Pittsburgh, Inc. (Todd), flagship unit of the group, is a member office of The Todd Organization, Inc. These companies design, implement, and administer corporate executive benefit pro-

Todd Pittsburgh Group

grams to attract and retain excellence in top management. It operates exclusively in this area based on 35 years of experience in the field, a record matched by few firms nationwide.

The need for Todd's service grows virtually with each Congressional mandate, change in accounting standards, and federal regulation that impacts retirement income and executive compensation. At the same time, competition for management talent across the business spectrum increases the importance of well-designed and skillfully executed benefit programs.

"It's axiomatic that businesses survive and prosper only through strong management direction. But the increasing velocity of change in executive benefits through governmental actions and general business

■ *Todd principals Steven C. Price, Richard B. Goodman and Eric P. Rader review Total Service Quality milestones report.*

dynamics means that corporations are challenged to provide attractive plans," said Steven C. Price, a principal of Todd Pittsburgh.

Price oversees Todd's operations and technical consulting services from an experience base in finance, tax, insurance, total quality management and systems.

"We exist solely to help companies by building benefit programs designed to meet the mutual strategic goals of the corporation and the executive," Price said.

Todd executives point out that while corporations devote much to the assembly and development of management teams, the design and administration of executive benefit programs may get less attention.

"Executive benefits often gets piecemeal attention from different disciplines within a company, such as the finance, treasury and human resource functions. Few people have their hands around the entire program," said Richard B. Goodman, a Todd principal. "Many executives may be in danger of not being able to reap rewards earned through years of company service. Governmental limits and certain aspects of compensation strategies can mean that traditional retire-

■ *Thorough planning is at the basis of all Todd programs.*

ment plans provide as little as 10 percent of a top executive's pre-retirement income."

The bulk of a senior executive's retirement income may be derived from non-qualified plans, which are unsecured "promises to pay" by the corporation. Sometimes executives don't know such promises can be altered or eliminated by corporate takeovers, management changes, or economic downturns.

With executives' post-retirement benefits financed through corporate capital, decisions about them are continually weighed against a company's liabilities and potential investments. For many companies, creative financing reduces the burden of benefit liabilities.

"As a matter of course, we look beyond the benefit plan on paper," said Eric P. Rader, a Todd principal. "We develop a range of analyses on all aspects of the benefit to determine if it is meeting the client's goals and objectives."

"Our expertise goes beyond looking at the tax and accounting implications. Many other aspects may be missed when plans are built on a series of ad hoc decisions based only on legislative changes," Rader said.

Typically, corporations leave design of executive benefit plans to outside professionals for whom this area is an adjunct to their

■ *Gary Warren, Todd client services director, explains the features of a split dollar benefit plan.*

core insurance, actuarial or financial consulting business. This approach may yield some executive benefit plans that are adequate in their initial design.

However, as questions and regulations arise over time about calculating benefit payments or accounting methods, the human resource department or corporate counsel may be left alone to interpret features and functions of the plans.

"We are set up to interpret and analyze our plans on an on-going basis, not just when they are installed. We don't leave clients to figure out what's next," Rader said.

The dynamic environment for executive benefit plans means that those set up only a few years ago may now be out of step with their original intent. The Todd Organization provides administration and communications for existing plans to modify them as warranted due to changing conditions.

Benefits consulting services grew rapidly during the 1980s as corporations implemented complex supplemental compensation and benefit plans for senior management. Changing tax laws and competition for executive talent fueled this growth, along with performance-based pay systems and the prevalence of corporate takeovers.

"This forced recognition that external forces have major impact on an executive's total compensation. At the same time, some supplemental plans were becoming the largest portion of an executive's current and deferred compensation," Goodman said.

The Todd Organization responded by adding analytical capabilities to assist the process of creating plans in an increasingly complex environment.

"The basic process doesn't change," Rader said, "but we must stay ahead of the way plans are financed, secured, administered and adapted in a changing climate."

From its inception in 1957, The Todd Organization grew nationally to ten offices in key cities across the United States by the early 1990s.

Todd Benefit Services of Pittsburgh, Inc.

Todd Benefit Services of Pittsburgh, Inc. (TBS), designs and implements traditional health and welfare benefit plans for its clients.

TBS helps organizations develop employee benefit plans that cost-effectively attract and retain valuable people.

TBS offers a full group insurance brokerage for employee benefits including group medical, self-funded plans, pensions and profit sharing, group life and accident coverage, disability, dental, vision, prescription drugs and long-term care.

For smaller companies, TBS provides services that might normally require the time of internal staff, including billings, claim resolution, utilization review and more. By using technology and a thoughtful process for design and review, TBS assists in controlling benefit costs through benefit design and alternative financing arrangements. This frees the clients from administrative time as

TBS steps in to solve problems, and negotiate with insurance companies, etc.

TBS reviews and refines plans to remain cost-effective and to answer changing objectives, and continually provides a readily-available liaison.

International Settlement Design, Inc.

Also affiliated with The Todd Organization of Pittsburgh, Inc. is International Settlement Design Inc., (ISD), an innovative structured settlement company servicing claims for insurers, self-insured corporations and government entities through its Pittsburgh headquarters and other offices throughout the United States, Canada and England. ISD began in 1980 as this industry was initiated.

Rather than lump-sum payments, parties in lawsuits may structure settlements to be paid over time through a variety of arrangements.

ISD develops economic evaluations, provides medical impairment analysis, and assists defense counsel at many stages of claims management. Like TBS, ISD draws on the accounting, finance, insurance, actuarial, tax and systems expertise of The Todd Organization of Pittsburgh, Inc. in developing appropriate settlement arrangements.

Staffed with experienced negotiators and dedicated to quality service, ISD assists with traditional uses of structured settlements for medical malpractice, personal injury and product liability and is at the leading edge of innovation in the areas of employment discrimination, workers' compensation and environmental litigation.

The Todd Pittsburgh Group with its commitment to technology, quality products and the process of plan design, brings significant expertise to help its clients meet the forthcoming challenges into the 21st Century. ▣

■ *TBS and ISD staff members frequently share information and resources to solve client problems.*

The Greater Pittsburgh Chamber of Commerce

Since its incorporation in 1878, the Greater Pittsburgh Chamber of Commerce has applied intelligence and cooperation to a vision of a viable business community and a dream of continual improvement in the quality of life for all residents of the region.

As a recognized leader in its field, the Chamber develops innovative membership benefits and programs in a continuing effort to address the most crucial needs of a diverse business community.

More than 2,500 individuals, from entrepreneurial to single-employee firms, belong to the Greater Pittsburgh Chamber of Commerce. The diversity of its members enables the Chamber to exercise great flexibility in developing ideas, pursuing initiatives and cultivating relationships toward the goal of continuing excellence in the Greater Pittsburgh business community.

The board of directors, composed of business and professional leaders from diverse sectors of the community, sets general policy for the chamber. Day-to-day operations are carried out by a full-time professional staff. Business people become involved in Chamber activities through committees ranging from government affairs issues and world trade to membership development and other

special projects. The Chamber's programs are as varied as the components of the regional economy.

Q-NET — Following its inception in June 1991, Q-NET became one of the fastest-growing programs offered by the Chamber. It encompasses a host of programs related to the Total Quality movement.

The Chamber's annual Greater Pittsburgh Quality Conference offers members an opportunity to learn about the Total Quality movement from some of the most highly respected corporations in the United States. The program spawned the Greater Pittsburgh Total Quality Award.

Through seminars and workshops, Q-NET volunteers deliver the message and vision to companies that have not yet discovered the benefits of the Total Quality philosophy.

WORLD TRADE ASSOCIATION — Another young venture of the Pittsburgh Chamber, the World Trade Association was founded to promote international economic relations and commercial cooperation.

WTA roundtables provide a forum for managers to explore the many aspects of conducting business across national borders. The association also sponsors the Chamber's International Business Breakfast Series in cooperation with the U.S. Department of Commerce and the District Export Council. It hosts visiting trade delegations, organizes special conferences and supports the mission of the Pittsburgh-Israel and Australian-American chambers of commerce.

■ *The goal of the Chamber is to develop ideas, cultivate business relationships and build a healthy competitive business environment. Photo by Roy Engelbrecht.*

DINAMO — Recognizing the importance of a modern, efficient navigation system, the Greater Pittsburgh Chamber of Commerce along with the governors of Kentucky, Ohio, Pennsylvania and West Virginia launched DINAMO, the Association for the Development of Inland Navigation in America's Ohio Valley.

Since its inception in 1981, DINAMO has dedicated itself to improving the economic climate in the Ohio Valley by urging Congress to expedite the modernization of the lock and dam system on the Ohio and its navigable tributaries, including the Monongahela and Allegheny.

The association's focus has been 16 sets of locks and dams, including eight in western Pennsylvania.

By the early 1990s, the U.S. Army Corps of Engineers had begun construction, design and study of improvements representing a $4-billion investment in the Ohio River system.

On the Mon, Allegheny and Ohio, river fleets moved more than $35.5 million worth of commodities past The Point in 1990, making Pittsburgh the nation's largest inland port. Nearly 48,000 jobs are connected directly or indirectly to river commerce in the Pittsburgh area.

EMPLOYERS & CHILD CARE — The project grew out of the late Mayor Richard Caliguiri's Task Force on Women in 1987.

Acutely aware of the challenges involved in balancing family and business responsibilities, the Chamber adopted the Employers & Child Care Project. In doing so, Pittsburgh became the first chamber in the state, and one of only a few nationwide, to recognize trends that are changing the conduct of business life in America.

The project is designed to educate employers about available child care support for their employees.

Through the work of the Chamber, the YWCA of Greater Pittsburgh, and the United Way, major child care consulting services and resource agencies in Allegheny County were consolidated under a new umbrella department called Child Care Partnerships.

Convinced of the worth of the endeavor, the Chamber has continued its support of Employers & Child Care, furthering the project's mission for years to come.

GOVERNMENTAL AFFAIRS — At the core of the Chamber's mission is its role as the business community's voice in the halls of government.

During the legislative session, the Chamber's Manager of Governmental Affairs continuously monitors the progress of business-related legislation and maintains contact with appropriate elected and appointed officials.

The Chamber lobbies officeholders directly and presents testimony whenever government committees solicit formal community reaction. Chamber positions on political issues are reviewed at one of seven policy committees. Members of the Chamber staff conduct research into legislative issues and analyze bills and proposed regulations.

As a stimulus to open debate on issues of interest to the business community, the Public Affairs Forum Series of the Chamber invites prominent government officials to address the membership over breakfast or lunch once a month.

Through its Political Action Committee, the Chamber supports candidates who clearly understand the needs of the business community and are critical to the passage of worthy legislation.

Through its special and ad hoc task forces, and coalitions, the Chamber also addresses special issues, such as the need for a statewide business court to supplant Pennsylvania's overburdened business dispute resolution system.

The Governmental Affairs program also brings Chamber members face-to-face with representatives and senators at annual receptions in Harrisburg and Washington. It coordinates conferences and roundtable discussions and provides a host of member services, such as supplying copies of legislation, arranging meetings with legislators and developing lobbying plans.

INTERGOVERNMENTAL COOPERATION — Keying on Pittsburgh's successful tradition of government-business partnerships, the Chamber's Intergovernmental Cooperation Programs work with people from both sectors to provide more efficient, cost-effective ways of providing services to citizens of the Pittsburgh area.

■ *The Greater Pittsburgh Chamber of Commerce also focuses on the continual improvement in the quality of life for all residents of the region. Photo by Roy Engelbrecht.*

LEADERSHIP PITTSBURGH — The Chamber launched Leadership Pittsburgh in 1984 in an attempt to broaden the base of the region's future business and civic leaders.

The ten-month program exposes 45 to 50 participants each year to key aspects of the community, including neighborhoods, hospitals, government agencies, businesses, schools, jails and soup kitchens.

PUBLIC RELATIONS — This department is instrumental in organizing functions and events that involve more than 5,000 Chamber members every year. The staff promotes support for Chamber activities, policies, and programs through contact with members, the community at large, and the news media. The Public Relations Department directs a variety of membership functions, including networking sessions, trade shows, and training seminars. The staff also conducts research and publishes an array of guides to Pittsburgh and its business community.

"The Chamber's approach in all of these areas is to develop ideas, cultivate business relationships, and work toward one common goal, a more healthy, competitive business environment in Pittsburgh," said Justin T. Horan, President. 🄍

■ *More than 2,500 individuals, from entrepreneurial to single-employee firms, belong to the Greater Pittsburgh Chamber of Commerce. Photo by Roy Engelbrecht.*

CHAPTER

The Professions

TWELVE

As a major center for corporations that increasingly depend on specialized skills, Pittsburgh counts its human resources as one of its most important assets.

Helping companies achieve the highest return on their investment in that asset is the job of Towers Perrin.

The international consulting firm advises employers in developing innovative strategies to respond to the human resource challenges that companies face today and will face in the future.

Towers Perrin was incorporated in 1934 and as the region's corporate activity expanded and diversified, Towers Perrin followed suit, opening its Pittsburgh consulting office in 1979.

At the same time, a new generation of flexible benefits is unfolding. Towers Perrin helps design plans that support a company's goal to be the employer of choice by addressing the full spectrum of work and family issues.

Seventy percent of the Fortune 1000 U.S. companies are among Towers Perrin's clients, and all kinds of organizations — public and private, for-profit and not-for-profit, small and large — turn to the firm's world-

■ *The Pittsburgh headquarters of Towers Perrin is located in the USX Tower, the tallest building in Pittsburgh. Photo by Roy Englebrecht.*

The local Towers Perrin office also tracks area trends in compensation and benefits. Through its annual Salary Planning Survey, for example, the firm informs local employers about competitive pay practices.

Keeping corporate management teams abreast of the evolving array of human resources strategies may be the mission of Towers Perrin. To carry it out, however, the firm relies on principles that have changed little over the last six decades:

"Our work must help our clients succeed. Meeting or exceeding our clients' expectations and contributing to their success are our highest priorities."

"We foster long-term client relationships. We can help clients best by focusing on their issues and needs from a long-term perspective."

"Through our people, we will differentiate our service and our firm. It is our people who must deliver the level of consulting services that will differentiate us in the marketplace."

"We must always operate as a well-managed, financially strong business. To maximize our ability to serve our clients and to reward our people, we must run our business the way we advise our clients to run theirs."

Through the twists and turns that tomorrow brings in human resources management, Towers Perrin believes that its clients will find those four standards to be familiar constants. ▣

TPF&C / A Towers Perrin Company

In keeping with the firm's philosophy of maintaining full-service offices, Towers Perrin staffed its Pittsburgh location with specialists in employee benefits, compensation, actuarial services, communications, asset management, and other human resources areas.

Towers Perrin in Pittsburgh serves more than 100 area employers. Through the firm's centrally located offices, clients have access to the full range of Towers Perrin capabilities, including performance management and work force effectiveness in addition to general management consulting.

The firm also provides risk management consulting services through its Tillinghast affiliate.

Among other responses to our clients' needs, Towers Perrin helps companies develop reward systems that enable employees to better focus on improvement in productivity, quality, and customer satisfaction. The approach emphasizes teamwork as well as individual performance.

Employee benefits, especially health care, are a dominant workplace concern today. Virtually no employer can afford to operate without a carefully considered benefits program.

With strategies such as managed care, Towers Perrin helps employers contain medical costs while improving the overall delivery of health care to employees.

wide team of nearly 5,000 employees located in 66 offices.

Despite its international perspective, Towers Perrin understands that the human resources challenges of individual companies spring from unique situations and that despite the increasingly global nature of business, corporate centers like Pittsburgh have needs that often reflect their regional economies.

That understanding is reflected in the many information-sharing seminars and briefings that Towers Perrin conducts as part of its commitment to the Pittsburgh area.

Since 1988, the Pittsburgh Flex Roundtable, sponsored by Towers Perrin, has provided a regular forum for area employers to share ideas about critical benefits issues.

Eighty-five area organizations participate in the quarterly Flex Roundtable sessions. Seminars on other critical human resource issues take place regularly.

■ *Pamela Thompson, Receptionist, Towers Perrin; Antoinette Petrucci, Vice President, Towers Perrin; Gary Matson, General manger, U.S. Employee Benefits, H.J. Heinz Company*

■ *The partners pride themselves on having built one of the most extensive computerized support systems in the profession which allows them to conduct research faster and better.*

Corporations around the country are discovering that the largest law firms in the biggest cities don't necessarily represent the best value in legal representation.

Burns, White & Hickton is one of the reasons for that awakening.

It is a new generation of law firm, formed in 1987 when five of Pittsburgh's brightest young legal minds recognized that success in their profession will increasingly belong to the firms that deliver not only effective but efficient service.

"Our philosophy is that we have no vested interest in the continuation of our clients' problems. Our focus is to quickly and effectively resolve our clients' disputes with minimal cost and minimal intrusion upon their production pursuits," said Dave Hickton, a founding partner and now one of 21 lawyers in the 80-person firm.

■ *Seated Left to right: Ralph F. Manning, Michael W. Burns, David A. Damico. Standing Left to Right: David J. Hickton, David B. White, Lisa Pupo Lenihan.*

Mike Burns, Dave White, Dave Hickton, Dave Damico, and Lisa Pupo Lenihan organized the firm.

They staked Burns, White & Hickton to their belief that legal clients, like the customers in so many other professions and industries, increasingly want value and will seek it out.

Burns, White & Hickton has a general trial practice that spans the country. Their cases include commercial disputes, personal injury, medical and other professional malpractice, railroad defense, worker's compensation,

occupational disease, products liability, general negligence, and insurance defense.

The addition of Ralph Manning as a sixth partner brought further expertise in corporate, commercial, and other transactional matters including experience in environmental and occupational safety and health, acquisitions, mergers and divestitures, real estate, banking, finance, and estate planning, among others.

But a lot of firms cover those areas.

Burns White & Hickton works to set itself apart by the character of its service and the method of the delivery.

The partners, for example, pride themselves on having built one of the most extensive computerized support systems in the profession. The motivation: efficiency, sufficient to prompt one client to compare the system to the computers at NASA.

"Computerization puts us in the position of organizing our approach to solving the client's problem and conducting research faster and better. That allows our lawyers more time to do what we do best, give careful, deliberative thought to the most effective strategy in any given case," according to Mike Burns.

The firm views its streamlined configuration as the underpinning of its strength: the ability to not only resolve individual cases, but to establish the means and methods of handling complex, multifaceted cases that touch numerous jurisdictions, plaintiffs, and legal disciplines.

"What we do best is take the large problem and attack the common themes in the plaintiffs' case, build themes in the defense case, acquire qualified experts, and most important in some instances, address problems in the business that underlie the legal case," said Dave White. "We can make the total problem smaller."

With that approach, the partners have expanded the firm from the 5 founders and the 15 original members of the support staff

to 21 lawyers and 21 paralegals with support from 40 others.

Growth for growth's sake is not a goal, whether it's in the number of lawyers on staff or the number of corporations on the client list.

Burns, White & Hickton

It is not unheard of for Burns, White & Hickton to turn down a request for representation or to consult with a client for a day or two in an attempt to correct the cause of legal problems rather than let a condition generate fees over a longer period.

The firm considers itself almost revolutionary in its approach to alternative billing. Few clients are billed by the hour. More often, they enjoy the budgetary protection of billing limits.

The firm's preoccupation with creating value for clients at the expense of fee-generating opportunities and its willingness to be known, consequently, as an oddity in the legal field may spring from the fact that the ages of the partners and the associates leave more good years ahead of them than behind them.

Only three of the lawyers in the firm were born before 1948, and the oldest was born in 1945. Yet all the partners had distinguished themselves before founding Burns, White & Hickton.

The six are managing Burns, White & Hickton so that anywhere in the country when the question becomes where to find value in effective, efficient legal representation, the answer will be "There's a small firm in downtown Pittsburgh ...."

■ *Mark A. Eck, Jane Ann Thompson and Louis C. Long, Senior Partners in the Pittsburgh office.*

■ *Donald W. Bebenek (seated), and George I. Buckler, Senior Partners in the Pittsburgh office.*

Responding to the needs of a changing business environment, Meyer Darragh's business practice group, which handles business law, tax and estate planning, and finance and banking, has recently added both international business and sports and entertainment practices to its roster of commercial services.

As Meyer Darragh enters its ninth decade of providing expeditious solutions to its clients' legal needs, the firm has rededicated itself to the goals of individualized service and timely resolutions. Meyer Darragh attorneys regularly evaluate each case, continually communicating progress so that clients may make informed decisions regarding the manner in which their legal matters should proceed.

Meyer, Darragh, Buckler, Bebenek & Eck

In 1913, when George Y. Meyer was a sole practitioner of the law, horse-drawn carriages were far more familiar than automobiles on the streets of Pittsburgh, World War I had not yet begun, and the renaissance that would transform the city from a smoky workshop into a gleaming corporate center was still several generations away.

As evolutionary as the city in which it is headquartered, the law firm of Meyer, Darragh, Buckler, Bebenek & Eck has grown to include over 60 attorneys and four branch offices. This commitment to a regional office approach provided the catalyst for expansion to Greensburg and Altoona, Pennsylvania and Charleston and Morgantown, West Virginia. By maintaining a full-time physical presence in regional locations, Meyer Darragh is well suited to deliver the highest quality legal service to its clients.

The firm's clients include local, regional, national and international corporations and a wide variety of product manufacturers. The firm's practice covers insurance defense and commercial litigation, product liability, general negligence, professional malpractice, toxic substances, workers' compensation, employment relations, environmental matters, civil rights, construction law, collection and foreclosure actions.

The firm is constantly implementing better ways to service its clients, arranging special court-administered settlement conferences in order to conclude litigation while resolving cases economically. In addition, Meyer Darragh utilizes various types of alternative dispute resolutions, including arbitration.

The firm maintains an extensive computer driven support system which allows it to manage efficiently the day-to-day information regarding each clients' work, regardless of the size or complexity of the problem. A state-of-the-art library, with computerized access to legal and information data bases, supports the firm's total quality approach.

Meyer Darragh is affiliated nationally with the prestigious American Law Firm Association (ALFA), an organization consisting of independent law firms located throughout the United States.

Reflecting a strong belief in the value of continuing education, firm attorneys present seminars in all areas of group practice and author an array of topical articles which appear regularly in commercial and legal publications.

A long-standing member of Pittsburgh's corporate landscape, Meyer Darragh has developed correspondingly strong ties with the community. Convinced that volunteering in the community is a worthwhile investment in the future, firm attorneys participate in pro bono projects and are actively involved in a variety of local civic, cultural, and nonprofit organizations.

As Meyer Darragh continues to mirror the evolution of the city in which it is headquartered, it strives to improve its service to its clients. The firm's cornerstone for the future is its promise of the highest professional efforts on behalf of its clients.

■ *John M. Noble, Senior Partner, Greensburg, PA office, George W. Lavender III and Robert P. Martin, Senior Partners in the Charleston, WV office.*

■ *Terry & Stephenson, P.C. executives analyze firm operations and develop client service plans.*

Of all the strengths that the accounting firm Terry & Stephenson P.C. offer its clients, the greatest is a well-developed understanding of the environment in which small and midsized businesses operate.

"We understand how tough it's getting out there," said Sam Stephenson, Pittsburgh-based partner in the certified public accounting firm.

"The ever-changing tax laws and the implementation of the many changes in the accounting rules have a major effect on profitability for small businesses particularly. If the accountants and advisers to small business don't keep abreast of these changes, they are unlikely to be able to deliver the level of quality service that a client should rightfully expect."

Terry & Stephenson is a minority-owned CPA firm serving a variety of public- and private-sector clients from offices in Pittsburgh and Denver.

"We've established ourselves as a high-quality professional services firm in each of our markets," said E. Alan Terry, managing partner.

In the 10 years after Terry founded the business, it grew from its lone original partner to an organization of 15 professionals, including Stephenson.

The firm has received a number of honors, including recognition from the City of Pittsburgh, the City of Denver, the U.S. Department of Commerce, and the Catholic Diocese.

The firm provides a full range of services: audit, review, compilation, accounting, income tax consultation and preparation, management consulting, financial systems analysis and software analysis, implementation, and support.

"We believe that it's not enough just to stress quality within our firm," said Stephenson. "We also see the importance of measuring that quality and verifying it to our clients. That's why we volunteered to join the AICPA Division of CPA firms and undergo periodic peer review."

Terry & Stephenson has been a member of the Private Companies Practice Section (PCPS) of the American Institute of CPAs since 1980, and received an unqualified report in its most recent peer review required for PCPS membership.

Members of the firm are active in the American Institute of Certified Public Accountants (AICPA), the Colorado State Society of CPAs, the National Association of Black Accountants, the Pennsylvania Association of School Board Officials, the Pennsylvania Institute of CPAs and the Pittsburgh Regional Minority Purchasing Council.

The firm brings an array of talents to its engagements, including auditing, accounting, tax consulting, and tax planning for the manufacturing, retail merchandising, real estate, and service industries, as well as the governmental and not-for-profit sectors.

Terry & Stephenson installs accounting systems and trains client personnel to operate them.

"We recognize the value that accrues to our clients through broad relationships with our firm," Terry said. "Management advisory services, for example, are a natural part of a client relationship and tend to have direct implications for the bottom-line. We're fully prepared to analyze and evaluate a company's lines of reporting and document flow as well as its security, pricing, and data processing practices in search of efficiencies and cost savings."

A CPA licensed in Colorado, Maryland, Ohio, and Pennsylvania, Terry holds a master's degree of business administration in finance from Indiana University, Bloomington, Indiana.

He began his career on the auditing staff of one of the big six international accounting firms with responsibility for Fortune 500 companies before joining Cummins Engine Co., where he advanced to senior financial planner.

Terry founded his firm after serving as manager of financial planning for the semiconductor division of Westinghouse Electric Corp. There he had responsibility for monthly, annual and long-range financial planning for both domestic and international operations.

Terry & Stephenson, P.C.

Stephenson is a Pennsylvania-licensed CPA with a B.S.B.A. degree in accounting from Bucknell University.

Before joining Terry & Stephenson in 1983, Stephenson was an audit manager for one of the big six international accounting firms in Pittsburgh. His responsibilities included audit fieldwork control, supervision, training, and management advisory services for companies in the manufacturing, retail, service, and financial services industries.

■ *Terry & Stephenson, P.C. professionals discuss inventory procedures with the chefs of a food service client.*

For decades, the major industrial companies of Pittsburgh and the world called on Kaiser Engineers to oversee construction of their largest plants and factories.

From the Monongahela Valley to Australia and Hong Kong, Kaiser planned and built the steel mills, aluminum smelters, and chemical plants that laid the foundation for the global industrial boom of the 20th century.

Today the company, now known as ICF Kaiser Engineers, continues to provide those giants of industry with state-of-the-art production facilities and technology, but with a twist that reflects the evolution of industries it serves.

ICF Kaiser Engineers, Inc.

■ *ICF Kaiser Engineers is managing the environmental site restoration program at the former U.S. Steel Duquesne and McKeesport Works to facilitate future economic redevelopment.*

While its industrial engineers are hard at work finding the best ways to build and manage the plants, ICF Kaiser's teams of environmental engineering specialists are helping many of those same companies demolish their aging facilities and cleanup the land on which they stood to prepare it for new commercial uses.

"We are without a doubt the company in Pittsburgh that is doing the majority of that work," said Bruce H. Laswell, group senior vice president of ICF Kaiser's Environment

■ *At Richmond Power & Light in Indiana, ICF Kaiser Engineers provided project management, licensing, and engineering design for the construction of the LIFAC air pollution control facility.*

Group. "We have the ability to convert an abandoned plant to a redeveloped industrial park, working with owners, developers, and bankers."

One example of that transformation is ICF Kaiser's cleanup of former USX Corp. steel mills in McKeesport and Duquesne, Pennsylvania. Working for the new owner of the land, the RIDC Southwestern Pennsylvania Growth Fund, ICF Kaiser is managing the restoration of 400 acres of former mill property that have since been occupied by several new smaller companies.

ICF Kaiser also participated in the revitalization of Herr's Island, the old Washington Landing in the Allegheny River northeast of downtown Pittsburgh. There, under the company's guidance, contaminated soil was removed and the Urban Redevelopment Authority of Pittsburgh built a marina and office buildings. ICF Kaiser designed a cleanup strategy that allowed the city of Pittsburgh to build tennis courts on part of the island that once had been uninhabitable because of past industrial uses.

As they work on environmental projects, ICF Kaiser's executives learn that their work is more than a nuts-and-bolts engineering task.

"Projects like that have a heavy community-relations flavor," said Laswell, adding that rebuilding discarded industrial sites brings jobs, contributes to broader economic development, and inspires a renewed sense of local pride.

While ICF Kaiser has built itself into one of the world's preeminent environmental engineering companies, it also continues to enhance its reputation as a ground-breaker on the industrial engineering side, with roots traceable back to the World War I era.

"We've been an industrial engineering firm in Pittsburgh for many years, and we've been an environmental firm in Pittsburgh for 15 years or so," said Paul DeCoursey, a Vice President of the Environment Group. "Combining the two lets us move ahead with Pittsburgh because it remains an industrial area, yet environment has become a big thrust. So our industrial clients, like Alcoa, Koppers, U.S. Steel, National Steel and LTV, for instance, are very much the same clients we deal with on the environmental side."

ICF Kaiser Engineers is based in Oakland, California, but Pittsburgh is home base for its divisions dealing with the steel, aluminum, and coal and mineral processing industries.

From offices in Four Gateway Center, about 250 ICF Kaiser planners, engineers, and support personnel help steel producers find more efficient ways to make metal and use the coke to fuel blast furnaces. They also assist utilities and other companies in finding ways to burn coal more cleanly and reduce pollution.

Realizing that coke production is becoming increasingly difficult as coke ovens get older and new clean air regulations make it very expensive to build new ones, ICF Kaiser has joined in the application of a technology by which pulverized coal is injected directly into blast furnaces. That reduces the amount of coke necessary for ironmaking and reduces the pollution control problems associated with cokemaking.

The company has taken an unusual step towards encouraging the use of pulverized coal injection technology. Within the fences of USX Corp.'s Gary Works in Indiana, ICF Kaiser designed, built, and arranged financing for a pulverized coal facility which reduces the use of coke by 25-30 percent. All USX had to do was promise to buy all the coal processed at the facility, which is owned and operated by ICF Kaiser and its partners.

As stiffer government clean air and clean water regulations require companies to work harder to clean up their air and water emissions, demand for ICF Kaiser's services increases. The company is among the leaders in designing and building air pollution control systems and water treatment plants for industrial clients worldwide, and ICF Kaiser executives expect considerable growth in those businesses during the nineties.

The chemical, pharmaceutical, and petroleum industries also have become major customers of ICF Kaiser because of the process engineering and environmental specialty ser-

vices provided by the company. Major projects are underway with PPG, Miles, Aristech, American Cyanamid, Shell, Arco Chemical, and Exxon that have a significant process and environmental component.

That growth is possible because of ICF Kaiser's solid background in engineering, planning, and construction. It is the largest subsidiary of Fairfax, Virginia-based ICF Kaiser International, Inc. The parent company was founded in 1969 as Inner City Fund, a four-person consulting firm that helped minority companies win government contracts.

Over the next two decades, ICF evolved into a major government consultant on energy and environmental policy issues. Business boomed, but contracts were being lost because ICF lacked engineering and construction expertise. So in 1989, it merged with Kaiser Engineers, a noted firm whose credits included Hoover Dam. It was founded in 1914 as the Henry J. Kaiser Co., a Canadian roadbuilding company in Vancouver, British Columbia.

By 1940, Kaiser had moved to California and was building ships, cars, steel mills, cement plants, aluminum smelters, and coal mines. In 1965, it was named the world's largest contractor by Engineering News-Record magazine.

But, during the late 1980s, Kaiser Engineers was cut loose from its former parent company and left with $70 million in debt from a failed leveraged buyout. It was in need of a partner to focus its engineering tal-

■ *For U.S. Steel's Gary Works, ICF Kaiser Engineers was selected to build a pulverized coal injection system to service four blast furnaces.* ents, and ICF came along at just the right time.

The combined company had to struggle to win new contracts, and even to keep existing ones but — by succeeding on a couple of major projects, including the $4.5 billion Boston Harbor cleanup — it eventually managed to revive itself. Today, the larger organization is a $675 million company with 4,000 employees in 90 offices around the world.

Just as ICF Kaiser was getting back on its feet, huge new markets began opening up with the fall of communism in Eastern Europe and the former Soviet Union. Hundreds of plants were in need of modernization and professional management, and factories that had operated with little or no environmental controls were in serious need of cleanup.

In 1990, ICF Kaiser was one of the first U.S. companies to sign a contract with an operating steel company in the Confederation of Independent States, providing a pollution control system on a coke plant.

ICF Kaiser helped the new owners of three major steel mills in the Czech Republic study how they should run the mills, which for years had been run and subsidized by the government. Not even the political turmoil following the rise of democracy has stopped

ICF Kaiser from growing its business beyond the old Iron Curtain.

Because a sister company operates as a global trading company, ICF Kaiser was able to accept payment in the form of metallurgical coal or coal tar when needs were urgent and hard currency was in short supply in the cash-strapped countries.

"Our work there is similar to what U.S. industries had to do in the 1950s and 60s," DeCoursey said. "Things are very bad. Industry in this country started cleaning up decades ago, and now Eastern Europe has to learn from our experience."

ICF Kaiser has made a long-term commitment to Pittsburgh because the company believes the Golden Triangle stands at the center of the industrial, engineering, and construction technology industry of the United States.

Pittsburgh is a source of high-quality technical talent and, with its high quality of life, the company finds that it's a good place to bring visitors and potential clients from around the world.

"It's startling to see the reaction of people from Czechoslovakia to the city of Pittsburgh," Laswell said. "They see the renaissance that has taken place here — one of the world's major industrial centers — and say 'if they did it in Pittsburgh, we can do it in Prague.' It's that kind of shining light." 〡

■ *Aerial view of Aristech Chemical Corporation's Haverhill, Ohio, plant, the location for an advanced industrial wastewater treatment facility being developed and designed by ICF Kaiser Engineers in association with Aristech.*

■ *Jim Stalder, managing partner.*

It began nearly a century ago. The United States Steel Corporation chose the public accounting firm of Price Waterhouse (named after British founders Samuel Lowell Price and Edwin Waterhouse) to serve as its auditors.

"The work involved in the accounts of subsidiary companies of the Steel Corporation located in the Pittsburgh area led to the leasing of quarters in the Peoples Savings Bank Building in May 1902 and the opening of the Pittsburgh office," wrote Chester DeMond, in the 1951 book *Price Waterhouse & Co. in America.*

Price Waterhouse

Like many businesses in Pittsburgh then, Price Waterhouse struggled at first. But by 1906, the office "began to receive so many appointments that it was necessary to extend the office facilities to four rooms and to increase the staff," DeMond wrote.

Today, Price Waterhouse, or PW, is the most widely known firm in the world of public accounting. As a full-service business advisory services firm, Price Waterhouse offers a full range of audit, tax, and management consulting services for organizations of all sizes in many different industries.

The firm was founded in London in 1849 and expanded to the United States in 1890 to serve clients whose operations had moved across the Atlantic.

The Pittsburgh office of Price Waterhouse grew from a staff of 6 employees to more than 230, serving a broad range of clients from entrepreneurial startups to Fortune 500 corporations.

In the 1990s, Price Waterhouse is proud to say that U.S. Steel, together with its parent, USX Corporation, is still one of its valued clients.

The firm's Pittsburgh office serves southwestern Pennsylvania, as well as portions of Ohio, West Virginia, and other neighboring states.

Growth for Price Waterhouse in Pittsburgh has come through not only the number of clients, but through the expansion of services. Along with the general areas of auditing, taxation, and consulting, the Pittsburgh office also specializes in international taxation, multinational corporations, middle-market and growing companies, manufacturing, retail, high technology, reorganization and litigation, and mergers and acquisitions.

The Pittsburgh office is one of 453 offices in 113 countries and territories employing 48,600 employees who serve some of the largest, most prestigious companies in the world. More Dow Jones industrial companies, more of the Forbes 100 largest U.S. multinationals, and more of the Fortune 50 exporters have engaged Price Waterhouse than any other firm.

Price Waterhouse believes these companies make the choice because of PW's reputation for quality and service, a reputation it earned by bringing to bear its resources and technical strength to find practical solutions to complex business problems.

The firm believes that the key to its success is its focus on global integration of its network of firms; selectivity in its markets, services, and clients; and reliance on nothing less than the best professional talent.

One of the most important factors that sets Price Waterhouse apart is management's belief that the firm's most valuable asset is its people. As a result, the professionals at PW enjoy the respect of their peers and an undeniable pride in being part of a first-class organization with the strongest reputation for quality and the best "brand name" in the profession.

As Price Waterhouse continues to serve clients in the increasingly challenging 1990s, it recognizes that quality and service are more important today than ever before and has reaffirmed its commitment to these areas — a commitment that has resulted in a number of firsts:

• Price Waterhouse is the first and only of the Big 6 accounting firms to have undergone a peer review and received an unqualified opinion and a "no comment" letter. This landmark achievement is an unprecedented confirmation of the quality of the firm's capabilities in the auditing arena.

• Price Waterhouse is the first firm to make its commitment to client service and quality a matter of corporate policy. Its chairman issued "The Client Bill of Rights," proclaiming personalized attention and professional excellence as its cornerstone.

Several years ago, the Pittsburgh organization embarked on a total quality journey to ensure that clients receive the best possible service. Total quality training became a

■ *Lori Durbiano, tax manager.*

requirement for all employees. Client satisfaction surveys are part of a program that tells PW's professionals how well they're doing and how to improve. The program established a process of continuous client feedback designed to ensure an understanding of what clients want, need, and value.

James C. Stalder, the Pittsburgh office managing partner, is a Northside native and Pennsylvania State University graduate who began his career with the firm as a staff accountant in 1962 and was admitted to the partnership in 1974. In 1988, he was named managing partner of the Pittsburgh office.

Stalder saw the office change significantly since coming on board in 1962.

"Although the firm has always been recognized as a leader in providing auditing and tax services, it has been exciting to witness

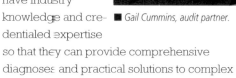

■ Top picture

Dave Smiddle(l), human resources director, and Dave Hamstead(r), audit partner, have been with the firm for more than 20 years.

■ Bottom picture

Price Waterhouse partner Tom Morgan discusses management consulting services with a client.

the development of a vast array of additional services — services that are being offered to our clients with the same high level of commitment to providing truly distinguished services," he said.

"It is the firm's goal to attract, develop, and retain individuals who have industry knowledge and credentialed expertise

■ *Gail Cummins, audit partner.*

so that they can provide comprehensive diagnoses and practical solutions to complex business problems."

PW-Pittsburgh is also very proud of its community involvement in the region. Its employees are active in more than 150 professional, civic, and community organizations. It's a commitment to the Greater Pittsburgh area and the region that is genuine and is indicative of the kind of leadership that Stalder provides, who himself is active in a number of diverse community, charitable, and professional organizations.

"I remain convinced that each of us has a responsibility to make a significant contribution to our local community and the organizations that make Pittsburgh a great place to live and work. In spite of our successes, this community faces enormous challenges that must be dealt with in the months and years ahead," he said. "With our broad-based financial and economic perspective, our people are well-equipped to participate in the identification and implementation of solutions to these challenges."

As Price Waterhouse prepares for the 21st century, it faces a formidable array of challenges and opportunities presented by the economic, business and political climates; the regulatory environment; competitive conditions, and, perhaps most importantly, client expectations.

"We recognize that we will not be able to capitalize on the opportunities or the challenges facing us by maintaining the status quo. We are, in fact, committed to continually improve the quality of services provided to our clients. We will be driven by our vision — to be the best professional services firm in the world — by the markets we serve, by our clients, and by our people. We will be recognized as the leader in every important aspect — quality, service, and value." **℗**

During the early years of the industrial age, workers were compensated with salaries or wages but not much more-a simple approach that was the standard until a few decades ago. As workers became more sophisticated, employers rolled out fringe benefits that grew into compensation packages designed to attract the best and brightest.

The increasing complexity of employee benefit packages demanded long-term attention and the support of specialists.

In 1940 Gregg Mockenhaupt, a pioneer in the employee benefit business, founded Gregg Mockenhaupt Associates to provide that support. The firm offered consulting and

MMC&P, Inc.

actuarial services to corporate employers. They also designed, installed, and administered pension, profit sharing, and group insurance plans.

■ *Jere Cowden and Paul Mockenhaupt, principals of MMC&P, work closely with clients, keeping them up to date on rapidly changing benefit and compensation trends.*

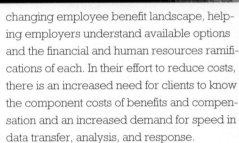

■ *MMC&P Client Service and Support Teams ensure a high level of service in all areas, while focusing on specific client needs.*

In 1983, sons Richard and Paul Mockenhaupt merged their company with Innovative Benefit Concepts (IBC), an actuarial and employee benefit consulting firm owned by Jere Cowden and John Parks. Since then, Mockenhaupt, Mockenhaupt, Cowden & Parks, Inc. (MMC&P) has experienced steady growth and earned an excellent reputation in the business community.

What began as a small company serving clients in western Pennsylvania has grown into one of the region's largest firms, offering employee benefit consulting and administration, actuarial services, and human resources and compensation consulting. MMC&P's client list includes corporations and public entities of all sizes from around the country. MMC&P is headquartered in Pittsburgh with offices in Cleveland, Ohio; Baltimore, Maryland; and Chicago, Illinois.

MMC&P has experienced this ten-year evolution by responding to their clients' needs. A contributing factor to the steady growth is a penchant for innovation and diversification and a strong focus on quality.

According to Richard Mockenhaupt,"We have the breadth of experience to offer an overall strategic approach to employee benefits. This is invaluable for creating new benefit plans or improving existing plans. You must look at the big picture."

Within the firm, which employs more than 115 people, there are three divisions: Corporate Client Services, Public Employee Benefit Services (PEBS), Employee Benefit Data Services (EBDS), and two specialty practices: Compensation Consulting and HMG Health Care Auditing, Inc.

MMC&P's Corporate Division serves corporate and tax exempt entities, providing proactive consulting through close strategic relationships with clients. MMC&P professionals keep pace with the rapidly

changing employee benefit landscape, helping employers understand available options and the financial and human resources ramifications of each. In their effort to reduce costs, there is an increased need for clients to know the component costs of benefits and compensation and an increased demand for speed in data transfer, analysis, and response.

As the critical issue of national health care moves from the theoretical stage to the strategic, it could change the way we buy medical coverage. MMC&P is experienced in the strategic approach to change.

Jere Cowden, Director of Corporate Client Services, feels that MMC&P is poised to meet these challenges. "As the marketplace demands change, the organizations that are able to adapt will fare best. We believe that our size, structure, flexibility, and strategic relationships will permit us and our clients to adapt to rapidly changing conditions while maintaining a high level of quality service."

Public Employee Benefit Services (PEBS) specializes in consulting and service to public sector employers. Benefit planning is extremely important to government employers as they struggle to maintain a high level of benefits on a prescribed fiscal budget. Richard Mockenhaupt, Director of PEBS, states, "We have the expertise to interpret and predict trends, monitor legislative changes that affect plans, and keep the public sector officials up to date on these issues. We can give them much needed support and help them develop an overall strategy for their particular situation."

Employee Benefit Data Services (EBDS) is an information management company providing administrative and data management services to trade associations and larger employers. According to Paul Mockenhaupt, who heads up the EBDS division, "Our division is in a unique situation. We're first a benefits company and second an information management company. When you put those two together, you'll see that we're providing the highest level of service with both sides complementing each other to the benefit of the client. We weld benefits, compensation, and data management."

The specialty practices of Compensation Consulting and HMG Health Care Auditing, Inc. address specific compensation, human resources, and health care claims auditing issues.

A competitive total compensation package does much to attract high quality employees. MMC&P's Compensation Consulting practice can help organizations develop a total compensation program that is unique to their needs, affordable, and highly perceived by their employees and prospective employees.

Cost control for health care benefits is a universal challenge. The specialty practice of HMG Health Care Auditing, Inc. was formed to respond to the challenge. MMC&P has developed computer systems specifically designed to monitor the payment of health care claims, auditing erroneous or duplicate payments. HMG consultants can also help you develop and monitor administrator standards to more effectively contain your health care costs.

As retirement vehicles become more complex and participants more sophisticated, employers must respond by offering state-of-the-art support systems. MMC&P has developed its newest product, DC Daily, in response to the growing need for daily valuation of 401(k)/defined contribution plans. DC Daily offers the unprecedented flexibility of choice among mutual funds, money managers, financial advisors and trustees. When this flexibility is paired with MMC&P's technical expertise and proactive consulting the result is quick and accurate resolution to complex retirement issues.

"Daily valuation gives a participant the option of making investment changes on a daily basis," states John Parks, President and CEO of MMC&P. "DC Daily is our response to this competitive national trend."

■ *John Parks, MMC&P's President and CEO, recognizes the importance of hiring qualified people and supporting them through training and a flexible, positive work environment.*

MMC&P's in-house data management capabilities enable the firm to find creative ways to bring information to clients-ways previously unavailable. The ability to custom design programs in response to unique needs ensures clients state-of-the-art design, recordkeeping, and administration.

MMC&P is an ESOP company comprised of a stable, energetic employee group. There is diversity in age, education and expertise. MMC&P employs actuaries, analysts and specialists, attorneys and accountants well versed in the administration of employee benefit programs, as well as consultants expert in benefit issues, human resources and compensation.

Two of MMC&P's most important assets are employees and clients. MMC&P recognizes the importance of hiring qualified people and then supporting them through training and a flexible, positive work environment. Clients cannot be well served without employees who are effective, productive and satisfied.

MMC&P's service philosophy is based on the team concept. Each team is a select group of people with whom clients can communicate about their unique needs. Client Service Teams consist of experts in each specialty, along with account managers and administrative support personnel.

Client Service Teams specialize in health and welfare and qualified retirement plan consulting including design, implementation, actuarial services, administration, recordkeeping and regulatory compliance for municipal, corporate, and tax exempt entities. Support departments provide legal, technical, communication, accounting, computer systems, and administrative services. These experienced and knowledgeable people work with the Client Service Teams to provide excellent service and quality products.

MMC&P plans to build upon their expertise by offering diversified services that afford the opportunity to become true strategic business and planning partners with their clients. Success is an elusive state, according to John Parks, and to maintain status quo in this decade of ever-increasing competition is to retreat. "We will constantly be alert to new opportunities and, at the same time, continue to improve our existing client service delivery systems," said Parks.

The diversity of its product line, experience, and expertise will continue to enable MMC&P to meet the needs and expectations of their clients. This diversity, along with creativity and a high degree of flexibility places MMC&P in a favorable position to respond to the dynamic nature of the employee benefit business. ▣

■ *Richard Mockenhaupt and the Public Employee Services Division specialize in an overall strategic approach to benefit planning for public sector employers.*

Kabala & Geeseman

Kabala & Geeseman is one of the area's premier "mid sized" law firms, having made a name for itself and a market niche by providing highly specialized services in a core group of related practice areas to professional and entrepreneurial clients.

The firm's lawyers represent business interests, ranging from professional practices in medicine, law, architecture and other fields, to high-technology start-up and real estate development. These closely held businesses all have a common need for experienced legal advice in the areas of tax, retirement planning, professional and business organizations, estate and financial planning. In addition, many of the professionals who require such services are physicians and other healthcare providers, who also need

highly specialized healthlaw counseling. Kabala & Geeseman has over 25 lawyers and legal assistants who provide this full range of services.

Controlled growth has allowed the attorneys in the firm to function in a coordinated team effort, combining expertise in multiple technical areas. The results include creative and practical solutions to problems that confront most business or professional endeavors. The attorneys are prepared to assist in all phases of business development, from incubation through implementation and growth to ultimate disposition, whether through sale, merger or transfer to future generations.

Since its inception, the firm and its members have achieved national recognition for the innovative quality of their practice, as evidenced by the firm's interstate client base and the many national specialty law meetings its lawyers have been invited to address. In addition, due largely to the systems engineering background of Edward J. Kabala, one of the firm's founders, cost effectiveness has been a crusade of the firm from its earliest days. In many areas, client expense is minimized through economies of scale, due to common interests of the firm's large client base.

Kabala & Geeseman's work in the tax and qualified retirement plan area for professional corporations is a good example of the firm's philosophy. In the early 1970s, Kabala & Geeseman was a leader in securing tax benefits that had not previously been available to professionals through incorporation.

Then, in the early 1980s, when Congress passed a succession of laws aimed at restricting tax benefits to both large and small businesses through qualified employee benefit plans, Kabala & Geeseman became an innovator in affordable compliance. The firm responded quickly with customized benefit packages and documents designed to accommodate clients of varying size, with tax and employee benefit problems. To reduce

expenses to individual clients, Kabala & Geeseman worked with the Internal Revenue Service to qualify for volume submitter status and spread the development cost among the more than 1,000 pension and profit sharing plans comprising its client base.

As the needs of its client base changed, the firm developed the expertise needed to serve those needs. When third party reimbursement and the complex Medicare fraud and abuse rules became a predominant concern of its health care clients, the firm developed the expertise to become a leader in reimbursement law, joint ventures and multiple provider practices.

The firm is an approved member of the consulting networks of both the American Medical Association and the Pennsylvania Medical Society.

Kabala & Geeseman's proactive approach allows for protective counseling that has secured numerous advantages for its clients. One facet of this approach is an extensive database that helps identify clients likely to be affected by specific changes in the law. The information encourages early awareness and effective preparation before compliance is mandated, so that appropriate planning can be undertaken.

When pension distribution rules became so complex that existing techniques were inadequate to analyze options and tax consequences, Kabala & Geeseman developed sophisticated proprietary computer software, which enables the firm to make complex financial and tax projections which in turn help its clients make knowledgeable decisions. The firm uses that software and the insights gained to provide analytical support to financial advisors and other law firms, as well as to clients.

Kabala & Geeseman has been guided by the principles that the only certainty is change, and the only identifiable trend is accelerating change. "In both cases," said Edward J. Kabala, "the best preparation is experience."

The emphasis on technical expertise and creative pragmatic problem-solving extends to all areas of the practice, including all types of business and transactional matters, commercial and real estate development, health care, employment law and employee benefits, estate planning and estate administration.

In each case, specific tax, securities, and succession implications affect the overall strategy.

"The fact is that we have the experience," said Robert G. Geeseman, another founding partner. "Not only do our clients rely on us, but many other firms turn to us for guidance."

All law firms strive to provide effective and competent counsel. Kabala & Geeseman places special emphasis on client access. As explained by partner Kenneth E. Lewis: "Evening and weekend calls and consultations are normal. The firm's attorneys are on call at all times because anything that is important to our clients is of critical importance to us."

Led by the six member Board of Directors, Kabala & Geeseman's specialized practice covers Pennsylvania, West Virginia, Maryland, Ohio and parts of several other states.

Edward J. Kabala, one of the founding principals, is active in the corporate, health care, employee benefits and estate administration fields, and is also a frequent author and lecturer on subjects affecting professionals. A 1964 graduate of the Pennsylvania State University, Kabala received his law degree from Duquesne University. He is a member of the American, Pennsylvania and Allegheny County Bar Associations, the National Health Lawyers Association, Academy of Elder Law Attorneys, Pennsylvania Society of Healthcare Attorneys and International Foundation of Employee Benefit Plans.

Robert G. Geeseman specializes in health care, taxation and professional corporations. He received his undergraduate degree in economics from Yale University and his law degree from the University of Michigan. Active in the American Bar Association since

■ *Michael A. Cassidy, Robert G. Geeseman. Photo by David Aschkenas.*
1969, Attorney Geeseman has served as chairman of the Professional Corporation Committee and chairman of the Retirement Committee. In addition to the American, state and county Bar Associations, he is a member of the American Judicature Society, the National Health Lawyers Association, and the Legal Advisory Board of the Small Business Council of America.

Michael A. Cassidy, specializes in the healthlaw and professional corporation areas. He is a member of the National Health Lawyers Association and the American Academy of Hospital Attorneys, and a director of the Pennsylvania Society of Healthcare Attorneys. Mr. Cassidy is also the past chairman of the American Bar Association's Antitrust Section Task Force on Hospital/Physician Joint Ventures, the past chairman and a current member of the board of the Allegheny County Bar Association Healthlaw Section, and served as a member of the Pennsylvania Department of Health MRI/CON Task Force. Mr. Cassidy has lectured and written in healthlaw areas on a national basis, speaking to the Nations Health Lawyers Association, the American Medical Association and numerous legal and medical professional societies.

Susan Foreman Jordan graduated magna cum laude from Brandeis University and received her law degree with honors from the National Law Center of George Washington University. She is admitted to practice in both Pennsylvania and West Virginia, and has been an instructor in the continuing education programs at Penn State and Robert Morris College. Ms. Jordan specializes in the areas of employment law and employee benefits and has lectured extensively in those areas to the American Society of Pension Actuaries, the Securities Industry Institute, Pennsylvania Bar Institute and other professional groups. Her publications have included articles in the Tax Management Compensation Planning Journal and ASPA Pension Actuary.

Kenneth E. Lewis practices in the areas of estate planning, administration and litigation. Mr. Lewis is a former member of the Legacy and Planned Giving Panel and the Board of Directors of the American Cancer Society. He is a frequent lecturer for the Pennsylvania Bar Institute, for which he has co-authored several publications, and numerous other community and professional groups.

Alan Z. Lefkowitz practices corporate and securities law and is a member of the Governing Council and former Chairman of the Corporation, Banking and Business Law Section of the Allegheny County Bar Association. He serves as Chairman of the Securities Law Regulation Subcommittee of that Section. He has lectured at the University of Pittsburgh Law School on corporate control and corporate succession matters and for the Advanced Technology Entrepreneurial Center of Pitt's Katz Graduate School of Business on business start-ups, venture capital financing and securities issues.

What began as a challenge to reform the tax laws to recognize professional corporations has evolved into a major law practice specializing in all aspects of business, health law, tax and estate planning, qualified retirement plans and employee benefits and commercial real estate transactions.

"We believe we're in just the right position to address those issues that most concern our clients and to actively assist them in finding solutions that are creative and make good business sense," said Kabala.

■ *Alan Z. Lefkowitz, Edward J. Kabala. Photo by David Aschkenas.*

"Complementing the Pittsburgh Renaissance"

Kirkpatrick & Lockhart is a Pittsburgh creation of the last half century. Founded by seven young lawyers on the eve of the first Pittsburgh Renaissance, Kirkpatrick & Lockhart has provided legal services to the Pittsburgh community throughout the period of Pittsburgh's rebirth and renewal.

The founding partners of Kirkpatrick & Lockhart were originally associated with another Pittsburgh law firm but left in the early 1940s to enter military service. Returning to Pittsburgh at the end of World

■ Robert L. Kirkpatrick

■ George D. Lockhart

Kirkpatrick & Lockhart

War II, they decided to establish a small general practice firm of their own. They began practice in 1946 under the name of Kirkpatrick, Pomeroy, Lockhart & Johnson.

Today Kirkpatrick & Lockhart is one of the largest firms in the country, with more than 325 lawyers in Boston, Harrisburg, Miami, and Washington, D.C., as well as Pittsburgh. The Pittsburgh office is now the largest law office in the city.

The founding partners believed that lawyers should have a broad grounding in the law, and they brought to their new endeavor experience in a wide variety of legal fields – corporate law, banking, municipal finance, estates and trusts, real estate, bankruptcy and reorganization, railroad and public utility law, and litigation in federal and state courts. The breadth of their experience and their associations

within the Pittsburgh community soon attracted clients to the firm.

Since its founding, Kirkpatrick & Lockhart's practice has been rooted in the activities and the life of the greater Pittsburgh community. The firm has advised a growing body of clients, including major corporations and financial enterprises; small businesses, partnerships and entrepreneurial groups; governmental units and municipal authorities;

educational, medical, charitable and civic organizations; foundations; and individuals.

The partners today believe that the practice will continue to reflect the life of the community. Thus, the opening of the Midfield Terminal both ratifies and anticipates trends in the practice of law. For while the firm's practice still has a local and regional core, it has expanded to include matters of national and international significance, many of which originate outside Pittsburgh.

■ Kirkpatrick & Lockhart is one of the largest firms in the country, with more than 325 lawyers in Boston, Harrisburg, Miami, and Washington, D.C., as well as Pittsburgh.

Today, Kirkpatrick & Lockhart serves clients whose operations are national or multinational in scope. Whether they produce stainless steel or robots, jet engines or computer software, banking products or health care services, the firm's clients face practical legal problems that cut across disciplines, embrace disparate areas of substantive law and require legal services in various locations throughout the nation and the world.

In rendering those services, Kirkpatrick & Lockhart draws upon lawyers from its different offices, lawyers who work together to meet client needs.

After nearly 50 years, the firm continues to believe that its lawyers must have experience in varied areas of the law, but it knows that the growing complexity of society and increasing legislative activity of governments at all levels require increased specialization. Breadth of experience and specialized skills are both necessary resources for a client facing an increasingly complex world with diverse, and sometimes conflicting, legal requirements.

In keeping with the vision of its founding partners, Kirkpatrick & Lockhart has made contributions to the Pittsburgh community that have not been limited to the legal services it provides to its business clients. Members of the firm have devoted substantial amounts of time to pro-bono, charitable, educational, governmental, civic and professional groups in areas of their particular interests.

Indeed, firm lawyers have devoted hundreds of hours to a pro-bono Pittsburgh legal initiative to protect the rights of battered women. They have participated actively in the leadership campaign of Neighborhood Legal Services and led all Pittsburgh law firms in contributions to the United Way.

Members of Kirkpatrick & Lockhart have served on the boards of 134 not-for-profit organizations and as President of the Allegheny County Bar Association, and they have addressed professional congregations from Munich to New York to San Francisco and ,of course, in Pittsburgh.

In light of the past half century, Kirkpatrick & Lockhart knows that change is inevitable. Pittsburgh has evolved greatly since 1946, and Kirkpatrick & Lockhart has changed – and grown – with the city. But Kirkpatrick &

Lockhart knows that some elements must remain constant in the practice of law: responsibilty, competence, integrity and hard work. These collectively have been the hallmarks of Kirkpatrick & Lockhart since its founding. They are the standards against which the firm confidently measures its future.

■ Members of Kirkpatrick & Lockhart have served on the boards of 134 not-for-profit organizations.

■ With JSA's expertise behind it, PNC Bank has transformed innovative banking concepts utilizing architectural and interior design at its North Hills Regional Banking Center. Photo by Lockwood Hoehl.

Somewhere between the strict function of a building and the boundless artistic possibilities for its appearance lies a design that is both efficient and handsome.

Finding it in a manner that advances the interests of the owner is a job for the architects Johnson/Schmidt and Associates (JSA).

"Our firm has always believed that we serve the interests of our client, whether it is a corporation or a government institution," said James B. Johnson, AIA, president and director of design.

"The challenge in designing a building is not whether an architect likes a particular style. The issue is to resolve all the factors — the activities that will go on inside, along with

Johnson/Schmidt and Associates

the features of the land and utilities that affect the site — in a design that is aesthetically pleasing."

"We've had the good fortune to have as our clients, over the years, owners who are realistic about cost and who allow us to create good designs, using good materials."

Serving as the foundation of JSA's architectural, engineering and interior design services is its commitment to quality. JSA's Quality Improvement Program addresses the quality of design, and documents communication and services offered.

With JSA's capabilities behind it, PNC Bank's Robinson Town Centre regional banking center was named Suburban Office Building of the Year by the Building Owners and Management Association.

In typical JSA style, the architects studied the owner's business strategy in order to transform the banking center concept into bricks and mortar that has helped set new standards in the banking industry. Once completed, JSA was commissioned to design an improvement on the concept at PNC's North Hills Regional Banking Center (see featured photo).

The firm's heritage dates to the late 1930s in Pittsburgh, where its founders, Roy Hoffman and Ken Crumpton, rose through the prestigious firm Jannsen & Cocken Architects.

They were classically trained architects who worked with steel, stone, wood, and glass to reproduce the grace and grandeur of the Classical European and Wren Colonial styles.

The firm achieved national recognition with the completion of five regional shopping malls, including South Hills Village, Monroeville Mall, and more than 13 million square feet of other retail projects across the eastern United States. It specializes in building technology for corporate, financial, retail, material handling, educational, and government organizations.

Besides Johnson, who joined the firm in 1957, the principals of JSA are Thomas W. Schmidt, AIA, executive vice president, secretary, and general manager; James V. Eckles, AIA, senior vice president; Edward A. Shriver, Jr., AIA, vice president and office manager; and M. Timothy Lawler, PhD, PE, principal engineer.

With 40 members, JSA has sufficient resources to undertake projects of nearly any size, but it is organized to function so that when owners engage the firm, they engage the principals as well. JSA's practice is to apply its best talent and principal involvement from every discipline to every project.

JSA tends to have long-standing relationships with clients. More than 75 percent of its annual commissions are from past clients.

JSA has served the May Department Stores Company, based in St. Louis, in the design of stores, corporate offices, and distribution centers for 20 years. Among recent May Company projects was the 1.3 million

square foot Lord & Taylor distribution center in Wilkes-Barre, Pennsylvania, office consolidations of several May Company divisions, store renovations, and new stores.

The firm consolidated on 16 acres at Solon, Ohio, two manufacturing plants of Kennametal, Inc. The 180,000-square-foot center, encompassing high-tech manufacturing, a computer center, food service, and management and engineering offices, was named to Industry Week magazine's "America's 10 Best Plants."

The firm's work is aided by extensive use of computers, including advanced software that is being developed in conjunction with research at Carnegie Mellon University. It is not uncommon for JSA clients to visualize a building with the aid of computer models before the first shovelful of dirt has been turned.

As the needs of its clients have expanded, so has the breadth of services offered by JSA. Where corporate owners once turned to architects to design a building, they now find that their needs are changing at such a rapid pace that they need professional help managing the use of their space as well. Some of the same technology that puts JSA at the cutting edge of architectural design also gives the firm capabilities in the unfolding area of facilities management.

"Technology is leading us into the next century. It has already had profound effects on the way we live and work, and the pace of change is accelerating," Johnson said. "Architecture has a role to play in that process, and our firm is casting seeds today that will bear fruit for our clients tomorrow."

■ *Photo by Roy Engelbrecht.*

CHAPTER
Building Greater Pittsburgh
THIRTEEN

The Pennsylvanian,
250-251

RUST Engineering,
252-253

Dick Group of Companies,
254-255

Limbach Company, 256

The Pennsylvanian, once a gateway between Pittsburgh and distant places, has now become a gateway between Pittsburgh's past and the city's future.

As Pennsylvania Station, this spectacular turn-of-the-century building was a thriving railroad hub. Under a domed, sky-lit portico, a circular driveway swirled with arriving and departing passengers.

Rechristened The Pennsylvanian, which opened in 1988, it remains a nexus of ground transportation. Buses, trains, and subway cars converge by road, rail, and tunnel. But its grand style is burnished these days for the tenants of its luxury apartments and offices and for the guests at receptions and banquets held in its grand concourse.

The Pennsylvanian

Where The Pennsylvanian became more than just a big, ornate apartment building and mass transit stop was in its power to inspire the city to contemplate the untapped potential in the mud-colored real estate lurking on the northeastern edge of downtown Pittsburgh.

In tandem with the nearby Benedum Center for the Performing Arts, Liberty Center, and Heinz Hall, The Pennsylvanian encouraged city planners to create the Pittsburgh Cultural District in an area along Liberty and Penn Avenues where massage parlors, strip joints, and drug dens squatted when the city wasn't looking.

Proponents of the Cultural District hoped to do for upper Liberty and the Strip District, (which flank The Pennsylvanian,) what Renaissance I had done for Pittsburgh's Point in bringing commercial development to a neglected area.

The Pennsylvanian has known neglect. The railroad station faded under

■ *While still a nexus for ground transportation, the Pennsylvanian offers luxury apartments, offices, and a beautiful location for receptions and banquets.*

decades of blackening soot and disuse. It almost disappeared entirely under the wrecking ball despite its roots in one of the 19th century's most prominent and powerful corporations.

The turn of the century was the height of the Golden Age of rail transportation, and to celebrate the power of their industry, railroad companies all over the country built cathedrals to their greatness in the form of opulent stations.

The Pennsylvania Railroad was one of the giants of the period, and Pittsburgh was making do with a large but mundane building. Compared to what was about to be built, it was little more than a train barn.

The Pennsylvania Railroad turned to D.H. Burnham & Co. of Chicago for a design for a new station in Pittsburgh. Burnham & Co. had planned the 1893 Chicago World's Fair and designed many of the early skyscrapers there.

Daniel Burnham gave the new station a Beaux-arts, neo-Baroque style that incorporated a brown brick and terra cotta shell. It was the vogue of the day. The building had two main parts, a 12-story office tower and the train shed. While the station opened October 1, 1901, the entire complex was not completed until 1903.

■ *The School House, formerly known as the Latimer School, was originally constructed in 1898. Historic Landmarks for Living renovated The School House on Tripoli Street in Pittsburgh's historic Deutchtown district in 1985, creating 77 luxury apartments. The large classroom windows were retained, flooding the apartments with light. A view of downtown Pittsburgh's skyline across the Allegheny River can be enjoyed from the upper floors.*

Pennsylvania Station took much of its glamour from the entryway, which consisted of a domed rotunda set on four arches, through which the two-story concourse received light.

The station twice survived natural disaster. On October 20, 1920 a landslide from an adjacent cliff caused damage estimated then at $1 million and closed the passenger area for seven months. By May of 1921, the station was fully operational. Sixteen years later, in 1936, the floods of that year closed the station for four days after a train wreck.

■ *Shadyside Commons, formerly the J. A. Williams warehouse, housing wholesale appliances, hardware and, at one point in its history, toys, was converted in 1986 to 148 distinctive apartments. Located on Amberson Avenue in the Shadyside area of Pittsburgh, this historic landmark which was built in 1903, features spiral staircases to lofts, wood beamed ceilings, brick walls, and a natural courtyard carved out of the center of the former warehouse.*

By 1947, the station was showing its age. The train shed was torn down and a new $27-million facility was built, making the station more quiet and giving it a more streamlined appearance. As the era of train transportation gave way to cars, trucks, and planes, Pennsylvania Station receded into history.

In 1963, the Grand Rotunda was listed in the Historical American Building Survey. Four years later the Pittsburgh History and Landmarks Foundation gave a historic designation to the station, acknowledging Burnham's contribution to Pittsburgh's heritage.

The low point for the building came in the 1970s. By then, the structure was unused and deteriorating through huge water leaks. City officials began to see the station as more of an eyesore than an architectural inheritance. Plans were made to replace it with a park.

According to Michael Gamble, property manager of The Pennsylvanian, Pennsylvania Station escaped the wrecking ball in 1985 and got a new lease on life after Historic Landmarks for Living in Philadelphia took on the $45-million job of transforming it into The Pennsylvanian.

The same company renovated the old Latimer School on the Northside and a year later opened Shadyside Commons from the ruins of the old J.A. Williams Warehouse.

Historic Landmarks for Living (HLFL) has renovated 20 buildings in Philadelphia and 6 in the Harrisburg area. It has also completed projects in Baltimore, Chicago, Milwaukee, and St. Paul. HLFL has dedicated itself to preserving and managing properties that will bring older architecture to a new generation.

In 1991, the Grand Rotunda received historic landmark status by the Pennsylvania Historic Landmark Foundation. Also that year the area's Building Owners and Management Association gave The Pennsylvanian its Special Purpose Building of the Year Award.

The Pennsylvanian still serves as a station for Amtrak trains, Port Authority Transit buses, and the steel-wheeled cars of the underground trolley system known as the T.

The office and residential portion of the building features marble floors, terra cotta pilasters, vaulted ceilings, and dramatic skylights. The 242 residential units include studio apartments, platform one-bedrooms, one- and two-bedroom units, one- and two-bedroom lofts, and two-bedroom townhouses.

A number of the 10th-floor apartments feature spiral staircases with lofts and hardwood floors. The 10th floor also has three apartments that were once Pennsylvania Railroad executive offices, where all the historic details have been preserved. The 12th and 13th floors have become one, with apartments arranged as two-story townhouses. A number of apartments have been set aside for short-term rentals with business travelers in mind.

The building also has a fitness room, a community room, and the concourse has the capacity to seat about 600 people for catered banquets and more than 1,000 for receptions. The Pennsylvanian was the site of the National Hockey League President's Reception when the league held its All-Star game in Pittsburgh.

■ *"The Pennsylvanian is the crown jewel of the company," says Scott K. Davis, regional property manager of the company.*

In the words of Scott K. Davis, CPM, regional property manager for Historic Landmarks for Living, "The Pennsylvanian is the crown jewel of the company."

Whether it's steel, breakfast cereal, chemicals, aerospace, or paper products, RUST has what it takes to design, build, and automate the factories that make the products demanded by an ever-more competitive world.

For nearly a century, RUST has been providing the latest in planning and design assistance, construction services, state-of-the-art process automation and production control technology.

"At one time, the RUST company was synonymous with the steel industry. But just like industrial America, which is constantly evolving to compete in global economy, we've built on our traditional strengths and diversi-

■ RUST has built and modernized mills for many of the nation's top steel producers.

RUST Engineering Company

fied into a wide range of capabilities that the times require," said Raymond E. Meyer, general manager of the Northeast region. With more than 35 years of experience, Meyer is the senior manager of RUST's Pittsburgh operations.

That diversity gives RUST expertise in many industries including the metals, chemicals, food and beverage, pulp and paper, energy, and aerospace sectors.

RUST is a company of RUST International Inc., one of the operating groups within WMX Technologies, Inc., the former Waste Management, Inc. WMX Technologies, with projected 1993 sales of $10 billion, is one of the world's largest environmental and infrastructure companies with major positions in remediation, alternative fuel cogeneration, air

■ RUST has constructed many major industrial projects.

pollution control technology, and water and wastewater treatment.

As WMX Technologies' Chief Executive Officer Dean L. Buntrock puts it, "There are very few environmental or infrastructure systems or services that we do not provide."

Within WMX Technologies' family of companies, Birmingham, Alabama based RUST is the principal supplier of technology development, and engineering and construction services. RUST currently employs over 12,000 people including 5,000 scientists, engineers, and project managers. Expected revenues for 1993 are $1.8 billion.

Pittsburgh is home to RUST Engineering Company's Northeast region, which is a full-service engineering office, located at 441 Smithfield Street. "The Pittsburgh office has a strong reputation in its own right as a part of RUST. But more than that, our office represents a doorway through which all the capabilities of RUST International Inc. and the operating companies of WMX Technologies are accessible to our clients," Meyer said.

RUST has built steel mills for USX Corporation and has performed food production plant study work for H. J. Heinz Company, two of Pittsburgh's biggest corporate names. Customers range from Coca-Cola and General Foods to NASA and The Timken Company. RUST's array of services also includes financing and equity investment projects.

RUST is a major participant in the pulp and paper industry. In fact, RUST has been involved in developing over 20 percent of the total new domestic capacity built between the mid 1970s and the early 1990s. This is a larger share than any other engineering firm in the United States.

In the chemicals industry, RUST has played key roles in major projects for Monsanto, Amoco, Hoechst Celanese, and many other companies. RUST recently completed construction of an activated carbon products plant in Mississippi for Pittsburgh-based Calgon Carbon Corp., and a polypropylene plant in Marcus Hook, Pennsylvania, for Epsilon Products.

In the energy industry, RUST has become the most experienced full-service contractor for the North American trash-to-energy industry. The company built the nation's first such plant in Saugus, Massachusetts, in the early 1970s, and later engineered improvements to the plant. Similar projects in Broward County, Florida, earned RUST the Florida Institute of Consulting Engineers 1992 Engineering Excellence Award.

RUST has done extensive work for U.S. government agencies, from the Postal Service, which sought help planning the upgrade of numerous mail handling facilities, to defense- and aerospace-related agencies. One aerospace project involved engineering

■ *The chemical industry is served by RUST. Photo by David C. Lewis.*

and construction of NASA's Advanced Solid Rocket Motor facility in Iuka, Mississippi. The booster rockets to be produced at this facility were designed to replace the space shuttle's twin solid rocket motors after the loss of the Challenger in 1986. RUST, acting as part of a team with Lockheed-Aerojet, provided much of the preliminary facility design work required for the proposal to NASA and continued as engineer for the project.

RUST is a technical leader in the use of three-dimensional computer aided design (3-D CAD). This advanced technology is used in a variety of industrial and environmental applications. This cutting-edge technology saves time and money by enabling planners to visualize, on a computer screen, a finished project in three dimensions.

A related CAD-based construction information system addresses design, construction, start-up, operations, and maintenance. It brings the benefits of three-dimensional computer modeling to construction personnel in the field, resulting in increased productivity and profitability.

Through its Enterprise Integration Center, which uses computer technology to simulate a company's work systems environment, RUST helps clients in many industries achieve competitive advantages in order management, inventory management, plant scheduling and management, production planning, laboratory automation, and maintenance.

RUST, with 90 years' experience as of 1995, is a company whose history involves three generations of the Rust family, the cities of Pittsburgh and Birmingham, and growth through a series of corporate mergers that have involved some of the most recognizable names in American industry: Swindell Dressler Company, M. W. Kellogg Company, Pullman, Inc., Litton Industries, Allied Signal, and Wheelabrator-Frye, Inc.

In Pittsburgh, around the turn of the century, a group of brothers founded Rust Boiler Company which manufactured and sold an improved and patented vertical steam boiler. When customers began asking for help with boiler erection and brickwork construction, the three brothers formed the Rust Engineering Company in 1905 and rapidly gained a reputation for technical expertise in their field.

In 1920, the brothers divided their business into three corporations with offices in Pittsburgh, Washington, D.C., and Birmingham. During the Depression, the Birmingham office changed its name to Rust Construction Company and concentrated on smaller projects, allowing the Pittsburgh office to focus on larger engineering projects nationwide. Engineering headquarters were moved from Pittsburgh to Birmingham in

1971, the year in which the company was acquired by Wheelabrator-Frye, Inc., now successor company, Wheelabrator Technologies.

RUST became part of WMX Technologies in 1990 through WMX's majority interest in Wheelabrator. In late 1992, WMX announced that RUST would become an independent division of WMX Technologies.

"It is RUST's personnel who provide time-proven experience in project development, project management, and engineering and construction services. And it is RUST's tradition of flexibility—quick and efficient direction of both engineering and construction resources to a project, regardless of size—that keeps the company competitive," Meyer said.

The fact that more than 80 percent of the company's project assignments come from repeat customers attests to RUST's success.

"The depth of those relationships has made us, in some cases, essentially a partner with the client, supporting them, working for their success. In fact, the trend towards partnering is nothing new to RUST. Clients have asked us to come back so often that partnering is really second nature to us."

■ *RUST Engineering Company's Northeast Office is located at 441 Smithfield Street.*

Noble J. Dick began his construction business in 1922 building garages and home additions in Indiana, Pennsylvania.

Today, under the leadership of his grandsons, David and Douglas, Dick Corporation is the Pittsburgh area's largest construction firm. The company has built or managed the construction of Pittsburgh's new international airport along with bridges, train stations, research centers, power plants, hospitals, and prisons across the United States.

Despite vigorous growth in the company and sweeping changes in the construction industry in the intervening years, Dick Corporation has been steadfast in its dedica-

Greater Pittsburgh International Airport New Midfield Terminal

The Dick Group of Companies

Dick Group of Companies

tion to excellence in the management of its assets and resources and in its approach to the marketplace.

``We like our clients to know that we are a well-established, deeply experienced construction company. We intend to be here for a long time. And we're financially sound, which is always a concern with clients today.

``More than that, we bring a highly qualified team to our projects. We like to think we have qualifications that some of our competitors don't,'' said David E. Dick, Chief Executive Officer.

The Dick Group of Companies is headquartered south of Pittsburgh in Large, Pennsylvania. The company includes groups that focus on commercial and institutional projects, the power and resource recovery industries, bridges and highways, and construction services.

Even though Dick Corporation was the largest construction firm in Pittsburgh and the 36th-largest in the United States in 1992, Douglas Dick, President, says the company does not embrace the notion that bigger is better.

``We did not structure the organization to be No. 1. in volume. Ranking has no bearing. What does it mean? Our objective is to not be big for the sake of being big,'' he said.

The family-run company regards its high ranking as a measure of its efficiency in meeting client needs and the quality of the services it provides.

The Dick Group of Companies embarked on another kind of growth when it embraced Total Quality Management, an approach to business that empowers individual employees to help lead the way to excellence.

``If your company's entire work force is encouraged to contribute ideas, rather than a company whose only ideas come from a few people at the top, you can develop a culture of excellence much more quickly,'' according to Douglas Dick.

``Communication is a big part of that process. In our company, management is not isolated. We have an organi-

zational chart, but we also have an open-door policy. Anybody could walk through my office door at any minute with a new idea. It could be someone who digs ditches or the chief financial officer.''

TQM goes hand in hand with Dick's belief that it delivers greatest value to clients when it is invited into a project at the earliest possible moment.

``Our experience and expertise covers the complete range of project stages from start to finish. The greatest and best use of our capabilities is to let Dick Corporation apply its knowledge to each phase. In that way, we provide continuity of control, assured execution, and optimum efficiency all the way from the design stage to occupancy,'' Dick said.

The family's approach to the business has allowed the company to grow to where it employs about 3,000 workers during the peak construction season.

``We've always hired the best talent we can get. As our employees grow in their work, they want bigger projects to challenge them. Dick Corporation grows as they grow,'' said Douglas Dick, President.

That approach has also enabled Dick Corporation to participate in a number of prominent projects, including those in the state and national capitals.

In 1982, the Pennsylvania General Assembly directed the Department of General Services to revive a plan to add new office space and a concourse linking the State Office Building to the Capitol Building in Harrisburg.

Kennametal, Inc.
Latrobe, Pennsylvania

The Dick Group of Companies

Dick's mission was to translate the elegance of the architect's vision into a complex of bricks and mortar. The work required the builder to institute operating efficiencies that allowed for cost-effective construction while preserving the architectural integrity of the Capitol complex.

One key was finding granite and glass that would provide continuity between the buildings. Artisans found the granite at the Vermont quarry that yielded the original stone. Solar-tinted glass was selected to reflect the building's image and raise energy efficiency.

The task in Harrisburg was to blend a new building with an old one. In Washington, D.C., the challenge was to restore an important building.

The Union Station Redevelopment Corporation chose Dick Corporation in 1986 to revive Union Station, the landmark turn-of-the-century rail station in the nation's capital.

With the date of the opening gala set when the project began, the Dick Corporation team had literally a million things to do all at the same time. The work of craftsmen had to be meshed with that of demolition and construction crews.

Because the 1908 design was not sufficient to carry loads produced by modern construction techniques or to accommodate the weight of the crane required to set structural steel, Dick engineers devised a dual platform system, which walked the crane down the concourse to distribute its weight.

To replace glass in the arched ceiling, Dick developed a process of laminating a new mesh-patterned glass, replicating the look of the old rolled glass. With that, Dick Corporation created a technology for historic glass.

Union Station reopened in September 1988, welcoming Amtrak and local commuter passengers along with millions of visitors to its new restaurants and mall.

Dick Corporation's greatest achievement may be its contribution to the rebuilding of Pittsburgh International Airport. Dick worked with Mellon-Stuart Company to prepare the 900-acre site for the 1.6-million-square-foot terminal along with roadways, parking areas, and the underground people-mover.

Dick also worked near the airport on the construction of White Swan Interchange, built on the site of the former White Swan Amusement Park on the Parkway West. The airport and highway opened in late 1992, slightly ahead of schedule.

The Dick Group also has broad experience in hospital and prison construction, including the new Allegheny County jail, and the building of highways, bridges, and resource recovery facilities.

After more than a decade of solid growth leading to the 1990s, Dick Corporation sees promising opportunities for the future.

"Probably the most active region for our company will be the Northeast," said Douglas Dick. "The company should be strong in the construction of infrastructure projects, hospitals, and office buildings. We also see opportunities in the construction of mechanical systems for the power industry."

Dick Corporation avoided overseas projects and exotic segments of the construction and industrial services markets. It has preferred to concentrate on the areas it knows best and where it can deliver the greatest value to clients.

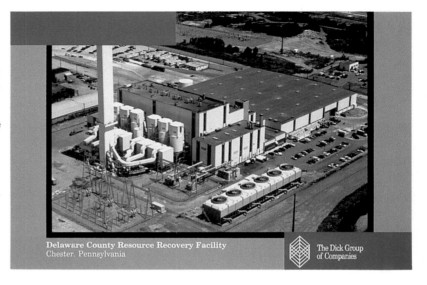

Delaware County Resource Recovery Facility
Chester, Pennsylvania

The Dick Group of Companies

"The only new area we are likely to enter is hazardous waste. That's going to be a huge market, given the demand in an increasingly environmentally minded society," said David Dick.

Meanwhile, in the construction business, the key to future work is the recent past.

"You have to sell on your past qualifications. You're only as good as your last job. Once you've established your qualifications for the project, the key is to determine what the owner is looking for. When you find that out, you can tailor the project to meet the need. In that regard, we're basically a service industry helping people who are looking to their own futures," said Douglas Dick.

West End Bridge
Pittsburgh, Pennsylvania

The Dick Group of Companies

■ Neal Sasser, chief executive officer, and his son Craig, project manager of Limbach, beneath portraits of the founding family. (left to right) Frank, Emil, Scott, and Walter Limbach. Photo by Roy Engelbrecht.

At the turn of the century, before the city of Allegheny became Pittsburgh's North Side, German immigrant Frank Limbach was already a renowned craftsman in his adopted homeland.

Apprenticing at an early age as a sheet metal craftsmen, Frank had come to America in the 1880s to work for several contractors in booming Pittsburgh. Having lost his job in an early union lockout in 1901, he responded in a very American way by opening his own business on Lowrie Street in the Troy Hill district.

His son, Emil, took leadership in the late 1920s and ran the company through the Depression years and into the 1950s, when

Limbach Company

■ At the turn of the century, Frank Limbach was already a renowned craftsman in his adopted homeland.

he turned it over to his sons, Walter and Scott. Today, the Limbach Company is one of the nation s top five mechanical contractors, according to Contractor magazine, with sales of more than $145 million and clients around the United States.

From its offices in Pittsburgh, Boston, Detroit, Columbus, Los Angeles and Orlando, Limbach has provided mechanical systems—heating, cooling, ventilation and plumbing—for some of the country's largest construction projects, including sports arenas, manufacturing plants, hospitals, institutions, high technology laboratories, defense projects, as well as commercial and retail facilities.

In 1992, Limbach participated in one of the major projects contributing to the resurgence of the Pittsburgh region's economy:

the renovation of the factory to be used by Sony Corporation to manufacture color televisions and television picture tubes in Westmoreland County.

Although this was a new plant for Sony, Limbach had been involved with the facility and its evolution for many years.

It was Limbach that provided the mechanical systems for the original building erected by Chrysler Corporation in 1968. Chrysler never used the plant and eventually sold it to Volkswagen of America in the mid-1970s. After VW vacated the plant a decade later, Limbach was called upon once again, this time by Sony to install the high-tech mechanical systems specially designed to manufacture televisions.

"We met all their technical criteria and assisted in making the renovation of this plant affordable. That's what Sony was looking for—value," said Limbach Co. Chief Executive Officer Neal Sasser, whose father, James, co-founded the mechanical division in 1946 with Scott Limbach.

Limbach's long-term work on the Sony plant, along with contracts to modernize food production facilities at the H.J. Heinz plant on the North Side, its work with Allegheny General, Children's and Presbyterian University hospitals and the Somerset County Prison and its renovation of Allegheny Center in Pittsburgh for Integra Bank exemplify the company's determination to provide creative solutions to customers' needs, Sasser said.

Like most companies, Limbach suffered during the economic downturn of the early 1990s. But as the economy improves and more of the firm's customers begin investing in renovations and new facilities, changes by Limbach during the 1980s have begun to pay off.

"We streamlined in some areas, but we also grew into new markets," Sasser said. "We grew in quality and diversified, while actually reducing our volume."

Perhaps the most significant change instituted by the company was the introduction of

an unusual franchising program—known as LINC—providing marketing, personnel, operations and accounting expertise to more than 160 heating and air conditioning contractors worldwide. LINC contractors provide HVAC maintenance on more than 70,000 buidings in the United States. More than 3,000 employees from as far as Australia, Asia and Saudi Arabia visit Pittsburgh annually in conjunction with LINC training.

Limbach also created the Affiliated Building Services division to provide long-term service and maintenance for large buildings or commercial sites that require an on-site workforce. ABS goes beyond mechanical maintenance to play key roles in electrical, general building maintenance and property management. ABS handles mechanical maintenance for the international airports in Atlanta, Newark, Boston and New York. The division operates in 17 states as well as a number of other countries.

"We service the mechanical systems we design and install, and we guarantee their efficient performance year after year," Sasser said. "This allows our customers to concentrate on their business, not on their buildings' environmental systems."

While Limbach's ambitions are global, it maintains a commitment to its community through direct support of local development initiatives typified by the Limbach Neighborhood Center a few blocks from where the company was founded.

"An unchanged principle throughout the changing times since 1901 has been Limbach's commitment to develop, train and invest in people. That tradition has enabled Limbach to expand beyond traditional contracting to take a position on the cutting edge of design-build expansion and post-construction services."

■ Photo at right by Roy Engelbrecht.

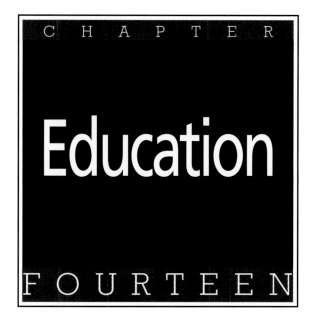

CHAPTER

Education

FOURTEEN

Robert Morris College, 260-261

La Roche College, 262-263

Indiana University of Pennsylvania, 264-265

For all of its seven decades in existence, Robert Morris College has been growing in search of better ways to meet the needs of its students.

The tradition promises only to intensify during the 1990s. Historically a business college with a focus on accounting, Robert Morris has responded to the needs of an evolving economy and the broadening interests of students by offering innovative degree programs in such areas as health services management, aviation management and sports management.

"In the future, you'll see more of this kind of diversification and more emphasis on graduate programs," said Dr. Edward A.

Robert Morris College

■ State-of-the-art technology prepares Robert Morris students for careers in any of downtown Pittsburgh's Fortune 500 companies. Photo by David J. Hiteshue

Nicholson, president of Robert Morris, "simply because that's where student interest is emerging." For example, annual enrollment in the Robert Morris MBA program doubled from the late 1980s to the early 1990s.

The college's ability to adapt to new academic demands attracted the recognition of hundreds of the nation's college presidents

and deans, who named Robert Morris the No. 1 "Up and Coming" specialty business college two years in a row in U.S. News & World Report magazine.

Recently, anticipating a continuing shift in the makeup of the economy, Robert Morris took steps to prepare for increasing numbers of students to enter the health services area. The shift was foreshadowed by a rapid growth of an undergraduate-level health services major, which attracted 150 students in the first two years it was offered. Because of that response, Robert Morris now expects to add a health services management major to its list of graduate-level business administration courses.

In its first 10 years, the sports management program at Robert Morris distinguished itself from those offered by other institutions in numerous ways, Nicholson said.

Unlike programs that focus on physical education, the Robert Morris program concentrates on the business of sports, including marketing, facility management and communication.

"A Robert Morris sports management major might end up as a sports information officer, in ticket sales, or in an accounting capacity with the Steelers or the Pirates," he said.

The sports management program is one that draws many students from outside the Pittsburgh area, making it a key component in the college's effort to expand enrollment of applicants from the eastern part of Pennsylvania, as well as from surrounding states and the rest of the country.

■ Robert Morris College's 230-acre main campus is located in suburban Moon Township just minutes from both downtown Pittsburgh and the Pittsburgh International Airport. Photo by David J. Hiteshue.

The college embraces its self-imposed "obligation to offer qualified individuals the means to start and the encouragement to continue the lifelong growth process through higher education." To accomplish its goal, the college enhances undergraduate and graduate programs with continuing education programs for professionals seeking required education credits or certification, individuals undertaking career changes and mature students returning to the classroom.

At all levels, Robert Morris places a strong emphasis on experience and hands-on learning, with emphasis on internships to ensure that students are fully prepared to enter the job market. "Throughout all of our programs we strive to provide a good blend of practice and theory," Nicholson said. "It's very often that employers will say the difference between Robert Morris and other institutions is that Robert Morris graduates are ready to go to work the day they graduate."

The Cooperative Education Program has placed students in internships at such companies as USX, Mellon Bank, Westinghouse, United Parcel Service, and Walt Disney World, as well as numerous accounting firms, hospitals and law offices.

Bolstering the internship program are faculty members who are eminently familiar with the practical applications of the subjects they teach.

"The typical Robert Morris professor has an advanced academic degree in addition to 10 or more years as a professional practitioner in his or her field," Nicholson said. "There's an emphasis in our curriculum on providing the skills necessary to be productive immediately," he said. "We're a teaching institution, not a research institution."

An appreciation for practical knowledge permeates Robert Morris College. In an era when information management is an increasingly critical corporate function, Robert Morris formed an institute to set worldwide standards for a user-friendly data management system known as MUMPS. The institute was placed under the direction of a former IBM scholar on MUMPS research. Created to track patient, physician and hospital records, the system was adopted by the European travel industry and showed promise for additional applications.

"As an institution that is attuned to the needs and direction of the business world, Robert Morris will likely undertake other initiatives like the MUMPS institute in order to share our areas of specialized expertise," said Jo-Ann Sipple, vice president of Academic Affairs.

In the Communications Department, students work in a state-of-the-art video production studio, where they have produced award-winning satellite education programs for the Public Broadcasting System.

In recognition of its strengths in that area, Robert Morris was chosen to document the construction of the new terminal at Pittsburgh International Airport and to document the redevelopment of the old airport terminal.

"The point is, these students are learning in the classroom by doing, and the quality of the work is outstanding," Nicholson said. "When they go out for jobs, they can use these videos as part of their portfolios. That typifies the Robert Morris philosophy."

■ *Students at Robert Morris College enjoy a variety of activities, including intramurals, Greek Life, theatrical productions and a Division I basketball team, a perennial participant in the NCAA Tournament. Photo by David J. Hiteshue.*

The school's faculty also has committed itself to instilling in students the importance of effective communications and writing skills in all fields of study.

The Writing Across the Curriculum program at Robert Morris has received national recognition for its emphasis on writing as a path towards better thinking in business, math and liberal arts. For example, a student studying cost accounting would use ungraded writing assignments to grasp the theory of overhead by outlining and analyzing the steps that determine production costs and selling price.

"We're not going to enter into the perennial bashing of why students can't communicate effectively; we're going to do something about it, regardless of their major," Nicholson said.

But even as the reputation of Robert Morris extends beyond the boundaries of southwestern Pennsylvania and promises to make essential contributions to future growth, the college also remains an important part of the region's past. Founded in 1921 as the Pittsburgh School of Accountancy, the school changed its name in 1935 to the Robert Morris School in honor of the Pennsylvanian who helped bankroll the American Revolution.

The school was purchased in 1962 by a nonprofit organization and, with the approval of the state Department of Education, became Robert Morris Junior College. In 1969, when it was granted the right to begin awarding the bachelor of science in business administration degree, the name was changed to Robert Morris College.

■ *With its accessible Pittsburgh Center, Robert Morris offers a convenient alternative for downtown workers beginning or completing a degree program. Photo by David J. Hiteshue.*

The college received approval in 1975 to prepare teachers of business and office education. In 1977, Robert Morris began offering the master of science degree and, in 1988, won the right to award the master of business administration (MBA) degree and the bachelor of arts degree with programs in English and Communication.

Robert Morris now makes its home on two campuses. The 230-acre campus in Moon Township, situated a mile from Pittsburgh International Airport, provides a vibrant academic setting for a resident student body. The Pittsburgh Center, located in the heart of downtown, serves commuter students from throughout the region for both day and evening classes.

During the 1992-1993 academic years, approximately 4,800 students were enrolled in the undergraduate programs, while graduate-level enrollment numbered about 700.

Robert Morris expects to continue its pattern of growth and innovative service. As development continues in the airport area, and as the Pittsburgh Center continues to draw new students, the college will continue to expand its business- and management-related curriculum to meet their needs, Nicholson said.

"These kinds of variations around the business focus of the institution really is the response Robert Morris has made to the change in the markets we serve," he said. "We're well-positioned to continue to serve those markets."

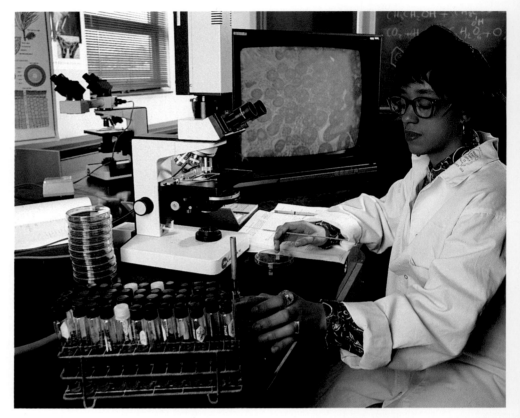

■ A strong Natural and Mathematical Sciences Division prepares La Roche students for our changing world.

Where Real Learning Prepares You for Real Life

La Roche College is an educational institution dedicated to balance. With a blending of liberal and professional education, La Roche strives to balance students' needs to learn and society's need for a well-prepared workforce. By emphasizing both the formal pursuit of a four-year degree and the personal search for meaning, the college helps students know themselves as well as the principles and practices of their selected professions.

La Roche College

"We want to graduate students who have a sense of their futures and have a well-grounded professional education that compliments their appreciation of the liberal arts," said La Roche president, Rev. Monsignor William A. Kerr.

■ La Roche strides into a new era under the leadership of President Kerr. Photo by Mark Lustgarten.

In 1992, 1763 students experienced this philosophy on La Roche's 100-acre wooded campus, located on the northern edge of Pittsburgh, 10 miles from the corporate towers of the center city.

La Roche administrators and faculty are well aware of the increasing concern among employers over the level of skill in language, math, and science that prospective employees bring with them as they enter the job market. "We feel very strongly that the basics need to be in place. People have to know how to read, write, and subtract before they can do some of the more complex things," said President Kerr. "We've got to get back to basics."

Named for Mother Marie de la Roche, founder of the Sisters of Divine Providence, La Roche is associated with the Roman Catholic Church and upholds a Catholic tradition. Its academic programs, enrollment policies, and campus life, however, are non-denominational. "Our association with the Catholic Church means that people have confidence in the academic work that goes on here. The tradition of Catholic education is a good one. It's important to our students and a selling point to the companies that recruit our graduates," said the new president.

Monsignor Kerr became president of the college in September 1992 after eight years as vice-president of university relations at The Catholic University of America in Washington D.C. Before joining Catholic U., he worked for 13 years at Florida State University, in campus ministry and as a faculty member. He holds a S.T.L. from Catholic University and a Ph.D. from Florida State.

La Roche offers undergraduate degree programs within the division of administration and management; social sciences, graphics, design and communication; humanities; nursing; natural and mathematical sciences; and graduate degree programs in Human Resources Management Nursing, and Health Sciences. "We're very strong in science and strong in graphic design and communications. We're strong in verbal arts and nursing, and we have a very successful program for communication skills," the president said. In addition, La Roche College, founded in 1963, will launch a Bachelor of Science Education program in the fall of 1993.

Today, La Roche sees its role as that of a community resource. "We're committed to the area," President Kerr said. "That doesn't mean we don't have students from all over the country and all over the world. We do."

■ *La Roche's College Center is the center of student life. Photo by E. Poggenpohl.*

The college maintains ties with St. Benedict the Moor School in Pittsburgh's Hill District and with Holy Rosary in Homewood. "As a suburban school, we feel we should be involved in those areas of the city where we can contribute the most," the president emphasized. The sense of community spills over into the administration's strategic planning. "As we look to strengthen academic areas where La Roche can excel, we do so always with an ear to the community," he said.

Links with the community are also evident in the encouragement all students receive to complete at least one supervised internship in a business or clinical setting. The internships are structured by faculty members, serving as mentors, and by employers. La Roche's connections with the business, research, and cultural communities in Pittsburgh give students a range of internship choices. Seniors may also participate in the annual Western Pennsylvania Association of Career Services Job Fair, where more than 100 regional companies interview candidates for as many as 2500 jobs.

La Roche's faculty members are known for their strong interest in their students' success. Incoming freshmen are paired with mentors from the faculty who help them set individual academic goals and plan strategies for achieving them. Mentors and students meet regularly over the next four years to discuss course selection, internships, and career alternatives. "I view La Roche as a college that has a caring, committed staff and faculty." the President continued, "We want to be a multicultural community to students. We're very committed to that. We want first to be a thriving college that's good at what it does. We're not trying to be everything to everybody.

If enrollment is any measure of the effectiveness of an institution's approach to higher education, then La Roche can take satisfaction in the surge that swelled the number of students from 1,280 students in 1980 to its current enrollment. Even though enrollment leveled off in the early 1990's, growth was taking other forms at La Roche, including an increase in the college's assets from just over $5 million in 1980 to nearly $24 million in 1992.

Along with greater recognition and a growing educational reputation, the college enjoys the financial stability associated with 23 years of consecutive balanced budgets.

Continuing expansion of the population in the North Hills communities that surround La Roche led administrators to expect renewed growth in enrollment in the mid-90s. Also the college is poised for growth with the construction of a Fitness and Sports Center, an expansion of student sports programs, to include men's and women's basketball, and a plan for a new computer-equipped academic building.

Additional interest in La Roche springs from members of society other than freshly minted high school graduates. "We have a lot of women returning to complete their educations, women who for one reason or another didn't earn their bachelors' degrees. A lot of people are enhancing their marketability by earning college degrees," President Kerr said.

"Whatever their motivation for coming to La Roche," President Kerr continued, "students find an atmosphere that fosters introspection which helps make college a rare and memorable period in their lives." Even a college president can get swept up in that atmosphere, as he was reminded one day in Academic Hall when he said, "hello" as he passed a group of students. One of then said, "Do you have time for a philosophical discussion?" Before he knew it, President Kerr was involved in a debate that refreshed his appreciation for the insight and conviction that students bring to issues like human behavior, the condition of society, and the direction of change in moral values.

The President continued, "I listened carefully to them. I thought to myself, 'How easy it is to misjudge people, especially young people, based on the way they dress or the way they wear their hair.'"

"I have to say that our students bring values that enrich the La Roche environment as much as La Roche enriches them through the academic programs that we offer. My guess is that as a society we're going to be involved in more intense discussion of issues like these in the coming years, and I think we'll be better off for it. I'm gratified that part of that dialogue will be taking place here," continued President Kerr.

■ *Small classes allow for personalized professor / student interaction. Photo by E. Poggenpohl.*

■ Photo by James Collins.

Pittsburgh's wealth lies not just within the Golden Triangle at the confluence of the Allegheny, Monongahela, and Ohio rivers but also in the rolling hills and river valleys that surround the city.

Fifty miles northeast of Pittsburgh, in the foothills of the Allegheny Mountains, lies the town of Indiana, Pennsylvania, the site of early glass factories and energy-rich coal mines, the Christmas Tree Capital, and the birthplace of legendary actor Jimmy Stewart.

There, too, is the site of Indiana University of Pennsylvania, the fifth-largest university in the state and a leading source of the talent that helps keep Pittsburgh's corporations, high-tech industries, schools, and government on the move.

Money Magazine's "Money Guide" has ranked IUP 22nd among all the nation's public universities and first in Pennsylvania.

"IUP has a lot to offer to the student who wants to explore a variety of career possibilities and have a good time while doing so," said Edward Fiske, former education editor of the New York Times.

"When it comes to costs, however, its tuition for out-of-state students rivals the in-state fees for many schools."

From 1875, when it was housed in a single building and had only 200 students, IUP grew to an enrollment of more than 14,300 students by the early 1990s, including students from nearly every state and more than 62 other countries.

Focusing on high-quality undergraduate education provided by a dedicated faculty in a student-centered environment, IUP also offers outstanding graduate programs at the master's and doctoral levels that help set it apart from other regional universities. IUP is the only state-owned university in Pennsylvania that offers doctoral degrees.

In 45 academic departments located within six colleges and two schools, IUP gives its students a choice of more than a hundred major fields of study. The university also has branch campuses at Kittanning and Punxsutawney.

Indiana University of Pennsylvania

IUP has a reputation to match its stature among regional universities. It has been recognized as a "best buy" by nearly every major college and university guidebook.

Among those citing the educational quality and cost-conscious pricing of IUP have been "Changing Times," The Kiplinger Magazine, The New York Times' "Best Buys in College Education," "How to Get an Ivy League Education at a State University," by Dr. Martin Nemko and Barron's "Best Buys in College Education."

The editors of Barron's said:, "For the followers of Big Ten athletics, there may be only one Indiana University. But for seekers of a top-quality education at a quality price, there's another contender for the Big Ten title, Indiana University of Pennsylvania. Just half the size of its giant cousin, IUP can still boast its share of `the biggest.'"

"Its internship program is the largest in Pennsylvania, larger than that of Penn State, which enrolls nearly three times more undergraduates. Its ROTC program is the fifth-largest in the nation."

Traditionally, one of every seven students is from Pittsburgh or Allegheny County, as are more than 10,000 of the university's 75,000 alumni.

Fifty-eight percent of IUP's first-year students were in the top 25 percent of their high school graduating class, and 90 percent were in the top two-fifths of the class.

The history of IUP is the chronicle of an institution that has evolved along with the needs of the society it serves. Originally known as the Indiana Normal School, it was later known as Indiana State Teachers College and Indiana State College. The name was changed in 1965 to Indiana University of Pennsylvania.

Several notable facets of the IUP experience contribute to its emergence as a university of national significance:

INTERNSHIPS — IUP has Pennsylvania's largest internship program. More than 50 percent of IUP's students prior to graduating

■ Photo by James Collins.

■ *Photo by James Collins.*

complete an internship at one of the Fortune 500 companies, at top accounting firms, banks, and other Pittsburgh regional businesses and at elementary and secondary schools throughout the state.

Placements also include the Carnegie and the Benedum Center in Pittsburgh, the Smithsonian Institution, the U.S. Chamber of Commerce, Disney World, and many of the nation's top resorts and hotels.

INTERNATIONAL EXCHANGES — Through an international exchange program, IUP students can elect to study at universities in England, France, Spain, Italy, Austria, Mexico, Australia, and other nations.

NATIONALLY KNOWN FACULTY — IUP has a long-standing reputation for attracting some of the top professors in their fields including nationally known experts in domestic violence, the alcoholic family, and research in the treatment of breast cancer, the spread of Lyme disease and DNA fingerprinting.

EDUCATION PIONEERS — Long a renowned institution for the training of teachers, IUP continues to serve as a pathfinder in teacher education. The university's College of Education has formed partnerships with big city, suburban, and rural school districts to elevate the art of teaching, involve increased minority participation, and assess the qualities needed by teachers, school principals, and school directors.

IUP's Urban Student Teaching Center in Pittsburgh helps develop special skills and attitudes needed to teach in inner-city schools.

PACESETTING PROGRAMS — No longer just an outstanding teacher training institution, IUP is among the elite in numerous other programs:

— Safety Sciences. The IUP Safety Sciences program, the first of its kind in the nation to be accredited and still among the largest, prepares graduates for management-level positions in government and industry. The department is the official Pennsylvania business consultant for OSHA, providing free on-site analyses for more than 6,000 businesses to determine environmental problems and help avoid costly citations.

— Criminology. IUP is one of only a small number of universities in the nation offering doctoral degrees in criminology. Many of the university's criminology graduates teach in other colleges and universities. In addition, many IUP graduates hold important positions in the FBI, the Secret Service, and state and local police bodies.

— Geographic Education. The national Council for Geographic Education, headquartered at IUP since 1988, works to enhance the status and quality of geography teaching and learning. The council develops policies for all aspects of geographic education for geography teachers nationwide.

— Minority retention and diversity. The Graduate School at IUP has won the Noel/Levitz national award for minority retention for compiling an 81-percent minority retention rate, an almost unheard-of accomplishment for a predominantly white university.

— Business Management and Services. The College of Business at IUP has developed a wide range of management support services, dedicated to enhancing the economic vitality of the western Pennsylvania region.

IUP students come from a wide variety of backgrounds but have several things in common — scholarship, enthusiasm, and the ambition to help others, whether through their chosen careers or through community service.

There are more than 200 student organizations recognized by the IUP Student Activities Board. Some of the ongoing community service programs sponsored by IUP students and organizations include Red Cross Blood Drives, an annual Walk to Pittsburgh for Children's Hospital, which raised more than $400,000 over the past 20 years, Big Brothers and Big Sisters, and numerous other community projects.

Its faculty, alumni, and students, its long-standing tradition, its service-oriented and research-supporting programs, and its commitment to western Pennsylvania's progress and culture make Indiana University of Pennsylvania a valuable part of the Pittsburgh success story. ▣

■ *Photo by James Collins.*

CHAPTER
Health Care
FIFTEEN

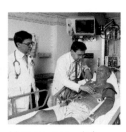

The story of Blue Cross of Western Pennsylvania is a story of people joining hands in time of hardship to find solutions for a brighter future.

The Great Depression of the 1930s brought an onslaught of economic hardships that made it nearly impossible for many persons to pay for medical care. Some hospitals stood on the brink of financial ruin.

With a spirit of community that is characteristic of western Pennsylvania, citizens joined forces to encourage state legislation to address the emergency.

As a result, on September 15, 1937, the Hospital Association of Pittsburgh, as Blue Cross of Western Pennsylvania was formerly

■ *To improve community access to primary care and other health-related services, Blue Cross has established Medicenters across the region in joint ventures with local hospitals.*

At the outset, experts predicted an eventual enrollment of 75,000 persons. That figure was surpassed within a year, and by the organization's fifth anniversary membership had reached 500,000.

In the association's first full year, it had agreements with 23 hospitals, providing payment of $6 per day for customer care.

customers in the form of payment for medical services.

With its financial success, BCWP has been able to continue to provide health care protection for people who don't have access to coverage or can't afford coverage from any other source.

Solutions That Make Sense

Armed with firsthand knowledge of employer and employee needs, BCWP has been able to respond quickly and accurately in finding solutions that make sense in benefit design.

To do this, the corporation continues to grow through the formation of subsidiaries and affiliates that offer a full range of cost-effective products and services to support and enhance the core business of health care coverage.

Blue Cross of Western Pennsylvania

known, became Pennsylvania's first nonprofit community health plan organization.

It began with a simple, yet crucial, mission: "to ensure that health care coverage would be available and affordable to all segments of the community."

■ *At the heart of Pittsburgh's Golden Triangle is Fifth Avenue Place, Blue Cross of Western Pennsylvania's corporate headquarters.*

Two years later, the roster included almost all hospitals in western Pennsylvania's 29-county area.

In 1940, companion coverage programs for doctors' services were made available through the Medical Service Association, which later became known as Pennsylvania Blue Shield. A year later, the Hospital Association of Pittsburgh gained authorization to use the legally protected "Blue Cross" symbol and, in 1963, officially became known as Blue Cross of Western Pennsylvania, BCWP.

Taking the Lead

BCWP has endured economic peaks and valleys, marketplace upheavals, health care reform legislation, and cultural change.

With more than 55 years of dependability, financial stability, and steady growth, the company has remained focused on its social mission and has emerged as the industry leader in full-service employee benefit programs for western Pennsylvania and beyond.

Today, BCWP provides benefits to close to 2.6 million customers. It is regarded as one of the most financially sound Blue Cross and Blue Shield Plans in the country.

BCWP also has the lowest administrative cost percentage of any large Blue Cross Plan. Through its efficiency, the corporation is able to return 96 cents of every premium dollar to

Products include life and disability insurance, third-party administrative services, health care cost and utilization management, health and wellness promotion and information systems.

While continuing to focus on the needs of western Pennsylvanians, BCWP saw unique growth opportunities for distribution of these non-health product lines in other regions.

Licensed by the Blue Cross and Blue Shield Association to use the Blue Cross name and mark only in western Pennsylvania and only in connection with its health care business, the corporation seized opportunity in 1991.

BCWP changed its legal name to Veritus, Inc. in order to market select products beyond western Pennsylvania. In western Pennsylvania, the company continues to provide health care coverage under the trade name Blue Cross of Western Pennsylvania.

From the Latin word meaning "true, real, genuine, well-grounded," the new legal name Veritus set in motion a long-term plan to remain competitive.

■ *Since its inception in 1985, the Caring Program for Children has provided health care coverage to more than 20,000 children.*

Veritus got under way immediately with the opening of several regional sales offices. Strategically located throughout the United States, the offices allow for an expanded revenue stream through broad national distribution of Veritus products. In that way, BCWP safeguarded its social mission and commitment to western Pennsylvanians for years to come.

Affordable, Quality Care

BCWP's comprehensive plan to help control health costs and improve the quality of care in western Pennsylvania is based on an approach known as health care management, which introduces better ways to coordinate the delivery of care, while making individuals wiser health care consumers.

Health care management is applied across all product lines to ensure recommended medical procedures are necessary and care is delivered in the most appropriate setting.

This is accomplished in several ways, from improved management of the use of services, to coordinating care through networks of primary and specialty physicians.

One health care management method zeros in on medical categories, such as maternity care and heart disease, that contribute significantly to rising health care costs. With on-site nurse reviewers, the corporation works with physicians and hospital staffs to evaluate cases to assure patients receive proper care.

Other programs stress second surgical opinion designed to emphasize less costly and equally effective nonsurgical procedures when available, and cost management that addresses areas of rapidly rising health care spending, such as prescription drugs and mental health and substance abuse treatment.

Healthier Lifestyles

Promoting healthy lifestyles is another proven way of managing health care costs and a vital component of BCWP's health care management philosophy.

For group customers, BCWP offers Lifestyle Advantage™, a program that gives employers a way to assess the general wellness of their work forces and identify controllable health risks through voluntary screenings.

The corporation's growing inventory of health promotion programs has helped employers build stronger companies by encouraging employees to adopt healthier lifestyles.

An example is the First Step™ maternity program, which fosters safe deliveries and healthy babies through a prenatal health education and support approach.

■ *A familiar sight to area residents, Blue Cross and Blue Shield cards are carried by more than 2.6 million customers.*

At the heart of community wellness is HealthPLACE®, a network of centers designed to help people maintain and improve their physical and mental well-being through education, training, and support.

Located throughout western Pennsylvania, HealthPLACE® uses a progressive approach to health promotion aimed at meeting the specific needs of each community.

Anticipating customer demand, BCWP also incorporated managed-care provider networks, which coordinate the delivery and financing of care, as part of its health care management strategy.

Keystone Health Plan West, a health maintenance organization (HMO), preferred provider organizations (PPOs), and Point of Service (POS) products are highlights of the BCWP network repertoire.

Although the networks differ in some ways, they share the common goal of reducing health care costs and maintaining quality medical services by channeling care to networks of physicians and hospitals.

For instance, with Keystone Health Plan West, a patient selects a primary care physician who coordinates all treatment, including inpatient and specialty care referrals. Unlike most facility-based HMOs, Keystone members receive care in the privacy of local participating physicians' offices.

The PPO programs offer savings for employers and greater freedom of choice for employees. The network includes community hospitals to provide convenient access to

■ *Sophisticated computer systems allow Blue Cross to custom-design products and services to meet the specific benefit needs of employers.*

Technological improvements to its Corporate Data Center allow for more effective product and service delivery, cutting in half the time it takes to transfer electronic data.

Critical to the corporation's continued success, these advancements in technology are the building blocks for the delivery of more flexible benefit products in years to come.

Government Partnerships

With an eye towards the future, BCWP continues to build on its long-standing business partnership with the federal government through the Medicare program.

One of the nation's leading Medicare intermediaries, BCWP has processed claims for hospital services for Medicare beneficiaries and the disabled since 1966.

Encouraged in recent years by the federal Health Care Financing Administration, HCFA, to enter shared claims processing agreements with other Medicare contractors, BCWP sought out affiliations with other Blue Cross and Blue Shield Plans. As a result of these partnerships, as well as enhancements to its Medicare claims processing system, BCWP now handles more than six million claims a year for beneficiaries in Arizona, Delaware, and the western, central, and northeastern regions of Pennsylvania.

BCWP has also joined with the Allegheny Health, Education, and Research Foundation and Mercy Health Plan of Philadelphia to develop Gateway Health Plan, a company that offers an extensive array of managed-care benefits to Medicaid recipients. The alliance reinforces BCWP's commitment to its mission by providing quality health care coverage to those most in need and who, often times, can't find providers to treat them.

The Hardest Hit

Through its leadership role in benefit design, health care management strategies, and government programs, BCWP is able to reinvest in the community through subsidized health care programs for the uninsured and marginally insured.

■ *The relationships Blue Cross has developed with area hospitals help manage the rising cost of medical services and enhance the quality of care for all Western Pennsylvanians.*

routine care, as well as the University of Pittsburgh's advanced health care facilities for specialty care.

Complementing the hospital networks are physician networks that include primary care physicians and specialists throughout southwestern Pennsylvania.

BCWP's Point of Service product is a marriage of open-access health care coverage and HMO plans. With POS, a primary care physician guides a customer's use of the provider network. POS participants receive a higher level of benefit coverage if they use primary care physicians within the network but also have the option to seek care outside the network.

Increasing the scope and complexity of BCWP's products and services requires enhanced data processing technology. To improve customer service and increase cost savings, BCWP consolidated six separate claims processing systems into one to handle all lines of business.

At its roots is a commitment to make coverage available to everyone on a continuous basis, regardless of age, occupation, or health condition, including those considered uninsurable or high risk by other insurers.

BCWP also employs the unique concept of community rating — spreading risk across a large pool of subscribers so that coverage is more affordable for everyone.

In addition, by subsidizing benefit programs, charging less for the programs than they cost to provide, BCWP gives children, the elderly, and the economically disadvantaged access to quality health care services as illustrated by the Special Care program.

Working with participating hospitals, BCWP developed Special Care, the region's first low-cost health care coverage program specifically for individuals and families without group coverage whose incomes are too high to qualify for state Medical Assistance, but are too low to afford other private health care insurance.

Serving as the model, BCWP's Special Care program has been replicated and expanded to cover residents statewide.

Created in cooperation with Pennsylvania Blue Shield and area hospitals, the Caring Program for Children is another innovative subsidized program.

Funded through contributions from community groups, foundations, unions, and individuals, the Caring Program provides free primary health care benefits to children of low-income families who do not qualify for Medical Assistance.

BCWP and Pennsylvania Blue Shield match all contributions dollar-for-dollar and cover administrative costs as well. Now replicated in 20 states, the western Pennsylvania program was the nation's first private initiative to fill this crucial children's health need.

So far, more than 20,000 children in western Pennsylvania have been helped through the Caring Program.

Beyond Health Care

BCWP's strong support of local civic activities extends from corporate programs to the personal commitment of its employees. The activities may vary, but the goal remains the same, to promote the health and prosperity of everyone in the region.

Whether it's a pledge for the corporate United Way campaign, a donation to Central Blood Bank, or lending a hand on a Junior Achievement project, employee support is always overwhelming.

In one such effort, BCWP employees led the way in the Boy Scouts of America Scouting for Food Campaign.

Gearing Up for Tomorrow

Built on a financially strong foundation, with a strategic plan in place and an ardent, experienced work force ready to meet the challenge, BCWP is well positioned to draw on its past to assure continued prosperity in the future.

Success in the years ahead centers on finding ways to provide better products with better services at lower costs for BCWP customers.

Forging ahead with the development of health care information systems and automated capabilities for improving productivity, the corporation will work in

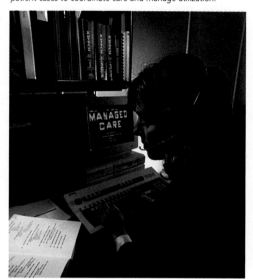

■ *Applied across all product lines, health care management helps customers avoid excessive health care expenditures by ensuring recommended medical procedures are necessary and that care is delivered in the most appropriate setting. Through one form of health care management, registered nurses review patient cases to coordinate care and manage utilization.*

tandem with health care providers to shape the future of the industry.

But only when a business becomes an integral part of the community it serves does it truly become successful.

With this in mind, BCWP will continue to evolve its health care management programs to ensure affordable care is available for all, tomorrow.

It will continue work with regional planning groups of health care providers, business leaders, and government officials to advance local solutions to community health care needs. New consumer advocacy initiatives to stay in close touch with the community are already under way.

These endeavors are vital as BCWP continues to pursue its unique mission in the 1990s.   **IB**

■ *HealthPLACE®, developed by Blue Cross in cooperation with its Health Education Center affiliate, features automated health displays, audio-visual tapes, health screenings, literature, classes and workshops aimed at helping people improve their physical and mental well-being.*

The University of Pittsburgh Medical Center

As one of the nation's premier academic medical centers, the University of Pittsburgh Medical Center (UPMC) is aggressively advancing biomedical knowledge through what it calls "translational science." Translational science is the process of taking a significant finding from the laboratory bench to the patient's bedside in the shortest possible time consistent with safety and scientific rigor. With a total of 1,236 medical-surgical beds and 279 psychiatric beds, UPMC encompasses a host of hospitals, specialized programs, and clinical facilities, including Presbyterian University Hospital, Montefiore University Hospital, the Pittsburgh Cancer Institute, and Western Psychiatric Institute and Clinic. UPMC employs more than 14,000 faculty and staff and offers some of the most advanced specialized facilities and equipment available. In a typical year, UPMC hospitals admit approximately 34,000 patients and see more than 400,000 outpatients.

UPMC also maintains cooperative relationships with Children's Hospital of Pittsburgh, Magee-Womens Hospital, and two Veterans Affairs Medical Centers. The medical center's affiliation with the University of Pittsburgh's Schools of the Health Sciences—Medicine, Nursing, Health and Rehabilitation Sciences, Pharmacy, Dental Medicine, and Public Health—generates a plethora of multidisciplinary research on the diagnosis, treatment, and prevention of a broad spectrum of diseases and health problems.

This dynamic environment supports hundreds of fruitful interdisciplinary investigations and has given rise to several major centers with substantial external funding. These include the Pittsburgh Cancer Institute; the Transplantation Institute; the Brain, Behavior, and Immunity Center; the Center for Neuroscience and Schizophrenia; the Alzheimer Disease Research Center; the University of Pittsburgh Heart Institute; the Pittsburgh Genetics Institute; and the Adolescent Alcoholism Research Center.

As part of its mission, UPMC is dedicated to training future generations of health care professionals. Nearly 1,000 residents and clinical fellows come to Pittsburgh every year for specialty training. In addition, the medical center shares biomedical insight and information with clinicians at local and regional health care facilities through its continuing medical education program.

UPMC values patient satisfaction among its highest priorities and strives to provide an environment that combines advanced diagnostic and treatment services with the most compassionate care possible. The medical center provides a full range of adult acute health care and offers many advanced medical-surgical programs. UPMC's clinical and research efforts coalesce around the following key areas:

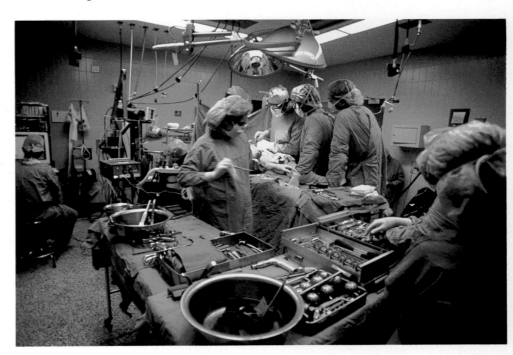

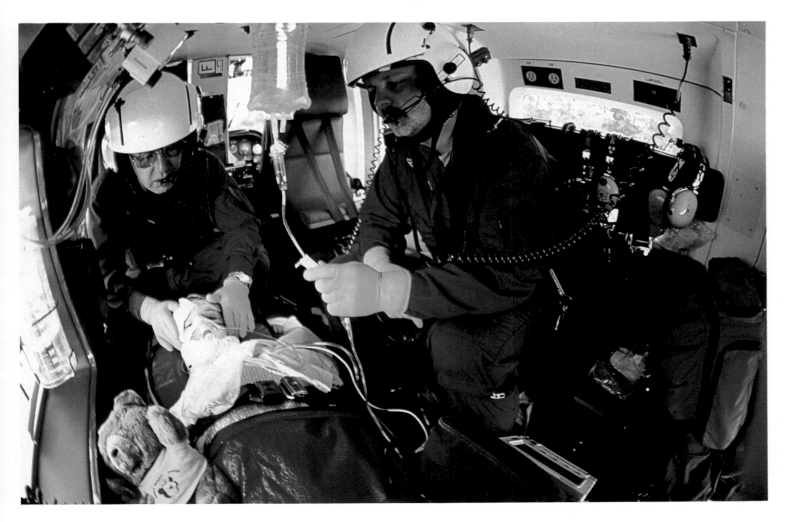

AIDS and HIV Infection: UPMC clinicians and researchers are at the front lines of the AIDS epidemic. The Pittsburgh AIDS Center for Treatment provides primary care to people who have the virus that causes AIDS. Researchers at the Pitt Treatment Evaluation Unit study new and effective therapies for AIDS and HIV and coordinate large-scale investigations into the nature and natural history of HIV infection.

Cancer: UPMC's cancer prevention, treatment, education, and research efforts are carried out through the Pittsburgh Cancer Institute (PCI), which has been designated by the National Cancer Institute as a comprehensive cancer center. PCI is one of only 28 such centers in the country. Since its creation in 1984, PCI has provided state-of-the-art diagnostic and treatment services to more than 6,000 people from western Pennsylvania and across the nation. PCI's work is shaped by far-reaching research, from early prevention and detection strategies to emerging forms of treatment like gene therapy, immunotherapy, and bone marrow transplantation.

Cardiology and Cardiothoracic Surgery: The University of Pittsburgh Heart Institute embraces a wide range of clinical programs and services, including prevention and intervention efforts. The Heart Institute's Chest Pain Center offers rapid triage, diagnosis, and care for people suspected of having a heart attack. The Heart Institute has also introduced innovations in cardiothoracic intensive care and the medical management of high-risk heart surgery patients. Research initiatives include the use of new cardiac imaging devices, the development of immunosuppressive agents for heart transplant patients, and clinical trials of medications to limit damage during and after heart attacks. Through the McGowan Center for Artificial Heart and Lung Research, the institute is pioneering the use of mechanical circulatory support technology for people with irreversible heart failure. A device known as the Novacor left ventricular assist system has been used more successfully and more often at UPMC than at any other medical center.

Environmental and Occupational Medicine: Preventing health risks associated with workplace and environmental hazards is

Members of the STAT MedEvac crew treat a pediatric trauma patient. STAT, a medical aircraft and helicopter service, is part of the Center for Emergency Medicine, a consortium of eight Pittsburgh area hospitals.

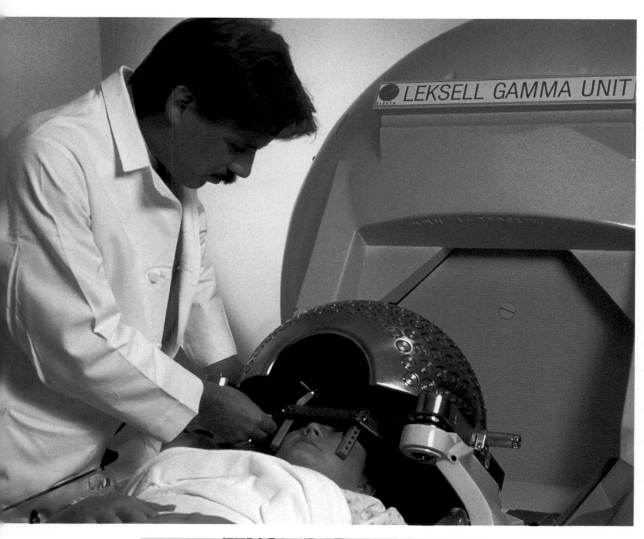

■ *A physician treats a patient with the Gamma Knife, a 20-ton, lead-shielded unit that delivers high doses of tumor-destroying radiation to pinpoint locations in the brain.*

the 100,000 or so genes in the human body. These efforts have made UPMC one of the premier centers for gene therapy research, a revolutionary new method in which a normal gene is substituted for an abnormal or malfunctioning one. Most of this research is carried out at the Pittsburgh Genetics Institute, an alliance of clinical geneticists and basic scientists at Pitt, Carnegie Mellon University, and several area hospitals.

Geriatrics: Through a wide range of geriatric programs and services, UPMC is helping to keep adults independent and active well into their older years. The Benedum Geriatric Center provides comprehensive health care to older adults by taking a family-based approach which examines the patient's total circumstances. Research on the aging process and the diseases that develop with age is conducted by geriatricians and gerontologists at the Alzheimer Disease Research Center and other affiliated programs.

Musculoskeletal Disorders: UPMC is dedicated to providing the most advanced medical and surgical care for people with musculoskeletal disorders and injuries through its Musculoskeletal Institute. The institute welcomes patients with complaints such as rheumatoid arthritis, osteoarthritis, and connective tissue diseases like scleroderma and systemic lupus erythematosus. Whether treatment requires intensive medication, implantation of artificial joints, corrective surgery, or rehabilitative regimens to improve the function of joint, bone, and cartilage, UPMC extends comprehensive, research-based care to each patient.

Neurosciences: By studying how the brain works, UPMC neuroscientists are shedding light on conditions as diverse as schizophrenia, autism, and Alzheimer's disease. Neurological research is carried out by the Center for Neuroscience at the University of Pittsburgh and the Brain, Behavior, and Immunity Center. In the clinical realm, more people seek specialized neurological surgery at UPMC than at any other medical center in the United States. Each year, UPMC

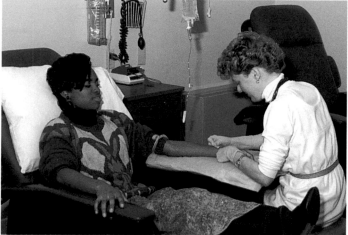

■ *Patient care remains the number one goal of UPMC. Each year, UPMC hospitals admit approximately 34,000 inpatients and treat more than 400,000 outpatients.*

one of UPMC's highest priorities. A major thrust of the medical center's efforts is the Center for Environmental and Occupational Health and Toxicology, which fosters collaboration among researchers in the fields of medicine, engineering, chemistry, and biology. The center also trains physicians in the treatment and prevention of occupationally or environmentally induced illnesses. A computerized system to predict the probable toxicity of virtually any organic compound was co-developed at UPMC.

Genetics: UPMC geneticists are striving to cure inherited diseases, such as Gaucher disease and Duchenne muscular dystrophy. Researchers actively participate in the Human Genome Project, a worldwide collaborative effort designed to map the functions of neurosurgeons perform about 3,000 major operations. Specialized services include stereotactic radiosurgery, microsurgery, the minimally invasive Gamma Knife, and the nationally renowned Center for Cranial Base Surgery.

Psychiatry: UPMC's psychiatric services are centered at Western Psychiatric Institute and Clinic (WPIC), a 279-bed center that is now part of Presbyterian University Hospital. WPIC incorporates 15 inpatient programs for children, adults, and the elderly. In addition, numerous outpatient programs allow WPIC to provide highly specialized diagnosis and treatment services. WPIC has been a leader in the treatment of depression and has been designated as a Clinical Research Center for Affective Disorders by the National Institute of Mental Health (NIMH). One of the nation's leading psychiatric centers, WPIC ranked first in funding from NIMH for the 1991-92 fiscal year.

Transplantation: UPMC performs more transplants and more types of transplants than any other medical center. Through the pioneering work of teams headed by

Thomas E. Starzl, M.D., Ph.D., the medical center's name is synonymous with organ transplantation. UPMC performs every type of major organ transplant—heart, pancreas, liver, lung, heart/lung, and kidney—and is the only transplant center performing multiple-organ transplants. On average, a major organ is transplanted at UPMC every 14 hours. Thanks to the efforts of UPMC researchers, cellular transplantation, especially pancreatic islet cell transplantation, has emerged as a viable new medical technology. A major xenotransplantation effort, which uses animal organs in humans, is examining novel ways to increase the pool of available donor organs.

Trauma and Critical Care: UPMC treats 70,000 emergency cases and 2,000 trauma victims a year. Emergency services are coordinated with Medic Command, the emergency communications center for the City of Pittsburgh Emergency Medical Services, a system of emergency care that provides a model for the nation. The Commonwealth of Pennsylvania has designated UPMC's University Trauma Center as a

Level I Regional Resource Trauma Center, the state's highest designation. Other unique capabilities in trauma and emergency medicine include programs in orthopaedic trauma, head trauma, and critical care. The Toxicology Treatment Program, located in the UPMC Emergency Department, is the region's only accredited toxicology treatment center.

Other innovative UPMC programs include the Digestive Disorders Center, the Sports Medicine Institute, and the Comprehensive Lung Center.

Considered in their entirety, the interdisciplinary nature of these and other UPMC programs reflects the spirit of service and discovery that characterizes the work of researchers, health care practitioners, and medical educators at the University of Pittsburgh Medical Center. ⬛

■ *The modular floor design of UPMC's Biomedical Science Tower permits flexible use of its 352,000 square feet of laboratory and office space.*

■ *UPMC hospitals, academic departments, centers, and programs have acquired some of the most advanced specialized facilities and equipment available and are applying them to the advancement of medical science.*

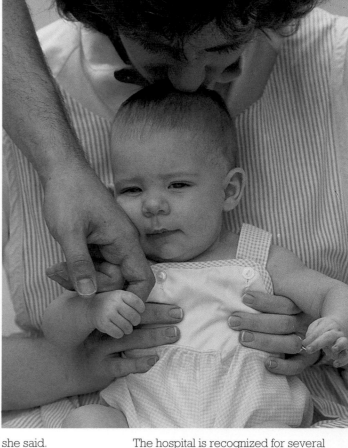

The Pittsburgh Mercy Health System is rooted in a 146-year tradition of meeting the health care needs of Western Pennsylvania. In 1847, seven Sisters of Mercy, having raised $3,000, traveled from Ireland and established the city's first hospital so that the growing numbers of laborers and immigrants would have access to medical care.

That humble facility served as a cornerstone on which an entire health care system was built. But it was not just brick and mortar that enabled Mercy to thrive and adapt to the changing medical needs of its community. In 1847, Mercy committed to a mission and value system that continues to guide it into the 21st century.

"Our mission is certainly spiritually based," said Sister Joanne Marie Andiorio, president of Pittsburgh Mercy Health System, citing Mercy's six corporate values: compassion, community, collaboration, stewardship, human dignity, and excellence. "Those values give rise to our dedication to meeting the medical needs of the underserved and our commitment to treating the whole person," she said.

The Pittsburgh Mercy Health System

Pittsburgh Mercy Health Systems, Inc.

Neither challenges to the health care industry, such as health care reform, nor chronic illness such as AIDS and Alzheimers, has lessened Mercy's conviction of its founding mission — to provide quality medical care through a special attention to patients' physical and emotional needs.

today represents a continuum of care. Through the years, the System has diversified to remain a leader in health care delivery. It includes the Mercy Psychiatric Institute, the Mercy Center for Chemical Dependency; Mercy Life Center Corporation, St. Joseph Nursing and Health Care Center and St. Pius Residence; the Pittsburgh Mercy Foundation and Mercy Ventures, a taxable entity that provides management services for a variety of health-related operations. These system components are borne out of several emerging community needs. They are: projected population growth; the aging population, increasing health care demands by the baby boom generation; public health goals; higher incidence of mortality and disease incidence among minorities and persistent poverty.Pittsburgh Mercy Health System also recommitted itself to meeting community health care need in 1993 when it agreed to acquire Divine Providence Hospital, located on the city's North Side.

Mercy Hospital of Pittsburgh, the System's flagship, exemplifies Mercy's mission of providing dignified care that furthers the social and economic opportunities of the community. It combines advanced technological resources available for diagnosis and treatment with human resources that guarantee patients compassion and kindness.

The hospital is recognized for several Centers of Excellence. Among them are: Mercy Heart Institute, Mercy Cancer Center, Mercy Trauma Program and Generations, a program focusing on women and children.

Mercy Heart Institute is a premier provider of quality cardiac care. With a full-range of services, the Institute cares for approximately 10,000 patients each year and was named by nationally known physician and author, Robert Arnot, M.D., as a National Center of Excellence in Coronary Artery Bypass Surgery and Angioplasty.

The Institute represents a new model of health care delivery in which physicians, nurses and management collaborate as a team to provide excellence in cardiac care.Mercy Heart Institute was the first to perform Excimer Laser-Assisted Coronary Angioplasty in the region and was one of a small group of hospitals to conduct FDA-authorized clinical research on this technology. The Institute is committed to research and is involved in the National Heart Attack Risk Study, and GUSTO, a research program that evaluated the effectiveness of TPA and Streptokinase — drugs used in the treatment of acute heart attack.

Mercy Heart Institute is composed of highly trained cardiovascular specialists who have expertise in the most advanced invasive and non-invasive diagnostic and treatment procedures. Some key services include but are not limited to: coronary artery bypass grafting, valve repair and replacement; ventricular aneurysm repair, abdominal and thoracic aneurysm repair, percutaneous transluminal coronary angioplasty, percutaneous transluminal coronary angioplasty, permanent pacemaker insertion, electrocardiography, thallium imaging and cardiac catheterizations.Like Mercy Heart Institute, the Mercy Cancer Center has also proven itself as a leader. In fact, Mercy Hospital was the first facility to offer radiation therapy in the 1950s. Today, the Mercy Cancer Center is guided by a highly trained and specialized team of physicians, nurses, educators, researchers and support staff. The Mercy Cancer Center offers patients a balance of sophisticated technological resources with compassionate care for nearly 1,000 new patients each year.

The Mercy Cancer Center treats all types of cancer and has clinical research programs in the following areas: head and neck cancer, brain tumors, breast cancer, prostate cancer and colorectal cancer. In fact, the Mercy Cancer Center is the first in Pittsburgh, and one of four centers nationally, to participate in an FDA clinical trial using 3-dimensional radiation and planning and treatment, radiosurgery and radioactive implants. This 3-D process enables physicians to precisely locate the tumor site and direct radiation only to the affected area. Cancer prevention and community outreach also play important roles at the Mercy Cancer Center.

Mercy's mission isn't limited to prevention, however. As Pittsburgh's oldest hospital, Mercy has been caring for trauma patients for over a century. And while the concept of treating the entire person has not changed, the severity of injury and level of technology available to treat such injury has increased significantly. Mercy is one of three Level 1 trauma centers in Pittsburgh and the only trauma center with an inpatient burn unit. The trauma program at Mercy is composed of a team of five certified trauma surgeons on-site 24 hours a day, a round-the-clock trauma team and an operating room dedicated solely to the treatment of traumatic injuries. It is also part of the Center for Emergency Medicine, which enables patients to be transported by helicopter from accident sites throughout Western Pennsylvania.

Mercy also uses the team concept in meeting the health care needs of women and children as they progress through various life stages. Generations is a collaborative effort between Mercy Hospital's Women's Health Center and Mercy's Children's Medical Center offering a full-range of health care services that include preventative, diagnostic, therapeutic and acute care for women and children.

Obstetrical services are unparalled and offer women specialized medical care in a comfortable, home setting. Examples of this approach include private, labor, delivery, recovery or labor, delivery, recover and post-partum suites and wooden cradles for the newborns. High-risk pregnancies are supported by a staff of neonatologists and perinatologists. And should an emergency arise, a Level III neonatal intensive care unit offers the newborn round-the-clock, specialized care.

The Center's Gynecological services address the multiple needs of women throughout their life. Advanced diagnostic and treatment available through the Center include: laproscopic surgical procedures, laser cone surgery, infertility diagnosis and treatment, and a dedicated gynecology patient unit.

■ *Sister Joanne Marie Andiorio, President of Pittsburgh Mercy Health System.*

The Mercy Children's Medical Center combines sophisticated diagnostic treatment with a patient-focused approach for children at birth through 21. The pediatric team is composed of board-certified pediatricians, sub-specialists and pediatric nurses available 24 hours a day. Services include: general pediatric care, a pediatric emergency center, a pediatric intensive care unit, an ambulatory pediatric unit, a short-stay unit and a comprehensive child life program for all pediatric inpatients.

Today, the Pittsburgh Mercy Health System continues the work of the original seven Sisters of Mercy and sees its task as sounding the call to service again for a new generation of men and women facing a world in need. The system will continue to meet the health care needs of its community by providing a continuum of services dedicated to the prevention as well as the treatment of disease. "Our mission is plain and simple — people caring for people," said Sr. Joanne Marie. "This is our history, our tradition and our future."

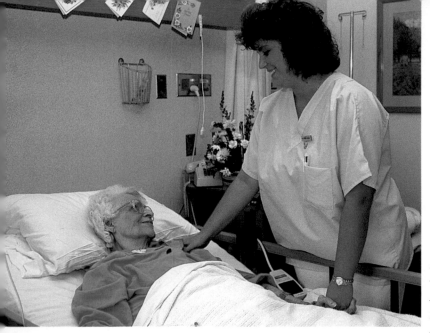

What do women want from a health care system?

Magee-Womens Hospital, the region's largest provider of health services for women and newborns, asks this question continually. Magee's programs are continually evolving

Magee - Womens Hospital

to meet the changing health care needs of women. It's a concept that Magee calls Womancare.ᔆᴹ

Magee serves the health care needs of women of all ages, and supports women in their roles as family health advisors, through educational classes, seminars, and special programs.

Commitment to women's health has been at the heart of Magee's mission since 1911, when the hospital opened its doors. At the time, obstetric and gynecologic standards nationwide were the lowest for all branches of medicine. Dr. Charles Zeigler, the first medical director, determined that Magee would become a teaching hospital that would "send the gospel of good obstetrics (and gynecology) far and wide."

Today, Magee is one of only a handful of nonprofit hospitals in the U.S. devoted to the care of women. Seeking input from women has become even more important with Magee's emerging role as a national leader in women's health.

The new Magee-Womens Research Institute is the only research facility nationwide devoted exclusively to women's health issues. And the hospital's ambulatory care model serves as a central referral point for the hospital's specialties.

At the same time, four health care specialties — genetics, oncology, infertility, and gynecology/uro-gynecology — are being developed as "centers of excellence," with state-of-the-art services, leading-edge research, and outstanding graduate medical education programs. While Magee enjoys an excellent reputation in each of these areas, the Center of Excellence concept provides a framework for the delivery of services, research, and professional education.

The 1990s will be years of incredible change at Magee, with new facilities and new services, directed by nationally and internationally recognized physicians and scientists, and enhanced by its affiliation with the University of Pittsburgh, a world-renowned center of academic medicine.

The future of women's health care bears a remarkable resemblance to the blueprint for Magee-Womens Hospital in the 1990s and beyond.

Here's a look at the hospital's specialties and its plans for the future.

Obstetric Services

Magee has one of the largest private obstetric services in the United States, with more than 9,000 deliveries each year, including more than 40 percent of the babies born to women living in the city of Pittsburgh.

The construction of a new labor suite will include the complete conversion to LDRs — private rooms where women spend the entire labor, delivery, and recovery period. Currently, Magee offers several LDRs, or women may choose to deliver in a traditional labor room.

For women requiring specialized high-risk pregnancy care, Magee offers the region's most comprehensive program, with nationally recognized perinatologists (specialists in pregnancy complications) and more education and support services than any hos-

pital in the area. Diabetes, hypertension, preterm labor, and repeated pregnancy loss are among the conditions managed successfully.

As the ob/gyn specialty hospital of the University's School of Medicine, Magee trains more than 650 physicians, nurses, and other health professionals each year.

Neonatal Intensive Care

Complications from prematurity, including low birth weight and respiratory distress syndrome, account for the majority of babies admitted to Magee's Neonatal Intensive Care Unit. The NICU, which treats approximately 1,200 babies each year, is the largest and busiest in the state.

Infertility Treatment

Magee's assisted reproduction program helps couples experiencing infertility. Gamete intrafallopian transfer (GIFT) and in vitro fertilization (IVF) are two successful methods of assisted reproduction available at the hospital and at a growing number of satellite facilities affiliated with Magee. A voluntary donor oocyte program provides eggs for women with premature ovarian failure or those women who cannot produce eggs.

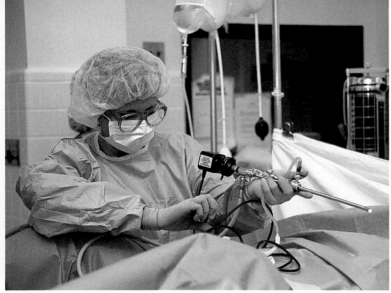

■ *In addition to general and gynecologic surgery, Magee offers many surgical services for the special concerns of women: urological dysfunction, breast cancer, plastic and reconstructive surgery, and more. The outpatient Surgi-Center is one of the busiest in Allegheny County, performing more than 5,000 procedures each year.*

Treating Women's Cancers

Women throughout the tri-state area come to Magee for the treatment of breast cancer and gynecologic cancers. In fact, Magee is one of the top 10 hospitals nationwide in the number of patients with gynecologic cancers who are treated, and among a small percentage of hospitals with a team of board-certified gynecologic oncologists. Its affiliation with the Pittsburgh Cancer Institute gives many patients access to promising new experimental therapies.

Magee's success in treating gynecologic cancers is based on a multi-disciplinary, team approach. While the gynecologic oncologist coordinates care, he or she is just one of many health professionals who care for the needs of the patient and her family, with compassion and sensitivity.

Magee's Breast Care Consultation Center is the region's first and most complete resource for women with known or suspected breast cancer. Women may be self-referred or referred by a physician to the center, where a team of breast cancer specialists provide information, diagnosis, and treatment consultation in a single location, during one appointment.

Surgical Services

In addition to general and gynecologic surgery, Magee offers many surgical services for the special concerns of women: urologic dysfunction, breast cancer, plastic and reconstructive surgery, and more. The Women's Continence Center treats causes of urinary incontinence and identifies women with more serious urologic problems. And the outpatient Surgi-Center is one of the busiest in Allegheny County, performing more than 5,000 procedures each year.

Genetics

Magee has long been a regional leader in genetics related to reproduction. In recent years, the Department of Genetics has expanded its focus to improving women's health by giving women the knowledge they need about their bodies and ways to stay healthy. The breast cancer risk analysis program, for example, provides information on a woman's chance of developing this disease. And Magee researchers are working to unlock genetic codes to cardiovascular and other diseases.

The department has expanded its role in other areas, as well, including screening newborns for metabolic disorders, genetic consultations for women, men, and children, and new methods of prenatal diagnosis.

In the Community

Magee's mission of providing quality health care extends into communities throughout western Pennsylvania. Each year, more than 40,000 people enroll in health education classes offered through the Department of Consumer Education. Taught by certified nurse educators at the hospital, at satellite centers throughout Allegheny County, and in schools and community centers, courses cover more than 30 topics, from prepared childbirth and adoption, to adolescent sexuality, menopause, and hysterectomy.

The hospital's comprehensive breast care system serves women at six city and suburban locations, and is one of the largest screening programs in the country.

Magee's Outpatient Clinic is a significant contributor to the health and well-being of women and infants in Pittsburgh. The important role of the Clinic is demonstrated by the growing number of women, with little or no health insurance, who seek obstetric and gynecologic care at this hospital facility. More than 30,000 visits are recorded annually. The hospital also operates a similar, freestanding clinic in the Hill District, prenatal care clinics in Clairton and Terrace Village, and sponsors numerous cooperative health education programs with local schools, including an on-site clinic at the Letsche School.

In Russia

Magee is a partner in an innovative program to bring modern obstetric practices and improved maternal and newborn health care to Russia. The first obstetric program funded by the United States Agency for International Development, the project provides childbirth education to women and their families and professional education to Russian physicians, nurses, and health personnel. A renovated and modernized Birth House was opened in 1993.

The Magee-Womens Research Institute

Finally, Magee is a leading advocate on behalf of increased federal funding for women's health research. For too long, women's health needs were, incorrectly, equated with men's. The Magee-Womens Research Institute, the only research center in the nation concentrating exclusively on women's health, has designed a research agenda that addresses major health problems that women may face during their lifetimes: cardiovascular diseases, menopause, breast cancer, preterm labor and preeclampsia, and autoimmune diseases such as rheumatoid arthritis and lupus.

By placing Magee's reputation and resources at the front of the research movement, the Research Institute will set the national standard for women's health research into the 21st century.

■ *Complications from prematurity, including low birth weight and respiratory distress syndrome, account for the majority of babies admitted to Magee's Neonatal Intensive Care Unit, which treats approximately 1,200 babies each year.*

Back in 1898, Pittsburgh iron magnate John Shoenberger foresaw a growing need for health care. His vision led him to found St. Margaret Memorial Hospital.

What Shoenberger did not foresee was the length to which future St. Margaret employees would go in order to provide the highest levels of care possible from a community hospital. Not only has St. Margaret Memorial offered quality health care to people in the tri-state area for nearly 100 years, but it continues to expand and improve its areas of expertise to meet the ever-growing needs of the community.

Located on a 21-acre campus near Aspinwall, this 267-bed acute care, community, and teaching hospital serves more than 100,000 residents in the surrounding north and east suburban communities.

The hospital's services and facilities include the specialties of general surgery, intensive-coronary care, emergency medicine, complete outpatient care, rheumatology, occupational health, and rehabilitation.

■ *For nearly 100 years, St. Margaret has consistently offered medical expertise, state-of-the-art technology and a tradition of warmth and compassion to patients of all ages.*

St. Margaret Memorial Hospital

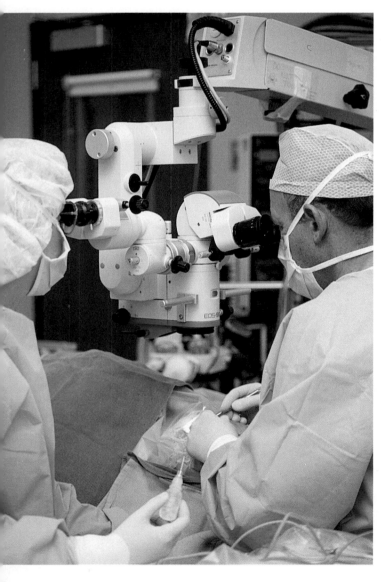

Several areas have been added or expanded in recent years, again in response to unmet community needs. A spine center and gerontology department have been added, while the hospital's orthopedic services, sports medicine center, and family practice residency program have been expanded.

Orthopedics and Sports Medicine

St. Margaret's medical staff includes 27 of the city's finest orthopedic surgeons who annually perform 2,300 orthopedic procedures, including 400 total hip and knee replacements.

Nurtured by the hospital's 30-year-old regional arthritis program and its extensive rehabilitation department, the orthopedic services offered at St. Margaret are listed among those most frequently used at western Pennsylvania and West Virginia hospitals, according to a recent Pennsylvania Health Care Cost Containment Council report. The quality of the orthopedic program also attracted medical education programs in Pittsburgh, which annually send 12 orthopedic residents to learn the newest techniques and advances.

■ *More than 400 physicians representing almost 40 specialities comprise St. Margaret's medical staff. Primary care doctors encompass the nucleus of the staff; specialities include rheumatology and orthopedics.*

St. Margaret's orthopedic surgeons staff another area, the Sports Medicine Center. St. Margaret boasts a comprehensive sports medicine program that opened in 1981 to serve the needs of Pittsburgh's professional, competitive, and recreational athletes. Because of the growing demand for this service, the hospital completed its state-of-the-art Sports Medicine Center in 1992. The 10,000-square-foot center can accommodate 200 people daily and offers the latest in sports medicine techniques and equipment.

The center also provides sports equipment modification, protective padding fabrication, splinting, and measurement and fitting of braces. Many of the specialists there have completed fellowships at nationally renowned sports medicine clinics and serve as team physicians for all of Pittsburgh's professional sports teams.

Other services available through the center include training sessions to teach coaches, team athletic trainers, and their student assistants preventive measures against injury; preseason screening for athletic teams; and community seminars.

The Spine Center

Back problems are complex. No single expert can be expected to have the right answer to treat the back. That's why St. Margaret recently formed the Spine Center, where patients can go to one location to see a specialist, or specialists, who best meet their needs. A team of neurosurgeons, orthopedists, physical therapists, radiologists, and rheumatologists combine their knowledge of the spine to offer the most up-to-date care. The Spine Center provides patients with a comprehensive spinal evaluation, recommendations for future care, rehabilitation, education, and follow-up as needed.

The center treats many types of back problems, including job-related back pain, injury from a sports or recreational accident, arthritis or osteoporosis, or injury from auto accidents.

Gerontology

A leader in specialized services for the elderly, St. Margaret developed a complete program of geriatric services to meet the needs of its patients over 55 and their families.

The hospital took great strides in gerontology in the 1980s and early 1990s. St. Margaret enhanced its circle of geriatric services, including the establishment of St. Margaret Classic Care — considered a breakthrough program in the area — in 1987. Classic Care is a geriatric specialty center, offering centralized, comprehensive, and continuous outpatient geriatric health services, consulting services, including insurance counseling, and a variety of specialty services, such as the Continence Clinic, Falls Clinic, and counseling for Alzheimer's disease, dementia, and depression.

Besides its treatment services, St. Margaret provides a variety of community education programs for seniors, their families, and health professionals, ranging from exercise and weight control to driving refresher courses, to insurance counseling.

Hospital-sponsored support groups for older adults and their families make living with such conditions as Alzheimer's Disease and arthritis easier. St. Margaret also provides skilled and intermediate nursing care to the frailest of the elderly at St. Margaret Seneca Place, a 180-bed nursing home in nearby Penn Hills.

In addition, the hospital is developing a care management program and retirement residence. The care management program

■ *St. Margaret believes in enriching the lives of older area adults and their families through a variety of programs and services, such as support groups, counseling, an exercise program, care management, and long-term care and retirement housing.*

will provide managed-home-care services for older adults. Seneca Hills Village retirement residence, a 105-unit complex, will be located on the Saltsburg Road site of the hospital's nursing home in Penn Hills. It is designed to provide a supportive, affordable residential living environment where seniors can maintain an active, quality lifestyle.

Family Practice

Through the hospital's three-year residency program, family physicians are taught to provide the best continuous, comprehensive, and personal health care for all family members. St. Margaret has been training family practice residents since 1971, only two years after family practice was recognized by the American Medical Association as medicine's 20th field of specialty. Along with less than 50 other hospitals in the United States, St. Margaret made a commitment to recruit quality medical students from around the country and teach them excellent, up-to-date, insightful medical care.

Since its beginning, the program, still the largest in Pittsburgh, has graduated almost 200 family physicians. More than one-third of those graduates have joined or begun practices in Allegheny County, particularly in the North Hills. To keep on top of the latest medical advances, techniques, and discoveries, the hospital sponsors continuing education lectures almost daily.

As part of the training during their second and third year at St. Margaret, residents spend considerable time seeing their own patients at the hospital's neighborhood family health centers in Lawrenceville and Bloomfield-Garfield.

Besides services and programs offered at St. Margaret's main campus, there are a number of satellite facilities, including the Doris Palmer Arthritis Center, St. Margaret Seneca Place Nursing Home, family health centers, a corporate care center, an occupational work center, the River Valley Rehab Center, the Medicenter, and the St. Margaret Memorial Hospital School of Nursing. **P**

■ *Since the hospital's move to Aspinwall in 1980, St. Margaret has continued to expand its services to meet area families' needs. This is accomplished in the 267-bed main structure and 100 and 200 Medical Arts buildings located on the 21-acre campus, as well as several satellite facilities throughout the city.*

Allegheny General Hospital: Continuing a Mission of Excellence

In 1832, Allegheny City—today, the North Side section of Pittsburgh—boasted 100 homes and 1,000 residents. Spring and summer that year brought with them a cholera epidemic that devastated the city. Residents fervently called for the establishment of a hospital, but as the epidemic waned and died, so did the urgency of their interest in a hospital. As Allegheny City grew and prospered during the next half century, community leaders recognized the need for care in a hospital setting that addressed a variety of health problems.

■ *Allegheny General Hospital is a 746-bed academic medical center that treats nearly 30,000 inpatients and 390,000 outpatients annually.*

Allegheny General Hospital

That need was met when two adjoining brick homes opened their doors for the first time as Allegheny General Hospital in 1885. In that 50-bed building, the hospital's founders set forth what would endure as Allegheny General's mission: promoting the general health of present and future generations in its communities. By adhering to this mission, Allegheny General Hospital played a role in the creation of Pittsburgh's distinguished health-care services legacy.

From its beginning, Allegheny General's leaders made a commitment to excellence in all facets of health care and to innovations in

■ *Life Flight was the first aeromedical emergency transportation system in the northeastern United States.*

the field of medical science. Each improvement to care throughout Allegheny General's history reflects that commitment. Within its first decade alone, for example, the hospital added a children's wing and a nursing school; it also used the horse-drawn ambulance, a forerunner to rapid access emergency care, and became the first hospital in the area to mount window screens and sanitize the surgical environment with carbolic acid spray.

More than 100 years later, Allegheny General Hospital's pioneering tradition of innovation in medicine and commitment to community remains strong. A 746-bed academic medical center, Allegheny General continues to provide Pittsburgh and the surrounding five-state area a comprehensive spectrum of health services, the teaching of humane and scientific medicine and the conduct of research that expands the frontier of medicine.

Exploration, Innovation

Great advances in both medicine and research occurred during the 1950s and 1960s, in the nation and at Allegheny General. Medical breakthroughs have continued throughout the past four decades, bringing to Allegheny General Hospital many "firsts"; such innovations exemplify the hospital's commitment to providing quality patient care and advancing the frontiers of medicine.

In 1961, an Allegheny General surgeon performed the state's first heart valve

replacement. One year later, the surgeon was part of the team that performed the city's first coronary bypass for coronary obstruction. In 1969, Allegheny General physicians performed the hospital's first heart transplant—the second in the state. Physicians at Allegheny General performed the nation's first double ventricular assist, an operation that proved that, under some circumstances, a damaged heart can rest and repair itself. Now, almost 1,500 open-heart procedures are performed annually by Allegheny General surgeons—the most in the state.

Advances in cardiovascular care continued at Allegheny General. In the 1980s, the hospital developed rapid coronary bypass techniques and laser applications for peripheral vascular surgery, as well as percutaneous transluminal coronary angioplasty. In the area of diagnostic procedures, Allegheny General Hospital was a pioneer of computerized echocardiography, which provides a two-dimensional moving picture of heart muscle in action. An Allegheny General physician performed the first echocardiogram in the United States. The number of heart catheterizations performed at the hospital, approximately 8,650 in 1992, was the most of any hospital in Pittsburgh and one of the highest in the state.

In 1974, the state's first computerized tomography (CT) scanner became operational at Allegheny General. In 1978, the hospital introduced Life Flight, the first aeromedical transportation system in the northeastern United States; by 1983, Life Flight had flown 4,700 flights.

In 1984, Allegheny General surgeons performed the nation's first percutaneous automated discectomy, a procedure for removing herniated back discs without major surgery. In 1985, an Allegheny surgeon performed the nation's first muscle-flap operation, in which back muscle is wrapped around a diseased heart and trained to beat.

The year 1986 brought the hospital accreditation as a Regional Resource (Level I) Trauma Center. Allegheny General was the first hospital in Pittsburgh to be verified by the American College of Surgeons, Committee on Trauma, as meeting the Level I criteria. Allegheny General became the first trauma hospital in the state to have a trauma intensive care unit, dedicated to caring for severely injured patients. The Trauma Center continues to be the busiest in Pittsburgh and sees the second largest number of patients of all hospitals in the state.

In 1990, the hospital became one of only 10 centers in the United States to study drugs that may reduce damage from spinal-cord injuries. One of the world's most comprehensive spina bifida centers opened at Allegheny General Hospital in 1991. One year later, hospital physicians learned through an Allegheny-based patient research study that a minimally invasive procedure known as percutaneous ultrasound-guided prostate cryosurgery may be an effective treatment for prostate cancer. Liquid nitrogen is used to destroy the cancerous prostate in this procedure, which helps patients who have not

■ *Advanced surgical techniques such as microdiscectomy — back disc surgery with the use of a microscope — are performed routinely at Allegheny General.*

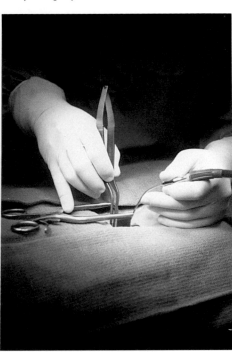

■ *Babies in the Level III Intensive Care Nursery — certified to provide the most crucial ventilatory care — are attended by experienced professionals who regularly handle critically ill children.*

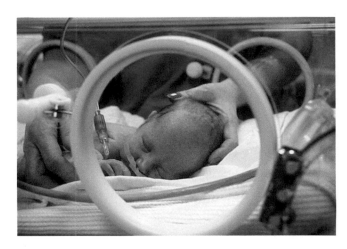

responded to conventional surgery or radiation therapy.

Anticipating Community Health Needs

Allegheny General Hospital offers a full spectrum of medical and surgical services that exemplify the depth and breadth of care available for any health concern, from the routine to the complex.

As forms of technology have evolved at Allegheny General, so have the number of services to meet patient needs. In recent years, several new services have been introduced. The hospital operates a Sleep Disorders Center, and a Clinical Electrophysiology Laboratory and Nuclear Cardiology Laboratory add new dimensions to cardiac care. A mobile lithotripter, shared with two area hospitals, enables the hospital to provide extracorporeal shock wave lithotripsy, which dissolves kidney stones through a noninvasive procedure. Allegheny General introduced the Pittsburgh area's first laser lithotripsy program and added transurethral ultrasound to its prostate program, complementing the comprehensive services available in the field of urology.

The hospital introduced several other patient-care programs in the early 1990s, including the Allegheny General Hospital IVF America Program—in partnership with Allegheny General's Department of Obstetrics and Gynecology—which offers in vitro fertilization to couples in southwestern Pennsylvania who have been unable to have children. Allegheny General offers a full range of obstetrics/gynecology services, serving as the site for more than 1,600 births in 1992. The hospital also operates a cytogenetics laboratory that helps physicians detect possible genetic abnormalities in fetuses. And a reproductive endocrinology program, begun in 1989, helps physicians diagnose and treat abnormalities specific to women's reproductive systems.

For the health needs of children and adolescents as they grow, Allegheny General's

Department of Pediatrics offers services in cardiology, surgery, endocrinology, infectious diseases, adolescent medicine, developmental pediatrics, pediatric cardiac angiography and a host of other health specialties. In addition, the hospital is part of an early childhood development program that focuses on behavioral disorders in children under 7, and an early intervention program instituted for autistic youngsters; both have won national acclaim.

In 1990, Allegheny General Hospital initiated the autologous bone marrow transplant program, which offers hope to cancer patients who are not responsive to other forms of treatment or are in an advanced stage of illness. The program now includes allogeneic transplants, or those that come from a patient's sibling or another individual with similar tissue.

The multidisciplinary Neuro-Oncology Program to support patients with brain tumors and other diseases was implemented in 1991, complementing established programs for epilepsy and stroke patients. The hospital also established a neuro-otology program for the treatment of diseases and conditions of the ear and balance systems. This program has been successful in implementing new technologies, including cochlear implants for both adult and pediatric patients.

Allegheny General's comprehensive range of orthopaedic procedures includes joint replacement, sports medicine, trauma, spinal surgery, hand surgery, orthopaedic oncology, pediatric orthopaedics, treatment of diseases affecting muscles, bones, ligaments and tendons, and management of deformity and growth-related problems. In addition, the hospital's Department of Orthopaedic Surgery is a major referral center in western Pennsylvania for patients who

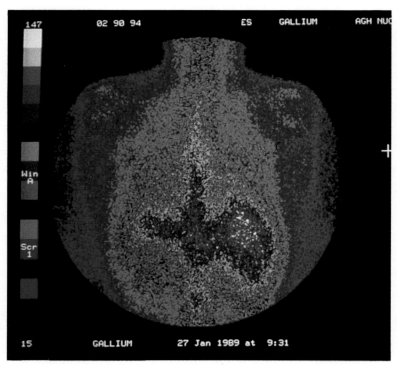

```
147        02 90 94              ES    GALLIUM       AGH NUC
Win
A

Scr
1

15        GALLIUM        27 Jan 1989 at   9:31
```

■ *Among the advanced diagnostic tests available at Allegheny General is SPECT scanning, which produces three-dimensional images of the brain and blood flow to various areas therein.*

with special needs, the hospital offers a 20-bed gynecology unit, postpartum and antepartum units, a perinatal special care unit and a neonatal intensive care unit. Other dedicated units at the hospital include a stroke unit and a bone marrow transplantation unit.

have sustained severe orthopaedic trauma injuries.

Services available in the area of respiratory therapy include two hyperbaric oxygen therapy chambers—the first in the Pittsburgh area. Allegheny General also is approved by the Commonwealth of Pennsylvania to perform kidney, heart, pancreas and single-lung transplants.

Allegheny General is recognized for its excellence in cardiology, cardiothoracic surgery, diagnostic radiology, gastroenterology, nephrology, neurology, neurosurgery, obstetrics/gynecology, oncology, ophthalmology, orthopaedic surgery, pediatrics, psychiatry, pulmonary medicine, transplant surgery and trauma (accredited as a Level I Regional Resource Center for adults and with special qualifications in pediatric trauma).

Indeed, Allegheny General offers people in need sophisticated medical, surgical and diagnostic programs. The hospital's critical-care capabilities include a 31-bed surgical intensive care unit, 20-bed trauma unit and 42-bed progressive cardiac care unit. Eight monitored maximum observation neurology beds and 42 other telemetry-equipped beds are available for patient care. The 12-floor inpatient building houses 20 operating suites, two cystoscopy rooms and a Labor, Delivery, Recovery and Postpartum Suite, which consists of private labor, delivery and recovery rooms. In addition, for women and babies

An array of sophisticated diagnostic procedures also is available at the hospital, including imaging technologies that help physicians assess the structure and function of organs or systems in the body. One such procedure is angiography, which enables physicians to view and detect abnormalities in the blood vessels of the heart, kidney and brain. Digital subtraction angiography, another diagnostic test, uses a computer to process images and subtract or remove unwanted background so that physicians may focus on a patient's blood vessels.

Urographic studies (which provide images of the urinary tract via X-rays), computerized tomography (CT) scanning of the body and brain, magnetic resonance imaging (MRI) and single photon emission computed tomography (SPECT) scanning are further examples of advanced diagnostic studies at Allegheny General Hospital.

By offering this spectrum of services, Allegheny General Hospital treats nearly 30,000 inpatients and 390,000 outpatients annually.

As medicine's innovations continue to take health professionals to new frontiers, it is important to note that services already in place at Allegheny General remain a focus.

For example, improving upon established technologies enabled Allegheny General in the 1970s and 1980s to follow up on research

that indicated medical illnesses such as head injuries, strokes or brain tumors could play a significant role in the development of emotional and behavioral problems. Allegheny General recognized the need for neuropsychiatric care and in 1988, Allegheny Neuropsychiatric Institute (ANI) was established to treat these problems in people of all ages.

This 94-bed hospital combines the expertise of a multidisciplinary treatment team with sophisticated brain imaging capabilities and studies to pinpoint the cause of patients' problems. Through its programs, ANI represents an avenue of care for patients with depressive disorders, problems with attention and concentration, memory deficits and motor-skills difficulties.

Allegheny General also expanded care for patients with special needs in 1991 when it opened the 119-bed Continuing Care Center. The center provides care for patients 18 and older in a homelike environment that fosters restorative care on a short-term basis.

Education of Health Professionals

Today's academic medical center environment attracts the best and brightest—as students and as teachers.

In support of its continuing commitment to education, Allegheny General Hospital joined with the Philadelphia-based Medical College of Pennsylvania in 1987; July 1988 brought the first Medical College students to the Allegheny Campus in Pittsburgh. Allegheny General serves as a clinical campus for Medical College students who come to Pittsburgh for required third-year clerkships in all clinical disciplines. Fourth-year students perform internships either in Philadelphia or Pittsburgh's Allegheny Campus.

Allegheny General supports graduate education for those medical students pursuing training in medical specialties. The hospital sponsors 15 residency programs and 7 subspecialty (fellowship) programs in cardiology, gastroenterology, hand surgery, medical oncology, nephrology, neuroradiology, and pulmonary disease.

The hospital abides by its responsibility to support community-appropriate education and the ongoing learning process for health professionals. To that end, Allegheny General

cal research in all neuro-science-related disciplines, including neurosurgery, psychiatry, neurology, neuroradiology, neuropathology, neuro-ophthalmology and neuro-otology. The center's research is led by an internationally recognized researcher in psychoneuroendocrinology.

The Allegheny-Community Clinical Oncology Program— which makes available to patients the latest cancer research protocols—operates at Allegheny General Hospital through a multiyear $1.2 million award from the National Institutes of Health. Through this program, Allegheny General Hospital is participating in the National Surgical Adjuvant Breast and Bowel Project's Breast Cancer Prevention Trial. The trial is evaluating whether the drug tamoxifen may prevent breast cancer development in women at increased risk for the disease.

In little more than a century, Allegheny General Hospital has moved from a time when similar health-care providers were little more than a series of sickrooms into the modern era of health science and technology. The hospital was, and is, a major contributor to Pittsburgh's reputation as an international center for health-service excellence. ▯

in 1988 created an educational environment: the George J. Magovern, M.D., Conference Center, which serves as the site for more than 2,000 educational programs each year.

In addition, the hospital's nationally accredited Continuing Medical Education (CME) program supports this commitment to furthering knowledge. More than 125 formal CME/continuing education programs were presented in 1992, including new initiatives on neuropsychiatry in clinical practice, codependency issues and infection control in dentistry.

Conduct of Research

In conjunction with the hospital's desire to forge new frontiers in medical education, its leaders also recognize that through innovative research, Allegheny General can improve the quality of health care. Science, in the form of laboratory medicine, took a great step forward in 1913 when the family of board member William Singer endowed a laboratory in his name. Further endowments eventually established the William H. Singer Memorial Laboratory and today's research component of Allegheny General Hospital— Allegheny-Singer Research Institute (ASRI).

Today, more than 100 investigators conduct research in 14 major disciplines at ASRI.

Recent research awards totaled more than $20 million. National sources of funding to ASRI include the American Cancer Society, the Department of Education, the National Cancer Institute and the National Institutes of Health. In addition, ASRI established new interdisciplinary research centers to address two major health areas—cardiovascular and pulmonary disease as well as neuroscience-related research.

The Cardiovascular and Pulmonary Research Center fosters the development of interdisciplinary research programs and encourages and supports investigator research in the cardiac, vascular, pulmonary and renal specialties. The center's director served as the former chief of the surgical branch of the National Institutes of Health's National Heart, Lung and Blood Institute.

The Neurosciences Research Center conducts, supports and develops basic and clini-

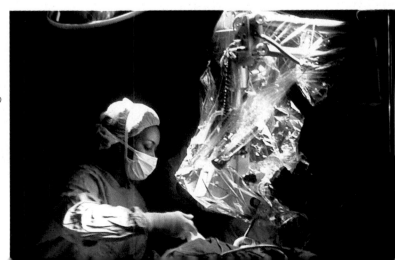

A cure for cancer. Genetic mapping. A diagnostic tool that pinpoints molecular change. A day when organs, even limbs, are salvaged from disease and trauma and restored to their full potential.

When dreamers dream of the future of health care, these are the wonders that come to mind and rightfully so. Medical technology, technique, and knowledge are advancing at a rapid pace. Many of today's visions promise to become reality in the near future.

Yet, for many health care leaders, the future focus is on balancing demands for universal access to health care with the pressure to control costs and maintain a high standard of quality.

In the wide-ranging debate over such questions, one voice brings reasoning inspired by the collective experience of hospitals and health care professionals in communities across western Pennsylvania and honed over years of collaboration toward common goals.

The author of that reasoning, the Hospital Council of Western Pennsylvania, believes there is no more compelling circumstance in which to speak out than that created by the nation's attempt to change the very nature of the U.S. health care system. Whatever measures adopted by the country under initiatives begun in 1993 by the Clinton administration, the results are likely to affect

Americans as profoundly as any breakthrough in medical technology.

Cooperation as A Vision of Reform

"We concluded some time ago that the new health care system should be quite different from what it has grown into during the past couple of decades," said Jack C. Robinette, president of Hospital Council.

"Whatever changes take place, we believe that at the core of the new system should be a new sense of collaboration, of cooperation between the health care community and the businesses, schools, and other human service organizations which serve the people in their local community."

The Council's prescription for reform can best be understood within the context of the western Pennsylvania experience. Throughout the history of this region, western Pennsylvanians have considered quality health care an unquestioned right. This is due in large part to the significant nonprofit hospital community serving this area and its commitment to provide care to all in need.

Interwoven with that network of nonprofit service is the Hospital Council of Western Pennsylvania, based in Warrendale, which represents more than 90 acute care and specialty hospitals and health care centers in the region.

The Council provides its affiliates with a wide range of programs, including group purchasing, information services, and strategic planning. Its most significant role in the 1990s may be to lead the exploration of new directions and workable solutions in the quest for a better, more effective health care system, one which is focused squarely on improving the health status of the people.

In the 1980s, increased financial pressure and decreased government support have compelled hospitals to look to concepts of free enterprise in order to meet the public's expectation of excellence. New management styles, program and product developments, sophisticated marketing techniques, and joint venturing are now part of the health care vocabulary. Yet, while one sector urges hospitals to "work smart," others decry a perceived blurring of the line between business and charitable institution.

The reality is that the Pittsburgh region's nonprofit hospitals hold a unique position in

Hospital Council of Western Pennsylvania

■ *Reaching beyond the traditional hospital role, health professionals from Suburban General Hospital in Pittsburgh hold a health fair for students at Avonworth Junior/Senior High School. The health fair is part of Healthy Communities for Western Pennsylvania, a community partnership program sponsored by The Hospital Council of Western Pennsylvania. Pictured with the students, are (center left) Jack C. Robinette, president of the Hospital Council of Western Pennsylvania, and next to him, Tom Hisiro, principal of Avonworth Junior/Senior High School.*

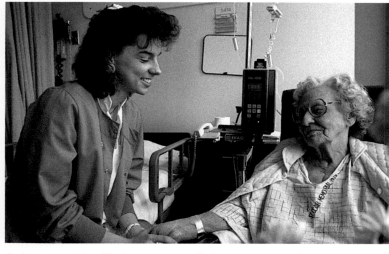

■ *Western Pennsylvania hospitals are widely known for both technological advances and, also for reaching out in a personal way to meet the healthcare needs of those living in the community.*

their communities. Their very nature distinguishes them from other "businesses." They strive to provide service based on human need, not on ability to pay. They function to heal the lives of individuals, not to mass-produce commodities. And they must work under regulations and standards that don't always promote financial stability.

At the same time, Pittsburgh's expectations of its hospitals are great. People expect immediate access to the most advanced technology available. They believe that hospitals must provide quality care for the poor and disenfranchised. And they demand that hospitals hold the line on the costs of health care. Fulfilling the demand for excellence amid profound economic and social pressure becomes, then, a critical balancing act.

As health care continues to grow as a dominant economic force in the region, the nation's health care initiatives become more important than ever to western Pennsylvania. The health care community has replaced employment in heavy manufacturing. The Council believes that economic revival can evolve fully only if the financial integrity of hospitals is ensured.

Robinette further acknowledges that there is no easy answer to this situation. But many western Pennsylvania health care institutions and communities have begun to take an important first step by developing effective working relationships with consumers, the business sector, the government, and other providers.

"Hospitals are moving toward the 'cooperative' model," Robinette said. "We have foreseen the creation of networks to promote health care and increase the effectiveness of health care delivery."

An Evolutionary Change

Say the word "hospital," and a very distinct image emerges in most people's minds. An imposing, complex structure. Medical professionals in white uniforms rushing from

one patient room to another as they administer care to the sick and injured. Electronic monitors, computerized diagnostic tools, and intricate life-sustaining machines.

But a new vision of hospitals has begun to take shape, in part through the influence of the Council. The hospital is an evolving community resource that breaks down the walls of traditional care delivery, making it more accessible to the community and, on many levels, more effective.

While new technology and the explosion of outpatient facilities enable hospitals to reach more people, the Council believes that a much more significant factor fueling the change is a universal realization that the health care system's values and characteristics must be reorganized on a national scale to meet the changing needs and expectations of the people it serves. Economic and social complexities demand a refocusing on the "basics"—and a more cooperative approach among all the stakeholders in the health care system to maximize the use of limited health resources through community partnerships and care networks. "Hospitals, their communities, and other related organizations cannot exist as islands," said Robinette. "By weaving their ideas, expertise, and resources into cooperative efforts, they have the potential to create a strong, effective bridge between what our health care system has been and what it needs to be."

Hospital Council members have forged strong and innovative links to their communities. At Punxsutawney Area Hospital, for instance, a program was developed to address a growing problem of teenage pregnancy in the local high school. Using tutors and special classroom education, the program dramatically reduced the number of teenage mothers who dropped out before graduation.

In Blair County, four competing hospitals have set aside their competitive differences and joined together to provide a self-esteem

program to prepare pre-school age children for entry into school. As part of the Council's Healthy Communities for Western Pennsylvania program, the consortium helps these children and their parents anticipate and address the challenges and pressures ahead of them.

By reaching out to hundreds of people—from elderly individuals finding peace, dignity, and understanding, to teenagers coping with drug and alcohol dependency—these "Hospitals without Walls" have worked closely with the communities they serve to extend themselves beyond the traditional paradigm of care delivery.

As a result, they have woven themselves even more tightly into the fabric of their communities and explored new ways to use valuable health care resources. Solid, progressive relationships are beginning to replace old barriers, and access to a wider, richer continuum of care has made seemingly hopeless issues more manageable.

Through the mutually beneficial partnerships that will surely result, answers can be found to the tough health care questions ahead. Only then can the viability of nonprofit hospitals be ensured and the public's right to quality health care for all in need be protected.

■ *Providing quality health care to people of all ages, from newborn infants to the elderly, is the goal of western Pennsylvania's health care community.*

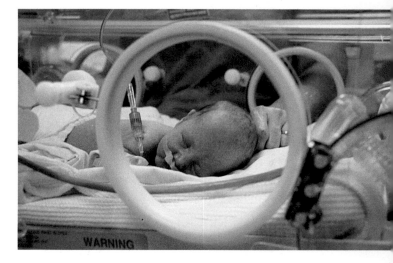

People are what make our health care system work. Without appropriately educated professionals, the impact of technological and scientific advancements developed in recent years would be greatly diminished.

Numerous factors affect the current need for human resources. Dramatic changes in technology—transplantation, genetics and microsurgery, for example—have created positions that did not exist a few years ago.

Also, with the end of the "baby boom," there simply are not as many new entrants into the work force as there used to be and these individuals have a great many career opportunities from which to choose.

The Center has taken a leadership role in developing innovative ways for schools and health care institutions to work together in providing the ever-increasing levels of skill and education required for the health care jobs of the future.

The Center's mission stresses the needs of today's health care labor force, and seeks ways to advance educational progress to effectively meet the challenges necessary to prepare highly qualified individuals for the health care workplace of the 21st century.

The keystone of this partnership model is the extremely successful "Adopt-A-School" program, which pairs health care facilities and school districts in 30 counties around western Pennsylvania.

conference center, offering students and their parents an opportunity to meet with and talk to many people already working in health care.

Mary Lou Murt, assistant director of nursing and Adopt-A-School facilitator at Mon Valley, called the program "an innovative and comprehensive strategy to recruit new professionals into health care careers."

After making students aware of how the health care system works, the next step is to assist them with more specific activities within the professions through classroom interaction and workshops.

At Braddock Medical Center, for example, Joseph McCarthy, a registered respiratory therapist and director of Cardiopulminary and Neurodiagnostic Services, visits high schools, including Steel Valley, Woodland Hills and East Allegheny, and talks directly with students about his profession.

McCarthy, who himself made a mid-career change into the health field, also teaches an actual part of the curriculum to junior and senior biology classes at East Allegheny, his alma mater. In his lectures, he

The Center for Health Careers

Finally, as the population ages, more and more people will require the services of the health care system. This increases the demand for health care professionals, even while the supply slowly diminishes.

In 1993, the Hospital Council of Western Pennsylvania published the results of Western Pennsylvania Healthcare Workforce 2000, a study which forecast the healthcare personnel needs of western Pennsylvania hospitals during the decade of the 1990s.

The study indicated that future growth in hospital employment would be highest in nursing and rehabilitation services. Emphasizing the continued movement toward primary care and preventive medicine, nurse practitioners and physician assistants also would be in greater demand.

Future investment in technology appears to be centered around electronic data interchange and enhanced diagnostic capabilities. These strong forces continue to reshape the future of health care, requiring an even more dedicated and talented work force.

To ensure an adequate supply of appropriately educated nurses, therapists and other health care professionals in the years to come, the Center for Health Careers was created in 1988 by members of the Hospital Council.

Central to the Center's mission and driving its success is the concept of partnership.

This program builds upon a systematic approach to health career development for students, emphasizing five key areas: awareness, exposure, exploration, preparation and training.

There are many examples of how these goals have been achieved throughout the region, but several programs exemplify the Center's mission in reaching out to students.

One of the most important steps in attracting new people to health care is to increase their awareness of how hospitals and other health institutions operate and what opportunities are available.

For example, at Monongahela Valley Hospital, junior and senior high school students gain first-hand experience about potential health care occupations through a series of field trips to various departments in the hospital and school discussion programs.

Mon Valley Hospital also has sponsored a Healthcare Careers Open House at its

■ One way in which Hospital Council's Center for Health Careers helps attract area students to pursuing health careers is through hospital and school sponsored "shadowing" experiences.

discusses lung anatomy, disease and diagnostic testing, and uses slides to illustrate lung function.

To allow for further exploration of health topics, the Center supports full-scale academic programs in the schools.

At St. Mary's High School, the Center cooperated with school administrators to create a cluster of year-long classes to educate students in wide range of health careers.

Students with interests ranging from nursing to pediatrics learn the history of health care and practical applications and skills, including how to take blood pressure and pulses, and how to draw a blood sample.

Other courses in the health-related technologies cluster at St. Mary's include medical terminology and anatomy. Students begin in their sophomore year, and by the time they are seniors they are prepared to spend part of their time working in health care institutions through co-op education programs at Andrew Kaul Memorial Hospital and area extended-care facilities.

Another component of the Center's drive to prepare students for the medical field involves educating them about the steps they need to take to prepare themselves for a career in health care.

At Sewickley Valley Hospital, teams of local junior and high school students participate in a unique quiz competition designed to emphasize the critical science and math skills necessary for success in health sciences training programs.

Based on questions developed by the hospital's Adopt-A-School committee, the students from Aliquippa, Ambridge, Freedom Area, Hopewell, Monaca, Northgate and South Side high schools are tested on their knowledge of health careers and general medicine.

■ *Each Fall the Center for Health Careers sponsors regional kick-off events to promote the "Adopt-a-School" program for area students. The program partners western Pennsylvania hospitals with area schools with the goal of attracting qualified students to health careers.*

Facilitator Georgene Snyder said Sewickley Valley set out to develop an educational program but, in the process, ended up with a program that was fun while also providing a learning experience.

The culmination of the Center's efforts focuses on facilitating student entry into training programs at the post-secondary education level.

Greenville Regional Hospital, part of the Horizon Hospital System, and the Center support a mentorship program which ensures that students understand what is involved with a particular health care career by arranging for students to follow along with, or "shadow," a working health professional.

The shadowing or mentor program, which involves a six-hour day with a health professional, allows trainees to experience such fields as nursing, physical and occupational therapy, radiologic technology, medical technology, respiratory therapy, pharmacy, medical records, biomedical engineering and physician assisting.

The program is available not only to high school students, but also to adults returning to the workforce. From this mentoring experience, the students were channeled into the hospital volunteer program and often into hospital internships. Two area colleges—Thiel and Gannon—have made the hospital mentorship an entrance requirement for admission to their health science programs.

The success of programs such as these is helping the Center expand its scope not only to attract students to the health care professions, but also to ensure that the education system prepares students to meet workplace needs and requirements.

The Center strives to be a visionary model of the power of collective action. By establishing productive partnerships with diverse groups of individuals and organizations, it has succeeded in providing the community with a positive, active solution to a pressing social issue. ▪

■ *One component of the Center's program is that of explaining the variety of health care careers available to students. Through publications, classroom visits and actual shadowing experiences with health care professionals, students have an opportunity to learn about careers such as physical and occupational therapy.*

The Western Pennsylvania Hospital has gained a national reputation as a renowned health care center for the treatment of cancer, at-risk pregnancies, diabetes and cardiovascular ailments, as well as for its innovative and aggressive approach to burn medicine.

Each year more than 140,000 people seek treatment at West Penn, located in the heart of Pittsburgh's Bloomfield section. While many patients are from the numerous, closely knit communities that surround the hospital, others travel great distances for the advanced care West Penn provides.

West Penn Hospital is a full-service, 542-bed referral medical center and teaching

West Penn Hospital

facility, employing about 3,000 people. The hospital complex encompasses approximately 1.2 million square feet and occupies two city blocks.

It is the primary subsidiary corporation of the Western Pennsylvania Healthcare System, a Pennsylvania nonprofit corporation. Other subsidiaries include the West Penn Hospital Foundation and West Penn Corporate Medical Services, Inc.

■ *A researcher examines Interleukin-3 (IL-3), a new cytokine under development at the Western Pennsylvania Cancer Institute. Cytokins are proteins in the blood that stimulate the growth and enhance the function of hematopoietic cells, which produce new blood cells in the body. When administered to people who suffer from lymphoma, the IL-3 may stimulate white blood cell recovery to help reduce infection following bone marrow transplantation.*

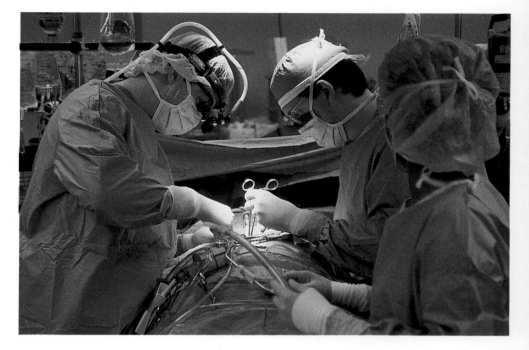

■ *A team from the Cardiovascular Institute performs a highly complex procedure to repair a thoracic aortic aneurysm. In addition to these procedures, West Penn cardiothoracic surgeons are on the leading edge of several other advanced techniques, including video-assisted thoracoscopic surgery and complex coronary artery surgery, such as coronary endarterectomy.*

But even as West Penn enjoys a reputation that reaches far beyond the nearby neighborhoods it traditionally has served, the institution has not lost sight of its role or its commitment to provide vital community services.

"We strive to serve the needs of our immediate neighborhood and to be a regional referral center providing state-of-the-art care for those in the outlying areas," said Charles O'Brien, Jr., Chief Executive Officer. "In the future, we intend to strengthen our role in both those areas."

West Penn works hard to live up to its designation as a regional medical and teaching center through its commitment to serving the needs of patients and other health care facilities from many surrounding counties and states.

Each year, hundreds of patients are brought to West Penn's Burn Trauma Center, including many from communities throughout Pennsylvania, Ohio, and West Virginia. Some patients come from overseas for burn treatment at West Penn.

Hundreds more critically ill infants from throughout the region are brought to the Neonatal Intensive Care Unit. The Western Pennsylvania Cardiovascular Institute and Western Pennsylvania Cancer Institute receive referrals for their diagnostic and treatment services from urban and rural hospitals throughout the tri-state area, and the Cancer Institute from across the country.

In addition to providing direct care to patients from outlying communities, West Penn's various departments and centers also send representatives to communities to provide specialized training and instructional programs for local health care professionals. The NICU, for instance, conducts training programs in techniques of neonatal and perinatal care, including neonatal resuscitation.

"Through these and other outreach programs, West Penn Hospital becomes a true partner in helping to improve the quality and delivery of comprehensive, state-of-the-art health care throughout the region," O'Brien said. Physicians at the Western Pennsylvania Cancer Institute initiated the first bone marrow transplant program in Western Pennsylvania in 1982, and transferred the program to West Penn Hospital in 1990.

As one of the major bone marrow transplantation programs in the state — and one of the top 20 in the country — the Cancer Institute receives referrals from throughout the Northeast. Patients undergo bone marrow transplants for treatment of a variety of cancers, including leukemia, Hodgkin's disease, and recurrent breast cancer.

The Cancer Institute's Clinical Trial Program is one of the first in the nation to test new colony-stimulating factors and anti-infection treatments such as the cytokine Interleukin-3 (IL-3). Cytokines are proteins in the blood that stimulate the growth and enhance the function of blood-producing cells in the body. When administered to people who suffer from lymphoma, a form of lymphoid cancer, the IL-3 may stimulate white blood cell recovery to help reduce infection following bone marrow transplantation.

To help find better alternatives for cancer patients, the Institute participates in a variety of research projects scientifically investigating more effective ways to strike back against many types of cancer.

As a result, the Institute can offer patients the benefits of a complete range of leading-edge technologies in the diagnosis and treatment of cancer, including newly developed tumor cell imaging techniques, bone marrow transplantation, use of dose-intensive chemotherapy and radiation therapy as well as new methods to stimulate the immune system to control minimal disease.

The Institute's comprehensive hematological services enable patients to have all coagulation and blood analysis and lab work professionally performed and interpreted in one location. Newer tests of bone marrow function including chromosomal analysis and stem cell assay facilitate more accurate diagnosis and guide treatment plans for patients with advanced bone marrow disorders.

The Center for Neuro-oncology at West Penn is one of 14 national members of the Brain Tumor Cooperative Group, sponsored by the National Cancer Institute, which coordinates trials of new therapies for treating malignant brain tumors. The center also is actively involved in investigations into the use of laser surgery for the treatment of brain cancer and the surgical implantation of biodegradable "wafers" into brain tumors.

■ *In West Penn's Neonatal Intensive Care Unit, highly sophisticated equipment monitors such physiological functions as respiration, pulse rate and PH levels, guarding against undetected apnea— life-threatening pauses in infants' breathing. The NICU at West Penn is one of the region's largest referral resources for sick newborns.*

For patients with cardiovascular diseases, the Western Pennsylvania Cardiovascular Institute at West Penn offers comprehensive patient care. The Institute is also very active in education and research in cardiovascular disease. It brings together a skilled medical and professional staff with state-of-the-art technology to provide patients with an array of services and a high level of care.

Patients can benefit from the specialized expertise of the Institute's four centers: the Cardiology Center, the Cardiothoracic Surgery Center, the Hypertension Consultation Center, and the Peripheral Vascular Center. Doctors at these centers perform the most advanced imaging, diagnostic and interventional procedures.

Complementing the Institute's sophisticated capabilities are a variety of support and community programs, including the Jane V. Love Cardiopulmonary Rehabilitation Center, a cardiac wellness program, and a women's heart risk assessment program.

West Penn is a tertiary care provider of obstetrical, neonatal and gynecological services. Staffed by an experienced team of board certified perinatologists and neonatologists, the hospital's regionally recognized Maternal and Neonatal Intensive Care Units receive critically ill mothers and newborns

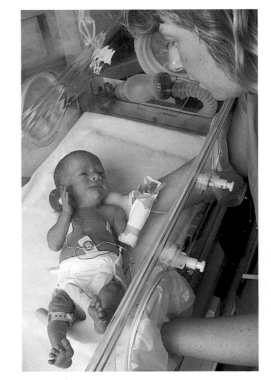

transported from other hospitals. For families with special concerns, the nationally recognized Reproductive Genetics Division offers genetic counseling and testing, including fetal ultrasonic evaluation, amniocentesis and chorion villus sampling (CVS), as well as environmental and occupational exposure risk assessment through the Pregnancy Safety Hotline.

A team of subspecialists provides tertiary gynecologic services which include the surgical, radiological, and chemotherapeutic treatment of advanced gynecological cancers using nationally recognized and coordinated treatment protocols, the diagnosis and treatment of urinary incontinence using sophisticated urodynamic testing techniques, as well as the diagnosis and treatment of children with gynecologic disorders and couples who are infertile. Using advanced

■ *West Penn's Radiology Department has achieved national recognition for its work in vascular stenting. It was one of the first five hospitals in the country to perform Palmaz stenting, and one of the first to use the Schneider Wallstent. Other advanced procedures offered for peripheral vascular disease include intra-operative duplex scanning of the carotid artery. This procedure ensures surgical accuracy and trascranial doppler monitoring to assess blood flow to the brain during carotid surgery.*

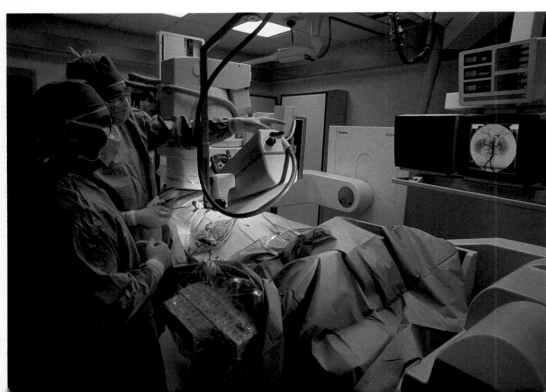

surgical techniques (i.e. video laparoscopic and laser surgery), postoperative recovery is rapid and hospital stay shortened. The hospital's Women and Children Division takes pride in providing unique, cutting edge services tailored to the needs of our families.

A commitment to women's health issues is reflected in the Breast Diagnostic Imaging Center (BDIC), which was created specifically with women's needs in mind. Realizing that some patients experience anxiety when

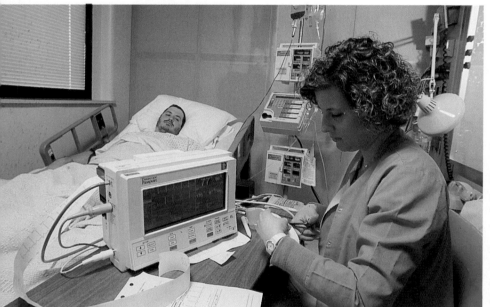

undergoing medical tests, the all-female BDIC staff strives to create a pleasant environment that will put the patient at ease.

West Penn's Medical Genetics Department is among the preeminent medical genetics departments in the tri-state area and is recognized nationwide as a leader in clinical genetics. To more effectively serve the genetic evaluation and counseling needs of patients in outlying areas, the Medical Genetics Department has established nine satellite clinics in communities including Erie, DuBois, Phillipsburg, and Beaver.

West Penn boasts that its Supplemental Newborn Screening program is one of the most widely used newborn screening programs in the country. More than 40 hospitals from Pennsylvania, New York, Ohio, and West Virginia use the program, which screens approximately 30,000 newborns each year for 12 potentially life-threatening inherited

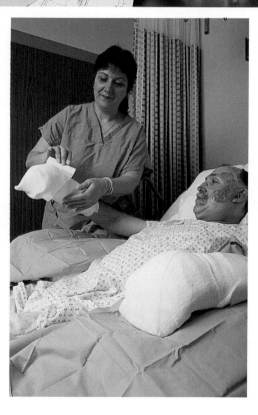

■ *Physicians at The Western Pennsylvania Cancer Institute initiated the first bone marrow transplant program in western Pennsylvania in 1982. Transferred to West Penn in 1990, the program now receives referrals from physicians throughout the Northeast. Patients of the Institute undergo bone marrow transplants for aplastic anemia, acute and chronic leukemia, Hodgkin's disease, lymphomas and other cancers of the blood.*

■ *The West Penn Burn Trauma Center has gained international acclaim for its level of sophistication in treating burn injuries. The 18-bed unit, which annually cares for some 400 critically burned patients and 500 lesser burned ones, is involved in an exchange program which enables physicians and other health care professionals to visit and study at the center.*

disorders. The program was selected by the state of Pennsylvania as a model for its proposed expanded newborn screening legislation.

The Department's Cytogenetic and Molecular Genetics Laboratories offer such advanced capabilities as chromosome analysis for identifying reproductive conditions and genetic disorders; detection of human papillomavirus, which has been closely linked to cervical cancer; bone marrow genotyping for monitoring the success of bone marrow transplantation; and DNA fingerprinting.

For families seeking a more traditional birthing experience, Birthplace, the only free-standing midwifery birthing center in Western Pennsylvania, is available at West Penn. Designed for low-risk pregnant families, deliveries take place in a Victorian home atmosphere located close to the hospital campus.

The opening in 1989 of the Joslin Center for Diabetes, an affiliate of the world-renowned Joslin Diabetes Center in Boston, reflects the hospital's commitment to enhancing the quality of diabetes care and management in the tri-state area.

Dedicated to excellence in diabetes care since 1898, the Joslin Diabetes Center in Boston is recognized around the world as the leader in diabetes treatment, research, and education. The Center at West Penn is one of seven Joslin affiliates. It offers patients access to a team of diabetologists who are board-certified in endocrinology, plus specially trained nurses, dieticians, nurse educators, and exercise therapists.

Patients of the Joslin Center for Diabetes at West Penn also have the opportunity to benefit from the aggressive clinical and laboratory research being conducted at the Boston Center. Many of the important innovations in diabetes care have resulted from Joslin programs, including laser treatment of diabetic eye disease, improved outcomes for diabetic pregnancies, and identification of immunological markers for diabetes.

The history of success in treating burn patients at the Burn Trauma Center has been enhanced by a commitment to research in areas such as wound care, resuscitation and psychological implications of burn injuries. The 18-bed Burn Trauma Center, which has

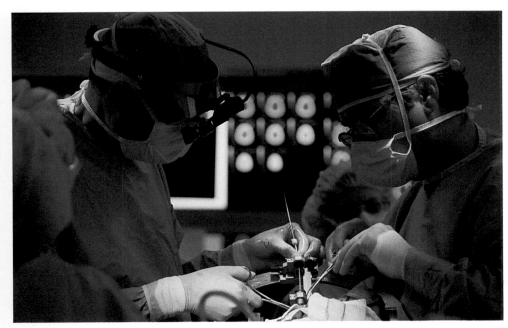

■ *A West Penn surgeon deftly plants a radioactive iodine "seed" into a brain tumor in a 60-year-old patient. This sophisticated procedure is one of several in clinical trial at West Penn's Center for Neuro-oncology. The center is also actively involved in investigations into the use of stereotactic laser surgery, oral tamoxifen therapy, and the surgical implanting of biodegradable "wafers" into brain tumors.*

earned international acclaim for its level of sophistication, annually cares for some 400 critically burned patients and 500 lesser burned patients.

The Burn Trauma Center is also involved in an exchange program which enables physicians and other health care professionals to visit and study at the center.

In addition to its advanced treatment expertise, the Burn Trauma Center's partnership in the Aluminum Cans for Burned Children Fund enables it to offer a variety of educational and charitable programs. These include a Scald Prevention program for parents, grandparents, day-care workers, and others responsible for watching young children; a Back-to-School program that has helped ease the return of burned children to the school setting; and a summer camp program where children with burns can interact and provide support for each other.

As a major regional referral center, West Penn Hospital recognizes that its responsibility as an educational and medical care resource extends far beyond its local communities and even the Greater Pittsburgh area. With this in mind, the hospital provides outreach programs with the purpose of supporting physicians, their patients, and their hospitals as they work to enhance the level and quality of health care they provide.

First Health Alliance is a partnership of more than 30 hospitals in western and central Pennsylvania, eastern Ohio, and northern West Virginia working together to make highly specialized medical care and education available in their areas.

Spearheaded by West Penn, one of the major objectives of the First Health Alliance is to make the advanced resources and expertise of major urban medical centers available to community and local hospitals.

''We believe this alliance provides one of our best opportunities to reach out to the other health care providers throughout the region,'' according to Ralph F. Hagemeier, who became West Penn's Senior Vice President of Network Development and External Affairs in early 1993. ''We can all benefit from the partnership it creates, and the result will be a higher level of health care for all our neighbors, near and far.''

The cornerstone of local health care in outlying communities is the primary care physician. West Penn Hospital is working to enhance the practice of individual physicians throughout the tri-state area through the Community Affiliate Program. Community Affiliate medical staff members receive Consulting Medical Staff privileges. They are offered a wide variety of benefits, including direct access to the medical expertise of West Penn Hospital Institutes, Centers and specialists; streamlined patient referral and information services; training programs for their staffs; and a variety of personal services.

West Penn's participation in the region's growth and prosperity dates back nearly a century and a half. The hospital was first incorporated in 1848, with its first building erected in 1850 on a site a few miles east of what is now Downtown Pittsburgh in the Polish Hill section of the city.

During the next 60 years, numerous buildings, including a School of Nursing building, were added to the original hospital complex. In 1886, The Western Pennsylvania Medical College, the forerunner of the University of Pittsburgh School of Medicine, was founded as an adjunct to the hospital. In 1912, West Penn relocated to its present location.

The hospital's increased physical plant continues to keep pace with the growth and increased sophistication of services provided.

A capital building program of more than $80 million is currently under way.

The building program includes the construction of a new nine-story patient care tower, a physician office building, a conference center, additional parking, and a redesign and expansion of existing facilities. The program is designed to increase emphasis on the key service lines of cardiovascular, cancer, maternal/infant, burn trauma, and diabetes/renal care; increase West Penn's efficiency; promote ambulatory care services, and prepare for future growth. Completion of the program is slated for 1996.

From its origins as a fledgling hospital serving the burgeoning eastern neighborhoods of Pittsburgh in the 1850s, West Penn has evolved into a nationally respected institution for leading-edge specialty care.

Despite this progress, West Penn has retained its historical identity and mission, continually striving, as the hospital's founders stated it, ''to be worthy of the age and vicinity in which we live.'' ▣

■ *As its name implies, the Patient Focused Care Unit brings most services, previously located in different areas of the hospital, right into the patient's room. This new approach, which West Penn was one of the first hospitals in the country to implement, reduces inconveniences for the patient, such as waiting in line or having to be transported from one area to another. Admissions, pharmacy, phlebotomy and physical, occupational and respiratory therapy are all located within the 49-bed unit.*

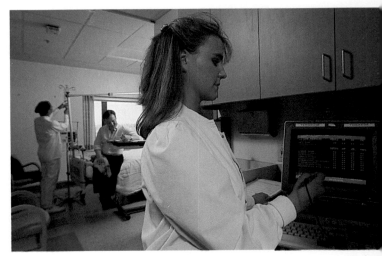

All photographs by David Aschkenas.

The population of the United States is aging so dramatically that we're amidst an "aging revolution." Never before in our history have seniors represented such a formidable group.

By the year 2030, over 25 percent of our population will be 60-plus. A surprising 8 million seniors will be over 85 years of age, thanks to major advances in health and medicine.

Today's elderly adults are different from yesterday's in that they are more independent, more demanding, more interested in a high quality of life, more open-minded to new possibilities and new challenges.

Lutheran Affiliated Services, or LAS, is a charitable, not-for-profit geriatric health care

■ *Lutheran Affiliated Services promotes seniors' health, wellness and self-care skills rather than treating aging as a disease.*

Headquartered in Cranberry Township, 25 miles north of Pittsburgh's Golden Triangle, LAS serves a metropolitan area with the most aged population in the nation, based on percentage of adults 65-plus.

Lutheran Affiliated Services

system pioneering innovative programs to address the needs of elderly adults. Affiliated with the Evangelical Lutheran Church in America, LAS carries out a tradition of service that dates back to 1893.

The LAS mission provides a ministry of long-term care, residential housing, geriatric services, and programs for older adults of all denominations in a Christian environment.

By the early 1990s, LAS was serving more than 1,000 residents in western Pennsylvania and the surrounding area.

LAS was established as a parent organization in 1986 to provide management and fiscal oversight for two premier long-term care and senior living communities and for several other subsidiary organizations — all dedicated to excellence in health care.

"The LAS strategy is based simply on moving the elderly service delivery system away from the traditional custodial model to a wellness model," explains Dr. Michael Hendrickson, LAS president and chief executive officer. "Instead of treating the aging process as a disease requiring constant treatment, the emphasis is placed on promoting a person's health, wellness, and self-care skills to maximize independence for as long as possible.

"We encourage seniors to live fully, take control of their lives, and feel good about themselves."

LAS has aggressively expanded its programs and facilities to meet the needs of the rapidly growing elderly population. In doing so, LAS has challenged traditional thinking and typical ways of providing care for older adults, creating new, breakthrough prototypes for adult care in the process. These prototypes have fired the imagination of geriatric professionals throughout the United States.

Programs of Excellence

Fundamental to the LAS approach is the creation of innovative Programs of Excellence to enhance the quality of life of older adults within caring communities.

The continuing care retirement community at LAS/Passavant Retirement Center in Zelienople, Pennsylvania, for example, allows elderly adults to "age in place," that is, to live in one location for the remainder of their lives with a continuum of services.

In a singular homelike campus, housing and care options for retirees range from independent cottage and apartment living to assisted living to intermediate and skilled nursing care.

Excellent health care and recreational activities are offered at every level.

Similarly, the state-of-the-art Alzheimer's Care Center at LAS/St. John in Mars, Pennsylvania, offers four distinct levels of care, from entry level to late stage. Residents may enter the center at any stage and become a part of a specialized, low-stress program promoting confidence and independence.

In contrast, other Alzheimer's centers often accept residents only at particular levels, or residents at all stages will be grouped together.

The LAS program for health assessment — the Geriatric Assessment and Care Planning Program — is another example of enhanced quality of life for aging residents. This new program breaks the mold of traditional geriatric assessment.

Explains Mildred Fincke, R.N., director of Clinical Services, "The goal is to establish and monitor a personalized care plan to

■ *At the LAS/Passavant Retirement Center, options for retirees include independent cottage and apartment living, assisted living, and intermediate and skilled nursing care.*

■ *Affiliated with the Evangelical Lutheran Church in America, Lutheran Affiliated Services carries out a tradition of service that dates back to 1893.*

maximize the independence and life satisfaction of every person living in an LAS community."

The comprehensive assessment is comprised of four basic components: physical, functional, psychosocial, and spiritual.

"Our program is special because it emphasizes the 'whole person,'" continues Ms. Fincke. "We're not just interested in the physical aspects that make a person who they are, but what they think, how they feel, and the values that are important to them. All of these factors contribute to a holistic approach to their well being."

Because many elderly adults now seek alternative living arrangements after their 80th birthday, LAS has anticipated a growing demand for assisted living. Assisted living residences provide renewed dignity and independence for older adults who need help with daily personal activities such as meal preparation, dressing, bathing, walking, and medication.

Historically, many elderly adults needing this type of care have entered nursing homes prematurely, even though their conditions didn't require clinical environments. The nursing home setting often proved detrimental to frail adults who weren't in ill health.

Responding to the demand for a new alternative — assisted living in a caring community — Lutheran Affiliated Services opened an important new prototypical facility for assisted living in February of 1993.

Newhaven Court at Passavant

Newhaven Court in Zelienople, is a free-standing assisted-living residence on the campus of the award-winning LAS/Passavant Retirement Center. Newhaven Court is yet another example of an LAS Program of Excellence, designed to meet the needs and desires of the frail elderly.

A product of more than 15 years of research and development conducted by Retirement Systems, Inc., RSI, of McLean, Virginia, Newhaven Court combines beautiful facilities and unique programs in a Caring Community Program that cultivates independence and well-being in ways never offered before.

RSI is a leading innovator of dynamic health and wellness programs for the elderly.

"The Newhaven Court residence itself — through value engineering and attention to human dynamics — is a key to the happiness the residents find there," explains Dr. Hendrickson.

"And the best news is the relative affordability. Our rates are extremely competitive. We strive to lead the industry in affordable retirement living."

Reminiscent of a finely furnished residential estate, Newhaven Court combines spacious common living areas such as the entry foyer, the grand stairway, the spacious dining room, health spa, and the library, with private, individual apartments clustered in cozy neighborhoods. Services include restaurant-style meals and help with laundry and housekeeping. Staff is available 24-hours daily to assist residents. And educational, recreational, social, and spiritual programming abounds.

Explains Robert Johnson, vice president of Marketing for LAS, The Caring Community Program at Newhaven Court provides a social and interactive environment while also

preserving personal privacy. It's a whole new approach to life for many seniors.

"Living at Newhaven Court is a balance of sociability and privacy, independence and assistance, individual pursuits and shared pleasures," says Mr. Johnson. "And to think that in the past, many of those adults had no alternative but a nursing home or round-the-clock home health care."

Mildred Fincke points to the health benefits, "It is very important to remember that a person's bodily health is greatly influenced by their emotional health. That's the beauty of clustering the apartments in Newhaven Court in neighborhood settings. A resident is surrounded by neighbors who care and socialize, yet privacy is still respected by providing individual apartments."

Two of the first residents at Newhaven Court were sisters who had lived side-by-side for 13 years in independent living cottages on the Passavant campus. "This new assisted living program at Newhaven Court is coming at an ideal time in our lives. We both realize that although we're still very active, we are slowing down a bit," said one sister.

The other sister agreed. "We've been on the waiting list since the very beginning, because we're planning for the future."

Adds William Pratt, LAS/Passavant executive director, "The beauty of the new facility complements the many wonderful programs being offered there. The assisted living program at Newhaven Court celebrates and

■ *Newhaven Court is an innovative, new alternative for the frail elderly. Newhaven offers assisted living in a caring, community environment.*

encourages life and independence instead of viewing the aging process as an illness."

LAS/Passavant Retirement Center

Newhaven Court is only one of many comprehensive programs available at Passavant Retirement Center — one of LAS' two premier communities. Passavant provides a full continuum of retirement care on 42 acres of picturesque country grounds in historic Zelienople, Pennsylvania.

Independent retirees may choose to live in apartments or in one of the 100 cottages, which range in size from efficiencies to large, three-bedroom homes. Assisted living programs are available in both Newhaven Court and in Passavant's main building near the "Main Street" mall, the central dining room, and the many recreation and activities centers. Intermediate and skilled nursing facili-

■ *Life at Newhaven Court uniquely combines spacious common living areas with private, individual apartments clustered in neighborhoods.*

ties are also located in Passavant's main building for temporary or permanent nursing care services.

Passavant's 650 residents choose the retirement lifestyle they prefer — and the level of services they require. Many residents pursue off-campus shopping and recreation on a regular basis. And right on the Passavant campus, there are activities to suit any fancy: from dancing to Bible study, ceramics to singing, college courses to movie matinees.

LAS/St. John Lutheran Care Center

LAS' other anchor facility is St. John — a 352-bed state-of-the art licensed nursing facility located in Mars, Pennsylvania. Founded in 1893, St. John builds on its tradition of excellence through three channels of service: long-term nursing care, treatment of Alzheimer's disease, and sub-acute and rehabilitative care in conjunction with area medical centers.

The facility goes beyond nursing care to extensive social service and pastoral care to provide for the complete person. Activities for residents include field trips, shopping, music, recreation, socials, and creative arts.

Long-Term Nursing Care

Long-term care is provided at St. John in both the intermediate unit and the skilled unit.

The intermediate care unit at St. John's is designed for residents who do not require the care of a registered nurse but need assistance in areas such as diet, care of sores, skin care, regulation of catheters or ostomies, dressing, feeding, personal hygiene, mobility, and general supervision.

The skilled care unit is appropriate for residents requiring more extensive skilled nursing care on a 24-hour basis. Patients must require active treatment of an unstable condition not requiring acute hospitalization, drugs requiring medical surveillance and monitoring, suctioning, tube feedings, physical therapy, occupational therapy, or speech therapy.

The Alzheimer's Care Center

Alzheimer's disease affects over 4 million Americans and is the fourth leading cause of death among adults.

Approximately 10 percent of the population over 65 is afflicted with Alzheimer's. A striking 47.2 percent of those over 85 are affected.

The Alzheimer's Care Center at St. John has evolved into one of the nation's largest and most progressive Alzheimer's caregivers. The latest expansion resulted in a program with four distinct levels of care and licensed for 113 beds.

"Through current research and interaction with residents, we have established a true continuum of care based on 'current best practice,'" explains Dr. Hendrickson. "This means that residents with Alzheimer's

■ *The LAS/Passavant Retirement Center enables seniors to "age in place," living in one location with a full continuum of human and health care services.*

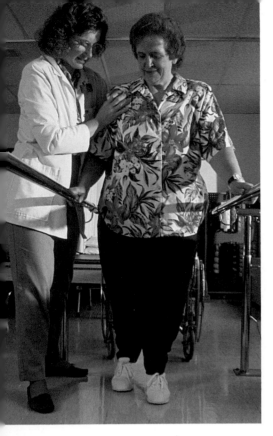

■ *LAS/St. John is a state-of-the-art specially care facility with three centers of healthcare excellence: sub-acute, Alzheimer's and long-term nursing.*

will receive the best care available at St. John, regardless of the stage or progression of their disease."

All levels of Alzheimer's care at St. John provide a home-like setting and encourage self-care including home-making and other familiar activities of daily living. A specially trained staff provides personalized care programs to help Alzheimer's residents cope with the symptoms of the disease — such as memory loss and disorientation.

All residents are assessed to determine their ability to share in larger activities at St. John. And the program accommodates transitional and family needs by providing flexibility for residents who desire to spend weekends at home with their families.

The Sub-acute Care Center

The St. John Sub-acute Care Center represents an innovative program designed to deliver residents the optimum level of recovery care, while offering savings of up to 50 percent over comparable services provided in hospital-based medical and rehabilitation facilities. Residents receive ventilator care, infusion therapy, post-surgical care, nutritional support, stroke care, and other specialized services.

St. John is evolving as a contracted provider of these services for hospitals, managed health care agencies, and other health care organizations.

Trinity SeniorCaring, Inc.

Based in Latrobe, this LAS corporation is now at the planning and development stage of creating new senior housing and assisted living facilities for elderly residents in the Latrobe area of western Pennsylvania.

Strategic Community-Based Health Care Affiliations

Lutheran Affiliated Services' strategic plan also includes the development of affiliations with other health care providers committed to delivering a wide variety of geriatric services to their geographic regions.

LAS is cooperating with strong regional hospitals to pursue the formation of unique health care affiliations. The goal is to create community-based, fully integrated continuums of care to meet the needs of senior adults. Such cooperations make LAS and its affiliates unique to the Greater Pittsburgh area, as well as one of the most progressive of such groups in the nation.

The new affiliations are dedicated to bringing about residential retirement developments and geriatric campuses that feature independent living, assisted living, and nursing care.

These new community-based partnerships will work cooperatively to share the resources and services of LAS and other providers for jointly developed programs. Hospital systems offer outstanding services in such areas as intensive care, emergency care, inpatient and outpatient acute care, rehabilitation, and transitional home care. LAS will contribute management and programming expertise in such areas as senior housing, assisted living, geriatric wellness and care management, specialized sub-acute services, long-term care, and innovative Alzheimer's treatment and education.

By the year 2000, it is estimated that over half of all health care expenditures will be dedicated to the needs of the elderly. LAS is positioning now to meet those needs with its Programs of Excellence.

The LAS Foundation

The LAS Foundation was activated in 1992 to implement a comprehensive development program for LAS and its affiliates.

"Our goal is to help support the LAS Programs of Excellence by securing funds from both private and public sources to support charitable care needs, program development, and capital projects," explains Ms. Barbara Trehar, president of the LAS Foundation.

"In a typical year, LAS communities provide nearly four million dollars in charitable care. No one has ever been asked to leave due to financial concerns," says Ms.Trehar.

Working closely with church congregations, private foundations, corporations, and individual donors, Ms. Trehar's efforts serve to ensure the health of an organization dedicated to the health and life satisfaction of seniors.

As LAS expands its mission and ministry into a second century of service, it is mindful of the traditions and sacrifices which brought the agency to its current position. As an emerging organization in the Greater Pittsburgh area, LAS declares that the greatest days for the organization — residents, families, and employees alike — lie in the days and years ahead. ■

■ *Seniors now represent such a formidable population group that demographers say we're amidst an "aging revolution."*

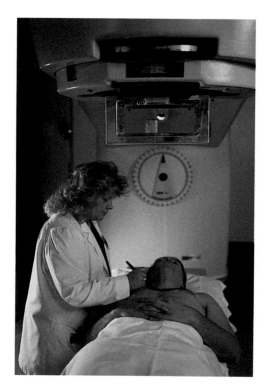

McKeesport Hospital

Commitment. It's the very heart of McKeesport Hospital's mission as a community-based health care provider. For 100 years, McKeesport Hospital has demonstrated its commitment to providing the very best in health care services to residents of southeastern Allegheny County and surrounding communities.

The Hospital's commitment spans a variety of areas, from providing the highest level of quality acute and community-based health care services, to the advancement of its clinical expertise through education and research.

Most of all, McKeesport Hospital remains committed to the communities it serves and the residents who live there. As it has done throughout its 100-year history, McKeesport Hospital continuously strives to strengthen its role as a major community resource and fully recognizes its charitable responsibilities. It is this commitment that has helped McKeesport Hospital to become one of Western Pennsylvania's leading community hospitals.

At the core of McKeesport Hospital's commitment is its highly trained staff of physicians and support personnel. These exceptionally skilled professionals allow the Hospital to combine human compassion with state-of-the-art technology in order to provide unparalleled service to its patients.

Founded in 1894, McKeesport Hospital is a 430-bed hospital located on a 4 acre campus 12 miles southeast of Pittsburgh. Its medical staff includes 250 doctors representing 37 specialties and sub-specialties.

The Hospital has built its commitment to providing superior health care services around five Centers of Excellence. These Centers of Excellence include Cancer Care, Elder Care, Cardiac Care, Rehabilitation Medicine and Psychiatry Services. Each Center of Excellence is designed to be sensitive to the variety of health care needs associated with care giving in its respective discipline.

The Cancer Care Center, McKeesport Hospital's Oncology program, takes a very personalized approach when diagnosing and treating cancer patients. It also utilizes some of the most sophisticated technology in radiation therapy and nuclear medicine.

Central to the Hospital's Cancer Care mission is its newly renovated oncology unit. This unique facility offers 22 beds for patients diagnosed with cancer, as well as outpatient chemotherapy and urgent care services. In addition, the unit provides superior educational and support services conducted by a specialized oncology team. This highly proficient unit complements a range of oncology services including prevention, detection, treatment, rehabilitation, continuing management, research and terminal care, as well as support groups which help to sustain a sense of determination in patients and their families.

Perhaps there is no greater need in the communities surrounding McKeesport Hospital than in the area of *Elder Care*. In recognition of this, eight Hospital physicians have become board certified in geriatric psychiatry. The Hospital's Elder Care program

focuses on wellness and in helping senior patients regain abilities associated with daily living such as shopping, cooking, bathing and living independently.

A key component in the Elder Care program is the Hospital's Golden Key Club, for seniors 55 years and older, which offers special benefits to members such as monthly lectures, free heath screenings, a newsletter, hospital discounts and an insurance information hot-line. An emphasis is placed on teaching people how to stay healthy through disease prevention and health promotion programs.

The *Cardiac Care Center* at McKeesport Hospital integrates the skills of a wide variety of specialists throughout the Hospital including cardiologists, surgeons, nutritionists, physical therapists and psychiatrists.

The Hospital took a major step forward in Cardiac Care in 1992 when it began offering cardiac catheterizations. The Hospital also offers outpatient cardiac rehabilitation services which allow cardiac patients to continue with their rehabilitation program after being discharged. This comprehensive multidisciplinary rehabilitation program includes exercise training, dietary lectures and psychological monitoring and assistance.

Rehabilitation Medicine offers extensive inpatient and outpatient programs. The inpatient program features a 14-bed rehabilitation unit and offers physical, occupational and speech and language therapy. Planned for the near future is a day-hospital program to help in the rehabilitation of patients suffering from arthritis, and following joint replacement and stroke.

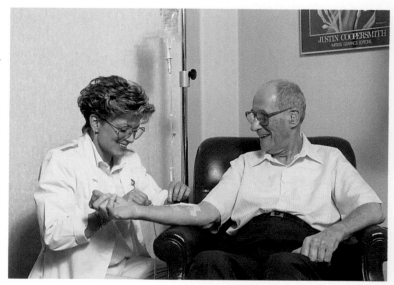

Outpatient rehabilitation services include outpatient physical and occupational therapy, as well as work conditioning services. The work conditioning program specializes in preparing patients with work-related injuries to return to their jobs with the awareness and physical conditioning necessary to reduce their risk of sustaining further injuries.

In *Psychiatry Services*, McKeesport Hospital offers its Hillside Psychiatric Treatment Program, which encourages patients and families to more fully understand their illness. Hillside is a 42-bed inpatient unit catering to the needs of adult and geriatric psychiatry patients. This program is being expanded to add outpatient assessment of psychiatric patients.

Often, physical symptoms will accompany psychiatric illness. Hillside can treat these physical symptoms as well as behavioral and emotional problems. Adult treatment can include group therapy with problem solving, learning and coping skills, family therapy, occupational therapy, individually designed therapeutic activities and behavioral contracts.

McKeesport Hospital's commitment to quality health care doesn't end with its five Centers of Excellence. Central to the Hospital's mission is its primary care program. In an effort to make this front-line service more available to a wider range of residents, McKeesport Hospital has established Satellite facilities specializing in care for the entire family, located throughout its service area.

Not only is McKeesport Hospital known for its superior medical care, it is recognized

for advanced teaching as well. Three Graduate Medical Education programs, Family Practice, Internal Medicine and General Surgery, give McKeesport Hospital the depth of coverage found only in the area's best hospitals. Twenty-four hour coverage, coupled with the most technologically advanced programs and equipment, provide the safest and most progressive environment health care has to offer.

For 100 years, McKeesport Hospital has been meeting the health care needs of the Monongahela Valley. Throughout this first century of service, the Hospital's mission has changed very little. That mission, quite sim-

■ *For one hundred years McKeesport Hospital has been meeting the health care needs of the residents of southeastern Allegheny County as well as portions of Washington and Westmoreland Counties. An array of services from outpatient surgery to inpatient rehabilitation are provided at the Hospital campus.*

ply, is to provide the highest level of quality services in a professional, cost-effective and caring manner.

As it prepares to enter its second century as a major provider of health care services, McKeesport Hospital will continue its commitment to quality care and advanced teaching. This commitment ensures that those communities comprising the Hospital's service area can expect to receive the very best in health care for many years to come. **P**

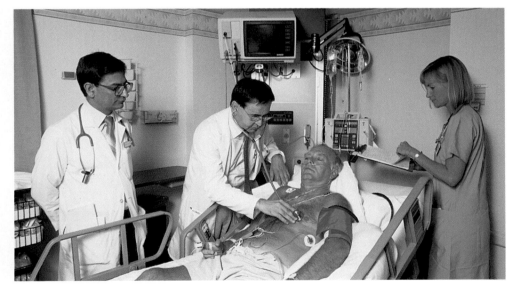

■ *Healing and learning go hand-in-hand at the McKeesport Hospital, where three graduate medical education programs give the depth of coverage found only in the best hospitals.*

CHAPTER

The Marketplace

SIXTEEN

Kaufmann's Department Store, 302-303

Joseph Horne Co., 304-305

Sewickley Car Store, 306-307

The Westin William Penn, 308

For the same reasons its founders were drawn to Pittsburgh more than 120 years ago, Kaufmann's Department Store has solidified its commitment to the Golden Triangle as the hub of the company's burgeoning retail empire.

Headquartered at the intersection of rivers, roads, railways and now airline routes, the city's dominant retailer has continued to strengthen its presence in Pittsburgh. From offices atop a 13-story flagship store in the heart of downtown, Kaufmann's now operates 40 stores and two distribution centers in four states. Annual sales top $1.2 billion.

The latest step in the consolidation was a merger, effective in early 1993, with the May Company, Ohio division, one of Kaufmann's

"The division, with all stores operating under the single name of Kaufmann's, will continue to carry the same high-quality merchandise known to both and embrace the same philosophy of providing quality service and merchandise to its customers," Tobin said.

Kaufmann's is proud to make its home in the city where it began and where it commands more than half the conventional department stores sales. Unlike officers at retailers whose corporate suites are far-removed from their stores, the executives at Kaufmann's thrive on their proximity to the sales floor, where they can see the merchandise, measure the flow of customer traffic, and gain inspiration every day.

Kaufmann's sense of style in running the company reflected the flair of his personal life. He maintained two offices in the upper floors of the downtown store—one a grandly appointed space and the other a monastery taproom which he had transported from Europe and rebuilt in Pittsburgh. He owned five homes, the most famous of which was "Fallingwater," the Frank Lloyd Wright-designed masterpiece built over a woodsy waterfall an hour's drive south of Pittsburgh.

In 1946, its 75th year of business, Kaufmann's joined The May Department Stores Co., setting it on a course of smart growth which continues to this day. By the early 1960s, the company had reached out to the suburbs where its customers were flocking by the thousands. Kaufmann's first suburban shopping mall store opened in Monroeville in 1961, and today more than two-thirds of its stores are located in these service-oriented regional centers.

Kaufmann's Department Store

sister companies in the St. Louis-based May Department Stores Co. The move brought 100 new hourly and salaried jobs to Kaufmann's central headquarters buying, merchandising, and sales support staff in Pittsburgh.

Kaufmann's also pledged to invest more than $150 million in the new combined division by 1996 to open six new stores and expand and remodel five existing stores.

New stores have been announced for Robinson Town Centre and Frazer Heights Galleries, two proposed malls in the Pittsburgh area, and one at University Town Center in Akron, which will replace an existing store. Multi-million-dollar expansions and renovations are under way or planned for Westmoreland Mall and Ross Park Mall in Pittsburgh, Mill Creek Mall in Erie, Irondequoit Mall in Rochester, and Walden Galleria in Buffalo.

William T. Tobin, president and chief executive officer of Kaufmann's, said the combined division will be better positioned to serve customers through its centralized buying, administrative, and marketing functions.

The consolidation, which is part of a company-wide effort by May Co. to reduce overhead, will save millions of dollars every year and make Kaufmann's operate more efficiently.

The company has long emphasized fashion leadership and customer service, and is widely recognized as one of the best merchandised department store companies in the nation.

No stranger to the international scene, Kaufmann's has historically produced a number of innovations. That leadership accelerated beginning in the 1920s under the spirited guidance of Edgar J. Kaufmann, the son of one of the German immigrant brothers who built the business in the 1870s.

It was the dashing "E.J." as he was fondly known, a product of Shady Side Academy and Yale, who endeavored to establish his family's business as a major player on the world fashion scene.

In 1926, an International Exposition of Arts and Industry was held throughout the store for a month. By 1927, Kaufmann had set up business offices in 27 foreign cities, and in 1928 he made the nation's first direct transatlantic call when he contacted the company's Paris office from Pittsburgh.

About that time, Kaufmann also oversaw the redesign of the downtown store's main floor, which has been regarded as a masterpiece of Art Deco style. The first floor aisles were constructed in a revolutionary wheel-and-spoke design to provide better traffic flow and more efficient display. The style was widely copied and still can be seen in department stores across the country.

In 1986, May Co. combined its Youngstown-based Strouss division with Kaufmann's, and in 1990 combined the Rochester-based Sibley's division with Kaufmann's. Today Kaufmann's runs stores in Pennsylvania, New York, Ohio, and West Virginia. Each one of them strives every day to fulfill the company's commitment to participate in the community and the economic vitality of its markets.

The community spirit dates to the days of Edgar Kaufmann, who believed the success of his company depended on the prosperity of the larger community.

He was a key player in the Pittsburgh Renaissance, a period of urban revitalization that transformed the downtown into a marvel of modern architecture after World War II and set the stage for second renaissance that raised Pittsburgh's image to new heights in the 1980s.

Kaufmann was one of six business leaders who founded the Allegheny Conference on Community Development, which sought to involve the captains of industry with the community's economic development. In addition to scholarship and other charitable funds, he also donated $1.5 million to help build the Civic Arena, and he bankrolled the Civic Light Opera.

The company has long boasted that its downtown store, which occupies an entire

city block in the same location it has occupied since 1877, is the largest between New York and Chicago. Its ornate bronze clock at the corner of Fifth Avenue and Smithfield Street is a landmark meeting place.

Under Kaufmann's roof, shoppers can find beauty salons, a dentist's office, and restaurants that prepare hundreds of thousands of meals a year, including legendary apple pies, for shoppers and office workers.

In addition to hundreds of sales associates whose mission it is to serve the customer, the behind-the-scenes staff includes hundreds of computer operators, painters, payroll clerks, electricians, secretaries, and others.

The more Kaufmann's has grown, the more it has established itself as one of the true traditions of Pittsburgh, rededicating itself every day to its informal credo: "A block long and a world wide." ◨

■ *The Horne's company is proud of its ability to anticipate the market's tastes and adapt quickly to them.*

Joseph Horne Co.

The decade of the 1990s dawned on tumultuous times for Joseph Horne Co., times that would require determination and shrewd maneuvering by the company's managers if Pittsburgh was to retain one of its oldest and most respected retailers.

Before it ended in 1992, the ordeal would test the loyalty of Horne's customers, the confidence of its lenders, and the mettle of its managers.

All three would pass the test, and the department store chain, whose 2,200 employees now operate 10 stores in Western Pennsylvania, would pass through the most precarious period in its 140-year history and move on to what promised to be a new era of stability and success.

"We're thrilled at the way things have worked out, and we're excited about the future of the Joseph Horne Co.," said Michael L. Pulte, president and chief executive officer.

The company's management team learned important lessons under difficult circumstances, lessons that make for more effective leadership, he said.

"We all grew beyond our expectations. We all learned how to make this company a survivor. We all learned to pull our oars to the same cadence, and we learned to have mutual objectives. We learned that the whole is more important than the parts."

The odyssey began with a leveraged buyout in December 1986 that put the company in the hands of private investors. By mid-1987, business conditions had deteriorated significantly. The stock market crash in October that year threw a dark shadow over the economy.

In July, 1988, Horne's was engaged in a proposed sale to Dillard Department Stores and the DeBartolo interests that nearly scuttled the company.

Hundreds of managers gave notice of their intention to leave, and 150 did depart.

Merchandise was not ordered at the rate it should have been, and inventories became extraordinarily thin.

By 1990, the company was beset by the daunting challenges of heavy debt, impatient lenders, legal logjams, and frustrated expansion efforts. If there was to be much of a future for Horne's, the company would have to make all the right moves. It did just that, and in rapid succession.

The first of the major financial hurdles was crossed in January 1992 with a $200-million restructuring of company finances.

The cornerstone of the arrangement was the exchange of $47 million in debt and preferred stock to common stock. The move freed Horne's from interest payments to its second-tier, or mezzanine, lenders.

It also strengthened the balance sheet sufficiently to convince the lead lenders to grant a five-year extension of term loans secured by real estate and a three-year extension of revolving credit secured by accounts receivable.

For generations of area residents, Horne's had been as much a part of Pittsburgh as the geology that brings the Monongahela and Allegheny rivers to a confluence at The Point.

It might be only a small exaggeration to say that the idea of Pittsburgh without Horne's was so alien as to be unacceptable, especially to the prime lender, Pittsburgh National, and the bank's chairman and CEO, Jim Rohr.

"They really looked on Horne's as something Pittsburgh needed to keep alive," Pulte said. "The mezzanine lenders were outstanding in their willingness to convert that debt to equity, and as the chief executive of the lead bank, Jim Rohr took a personal interest. He was outstanding."

The credit arrangement improved the company's net worth by 50 percent and avoided any need to reduce the work force or roll back wages.

With its finances in place, Horne's then moved on to address another big challenge. Only a month after reaching agreement with its lead lenders, the company settled its protracted lawsuit with the Youngstown, Ohio-based Edward J. DeBartolo Corp. and Little Rock, Arkansas-based Dillard Department Stores.

The case arose after DeBartolo and Dillard abruptly called off the 1988 agreement to buy the chain for $234 million. At the heart of the settlement was an agreement by DeBartolo and Dillard to buy the assets and receivables of five Ohio stores from Horne's for about $24 million.

The cash freed Horne's to pay debt. It also allowed the company to ease out of Cleveland and Youngstown, two recession-gripped markets where the name Horne's did not enjoy the recognition and customer loyalty that were major strengths in Western Pennsylvania.

"It made a lot of sense for us to leave Ohio and focus our efforts on Western Pennsylvania," said Pulte. "We never really got a foothold in Cleveland. We were the new kid on the block."

■ *President and Chief Executive Officer Michael L. Pulte*

With the sale of the Ohio stores, Horne's was comfortably configured the way it had been previously, a 10-store chain with eight locations in the Pittsburgh area and two in Erie. The company could once again focus on the region where it started in business in 1849.

Senior managers live in the Pittsburgh area as do members of the board of directors. Their understanding of the region's history, its changing economy, and its future prospects gives Horne's an ability to anticipate the market's tastes and adapt quickly to them, according to Philip S. Rossin, senior vice president for marketing.

"The people who lead our organization are people who know the Pittsburgh region, understand our market, and are in touch with our customers. We're all based right here. That's a distinct advantage," Rossin said. "We don't need approval from distant sources."

In an effort to reach out to its loyal customers and attract new ones, Horne's embarked in late 1992 on a year-long adver-

tising and marketing campaign built around the theme "Have you seen us lately?"

The campaign reintroduced Horne's as a retailer offering everyday competitive prices on moderate to better fashion merchandise in a setting that appeals to a diverse clientele.

In line with that mission, the company installed a $4-million computerized cash register system capable of reading magnetic stripes on credit cards. The system allowed faster, more accurate sales transactions and more efficient inventory control.

"This system will allow us to be more flexible so we can react to the market quickly," Pulte said. "We will be able to tell what we sell now by size, color, and style."

Horne's also mailed out more than half a million new magnetically coded charge cards with a discount coupon, a move that was timed to spark sales volume in the fall and holiday shopping seasons.

Horne's also announced that it would honor VISA and MasterCard to make shopping more convenient.

The company's ability to maneuver towards growth was forged over more than a century of service in a region whose economy seems to remake itself every few generations.

That kind of responsive retailing springs from a management tradition born when the 23-year-old Joseph Horne began doing business in downtown Pittsburgh in a three-story building on Fourth Street. The gleaming, glass-walled PPG Place was built on the site in the 1980s.

"Together with our employees, shareholders, and lenders, we have achieved a number of important goals," said Chairman Pulte. "We have succeeded in making Horne's a stronger, more focused company that can serve its loyal customers better than ever before."

The experience also brought lessons that can serve Pulte well for a long time.

"I learned, among many things, to take my responsibilities seriously but not myself." ▣

■ *Bob Nikel driving his Porsche 944 Turbo escort car at 24-hour run at the Mid Ohio Racetrack.*

The Sewickley Car Store is a landmark on Ohio River Boulevard at the Sewickley Bridge. The prominent location probably is the least of the ways in which the business stands out.

"I don't think of this as your average automobile dealership," said owner Bob Nikel.

Nikel and his team of hands-on managers and technicians run the kind of organization that car owners search for and tell their friends about when they find: that small, expert garage whose technical sophistication is unsurpassed and whose success in satisfying customers is inspired by a love of cars.

If the staff and management were driven by ordinary motives, the Sewickley Car Store

Sewickley Car Store

■ *The Sewickley Car Store lineup: Audi, Porsche, and BMW. Photo by Roy Engelbrecht.*

could sell any make of car. But because it is precision machines rather than profit margins that make this group tick, Nikel's organization deals in three of the world's finest automobiles—Porsche, Audi, and BMW.

Porsche earned its reputation in racing and with innovations in sports car technology.

Audi complements the Porsche tradition with sedans engineered to make the average driver a better driver. For example, the all-wheel-drive Quattro, a highly popular car in the hilly terrain of western Pennsylvania, set a new standard as a true sports sedan when it was introduced in 1983.

BMW is renowned for excellence in a broad range of vehicles, from sports sedans to top-of-the-line highway cruisers.

"All three of those lines offer unparalleled safety," said Nikel. "Our products are technologically ahead of the rest of the auto industry, and we support our customers with service that we consider to be well above the industry norm."

The Sewickley Car Store is nothing if not a reflection of the character of the people who run it.

"When Bob Rost and I opened for business in 1976, our goal was to make this dealership one of the best in the country. We wanted our staff to be committed to the product and the customer, and we wanted our product to sell on service, not on salesmanship," Nikel said.

His approach to the business led Nikel to insist that his employees take personal responsibility.

"Nobody is perfect. If we make a mistake, it is a matter of pride in our craftsmanship that we step up to the plate. We don't make excuses. Without question, that approach has paid off for the reputation of our organization, and it has paid off for our customers."

Nikel has staffed the Sewickley Car Store with people who share his love of quality automobiles and his business philosophy.

Some, including Porsche and Audi technicians Joe Weber, Bruce Gifford, and Byoung-Chin An have been with Nikel since he opened the dealership in 1976. Joe Scarfone, general manager of BMW sales and used car sales, began in 1976 and worked through various departments to become Nikel's only co-owner.

E. Paul Dickinson, Porsche-Audi service manager, has known Nikel since the early 1970s. They were racing associates long before they were business associates.

Dickinson holds numerous Solo II championships with Porsche 911s and 944s that were built by Nikel.

The technicians who kept Dickinson in the hunt for national championships are members of the same team that go to work for customers when their cars need attention. They may very well be the most highly trained service team in the tri-state area.

And there's no mistaking the reflection of Dickinson's competitive spirit and love of fine cars in the personal attitudes of the rest of the Sewickley Car Store staff.

"When someone has no special interest in the work they're doing, when it's just a job, it shows," he said. "We love great cars and we love racing, and when customers walk in here, they find a friendly, enthusiastic atmosphere. This dealership is home for one of the great interests in our lives. People are welcome in our home any time."

"The same attitude is apparent all the way down to the lot attendants," said Dave Plattner, Porsche-Audi sales manager.

"A lot of people like being in the car business. Everyone here universally loves being in the car business but also loves cars. There's a difference," said Plattner, a self-professed "car nut" who waited years for an opening on Nikel's staff.

Like Plattner, many other employees wait for an opening to join the staff or to move up.

One Porsche-Audi salesman was attracted to the organization as a driver for the dealership's towing service. He started working for Nikel as a technician and later moved into sales.

A parts department employee started at the dealership washing cars, moved up to detailing, and then into parts.

"There are a lot of stories like that around here," Plattner said.

One of them belongs to Scarfone. His first job was at the parts counter. He graduated to parts manager, later moved into sales, then became manager of BMW sales and used car sales.

In Scarfone and Nikel, the Sewickley Car Store's top two managers are products of the "back end" of the business, the dirty fingernail area.

"It's a perspective that few people in general management and sales have in this business. It's born of a love of the car as opposed to just love of money," Scarfone said. "Between the two of us, we formed the nucleus for a business that sells and services cars. That's what we like to do, and it just so happens we've been able to make our living at it."

"When you love the cars you sell, they're easy to sell and easy to fix. It all falls into line."

BMW Service Manager Ray Gonzalez is cut from the same mold. He has a lifetime of European car experience and has devoted himself since 1978 to BMW products. A former racer and past president of the Porsche Club, his customer sensitivity and technical expertise have earned Gonzalez a reputation as the top BMW service manager in the Pittsburgh region.

"I like coming to work. My wife accuses me of being in love with my job, and there's some truth to it," he said.

Having worked in service at other dealerships in the Pittsburgh area, Gonzalez says unequivocally that the Sewickley Car Store takes a rare attitude about its customers.

"Our primary objective is to fix the car and fix it right, not to charge for the seven or eight hours it took to fix it but the $200 we quoted. A lot of places don't look at it that way, and that's why you hear the kind of stories you do when you ask people about their car dealer," he said.

"We put the relationship with the customer before profit because we know that's the best way of assuring that business will come to us. We don't look at the customer as a dollar bill."

The man who assembled the Sewickley Car Store team grew up with a wrench in one hand and a gear shift in the other. Nikel was bitten by the car bug during his junior year in high school. He bought a 1946 Ford that quickly became a racing laboratory, housing at various times Mercury, Oldsmobile, and Cadillac engines.

"Back then, my goal was to become one of the best technicians around."

Nikel's goals haven't changed much since then except that he applies his considerable skills at his own dealership.

He began his career as a mechanic for Stoddard Imported Cars in Cleveland and soon became service manager. The owner, national racing champion Chuck Stoddard, introduced the young Nikel to the thrill and challenge of auto racing.

Since then, Porsche racing has made a deep impression on Nikel, whose respect for machines, engineering, and safety are all reflected in the cars he races, sells, and services.

Nikel has campaigned cars starting with a Fiat Bianchino, a Porsche 914 2-liter, a 914.6, 924, and 944s in 24-hour endurance racing.

Along the way, he acquired one Porsche that he would not let go, one of the original fifteen 911 RSRs that competed in the International Race of Champions series in 1973-1974. Nikel's is the No. 2 car that Peter Revson raced to second place in the final round at Daytona.

"We built a Porsche 924 racer here, which I campaigned as a GT3 for years. We had two 924s when they first came out, and we ran those in club races. When the 944 was introduced by Porsche, we took one of the first ones. Paul Dickinson campaigned that car and won a national championship in the Pro Solo Series the first year out."

Nikel shares his racing skills with novice and aspiring drivers at Porsche and BMW schools on the East Coast.

He decided to relocate and open his dealership in Sewickley after realizing that customers were traveling 150 miles from Pittsburgh to bring cars to him for service in Cleveland.

When he came to the Pittsburgh area, Nikel brought with him a belief that has served him well ever since: "Do the utmost for your customers, and they'll be your best advertising." ▣

■ Byoung-Chin An (left) and Joe Weber (right) are both master technicians with Sewickley Car Store. Photo by Roy Engelbrecht.

■ BMW Service Manager Ray Gonzalez (left) and Ken Anderson, master technician, at the BMW diagnostic center. Photo by Roy Engelbrecht.

■ *Spacious guest rooms feature Drexel Hertiage furniture, marble baths with hair dryers, in-room movies and express check-out.*

1916...the world was at war; in Pittsburgh steel was king; the cornerstone was laid for a new City-County Building; the Mellons purchased a prime downtown site for the construction of a new bank building, and The William Penn Hotel was completed at a cost of six million dollars.

Built by Pittsburgh industrialist, Henry Clay Frick, the original building on William Penn Way was, with 1,000 rooms, the largest hotel between New York and Chicago. With its Georgian lobby and Italian Renaissance Ballroom, it is a classic example of old world elegance and timeless design. It was famous, not only for its beauty, but as an example of progress, with "certified lighting and a bath in every room." Pittsburgh, a city of million-

dles...its opening is an epoch in the history of the city as a community."

In 1993, The Westin William Penn continues this tradition of excellence. Named in 1993 as the "Best overall hotel, best service, best dining in Pittsburgh by the Pittsburgh Post Gazette, the hotel prides itself on its impeccable reputation for service. Also named by Mid-Atlantic Country Magazine in

Located in the center of Pittsburgh's vital downtown business and cultural district, the hotel has earned a reputation for being the place in Pittsburgh for conventions, business meetings, wedding receptions, or just a great night's stay. It's success is the result of a dedicated staff's commitment to "delight and astound" it's guests.

After a $30 million renovation, 595 spacious guest rooms feature Drexel Heritage Furniture, marble baths with hair dryers, and Caswell and Massey amenities. All rooms have a choice of over 60 in-room movies with color cable television. Crown Service Rooms offer a complimentary afternoon tea, cocktail and shoe shine, continental breakfast, and newspaper. State of the art services, such as Voice Mail, AT&T Language Line, and express check-out bring today's convenience to these classic accommodations.

The Westin William Penn

aires and immigrants who had little time for luxury and no need of frills, nonetheless, welcomed the new hotel. The opening announcement in the Gazette Times of March, 1916, described it as "...a house of a thousand guest rooms, without need of can-

their February, 1993, edition as one of the "50 Finest Hotels and Resorts of the Mid-Atlantic", The Westin William Penn exemplifies a commitment to total quality management.

With over 50,000 square feet of meeting space, an Executive Fitness Center, a full service business center, and in-house audio-visual and teleconferencing capabilities, The Westin William Penn hosts meetings from 10 to 1,200 with ease.

To further enhance a visit, guests may enjoy superb regional cuisine in the newly restored Georgian Terrace Room, or relax in the sumptuous Palm Court Lobby over a luscious Afternoon Tea with entertainment by concert pianists. Jazz lovers may stop by on Thursday or Friday evenings to hear Joe Negri, a local favorite, play soft blues or hot licks in the Palm Court.

The Westin William Penn, the home of Pittsburgh's past, continues to move enthusiastically toward the future as a vital part of the Pittsburgh community.   ▣

■ *The Westin William Penn is a classic example of old world elegance and timeless design.*

Bibliography

Bilstein, Roger E., <u>Flight in America, From the Wrights to the Astronauts</u>, The Johns Hopkins University Press, 1984.

Trimble, William F., <u>High Frontier, A History of Aeronautics in Pennsylvania</u>, University of Pittsburgh Press, 1982.

Harrington, James P., Smith, Frank Kingston, <u>Aviation and Pennsylvania</u>, Franklin Institute Press, 1981.

_____, "Business Hub of the Northeast," Penn's Southwest Association, 1992.

_____, "A Statistical Profile of the Pittsburgh Metropolitan Region," Greater Pittsburgh Office of Promotion.

_____, "Western Pennsylvania Businesses with Investment from Foreign-Based Companies," KPMG Peat Marwick, 1992.

_____, "Technology and the Health Sciences," <u>Pennsylvania Technology</u>, Pittsburgh High Technology Council, Second Quarter 1990.

_____, "The Case for Internationalizing the Pittsburgh Region," The Pittsburgh International Initiative of Western Pennsylvania, 1991.

Starling, Judy, et.al., "Labor Climate in the Pittsburgh Primary Metropolitan Statistical Area," The Center for Labor Studies, The H. John Heinz III School of Public Policy and Management, Carnegie Mellon University, 1992.

_____, <u>1993 Book of Lists</u>, The Pittsburgh Business Times, 1992.

Index

Pittsburgh's Enterprises Index

This book was set in Rockwell Light, Rockwell Light Italic, Frutiger Roman, and Frutiger Light Italic at Community Communications, Montgomery, Alabama. Printed on 80lb. Warren Flo Text by Hoechstetter Printing Company, Inc.